The Devil Drives

A Life of Sir Richard Burton

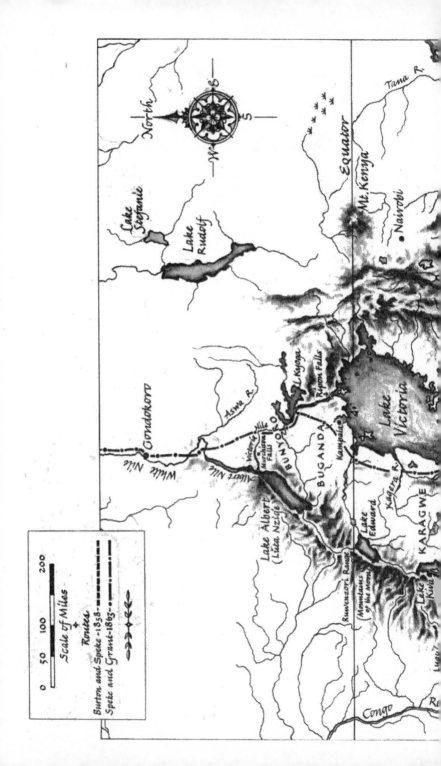

Indian Ocean

The
NILE SEARCH
1858·1863

Mombasa
PEMBA
ZANZIBAR ISLAND
Dar es Salaam
Mafia I.
Kilwa (Quiloa)
Ruvuma R.
Arumid
Pangani R.
Ngera
Zanzibar
Bagamoyo
Zungomero
Rufiji R.
Wami R.
Dodoma
Kisigo R.
Njombe R.
Kanyenyeri
Tabora (Kazeh)
Ruegura R.
Lake Rukwa
Msene
Ujiji
Ujimbo
Ugalla R.
Lagosa
Malagarasi R.
Lake Tanganyika
Lukuga R.
Lake Mweru
Lake Bangweulu
Chitambo's
Luvua R.
lualaba (Congo) R.

The Devil Drives

A Life of Sir Richard Burton

BY FAWN M. BRODIE

W · W · NORTON & COMPANY

New York   London

To Bernard

COPYRIGHT © 1967 BY FAWN M. BRODIE

First published as a Norton paperback 1984

Library of Congress Cataloging in Publication Data
Brodie, Fawn McKay, 1915–1981
The Devil drives.
Reprint. Originally published: New York: Norton, 1967.
Bibliography: p.
Includes index.
1. Burton, Richard Francis, Sir, 1821–1890.
2. Explorers—Great Britain—Biography.   I. Title.
G246.B8B7   1984   941.081′092′4 [B]   84-7989

ISBN: 978-0-3933-01-66-3

Printed in the United States of America

W. W. Norton & Company, Inc.
500 Fifth Avenue, New York, N.Y. 10110
W. W. Norton & Company Ltd.
37 Great Russell Street, London WC1B 3NU

6 7 8 9 0

CONTENTS

ILLUSTRATIONS

ACKNOWLEDGMENTS

RICHARD BURTON published forty-three volumes on his explorations and travels. He wrote two volumes of poetry, over a hundred articles, and 143 pages of autobiography. In addition, he translated sixteen volumes of the *Arabian Nights*, six volumes of Portuguese literature, two volumes of Latin poetry, four volumes of folklore—Neapolitan, African and Hindu—all of which have extensive annotations that help to illuminate Burton's character. These works, plus the biography written by his wife, form the basic collection of source material for a life of Burton. But there is also significant material scattered in many places.

Although Lady Burton burned almost all her husband's journals and diaries after his death, and whatever else she thought might be misused, a surprising amount of manuscript material escaped. There are five important manuscript collections, hitherto largely unmined by Burton biographers. The Royal Anthropological Institute in London, which houses Burton's immense private library, has clippings, letters and boxes of material Burton had assembled for future volumes, as well as manuscripts in his own hand. Professor A. H. Christie, Director of the Institute, and Miss B. J. Kirkpatrick, Librarian, extended to me extraordinary courtesies during my stay in London, provided photostats, and gave me the benefit of their extensive knowledge of Burton himself. The most important collection of Burton's own letters is in Trinity College Library, Cambridge. It consists of forty salty communications to Lord Houghton (Monckton Milnes). Mr A. Halcrow, Librarian, kindly provided me with Xerox copies and permission for quotation. The Henry E. Huntington Library in San Marino, California has many letters from Richard and Isabel Burton dating from 1885 to 1892, as well as unpublished Burton manuscripts. Permission to consult and to quote from these was given me by Librarian Mary Isabel Fry.

There are two important private collections, one owned by Mr Edwards H. Metcalf of San Marino, California, the other by Mr Quentin Keynes of London. I have benefited from Mr Metcalf's large collection of letters to Burton, and from his correspondence between Lady Burton and Leonard Smithers, and numerous letters by Burton himself. Mr Keynes, too, was most generous in letting me see his manuscripts, and also granted permission for numerous quotations. He has many documents which until recently belonged to Lady Burton's heirs, including numerous Burton letters, several important letters of John Speke with Burton's scribbled tentative reply at the end of each letter, fascinating manuscripts dating from Burton's early years in India, and other varied materials illuminating almost every period in Burton's life. Thanks to his kindness, I have been able to solve certain mysteries and greatly to enrich my understanding of certain crucial episodes in Burton's life. To Mr Keynes, too, I owe a memorable evening spent with him and Mr and Mrs Alexander Maitland, which included a trip to Burton's exotic tomb at Mortlake.

Mr Maitland, who is writing a biography of John Hanning Speke, clarified ambiguities about Speke's death, and provided me with a copy of an important Speke letter. Mrs Dorothy Middleton, Assistant Editor, Royal Geographical Society, kindly sought out for me numerous illuminating letters written by Burton and Speke now in the Society's archives, and gave me additional information on Speke and his family. Miss P. J. Willetts of the British Museum Manuscript Department took time one busy afternoon to seek out for me eighteen pages of manuscript in Burton's largely illegible hand, and to arrange for photostating. These turned out to be a rare discovery. They proved upon examination to be journal and diary entries made on board ship during Burton's journey to the United States in 1860. They are the only pages of Burton's forty-year journal collection to have survived. Norman Penzer for a time owned one of Burton's journals, written during 1876, but this was destroyed when Penzer's London home was burnt during World War II. Miss Willetts also arranged for me to use the manuscript diary of Sir Charles Napier.

Mr Stanley Sutton, Librarian of the India Office, kindly instituted a search for Burton's intelligence report on the Karachi brothels made at the request of his commanding officer, Sir Charles Napier, which had badly damaged Burton's Indian Army career. When it could not be found in the India Office archives, Mr Sutton asked Mr P. M. Joshi, Director of the Bombay Record Office at Delhi, to have a search made there. When this failed, a third search was made for me by Muhammad Sadulla, Keeper of the Records, Government of West Pakistan, at Lahore. Unfortunately this too proved fruitless, and one must assume that the manuscript was indeed destroyed, as Burton's bibliographer, Norman Penzer, suspected.

I wish to thank also Mr Philip Van Doren Stern, from whom I was able to purchase an almost complete set of Burton's books. One of these, *First Footsteps in East Africa,* contained two pages in Latin of Burton's Appendix IV on infibulation, an appendix which the printers had refused to bind into the first edition, and which hitherto had been thought lost altogether. I am grateful also to Mr Jim Hatch, for hospitality and aid in Cairo, and to Mr Gordon Waterfield, editor of the 1966 edition of Burton's *First Footsteps in East Africa,* for permission to see his proofs in advance of publication. Miss J. Hermann permitted me to see the Burton books and relics at the Dulwich Library. Special courtesies were extended to me by Lady Margaret Keynes, Mr Robert G. Sawers of Routledge and Kegan Paul Ltd., Professor A. S. Tritton, and Professor Michael Howard of London University, David Wheeler of the British Broadcasting Corporation, Mr Jerrold Cooper, Mr Dale L. Morgan, and Dr Edward Shapiro. Dr Ralph Greenson, Clinical Professor of Psychiatry at the University of California at Los Angeles, and Dr Nathan Leites, of the University of Chicago, read extensively in my manuscript and gave me invaluable aid in defining clinically some of the complexities of Burton's personality, and additional significant aid in this area came from Dr Lewis J. Fielding and Dr Maimon Leavitt.

My eldest son, Richard Brodie, pawned his guitar one Christmas to buy me a Burton letter which I cherish; Pamela Brodie found for me a special Nile story, and together with Bruce Brodie they have endured with their usual amiability the difficulties engendered by their mother's writing. My husband, Bernard Brodie, has tolerated endless "Burton talk" with good humour, and has given the manuscript his characteristic thorough and perceptive scrutiny and criticism.

There have been ten biographies of Sir Richard Burton and two of Lady Burton. This book is primarily about Richard Burton, but it is also secondarily about his wife. If at times Isabel Burton seems unnecessarily to dominate a chapter, it is because she was an exceptional woman in her own right, and because the marriage was in most respects extraordinary. It is also because she was as free in communicating her own feelings as Richard was secretive, and her feelings are often the only clue we have to the true nature of his.

Fawn M. Brodie
Pacific Palisades,
California

January 1967

The Devil Drives

A Life of Sir Richard Burton

The Devil Drives

Starting in a hollowed log of wood—some thousand miles up a river, with an infinitesmal prospect of returning! I ask myself "Why?" and the only echo is "damned fool! . . . the Devil drives."[1]

S O RICHARD FRANCIS BURTON, preparing for an exploration of the lower Congo in 1863, wrote to Monckton Milnes from the African kingdom of Dahomey. Asking himself why he risked life and sanity to penetrate the unknown jungles of Central Africa, he repeated a question that had tormented him upon his earlier voyages. His answer, "the Devil drives," applies not only to his geographical discoveries but also to the whole of his turbulent life. The nature of his demon, the source of his restlessness, and the nourisher of his courage, baffled his friends his wife, and later his biographers.

Moreover, though Burton scoffed at all forms of religious superstition—whether the fetishism of the Fan cannibals or the death ceremonies of his own Church of England—he dwelt fascinated upon all things accounted devilish in his own time. Once he even contemplated writing a biography of Satan himself. "It is interesting to note the superior gusto with which Eastern, as well as the Western tale-teller describes his scoundrels and villains," he wrote, "whilst his good men and women are mostly colourless and unpicturesque. So Satan is the true hero of Paradise Lost and by his side God and man are very ordinary; and Mephistopheles is much better society than Faust and Margaret."[2] Burton's own visage seems to have conjured up thoughts of Satan; Swinburne said that he had the jaw of a devil and the brow of a god; and the Earl of Dunraven wrote that Burton "prided himself on looking like Satan—as, indeed, he did."[3]

But Burton's preoccupation with things Satanic was only one aspect of the man. In the catholicity of his interests he seemed to have been a true man of the Renaissance. He was soldier, explorer, ethnologist, archaeologist, poet, translator, and one of the two or three great linguists of his time. He was also an amateur physician, botanist, zoologist, and geologist, and incidentally a celebrated swordsman and superb raconteur.

"Discovery is mostly my mania," he wrote.[4] And in a world where there seemed to be very little left to be discovered, he sought out the few remaining mysteries. He penetrated the sacred cities of Mecca and Medina at great risk and wrote detailed descriptions. He was the first European to explore the forbidden Moslem city of Harar in Somaliland, which promised death to any infidel. Then he turned to the mystery that had fired the curiosity of Alexander, Caesar, and Napoleon, "the greatest geographical secret after the discovery of America," the source of the White Nile. Enduring great hardship, he succeeded with John Hanning Speke in discovering Lake Tanganyika, but just missed Lake Victoria, a failure that embroiled him in controversy and tragedy.

But Burton's real passion was not for geographical discovery but for the hidden in man, for the unknowable, and inevitably the unthinkable. What his Victorian compatriots called unclean, bestial, or Satanic he regarded with almost clinical detachment. In this respect he belongs more properly to our own day. But he was trapped in a century where few men truly understood his talents; he was confined and penalized by the pruderies of his time, praised only for his most obvious exploits, and generally condemned for a curiosity as prodigious as it was penetrating.

During his later years he railed against the "immodest modesty," cant, and hypocrisy of his era. He took it upon himself to bring to the West the sexual wisdom of the East, where acceptance of the naturalness of the art of love came close to religious exaltation. Precursor of Havelock Ellis and Sigmund Freud, he anticipated many of their insights. He translated his sixteen-volume edition of the unexpurgated *Arabian Nights*, larded with ethnological notes to make it a veritable treasure house. He risked prosecution and imprisonment to print, secretly, several translations of Oriental erotica, one of which, *The Perfumed Garden of the Cheikh Nefzaoui*, also called *The Scented Garden*, he was working on when he died.

His other writings were prodigious in quantity and extraordinarily varied in content. He shines therefore in three constellations of gifted men. He is among the first rank of British explorers, together with David Livingstone, Henry Stanley, Samuel Baker, and John Hanning Speke. He was one of that group of gifted British scientists, many of them "amateurs"—Charles Darwin, Francis Galton, Charles Lyell, James Frazer, Flinders Petrie, Arthur Evans, A. H. Sayce, and Thomas Huxley—who pushed back the frontiers of man's knowledge of man in an explosion of enthusiastic discovery. And thirdly, he was a literary figure of great distinction.

"He was fond of calling himself an anthropologist," J. S. Cotton wrote in the *Academy* at his death, "by which he meant that he took for his domain everything that concerns man and woman. Whatever humanity does he refused to consider common or unclean; and he dared to write down in black and white (for private circulation) the results of his exceptional experience. . . . His virility stamped everything he said or wrote. . . . He concealed nothing; he boasted of nothing. . . . But to those who were admitted to his intimacy, the man was greater than what he did or what he wrote."[5]

His wife wrote that except in a gathering of his best friends "he would throw out his quills like a porcupine."[6] But there were many such gatherings, and it is astonishing how many nineteenth-century Englishmen in their reminiscences devoted pages to a single evening with Richard Burton. Bram Stoker, though at first repelled by his "iron countenance," wrote that "as he talked, fancy seemed to run riot in its alluring power; and the whole world of thought seemed to flame with gorgeous colour." Lord Redesdale noted that "the thing which he loved above all others was to astonish, and for the sake of that he would not hesitate to violate the virtue of the pure maiden who dwells in a well."[7] When a young curate asked him once if he had shot a man near Mecca, he replied mischievously, "Sir, I'm proud to say that I have committed every sin in the Decalogue." Still Burton could be stung by the consequences of his own tall tales about himself. Once in a crowded party he overheard a woman say, "There is that infamous Captain Burton. I should like to know that he was down with some lingering illness." Burton turned to face her and said gravely, "Madame, I have never in all my life done anything so wicked as to express so shocking a wish as that."[8]

Ouida, the fashionable female novelist of the time, wrote that Burton "looked like Othello, and lived like the Three Mousquetaires blended in one."[9] Frank Harris wrote a memorable essay on Burton, which he included in his *Contemporary Portraits*, along with Carlyle, Whistler, Swinburne, Rodin, and Anatole France. He had met him first at a London party:

Burton was in conventional evening dress, and yet, as he swung around to the introduction, there was an untamed air about him. He was tall, about six feet in height, with broad, square shoulders; he carried himself like a young man, in spite of his sixty years, and was abrupt in movement. His face was bronzed and scarred, and when he wore a heavy moustache and no beard he looked like a prize-fighter; the naked, dark eyes—imperious, aggressive eyes, by no means friendly; the heavy jaws and prominent hard chin gave him a desperate air. . . .

Burton unbuttoned, and talked as only Burton could talk of Damascus and that immemorial East; of India and its super-subtle people, of Africa and human life in the raw today as it was twenty thousand years ago. . . .

Burton was of encyclopaedic reading; knew English poetry and prose astonishingly; had a curious liking for "sabre-cuts of Saxon speech"—all such
words as come hot from life's mint. . . .

A western lynching yarn held him spell-bound, a *crime passionel* in Paris
intoxicated him, started him talking, transfigured him into a magnificent
story-teller, with intermingled appeals of pathos and rollicking fun, camp-
fire effects, jets of flame against the night.

His intellectual curiosity was astonishingly broad and deep rather than
high. He would tell stories of Indian philosophy or of perverse negro habits
of lust and cannibalism, or would listen to descriptions of Chinese cruelty
and Russian self-mutilation till the stars paled out. Catholic in his admiration
and liking for all greatness, it was the abnormalities and not the divinities
of men that fascinated him.

Deep down in him lay the despairing gloom of utter disbelief. . . . Burton's
laughter, even, deep-chested as it was, had in it something of sadness.[10]

As a brawler in his youth, and a literary brawler in maturity, Burton
made many enemies. He could dismiss the editor of the *Pall Mall
Gazette* for his "malevolent insipidities," and demolish the reputation
of an author by writing in a review, "This book has been carefully
purged of everything valuable." He attacked Henry Reeve, editor of
the *Edinburgh Review*, as "a cross and cross-grained old man whose
surly temper is equalled only by his ignoble jealousy of another's
success."[11] But much of this cudgeling was in response to venomous
attacks upon his *Arabian Nights*. After its publication he was called
"an authority . . . on all that relates to the bestial element in man,"
and "a man who knows thirty-five languages and dialects, especially
that of pornography." Henry Reeve called his *Nights* "one of the most
indecent books in the English language," and "an extraordinary
agglomeration of filth."

Burton's marriage was no less fascinating than his explorations. His
friends and biographers have been sharply divided into those who
admired and those who detested his wife. Isabel Arundell Burton was
a member of the Roman Catholic aristocracy, in her youth a girl of
considerable beauty, and all her life the possessor of a proud, independent, and romantic spirit. W. H. Wilkins, her first biographer,
described her relations with her husband as "more like a poem than an
ordinary marriage." Ouida, who was friend to both, insisted theirs was
"a love marriage in the most absolute sense of the word."[12]

Burton's niece, Georgiana Stisted, on the other hand, who wrote an
effusive biography of her uncle, described the marriage as "a serious
imprudence." John Payne, rival translator of the *Arabian Nights*, told
the biographer Thomas Wright that Isabel "was answerable for most

of Burton's troubles. She didn't know the difference between truth and falsehood. . . . She and Burton never understood each other." Lord Redesdale wrote that "Burton was a model husband, and his wife adored him," but he believed Isabel to have been a snob who did Burton great damage in his foreign office posts. Others called her silly, fatuous, superstitious, and a bigoted Catholic. Swinburne at first called her "the best of wives," but turned against her savagely after Burton's death.[13]

Troubled by her husband's preoccupation with erotic literature, Isabel repeatedly urged him to abandon his translation of *The Scented Garden* and turn instead to his own memoirs. Finally he said to her, "Tomorrow I shall have finished this, and I promise you that after this I will never write another book upon this subject. I will take to our biography." The next day he was dead. Within a fortnight Isabel Burton had destroyed the manuscript. "Sorrowfully, reverently, and in fear and trembling," she wrote, "I burnt sheet after sheet, until the whole of the volumes were consumed."[14]

Later she set about writing the biography of her husband, describing him as "the most pure, the most refined, the most modest man . . . that ever lived." She insisted, "There is one thing that I feel I *am* fit for, and that is to lift the vail as to the *inner* man." Afterwards she took the forty-year accumulation of his journals and diaries and burned practically everything.

Burton had kept two sets of journals, one the detailed account of his travel experiences, which included his anthropological notes, summaries of books he had read, and impressions of conversations with many of the most influential people in England. The other set consisted of his intimate diaries, which he always kept under lock and key. From the few portions his wife singled out for quotation, and from several pages preserved in the British Museum, we have reason to believe that these diaries were a record of his pain, heartbreak, and humiliation, as well as his exaltation. A few documents and a good many letters escaped the holocaust. So the loss was not total; it was simply irreparable. There would have been a loss of comparable magnitude had Boswell's widow built a bonfire at Malahide Castle.

A fine oil painting of Sir Richard Burton painted by Sir Frederick Leighton in 1876 hangs today in the National Portrait Gallery. It is a strong portrait, as befits the man, showing the ruddy complexion, full beard and moustache, and fierceness of eye. Burton is in good company, in the same room with Matthew Arnold, Charles Dickens, John Ruskin, and Dante Gabriel Rossetti. Above him is Sir Charles Lyell, British geologist who was buried in Westminster Abbey. Across the room is the beguiling portrait of the three Brontë sisters done by their brother, Patrick Branwell Brontë. Burton seems to be staring at Ruskin, whose bland, blue eyes and benign countenance are in sharpest contrast with his own baleful glare. It is a curious accident that Burton should seem to be looking directly at the one man guilty of exactly the same kind of post-mortem burning as his wife. Ruskin had been made executor of the estate of the painter J. M. W. Turner, and in going through the collection of his canvases in 1857, he discovered a group of paintings Turner had made of sailors and prostitutes on the London docks. He burned them all.

Isabel knew the story well. "Turner's executors burnt a few of his last pictures under similar circumstances to leave his reputation as a painter at its zenith," she wrote. "I acted from the same motive."[15] Though the burning insured Isabel Burton's position as Richard Burton's most important biographer, it nevertheless underlined her incomprehension of the true nature of his "demon," and made everything she wrote suspect, especially her portrait of "the inner man."

The Merest Trifles

How strange are the tricks of memory, which, often hazy as a dream about the most important events of a man's life, religiously preserve the merest trifles.

Richard Burton, *Sind Revisited*[1]

*I*N HIS BOOKS Richard Burton wrote in exuberant detail about every-thing save the people who touched him most deeply. We hear him marvelling at the desert stars over Mecca, cursing the imbecility of British generals in the Crimea, raging at the mutilation of Sudanese boys for sale as eunuchs in Zanzibar, and defending the purity of the *Kama Sutra*. But among all the thousands of pages of his lively prose, including 143 pages of autobiography, he devoted fewer than three pages to his mother, scarcely more to his father, and only fleeting references to his wife. His anecdotes about his mother are written lightly, with little apparent feeling. The first, and probably the most significant, is a story of betrayal. We do not know who told him the story, or how many times in his childhood he heard it repeated. But at age fifty-five, when Burton came to write about his mother, the first fact he recorded was that she was responsible for his being cheated out of £80,000.

This money was the legacy of his grandfather, Richard Baker, an English country gentleman of substantial means, who lived with his strong-minded Scottish wife Sarah at Barham House, Hertfordshire. To his three daughters Baker had given a considerable dowry when they were married, and he expected to divide the remainder of his property among these daughters and his only son, Richard Baker, jr, the child of his first wife. But Baker had difficulties with his son, and after his daughter Martha gave birth to his first grandson and named him Richard, he began to think seriously of disinheriting the youth in favour of the new infant.

Richard Francis Burton was born at Torquay, March 19, 1821,[2] baptized at Elstree, and for a time lived in his grandfather's house. Before he was a year old his parents moved to France, but returned with him for long visits. Burton tells us that his earliest memory was "being brought down after dinner at Barham House to eat white currants, being seated upon the knee of a tall man with yellow hair and blue eyes." The grandfather delighted in Richard's hair, which was red at birth and only later changed to black, as well as in his precocity. "I was intended for that wretched being, the infant phenomenon," Burton wrote wryly, "and so began Latin at three and Greek at four." The grandfather's affection deepened as his troubles with his own son multiplied, and these difficulties came to a climax when the boy was three and a half. Martha Burton returned again to Barham House, this time for the birth and baptism of Richard's younger brother Edward. Burton gives us a truncated story of what happened, writing with a staccato quality, as if he were getting the memory past him as fast as possible.

My mother had a wild half-brother—Richard Baker, junior, a barrister-at-law, who refused a judgeship in Australia, and died a soap-boiler. To him she was madly attached, and delayed the signing of my grandfather's will as much as possible to the prejudice of her own babe. My grandfather Baker drove in his carriage to Messrs Dandy, his lawers, with the object of signing the will, and dropped dead, on getting out of the carriage, of ossification of the heart; and the document being unsigned, the property was divided. It would now be worth half a million of money.[3]

Richard Bark, jr duly inherited his share, and promptly lost the money to a French swindler, Baron Thierry, who subsequently set himself up as a king on a South Sea island and came to a Burtonesque end when he was devoured by cannibals. Beyond this we know nothing of young Baker's life, but it is worth noting that where "wild" was the appropriate word for the half-brother to whom Burton's mother was "madly attached," wild, too, became a fitting adjective for her son. How much Martha Baker's unspoken fascination for delinquency was responsible for her son's persisting inclination towards it, we are to see in Richard's life.

Burton prefaced the second anecdote about his mother with an account of his wildness as a young boy in France. "I was a boy of three ideas," he wrote. "Usually if a child is forbidden to eat sugar or to lap up the cream he simply either obeys or does the contrary; but I used to place myself before the sugar and cream and carefully study the question, 'Have I the courage not to touch them?' When I was quite sure of myself that I had the courage I instantly rewarded resolution by emptying one or both."[4] He described himself and his brother as "perfect devilets," fighting the French gutter boys, tricking the brutal schoolmasters, upsetting and pommelling their female servants, and taunting the aged concierges, who screamed predictions that they would end up at the guillotine.

"Our father and mother had not much idea of managing their children," he wrote. "It was like the old tale of the hen who hatched ducklings. By way of a wholesome and moral lesson of self-command and self-denial, our mother took us past Madame Fisterre's windows, and bade us look at all the good things in the windows, during which we fixed our ardent affections upon a tray of apple-puffs; then she said, 'Now, my dears, let us go away; it is so good for little children to restrain themselves.' Upon this we three devilets turned flashing eyes and burning cheeks upon our moralizing mother, broke the windows with our fists, clawed out the tray of apple-puffs, and bolted, leaving our poor mother a sadder and wiser woman, to pay the damages of her lawless brood's proceedings."

"Talking of the guillotine," he went on, "the schoolmaster unwisely allowed the boys, by way of a school-treat, to see the execution of a woman who had killed her small family by poisoning, on condition that they would look away when the knife descended, but of course that was just the time (with such an injunction) when every small neck was craned and eyes strained to look, and the result was that the whole school played at guillotine for a week, happily without serious accidents."[5]

The special interplay of these old memories, with the primitive themes of temptation, denial, smashing, poisoning, and decapitation—all having to do with his mother—are no less remarkable than the light-hearted tone of the writing, and the haste with which he dispatches a description of what may well have been the most awesome spectacle of his life. There is no blood in these recollections, either blood on his fists, as there must have been if he truly smashed the pastry shop window, or blood spurting from the woman's head as it fell into the basket. Sometime early in his life Burton had learned to detach himself from anxiety by assuming the role of observer. So horror was transmuted into excitement, and even the execution of "a mother" became a kind of game.

Burton's niece, Georgiana Stisted, described Burton's mother as "a gentle and intensely unselfish woman" who led "a harmless and amiable life." She described her as "tall, graceful and attractive, with tiny hands and feet and a mass of luxuriant brown hair." Burton used only the adjectives plain, thin, and delicate, and before his marriage the adjectives he usually employed to describe British women were hysterical, highly nervous, dyspeptic, and thoroughly civilized, with the latter always a pejorative term. Georgiana also wrote that Burton "adored his mother, thinking nothing in heaven or earth too good for her." Martha Burton was married to a man who was something of a prig, and apparently had imprisoned herself in a reputation for gentleness and generosity. So it was not surprising that she came to take a secret pleasure in the wild indiscipline first of her half-brother and then of her eldest son.

In one of his early Indian travel books Burton revealed that as a child he suffered from recurrent nightmares. "Did you ever," he wrote, ". . . when abandoned by your nurse to the horrors of a big black bedroom see a grinning face advancing towards you from the distant apex of the huge cone which lay before your closed eyes—advance gradually, but unavoidably, till, in spite of your struggles, its monstrous features were so close to yours, that you could feel them; then, almost suddenly, start back from you, flit away, diminish till nothing but the dark eyeballs remain in sight, and disappear presently to return with all its terrors?"[6]

In the same book he described his astonishment as a young soldier in India in the "all-absorbing passion" of the Hindu mothers for their children, contrasting their behaviour with that of British mothers in a passage that is remarkable not only as a piece of comparative ethnology but also as a poignant personal document:

> To the Hindu mother the child is everything. From the hour of his birth she never leaves him day or night. If poor, she works, walking about with him on her hip: if rich, she spends life with him on her lap. . . . When he is sick, she fasts and watches, and endures every self-imposed penance she can devise. She never speaks to or of him without imploring the blessing of Heaven upon his head; and this strong love loses nought when the child ceases to be a toy; it is the mainspring of her conduct towards him throughout life. No wonder that in the East an unaffectionate son is the rare phenomenon: and no wonder that this people when offensively inclined always begin by abusing one another's mothers.

In western civilization, on the other hand, he continued,

> The parents are engrossed by other cares—the search for riches, or the pursuit of pleasure—during the infancy of their offspring. In the troublesome days of childhood the boy is consigned to the nursery, or let loose to pass his time with his fellows as he best can; then comes youth accompanied by an exile, to school and college . . . there is little community of interests and opinions between parent and child—the absence of it is the want of a great tie.

Later he wrote, "Nothing astonishes Hindus so much as the apparent want of affection between the European parent and child."[7] Noting that many mothers among primitive peoples nursed their children into the second and even third year, he counted it healthy and a great boon to the child. In Medina, he described a pilgrim mother meeting her two sons. The youngest was "weeping aloud for joy as he ran around his mother's camel . . . standing on tiptoe, she bending double in vain attempts to exchange a kiss, while the surly elder brother stood by watching." "Truly," he wrote, "the Arabs show more heart on these occasions than any Oriental people I know."[8]

It is a mistake, however, to take Burton's wistful intimations of abandonment and deprivation wholly at face value, even though hunger for the forbidden and the lost seemed to be with him always. As we shall see, except for a single critical year at school in England when he was nine, Burton lived with his mother until he was nineteen. Moreover, between ten and nineteen he was tutored at home, and therefore was near her constantly. When finally he left for the university, according to his niece, his mother said it was "just as if the sun itself had disappeared."[9]

That Burton *felt* cheated, deprived, and unsure of her affection, however, there can be no doubt. Very early it was reflected in a special kind of delinquency.

> Like most boys of strong imagination and acute feeling [he wrote] I was a resolute and unblushing liar; I used to ridicule the idea of my honour being in any way attached to telling the truth, I considered it an impertinence the being questioned, I never could understand what moral turpitude there could be in a lie, *unless it was told for fear of the consequences* of telling the truth, or one that would attach blame to another person. That feeling continued for many a year, and at last, as very often happens, as soon as I realized that a lie was contemptible, it ran into quite the other extreme, a disagreeable habit of scrupulously telling the truth whether it was timely or not.[*]

Actually Burton never wholly abandoned lying. As an adult he attributed to himself killings and cannibalism that were wholly fabrications. He lied to shock, to amuse, and above all to catch and hold an audience. And in a deeper sense, since his lying made all reality relative, it also made the truth he could not bear to face less painful. As a young man he began to watch other men lie, and to examine the phenomenon perceptively in his writing. Of lying among the Sindians in northern India he said, "Where truth is unsafe this must be expected from human nature." Again he wrote, "They deceive because they fear to trust. They boast, because they have a hope of effecting by 'sayings' what there are no 'doings' to do."[10]

Late in life Burton wrote, "A man is mostly what his mother makes him."[11] Certainly his mother was his first and most important audience. Although in the beginning the lying may have been an effort to impress

---

[*] Isabel Burton, editing her husband's memoir, entered at this point a characteristic footnote: "From that moment he became a man wholly truthful, wholly incorruptible, who never lost his 'dignity', a man whose honour and integrity from the cradle to the grave was unimpeachable." Isabel Burton: *Life of Captain Sir Richard F. Burton*, I, 21n.

by "sayings" as he could not by "doings," he soon came to entertain her with true madcap adventures. And there developed a secret alliance between them. On his journey to Mecca, in describing the affection of an Arab mother for her son, he wrote, "Like all mothers, she dearly loved the scamp of the family."[12]

A third episode, which took place when Richard was fifteen, shows that the corrupting quality of his mother's indiscipline continued through his adolescence. A Jamaica Irishman wintering, like the Burtons, in Pau in southern France, one night offered the two boys all they could drink. "Edward, not being very well, was unusually temperate," Burton wrote, "and so I, not liking to waste it, drank for two." He went home deadly pale, with staring eyes, and his mother thought he had contracted cholera. "But other symptoms puzzled her," Burton confessed. "She fetched my father, who came to the bedside, looking carefully for a minute at his son and heir and turned upon his heel, exclaiming, 'The beast's in liquor.'"

His mother reacted first with a flood of tears, then with a surreptitious financial offering, and finally with an apparently irrelevant interdiction, this time a naughty book. She "presented me with a five-franc piece," Burton said, "making me promise to be good for the future, and not to read Lord Chesterfield's 'Letters to his Son,' of which she had a dreadful horror. It need hardly be said that the five francs soon melted away in laying in a stock of what is popularly called 'a hair of the dog that bit.'"[13] And it can be taken for granted that he read Lord Chesterfield immediately.

The contrast between his father's contempt and his mother's compassion in this episode stuck like a burr in Burton's memory. He described it in his memoir, at fifty-five, and referred to it again at sixty-three, when, in translating the *Arabian Nights*, he stumbled upon a similar story. An Arab youth, Nur al-Din, comes home drunk with wine, and his father suspiciously asks what ails him. The protecting mother interjects deftly, " 'Twould seem his head acheth for the air of the garden," but the father will not be evaded and loudly berates the youth. "How true to nature the whole scene is," Burton wrote in a footnote, "the fond mother excusing her boy and the practical father putting the excuse aside. European paternity, however, would probably exclaim, 'The beast's in liquor!'"[14]

Burton's final reference to his mother, describing the parting when he left her in Italy at nineteen and went off to Oxford, is bitter. "The break-up took place about the middle of the summer. It was comparatively tame. Italians marvelled at the Spartan nature of the British mother, who, after the habits of fifteen years, can so easily part with her children at the cost of a lachrymose last embrace, and watering her prandial beefsteak with tears. Amongst Italian families, nothing is more common than for all the brothers and sisters to swear that they will not marry if they are to be separated from one another."[15] If, after all these years of proximity he found her grief on parting thin, one can well believe that his mother over the years had been seductive as well as denying. He vowed on numerous occasions—as his niece reported—that he would never marry at all.

As we shall see, he spent two years at Oxford and then seven in India, returning at the age of twenty-eight. He lived briefly in England and then moved to France, where his mother and sister joined him. His father, except for brief visits, chose to remain in Italy. This curious arrangement was maintained for four years. Then in 1853 Burton went off to explore what he called "the mother city of Islam," forbidden to all non-Moslems. Before he returned his mother was dead. He did not marry for another seven years—by then he was almost forty.

Joseph Netterville Burton, Richard's father, was of mixed English, Irish, and possibly French blood, and claimed to be closely allied with if not actually a member of the British aristocracy. Sir Edward Burton, "a desperate Yorkist," had been knighted by Edward IV, and Sir Thomas Burton had been created a baronet by James I. However, there was a gap in Burton's lineage prior to 1750, and one had to go back to 1712 to establish connection with a line claiming the honours of a baronetcy. Richard Burton's grandfather was the son of an English clergyman who had emigrated to Ireland and married a girl of Irish, or Irish-French descent. His son Joseph grew up on what Burton described as an impoverished Irish estate, and left it to join the British army at seventeen. He rose to the rank of Lieutenant-Colonel—which in the days of purchased commissions would suggest considerable wealth.

When Burton wrote about his father in his memoir, he noted first that he was "considered a handsome man, especially in uniform, and attracted attention even in the street." He described him as "more of a Roman in appearance than anything else, of moderate height, dark hair, sallow skin, high nose, and piercing black eyes," most of which suggests a resemblance to himself. But Burton would have us believe that from a very early age he accounted himself ugly, unlike his father and younger brother.

"As handsome men generally do," Burton wrote of his father, "he married a plain woman, and . . . the children favoured, as the saying is, the mother." "Our parents," he continued, "very unwisely determined to correct all personal vanity in their offspring by always dwelling upon our ugliness. My nose was called cocked; it was a Cross which I had to carry, and was a perpetual plague to me; and I was assured that the only decent feature in my face was my teeth. Maria, on account of her fresh complexion, was called Blousabella, and even Edward whose features were perfect, and whom Frenchmen used to stop and stare at in the streets, and call him 'Le Petit Napoleon,' was told to nauseousness that 'handsome is as handsome does.' "

Although Burton's numerous portraits and photographs testify to a rugged, masculine face that for all its fierceness was also boldly handsome, there is evidence of his great dissatisfaction with it. He grew a moustache, later a beard, each of which was frequently changed in length, shape, and size, as if to dramatize the persisting discontentment with his face, or perhaps more importantly with his total self. When starting off as a young officer for India at twenty-one, he shaved off his hair altogether—to keep his head cool, he said—and carried a wig. At fifty-five, when Sir Frederick Leighton was painting his portrait, he said to the artist, "Please don't make me ugly, don't."[16]

But Burton never carried himself as an ugly man. And it is quite possible that his preoccupation with his face was connected with his consuming desire to disassociate himself from his father in this as in every other respect. Like his father he too attracted attention in the street, not for the perfect features but rather for an extra dimension in size and bearing, and for an absolute originality in face and character. Young Laura Friswell, aged nine, saw him as "a bold, bad bandit," and Harold Nicolson, even younger, never forgot his "questing, panther eyes." Ouida wrote, "His mere presence in a club-room made the ordinary club-men seem small." Arthur Symons, poet and critic, said that he had "a tremendous animalism, an air of repressed ferocity, a devilish fascination."[17]

Georgiana Stisted tells us Burton said that "his father was the most moral man he had ever known; and would often add, in his curious, abrupt way, 'Nice to be able to feel proud of one's parents!' " Many biographers have cited this statement as evidence that he was indeed proud of them, but since his intonation went unrecorded, no one can be certain whether Burton was really expressing pride, or simply noting ironically his lack of it. Burton himself described his father as "a highly moral man," but added the immediate qualification that though he was too moral to be seen in a gambling room, he was a plunger on the Stock Exchange with "a decided taste for speculation," and "utterly reckless where others would be more prudent." "Happily," the son continued, "he could not touch his wife's property, or it would have speedily melted away; yet it was one of his grievances to the end of his life that he could not use his wife's money to make a gigantic fortune."

If we are to accept his son's account, there was little to admire about Joseph Burton aside from his good looks. His military rank, as we have seen, argued nothing but the means to purchase it. Moreover, his professional career was cut short by a gesture his son found incomprehensible. In 1820, while stationed in Genoa with a contingent of British troops, he was trapped in the intrigue surrounding the estrangement of King George IV and Queen Caroline, who was at this time also living in Italy. Rumours that she had an Italian lover filtered back to England, and the king, seeking an excuse for divorce, had her tried by the House of Lords for adultery. It was of course the *cause célèbre* of its day. Several British officers stationed in Italy were ordered to appear as witnesses against her, among them Joseph Burton. Believing her, as did most Englishmen of the time, to be innocent (she was indeed, acquitted),[18] he refused to testify. The Duke of Wellington, then prime minister and opposed to the queen, penalized Burton by putting him on half pay, and thereafter—as the son heard the story—"he lost all connection with the army." Instead of making some attempt to mend his career, he decided to leave England altogether. This was 1821, the year of Richard's birth.

Having affectionate memories of southern Europe, Joseph Burton chose to live on the continent, first in central France, where the food was good, the necessity for keeping up appearances less troublesome, and where he could live decently—if parasitically—upon the income from his wife's inheritance. They moved to Tours when Richard was but a few months old. His father never worked again.

Richard later described the milieu into which his parents settled in Tours with a sharp eye for its scale of values.

> It contained some 200 English families . . . an oasis of Anglo-Saxondom in a desert of continentalism. . . . They stuck to their own Church because it *was* their Church, and they knew as much about the Catholics at their very door, as the average Englishman does of the Hindu. . . . They were intensely national. Any Englishman in those days who refused to fight a duel with a Frenchman was sent to Coventry, and bullied out of the place. English girls who flirted with foreigners, were looked upon very much as white women who permit the addresses of a nigger, are looked upon by those English who live in black countries.[19]

They lived in a small chateau which they called Beauséjour, on the right bank of the Loire, with a garden, vineyards, and a captivating view. Later, in his long poem *The Kasidah* Burton wrote:

> Ah! gay the day with shine of sun, and bright the breeze,
>   And blithe the throng
> Met on the River-bank to play, when I was young,
>   When I was young.

There were horses and dogs, snail-hunting and picnicking, with nearby shops like that of Madame Fisterre, the maker of admirable apple-puffs. The great old chateaux of the French kings and high nobility dotted the river nearby, and Richard grew up with these castles to illuminate his fantasies. It is not surprising that he listened enraptured to a family legend that the *Roi Soleil* himself, Louis Quatorze, may have been his own ancestor.

There is hardly anyone who does not early in life imagine himself to be the child of a king, cast by mischance into the laps of the pedestrian parents who are rearing him. So beguiling is this fantasy that countless families in Europe and many in America pride themselves on having a drop of royal blood. The Burton genealogy was surprisingly explicit save for the inevitable flaw, which came in the beginning. Louis XIV was said to have fathered the son of the Countess Montmorency, though the king never acknowledged him. The boy, Louis le Jeune, grew up a Huguenot. Fearful for the safety of his own son, he was said to have smuggled him to Ireland with the aid of a Lady Primrose, who adopted him. This boy, Drelincourt Young, grew up at Armagh and eventually married and begat Sarah Young, who was unmistakably Richard Burton's paternal great-grandmother.

Burton took the story seriously, noting that his Grandmother Burton's portrait showed "the regular Burton traits, the pear-shaped face and head which culminated in Louis Philippe's." Isabel Burton insisted on tidying up the record by saying what is nowhere else recorded, that Louis XIV had "morganatically *married* the Countess," but Richard was untroubled by the taint of illegitimacy in his heritage. When discussing the matter once with Sir Bernard Burke, who expressed astonishment that Burton, being connected with so many of the best families, should trouble about what could "only be a morganatic descent at best," Burton replied, "Why! I would rather be the bastard of a King, than the son of an honest man."[20]

Joseph Netterville Burton was doubtless honest, and in the English colony of Tours respected and respectable. Throughout his son's childhood, he was content to hunt boar in the forest, to attend soirées, to dabble in chemistry, and to drink with the Italian and Irish expatriates, whom he particularly liked. He struggled valiantly but ineptly with the education of his sons. Richard in his memoir gave no hint of any mutual affection, instead complained of the want of understanding, of the perpetual "scolding and threatening," and "the usual parental brutality." Later he quoted John Locke with approval: "*Beating* is the worst and therefore the last means to be used in the correction of children."[21] Throughout his whole childhood, he said, one governess, a remarkable Miss Morgan, was "the only one who ever spoke to us children as if we were reasonable beings."

He never forgave his father the character of his education. And whatever his father most liked to do he would first try and then come to detest. He hunted every variety of animal in India, but abandoned hunting altogether with contempt save for hunting with a falcon, which held his interest longest, perhaps because it was the bird and not he that did the killing. Where the father was superstitious, hypochondriacal, and prey to the exponents of every medical nostrum, Richard became a serious student of medicine—and his brother a practising physician—with a blistering contempt for the quackery inside and outside the profession. Where his father frittered away both time and money, giving himself up wholly to sloth in the end, the son worked as if pursued by a demon, for long periods incapable of even momentary idleness. Significantly, when Burton chose a pseudonym under which he published some of his poetry, he settled on Baker, the maiden name of his mother.

And yet Burton paid his father the compliment of identification in one of the most crucial decisions of his life, when he insisted on becoming a soldier. True, this, too, was against his father's wishes, for with singular obtuseness the elder Burton hoped to turn him into a clergyman. Affection for the uniform was not Richard's alone; Edward also, as a surgeon, went into the army, and Maria married a lieutenant-general.

When, finally, Richard Burton went off to India in uniform, he watched the behaviour of Hindu fathers with their sons with no less absorption than he watched the mothers. In 1847, at twenty-six, in a foretaste of the great translating of his later years, he sat down in Bombay to translate the charming *Pilpay's Fables* into English. If one looks today in the Royal Anthropological Institute in London at this still unpublished manuscript, with its crabbed handwriting and its key passages blackly underlined, one notes that this, Burton's first serious literary effort, began with the story of a father and two sons. "Alas," complains the Raja Chandra-Sain, "there are four qualities collected in my sons, namely youth, wealth, pride, and ignorance—any one of which is sufficient to bring a man to ruin and *utter confusion.*" And the problems of this story begin when the sons—as Burton translated and underlined the act—*stand disrespectfully in his presence.*

The Impact of France

My misfortunes in life began with not being a Frenchman.

Richard Burton to John Payne, January 19, 1884[1]

*W*HEN RICHARD WAS nine his parents left Tours, though the reason is obscure and seems to have remained always obscure to the son. He insists that his father had been happy there, and that life had been "gay and pleasant." He could not know that this would be the beginning of an incessant wandering—fourteen moves in ten years—that would scar him in a special fashion for life. Though he recorded his "wild delight" in escaping school and masters, his memoirs also reflect the ancient pain of this first uprooting.

Travelling with a family was "a severe affliction," he said; it meant refurbishing old carriages, stuffing miscellaneous luggage into innumerable receptacles, and auctioning off to greedy strangers everything that could not be carried. Then came the journeying "along the interminable avenues of the old French roads, lined with parallel rows of poplars, which met at a vanishing point in the far distance." The inns were small and wretched, with damp sheets, frigid bedrooms, and an inevitable two-hour wait for dinner. Burton remembered his parents arguing with rapacious landladies, one of them, her arms akimbo, roaring, "If you are not rich enough to travel, you ought to stay home."[2]

It was a frightening year on many counts; in 1830 France was in upheaval, with revolution hurtling Charles X from the throne, and a cholera epidemic decimating the nation. The frantic Burton flight was without obvious destination. It ended in Chartres when Richard's mother became critically ill, and Grandmother Baker was sent for to rescue the paralysed family. This sturdy Scotswoman, who detested the French, and who never failed on crossing the Channel to "inflate her nostrils" and quote her favorite Cowper, "England with all thy faults, I love thee still," now packed up the whole family for a return to Brighton. The Burton children, their noses stuffed with camphor to ward off infection, rode wide-eyed through Paris, seeing bullet holes in the walls and the skeletons of burned houses.

Back in England Joseph Burton for the first time seems to have faced seriously the question of a British education for his sons. Despite his childhood in Ireland, he proved now to be ambitious for them in exactly the fashion of the class to which he pretended—it had to be Eton and Oxford or Eton and Cambridge, with no alternative even to be considered. As preparation for admission to Eton, he settled on an obscure institution in Richmond run by the Reverend Charles Delafosse. Richard recognized later that in theory this was sound planning. "To succeed in English life," he wrote, "boys must be brought up in a particular groove. First the preparatory school, then Eton and Oxford, with an occasional excursion to France, Italy, and Germany . . . to find out that England is not the whole world." What Joseph Burton had not reckoned with in his sons was the already overpowering impact of France.

From the first moment of docking they detested England. They shuddered at the cold grey seas, the smoke-filled air of Brighton.

Everything appeared so small, so prim, so mean, the little one-familied houses contrasting in such a melancholy way with the big buildings of Tours and Paris. We revolted against the coarse and half-cooked food, and, accustomed to the excellent Bordeaux of France, we found port, sherry, and beer like strong medicine; the bread, all crumb and crust, appeared to be half baked, and milk meant chalk and water.

At boarding school what was bad turned to execrable—"stick-jaw pudding," meat cooked "black out and blue inside, gristly and sinewy," with grapeshot potatoes and the hated carrot, and on Saturday, "a peculiar pie, which contained all the waifs and strays of the week." The headmaster, Delafosse, Burton said, was "no more fit to be a schoolmaster than the Grand Cham of Tartary." "Instead of learning anything at this school, my brother and I lost much of what we knew, especially in French, and the principal acquisitions were, a certain facility of using our fists, and a general development of ruffianism." The school was "a nightmare," the "Blackshop of Charles Dickens."

His sister Maria, he wrote, "says that I was a thin, dark little boy, with small features and large black eyes . . . extremely proud, sensitive, shy, nervous, and of a melancholy, affectionate disposition." In the British school he became fierce, surly, and desperate. "I was in a perpetual scene of fights; at one time I had thirty-two affairs of honour to settle." Finally, he said, he was "beaten thin as a shotten herring, and the very servant-maids, when washing me on Saturday night, used to say, 'Drat that child! what has he been doing? He's all black and blue.'" Edward, he said, "fought just as well as I did, but he was younger and more peaceable." Later, in reflecting on the brutalizing effect of boarding schools, he noted shrewdly, "Such is the effect of a boy's school after a few months' trial, when the boys learn to despise mother and sisters, and to affect the rough as much as possible, and this is not only in England, but everywhere the boy first escapes from petticoat government. He does not know what to do to show his manliness."

The Richmond preparatory school was perhaps not much worse than others of the time, and had Richard remained, learning to meet the routine sadistic hazing with dodging and good humour, he might have found the second year tolerable and in due time have entered Eton. But a severe epidemic of measles struck the school and several boys died. Richard and his brother were sent home temporarily, and their Aunt Georgina, appalled by her older nephew's cadaverous appearance, urged his parents to take the boys out altogether. Joseph Burton, who disliked England no less heartily than his sons, was now easily persuaded. "He was sighing for shooting and boar-hunting in the French forests," Burton wrote, "and he felt he had done enough for the education of the boys, which was turning out so badly. He resolved to bring us up abroad, and picked up the necessary assistance for educating us by tutor and governess."

Burton later looked upon this step as a fatal error. "A man who brings up his family abroad, and who lives there for years, must expect to lose all the friends who could be useful to him when he wishes to start them in life. The conditions of society in England are so complicated, and so artificial, that those who would make their way in the world, especially in public careers, must be broken to it from their earliest day. The future soldiers and statesmen must be prepared by Eton and Cambridge. The more English they are, even to the cut of their hair, the better." But at the moment, when his family embarked for France, he and his brother were ecstatic at their liberation. "We shrieked, we whooped, we danced for joy. We shook our fists at the white cliffs, and loudly hoped we should never see them again. We hurrah'd for France, and hooted for England, 'The Land on which the Sun ne'er sets—nor rises,' till the sailor who was hoisting the Jack looked upon us as a pair of little monsters."

The measles epidemic was probably the most critical single accident in Burton's life. "In consequence of being brought up abroad," he wrote, "we never thoroughly understood English society, nor did society understand us." And at another time, even more grimly, he said, "England is the only country where I never feel at home."

But Richard Burton did not emerge from his years in France as a Frenchman. Instead he grew up ambivalent about both nations, lacking any strong sense of national identity, counting himself, as he put it, "a waif, a stray . . . a blaze of light, without a focus." However, he had learned that escape from nightmares was possible, and it is not altogether surprising—especially since the pattern was reinforced by his father's wanderings—that in later years whenever Burton found life intolerable, he invariably sought relief in flight, if possible to another country.

Crossing the Channel was not identical, however, with going home, as the Burton children discovered to their chagrin. Instead of returning to Tours they stopped in Orleans, "a horrid hole," and then moved on down the Loire to Blois, which had a sizable British colony. Richard mentions the old royal chateau town with indifference—"when one describes one colony one describes them all," he said—and only Beauséjour seems to have been permanently lodged in his heart. Many years later, when about to start his memoirs, he returned to the little chateau, pleased to find the beauty undiminished and to escape the disillusionment that usually accompanies such journeys into one's past.

At Blois Richard first uneasily sensed in his parents the beginnings of degeneration.

> Our father and mother were imperceptibly lapsing into the category of professed invalids, like people who have no other business in life except to be sick. . . . They tried every kind of drug and nostrum known, and answered every advertisement. . . . They had a kind of rivalry with other invalids; nothing offended them more than to tell them that they were in strong health, and that if they had been hard-worked professionals in England, they would have been ill once a year, instead of once a month. Homeopathy was a great boon to them, and so was hydropathy. So was the grape-cure and all the humbug invented by non-professionals, such as the hunger-cure and all that nonsense.

There was a searing family crisis in Blois, when the elder Burton resolved to move to Italy. Grandmother Baker, visiting at the time, trumpeted, "You'll kill your wife, sir," and tactlessly accused her son-in-law of wanting to return to a mistress of earlier days. Richard, who heard more than he should of the adult squabble, described the mistress ambiguously as "a young Sicilian woman who received the Englishman's pay and so distributed it as to keep off claims." Grandmother Baker was packed off to England, and the Burtons set out for Italy in a series of slow moves, which indicate that whatever the obscure object of his search, Joseph Burton had settled into wandering as a way of life. Every stop proved somehow distasteful. Lyon was "a perfect den of thieves," and Livorno "the headquarters of brigands." In Pisa they lived on the wrong side of the Arno; in Siena the expatriate English were "fugitives from justice, social or criminal," and Rome was "a piggery."

But along with the grumbling in Burton's memoir—surely the child's echo of the perpetual parental complaining—he communicated also his own excitement and delight at countless new discoveries. If he found Siena "one of the dullest places under heaven," he also adored Perugia. He became a "walking catalogue" of art in Florence, and went from church to palazzo and from ruin to ruin in Rome with "peculiar ardour." He learned also to swim, dance, and shoot, and to play chess two games at a time with his eyes blindfolded. He learned to draw with such skill that he was able later to illustrate his own travel books. Edward became a competent musician, but Richard's violin lessons ended when, in a fit of violent anger because his master complained of sour notes, he broke the instrument over the old man's head.

He became a passionate fencer, picking up the best of both the French and Neapolitan techniques, and combining them in such fashion that he became, eventually, one of the outstanding swordsmen of Europe. "Fencing," he said, "was the great solace of my life." At fifteen he planned to write a book on technique; forty years later, in 1876, he did write a 59-page instructional manual on a wholly different kind of sword-play, *A New System of Sword Exercise for Infantry*. By then he had become so fascinated with the sword as a symbol that he wrote a 300-page piece of socio-historical research, *The Book of the Sword*— erudite, sophisticated, occasionally mystical. The sword is "a gift of magic," he said, "one of the treasures sent down from Heaven," "a creator as well as a destroyer," "the key of heaven and hell."[3]

But as a boy he looked upon it merely as an instrument of pleasure. Once when he and Edward were fencing without masks, his foil (no doubt button-tipped) went down the younger brother's throat. It "very nearly destroyed his uvula," Burton wrote, "which caused me a good deal of sorrow." The memory must have returned to haunt him later when Edward, as a young surgeon in Ceylon, received a brain injury that left him a life-long mute. When Richard began his memoir, he had long since come to terms with Edward's fate, and when he mentions him at all it is with tenderness.

In his memoir he scarcely notices his sister Maria, except to record that he borrowed her savings to buy secretly a forbidden case of pistols, but it is clear that the three children turned to each other for the affection and communication so lacking in their constantly changing and always foreign environment. "It is a common saying in the family," Burton's niece wrote dryly, "that the Burtons understand only each other."

As they wandered over the continent governesses came and went, most of them quickly, as they found their task to be, in Richard's words, "absolutely impossible." The boys, aged ten and seven, were entrusted to a tutor, an Oxford graduate named H. R. DuPré, described as "an awkward-looking John Bull article," with narrow forehead and thick lips, "who wanted to see life on the continent, and was not unwilling to see it with a salary." From the beginning Richard detested him. He had permission to beat his pupils with a horsewhip, and did. The permission continued for nine years, though the beatings diminished as the boys became handy with their fists. So to the beatings Richard received from his father, and to those received in the English preparatory school, were now added the beatings from his English tutor. It is hardly surprising then that he came to associate the land of his birth with punishment.

Why DuPré chose to stay with the Burtons so long, and why the parents retained him in the face of the boys' hatred are equally mysterious. By the time Richard was eighteen DuPré was no longer a threat or a teacher. "We had thoroughly mastered our tutor," he wrote, "and threw our books out of the window if he attempted to give a lesson in Greek or Latin." Richard did, however, emerge from these years with a precocious cosmopolitanism—a familiarity with European art, architecture, and geography gained first-hand, an intimate knowledge of social behaviour in half the provinces of Italy and France, and an unusually explicit schooling in sexual matters learned mostly from Italian medical students. His extraordinary promise, as evidenced by his intellectual energy and prodigious curiosity was, however, very nearly wrecked by the indiscipline and dilettantism of his education.

What saved Burton, and pointed the direction of his subsequent career, was his extraordinary linguistic gift. Nimble and quick with the French he had learned at Tours, he developed also a flawless ear for French dialects as his family moved ever southwards. At Pau he learned Bernais, a mixture of French, Spanish, and Provençal. He learned Italian in northern Italy, and a smattering of spoken Greek in Marseilles. In the long stay in Naples he so mastered the Neapolitan dialect that he was equipped in later years to make the finest English translation of Giovanni Battista Basile's *Il Pentamerone*, a collection of Neapolitan folk tales that rivaled those of Boccaccio. Eventually he picked up Spanish and some German, and became proficient in Portuguese.

During his adolescence he constantly pushed outward, warm-hearted and eager, hungry for communication. Inevitably his attacks on the new language or dialect were rewarded with friendship and admiration. "The country folk were delighted when addressed in their own lingo," he wrote. "Nothing goes to the heart of a man so much as to speak to him in his own patois." Where his parents were imprisoned in their illnesses and expatriate rituals, the boy became free for experience and friendship. Not only did he become inured to the successive uprootings, but he also developed a talent for taking the measure of a new city without prejudice or dread. Sometime during these years he adopted as his motto: *Omne solum forti patria*, which he translated: *For every region is a strong man's home.*

He moved in and out of the little English colonies, garnering the maximum from the temporary friendships, falling in love with a succession of British girls and occasionally with an Italian, Edward duly imitating him. All the girls were strictly watched by their parents, and little came of the amours save regretful references in his autobiographical fragment. Naples he loved best as the least strict of all the Italian cities, the site of his most celebrated adolescent escapades. Here the housing was good, the servants inexpensive, and his parents had some status through unexpected connections at the court of Frederick II, King of Naples, who, despite a reputation for cruelty and treachery, tolerated the English and was considered by the local British colony something of a *bonhomme*.

Richard explored the whole Sorrento peninsula, climbing the ash-covered slopes of Vesuvius many times, taking twenty minutes to reach the crater and four to come down—"You could only feel incredulous that it was possible to run at such a rate," he wrote. He tried to climb down into the ever-steaming crater, and had to be forcibly hauled up. Once during an eruption, with the lava flowing all the way to the sea, he and his brother jumped on top of the blackening fire stream and burned their boots, deriding the friends who dared not follow.

It was in Naples, too, that he and Edward, their knives in their belts, invaded one of the prostitute areas and spent their pocket money treating the neighbourhood. "The orgie was tremendous," he wrote with satisfaction, "and we were only too lucky to get home unhurt, before morning, when the Italian servant let us in." Though only fifteen and barely twelve, the brothers became enamoured of two "syrens" in the area and wrote them passionate letters. Their mother, discovering the correspondence, and realizing from the nature of the girls' replies that they were prostitutes, was horrified. "A tremendous commotion was the result," Burton wrote. "Our father and his dog, DuPré, proceeded to condign punishment with the horsewhip; but we climbed up to the tops of the chimneys, where the seniors could not follow us, and refused to come down till the crime was condoned." It was this episode, Burton noted drily, that "disgusted our father of Naples, and he resolved to repair to a pure moral air."[4]

So they moved north and across the border into France. Before they left a severe outbreak of cholera spread through the city, the death toll at its highest reaching 1,300 in a single day. The epidemic brought panic and paralysis, and a rumour spread that the disease was not cholera but mass poisoning, for which the government was somehow responsible. Several doctors were murdered, and a mob gathered in the market square threatening revolution. At this point, as Burton tells the story, "the King himself drove up in a phaeton and jumped out of it entirely alone, told the citizens to put up their ridiculous weapons, and to show him where the poisoned provisions were, and, seating himself upon a bench, ate as much as his stomach would contain. Even the *lazzarone* were not proof against this heroism, and viva'd and cheered him to his heart's content."

Richard found the king's behaviour magnificent. To show his contempt for his own parents' panic—perhaps also to allay his own anxiety about dying through a conspicuous act of courage—he resolved upon a dramatic gesture of his own. As usual, he involved Edward as co-conspirator and witness. Knowing that the corpses of the poor were regularly gathered in carts in the dead of night and taken outside the city for mass burial, he persuaded an Italian servant to get two costumes appropriate for undertakers' mutes, and then the two boys, dressed like *croquemorts*, slipped out and passed themselves off as assistants to the men engaged in the grisly labour. It was the first of Richard Burton's many successful disguises, and resulted in what may well have been the most traumatic night of his whole adolescence.

Outside Naples was a large plain, pierced with pits [he wrote], like the silos or underground granaries of Algeria and North Africa. They were lined with stone, and the mouths were covered with one big slab, just large enough to allow a corpse to pass. Into these flesh-pots were thrown the unfortunate bodies of the poor, after being stripped of the rags which acted as their winding-sheets. Black and rigid, they were thrown down the apertures like so much rubbish, into the festering heap below, and the decay caused a kind of lambent blue flame about the sides of the pit, which lit up a mass of human corruption, worthy to be described by Dante.

It was a courageous and macabre adventure, worthy of Burton in Mecca and Burton in Africa, and he told it for posterity at fifty-five with a grave relish, doubtless a faithful enough echo of what he had told to his horrified parents when he was just fifteen.

Oxford

THE REMARKABLE THING about the Burton family is that it held together until Richard was nineteen. But by 1840, as Burton wrote, "it was ripe for a break up." "Our father, like an Irishman, was perfectly happy as long as he was the only man in the house, but the presence of the younger males irritated him. His temper became permanently soured. He could no longer use the rod, but he could make himself very unpleasant with his tongue." Since there was no formal schooling the boys were constantly at home, and "we were not pleasant inmates."

The last winter together was spent in Pisa, where Burton went for a time to the University. Here he and Edward became friends with a group of Italian medical students and were soon experimenting with opium as well as alcohol, and carousing in the streets. One fight brought the local police. "My legs were the longest, and I escaped," Burton wrote, but Edward landed in jail. When their stony-faced father went to rescue his son, he found the youth light-heartedly treating the other prisoners to the contents of his pocket flask of Jamaica gin. Joseph Burton seems finally to have admitted that it was time to abdicate his role as educator, and announced that this was the last straw and the youths must go to school in England. Richard begged to go to the university in Toulouse, but his father was adamant. It was to be Oxford for Richard and Cambridge for Edward, with careers as clergymen for both.

In the autumn the youths set out for "the chill and dolorous North," casting "longing eyes at the charming country which we were destined not to see again for another ten years."[1] Once they were back in England the old dislike returned with redoubled violence. "Everything appeared to us so small, so mean, so ugly," Burton wrote. "The faces of the women were the only exception to the general rule of hideousness. . . . The little bits of garden were mere slices, as if they had been sold by the inch. . . . And there was a desperate neatness and cleanness about everything that made us remember the old story of the Stoic who spat in the face of the master of the house because it was the most untidy place in the dwelling." Only the massive, gracious buildings of Oxford reconciled him to staying, though the little cardboard-like houses clustering around them reminded him "of swallows' nests planted upon a palace wall."

Settled in Trinity College, he immediately established a reputation for irreverence and rebellion. He refused to be "sentimental, tender, and aesthetic" about the university, preferring to call the caps and gowns absurd, the students' rooms dog-holes, the cheese beeswax, and the meat fit only for cannibals. Having arrived with an impressive moustache, "the envy of all the boys abroad," he was affronted at all the clean-shaven faces, which made him feel he was back among school children, and when within the first hour of his arrival, one of the upperclassmen laughed at it, Richard challenged him to a duel. This gesture, which would have been appropriate at Heidelburg or Bonn, was greeted with absolute incomprehension at Oxford. Explanations succeeded, and he went his way sadly, convinced, he said, that he had fallen among grocers.

Actually it was against the university rules to wear such a moustache, but Burton refused to be shaved until handed down formal orders from the college authorities. This was the first of several acts of bravado for which in the end he paid a heavy penalty. All his rebellion, however, was now against the dons rather than his fellow students, few of whom, learning of his reputation as boxer and fencer, chose to test his strength. He was now about six feet tall, with immense shoulders and massive head, and his facial sculpture already showed something of the ferocity that in later years became indelible. Burton, said one of his acquaintances, "was, without doubt a terrible fighter." His friends called him Ruffian Dick, not because he acted the ruffian, but in a "playfully complimentary" fashion, referring to two famous pugilists of the day who went by the nicknames of "Old" and "Young Ruffian." The term referred only to their style of fighting.[2]

At Oxford Burton quickly learned what he had failed to perceive at the age of nine, that English youths "begin by being tossed, and then toss others in a blanket." Once he submitted with good humour he was soon accepted and popular, with a respected reputation for his liquor capacity and his ingenuity in devising practical jokes. He stood on his feet long enough and late enough to put the Welsh boys to bed; he smuggled in forbidden air canes, and shot down the rooks circling above the masters as they played at bowls. He climbed down a rope at night into the Master of Balliol's garden, plucked the finest flowers and planted in their place "great staring marigolds," writing with relish that "the old gentleman's countenance when he saw them next morning was a joy forever."

His reputation for wit and high spirits soon won him numerous dinner invitations in the town, particularly at the home of the Duke of Brunswick, where he met the most celebrated of the Oxford scholars, Thomas Arnold, John Henry Newman, and Benjamin Jowett. He was personally impressed only by Newman, but came away from Oxford with a respect for the thoroughness of their classical learning and for the discipline that lay beneath it.

At Oxford, too, he made the first friendships that would endure through life, among them the fencing master, Archibald Maclaren, and the Reverend Thomas Short, his tutor, who treated his infractions of discipline with a lenient hand. His best friend was Alfred Bates Richards, a big, rangy, muscular student who could outbox Burton but never master him with either foil or broadsword. Later, as the editor of the *Morning Advertiser*, Richards wrote an illuminating sketch of Burton. Of the Oxford days he said, "I am sure, though Burton was brilliant, rather wild, and very popular, none of us foresaw his future greatness, nor knew what a treasure we had amongst us."[3]

Burton seldom wore his genius on his sleeve, preferring, as Francis Galton noted, "dressing himself, so to speak, in wolf's clothing, in order to give an idea that he was worse than he really was."[4] His only ambition seemed to be acquiring a reputation for wildness and eccentricity —the result in part of his mother's sly delight in folly, and of his father's corrosive petulence, which he mistook for contempt, and for which he paid with contempt in return. Moreover, having never been in a proper school, Burton had no experience measuring himself scholastically against his fellows. He possessed conviction but no proof of his superiority. He was certain only that he had been educated badly, and with this the unperceptive Oxford professors readily agreed.

Richard's father insisted from the beginning that he try for a fellowship. He applied and was turned down. But by one of those twists of fate that plagued Burton often in his life, the failure resulted not from the defects but from the very superiority of his education and talent. For it was in Greek and Latin, which by now he knew thoroughly, that he failed to satisfy the dons. Burton could not only read and translate ancient Greek, he could also speak some modern Greek, which he had learned from Greek merchants during a sojourn in Marseilles. This he could not resist demonstrating during the examination. "The devil palpably entered into me and made me speak Greek Romaically by accent, and not by quantity, even as they did and still do at Athens," he said. But the examiners, instead of being impressed by his linguistic ability, saw only gross errors of pronunciation.

Then when he went on to converse in "Roman Latin—real Latin" instead of the anachronistic Anglicized Latin taught only in Britain and understood only by Englishmen—a remnant of an old distinction between Protestants and Catholics—the dons laughed at him. DuPré should have taught him what to expect, but apparently had not, or else Burton relished disregarding him. And he may well have indelicately paraded his contempt for the Anglicized Latin during the examination. The true Roman Latin pronunciation would eventually be adopted in all British schools, but meanwhile Burton failed to get the fellowship, which went instead to an inferior student who, as Burton put it contemptuously, "turned a chorus of Æschylus into doggerel verse." This was the first of several rivals in Burton's life who would carry off a prize he deserved. The failure generated a rage that had quiet but destructive consequences.

Disconsolate and bitter, he decided now not even to try for the coveted "first class." "I did not care to begin my life with a failure," he wrote by way of explanation. It is significant that Burton never again competed with undistinguished and mediocre men in conventional fields, turning instead toward the exotic. He had failed his father, who had "set his heart" upon the fellowship; he had also defeated him, and when Burton said "the devil palpably entered into me and made me speak Greek Romaically," he dimly recognized the force of a wish to fail. Still he felt immense respect for Oxford—as he may still have felt for his father—and the defeat festered.

It did not help when he looked about him and saw the sons of noblemen—distinguished from others by the gold tufts on their mortar board hats—granted academic honours almost automatically. "With a smattering of letters, enough to enable a commoner to squeeze through an ordinary examination," he wrote, "gold tuft took first class, and it was even asserted that many took their degrees merely by sending up their books." Oxford, he concluded, "with notable exceptions, was a hotbed of toadyism and flunkeyism," and he agreed with a contemporary definition—"a place to make rather ignorant gentlemen."

Though defeated in the field of his greatest talent, Burton did not flee from languages but shifted instead to an exotic tongue—Arabic. There were no classes for undergraduates in Arabic at Oxford, and when he approached the regius professor who might have helped him, he was told that "it was the duty of a professor to teach a class and not an individual." More determined than ever, once the right to learn was denied him, Burton began to teach himself. A friendly Spanish Arabist, Don Pascual de Gayangos, whom he met at dinner, noting that the youth wrote his Arabic letters from left to right, laughingly pointed out the error and showed him how to copy the alphabet.

A new language meant something special for Burton; it was both a challenge to his ambition and a healing of the wounds to his self-esteem. There must also have been the fantasy common to those who fail at school, the dream of some day besting the professors at their own game. Scorned by the scholars, he would one day be the greatest of them all. The honours in Latin and Greek he would leave to the formidable Jowett and Newman,* but in the exotic Arabic he could shine—as he had shone as a boy in the Bernais and Provençale dialects. In any case, out of this crisis of failure an Arabic scholar was born whose name would one day reign over all others as translator and propagandist for the literature of the East.

Along with his bitterness against the language examiners, Burton had developed too a raging contempt for their teaching methods. Their philology, he said, was ridiculous, and they failed to use man's capacity for reason. Properly scorning the hundreds of schemes for transliterating Arabic into Latin letters, he evolved a language learning technique entirely his own. He learned it as a child does, he wrote, as a work of pure memory, but with every artificial assistance possible. This technique, which must have begun without conscious planning as he picked up languages in southern Europe, became so perfected at Oxford and later in India that Burton eventually could learn a new language in two months.

I got a simple grammar and vocabulary, marked out the forms and words which I knew were absolutely necessary, and learnt them by heart by carrying them in my pocket and looking over them at spare moments during the day. I never worked for more than a quarter of an hour at a time, for after that the brain lost its freshness. After learning some three hundred words, easily done in a week, I stumbled through some easy book-work (one of the Gospels is the most come-atable), and underlined every word that I wished to recollect, in order to read over my pencillings at least once a day. Having finished my volume, I then carefully worked up the grammar minutiae, and I then chose some other book whose subject most interested me. The neck of the language was now broken, and progress was rapid. If I came across a new sound like the Arabic *Ghayn*, I trained my tongue to it by repeating it so many thousand times a day. When I read, I invariably read out loud, so that the ear might aid memory. I was delighted with the most difficult characters, Chinese and Cuneiform, because I felt that they impressed themselves more strongly upon the eye than the eternal Roman letters . . . whenever I conversed with anybody in a language that I was learning, I took the trouble to repeat their words inaudibly after them, and so to learn the trick of pronunciation and emphasis.

Burton readily admitted the distinction between "learning" a language and mastery of it. And he pointed out, too, that he would forget the most recently learned language when attacking a new one. The Arabic begun at Oxford certainly did not have its neck broken in two months. Nevertheless, when he joined his parents in Germany for a holiday, he had something positive to lay at his father's feet along with

---

* Shortly before his death he did turn to the serious translation of Latin poetry, but chiefly that poetry which had been considered too indelicate for British taste.

the fellowship failure. In Heidelberg he confessed his depression over his Oxford career and begged for permission to go into the army, "that failing, to emigrate to Canada or Australia." Edward, too, tired of being tutored by a humourless clergyman in preparation for entering the university, "swore he would rather be a 'private' than a fellow of Cambridge."

But their father, Burton wrote, was inexorable. "He was always thinking of that fellowship." So Richard returned to Oxford. "I went there with no good will, and as my father had refused to withdraw me from the University, I resolved to withdraw myself." Three brothers among his friends, sons of an Indian army colonel, were planning to enter the Bombay army and begged him to join them. The British East India Company was gradually extending dominion over northern India into Sind. Here there was fighting and a chance for glory, and Burton decided he must go there at all costs.

He deliberately planned to get himself rusticated from Oxford, not expelled, and drew a careful distinction between them. "The former may happen in consequence of the smallest irregularity, the latter implies ungentlemanly conduct." He gave bigger and more opulent wine parties; he circulated caricatures of Heads of Houses, parodies, epigrams, and epitaphs, but nothing happened. Finally, in open defiance of a college order forbidding undergraduates to attend a steeplechase, he persuaded several youths to accompany him in a tandem, and "when they should have been attending a musty lecture in the tutor's room, they were flicking across the country at the rate of twelve miles an hour."

The next day, brought before the college dignitaries, Burton protested that they were being treated like children. "Trust begets trust," he said, and insisted that attending a race was no breach of morality but a test of their maturity. It was no doubt a fine and eloquent speech, but the dons felt that "to commit a crime and to declare it a virtuous action" was arrogance beyond condoning. All the other culprits they simply suspended; Burton they expelled.

The youths hired a tandem to leave in style, stowed their luggage in it, and bade farewell with the driver steering the high-trotting shaft horse over the beds of the best flowers, while Burton hooted his loudest on a tin trumpet and kissed his hand to the shop girls. Watching so light-hearted an exit from High Street up the Queen's Highway to London, few could have guessed that Richard Burton was sick with rage. "In my anger," he wrote frankly in his memoir, "I thoroughly felt the truth of the sentiment—

> 'I leave thee, Oxford, and I loathe thee well,
> Thy saint, thy sinner, scholar, prig, and swell.'"

In greeting his fond aunts in London, he could not at first bear to tell the truth, and invented a tale about being given a vacation for having taken "a double-first with the very highest honours." At first believing him, they celebrated with a dinner party, which in the end only served to add a sense of outrage to their disappointment—thus doubling the punishment for Richard, who cared for their good will. The faithful Edward, who had by now matriculated at Cambridge, speedily followed his brother's example, though with less of a flourish.

Eight years later, in 1850, after an acute personal crisis in India, Richard Burton returned to Oxford, faced again at twenty-nine with the agonizing decision of what to do with his life. "Like the prodigal son," he wrote, "I returned to Alma Mater with a half-resolution to finish my terms and to take my bachelor degree. But the idea came too late. I had given myself up to Oriental studies, and I had begun to write books." To this Isabel Burton added a footnote. She wrote it with her characteristic disarming simplicity, but in linking Oxford with Burton's father she managed uncharacteristically if accidentally to be profound: "How often I have heard him regret that he did not do this, and I can testify that at the bottom of his heart he loved Oxford, but he could not obey his father, and also carry out the destiny for which he was best fitted and obliged to follow."

V

Fact and Fiction in India

I loved—yes, I! Ah, let me tell
The fatal charms by which I fell!
Her form the tam'risk's waving shoot,
Her breast the cocoa's youngling fruit;

Her eyes were jetty, jet her hair,
O'ershading face like lotus fair;
Her lips were rubies, guarding flowers
Of jasmine dewed with vernal showers.

Richard Burton, *Stone Talk*[1]

*D*URING BURTON'S YOUTH British power in India had extended north
like a giant octopus, with tentacles pushing up the Bolan and
Khyber passes into the mountains of Afghanistan. As was customary
with the military officers of the East India Company, they signed
treaties with the local Ameers and then pulled back the striking force,
leaving only a token garrison of mixed British and Indian troops, with
a civilian governor to recover taxes and enforce British ideas of justice.
No one in England or India was prepared for the massacre of January
1842.

Uniting in unexpected strength the Afghans threatened Kabul. The
doddering General W. G. K. Elphinstone (who had been best man at
the wedding of Burton's parents) agreed to evacuate the country, and
over sixteen thousand men, women and children—700 British troops,
4,000 Indian troops, and 12,000 followers—fled the city into the fearful
January storms. Many froze to death in the mountain passes, others
were captured or slain, and only one survivor reached Jalalabad to tell
the story. The British public, which had watched the extension of
empire in India with easy complacency, clamoured for revenge, and
recruitments for the Indian Army soared. This crisis, coming shortly
after Richard Burton's expulsion from Oxford, worked in his favour.
It was now easy for Joseph Burton to capitulate to his son, and after
some manoeuvring he purchased a commission for him in the Bombay
army at a cost of £500.

Immediately Richard abandoned a new enthusiasm—astrology and the literature of the occult—and plunged into the study of Hindustani —the most important and widespread of the Hindi dialects—working under the gifted Orientalist, Duncan Forbes, of King's College in London. "In India two roads lead to preferment," Burton later wrote. The first is "getting a flesh wound, cutting down a brace of natives, and doing something eccentric, so that your name may creep into a despatch. The other path, study of languages, is a rugged and tortuous one, still you have only to plod steadily along its length, and, sooner or later, you must come to a 'staff appointment.'" The third road— using influence—he disdained. Though his father had relatives in India, among them a general and a judge in Calcutta, Burton was determined to lick no boots. "A man proves his valour by doing what he likes," he said.[2] It was a bold but impolitic formula for army life.

When the *John Knox*, carrying Ensign Burton and a shipload of fellow officers and men docked in Bombay October 28, 1842, one soldier shouted ashore, "What news from Jalalabad?" At the answer, Burton wrote ironically, "All hopes fell to zero. . . . The campaign was finished. . . . Ghuzni had fallen, the prisoners had been given up . . . and there was no chance of becoming Commanders-in-Chief within the year."[3]*

His first days at Bombay were all disenchantment. The romantic East seemed only dinginess, filth, and stench. The streets were common sewers, and even the lone cathedral tower, built by the Portuguese, seemed to him "splotched and corroded as if by gangrene." The spectacle of natives imitating European dress offended him. The first sight of a Sepoy in faded scarlet and blue dungarees "nearly drove me back to the *John Knox*," he wrote, deploring the abandonment of the native dress, with its white cotton jacket, graceful coloured waistcloth falling to the ankles, and bright cloth slippers.

The want of privacy, always an affliction to Europeans in the Far East, appalled him. After a few nights in a hotel, where drunken guests stood on chairs and shouted obscenities over the thin cloth partitions, he felt sick with rage. Walking along the seashore to escape, he stumbled upon the Hindu funeral burning ground, and stood in fascination, watching heads and limbs tumbling off the pyres. A kindly garrison surgeon gave him quarters in a sanatorium by the sea. Though infested with lizards and bandicoot rats, and close to the smell of roast Hindu when the wind was right, it was a haven. The inmates,

* Burton learned later, with great resentment, that officers of the Bombay army, which was technically under the semi-official British East India Company rather than the regular British army, were severely discriminated against in the latter organization, and had almost no chance for advancement beyond the rank of Captain, regardless of the degree of war service.

some of whom were not very ill, led what Burton called "a roystering and rackety life," and were happy to lead him into "all kinds of mischief, introducing me to native society of which the less said the better."

Later in Baroda, where he was stationed with the 18th Native Infantry, he could see that the average officer lived rather handsomely. He had "a horse or two, part of a house, a pleasant mess, plenty of pale ale, as much shooting as he can manage, and an occasional invitation to dance, where there are thirty-two cavaliers to three dames, or to a dinner party when a chair unexpectedly falls vacant." The subalterns had at least five servants; one stood behind his master at meals, turbaned and gorgeously dressed, ready to place silver lids on the tumblers to keep out the insects. "But some are vain enough to want more," Burton wrote, "and of these fools was I."[4]

Most Englishmen who survived the fevers and climate of India lapsed after a year or two into fatalism, ennui, or debauchery, but with Burton seven years of service saw no diminution either of his ambition or his curiosity for the exotic. His preoccupation with languages now became a passion. He had barely landed in Bombay before seeking out the finest language-master in the city, a white-bearded Parsee priest, Dosabhai Sohrabji, who recognized the young ensign's linguistic genius and described him as "a man who could learn a language running." "I remained friends with the old man," Burton said, "till the end of his days."

Most of Burton's fellow officers, with traditional arrogance, looked upon the natives as "niggers" and savages, and accounted the officers who bothered to learn their language eccentric if not dangerous. "There was not a subaltern in the 18th Regiment, Burton said, "who did not consider himself capable of governing a million Hindus." He knew from his childhood the incomprehension, hostility, and contempt of any people for the foreigner who cannot speak his tongue, and this he could no more endure in Asia than in France. "I threw myself with a kind of frenzy upon my studies," he wrote. "I kept up the little stock of Arabic that I had acquired at Oxford, and gave some twelve hours a day to a desperate tussle with Hindustani."[5]

Five months after his arrival in Baroda in April 1843, he obtained leave for official testing. Facing him in Bombay was Major General Vans-Kennedy, a fine Orientalist who knew Hindustani and Persian intimately, as well as Gujarti, Sanscrit, and Arabic. Preferring the society of natives, he lived in a "tumbledown bungalow in a tattered compound," with an incomparable collection of books and manuscripts. A tough examiner, he insisted that Burton and the eleven other officers translate from two books and a sample of native writing, that they engage in conversation and write a paper. Burton finished first out of the twelve, winning the respect and friendship of Vans-Kennedy, and went back to his first staff appointment, regimental interpreter.

Immediately he plunged into the study of Gujarti, which was spoken by the local Parsees, and began elementary lessons in Sanscrit. Within seven months he was back before Vans-Kennedy, whom he had come to admire as he could not admire his father, and again he passed first. This time he outdistanced Lieutenant C. P. Rigby, one of the finest linguists in the Bombay army, who later became one of Burton's implacable enemies. In the next year he passed first in Marathi, outdistancing six. It was as if no amount of examination passing could exorcise the memory of his Oxford failure. Each return to Vans-Kennedy deepened their friendship. Increasingly he identified himself with this military scholar, accumulating Oriental books and manuscripts, and so mingling with the natives that his fellow officers began to call him "the white nigger." Later, in describing these Indian years, Burton pronounced the sobriquet "ominous," and it was.

He took to languages in India as other men to liquor, intoxicated by the sense of mastery and the exhilaration of unlocking mysteries. Late in 1844 he took up Persian, and eventually went on to Sindi, Punjabi, Telugu, Pashto, Multani, Armenian and Turkish. Perhaps language mysteries were a substitute for mysteries more primitive; foreign tongues may have taken on for him a libidinal quality, particularly since he grew up without a true mother tongue. The Arabic language, which he came to cherish above all others, he once described as "a faithful wife following the mind and giving birth to its offspring."[6] Eventually he became one of the three or four great linguists of his time, mastering in the end twenty-nine languages and enough dialects to add up to more than forty.[7]

In Baroda, partly as a joke but also with serious intent, he collected monkeys of different ages and species, took them into his house and tried to unlock the mystery of *their* language. Calling them doctor, chaplain, secretary, and aide-de-camp, he gave them stools to sit on and bowls to eat from at the table. His servants waited upon them with decorum, and he kept order with a small whip. Isabel Burton tells us that "one tiny one, a very pretty, small, silky-looking monkey, he used to call his wife, and put pearls in her ears." He collected a vocabulary of sixty sounds before abandoning the study for that of another human language, but his notes were destroyed in a warehouse fire in London in 1861.[8]

Burton was not a pedant with languages but a libertine—mastering, using, and abandoning. Though he spent many hours in these pursuits, they were for him neither an escape from nor a substitute for living, for he sampled everything in India with great gusto—the conventional and unconventional, the respectable and the tabooed. Without the language mastery there would have been no easy open door to his multi-form adventures. "In those days," he wrote, "sensible men who went out to India took one of two lines—they either shot, or they studied languages." In the beginning he shot partridges, bison, boars, cheetahs, even tigers, though he came to despise all such sport. His wife tells us that "one of his greatest remorses was shooting a monkey." "It cried like a child," he said, "and I can never forget it."[9] He watched the popular native spectator sports—fights between elephants and tigers, or tigers and buffaloes. He tried riding alligators; he took lessons from a snake-charmer. He learned the Sepoy wrestling techniques and their horsemanship, which he thought superior to the British. In return he taught the native troops under his command to improve their swordsmanship.

The band concerts, billard playing, and prim picnics arranged by British "society" he found intolerable. British women in India, he wrote, often became "fanatically one-idea'd, pharisaical," overwhelming a man with lectures about his immortal soul and oral treatises on the proper behaviour of a Christian in a heathen land. Men and women alike, he wrote, "looked upon the heathen around them (very often far better than themselves) as faggots ready for burning."[10]

Clandestine intrigues among the British, however, he found common enough. "India was the classic land of Cicisbeism," he wrote, "where husbands are occupied between ten am, and five pm at their offices and counting-houses, leaving a fair field and much favour to the sub unattached." But Burton's taste was for more exotic pastures. In his seven years in India he had at least three love affairs, but none was with a "one-idea'd pharisaical" English woman. Details of these amours are brief, fragmented, and in one instance deliberately disguised. The first one, to which he admitted with surprising frankness, involved a native mistress in Baroda. He wrote of her tersely, seemingly without feeling:

The *Bibi* (white woman) was at that time rare in India; the result was the triumph of the *Búbú* (coloured sister). I found every officer in the corps more or less provided with one of these helpmates. We boys naturally followed suit; but I had to suffer the protestations of the Portuguese *padre*, who had taken upon himself the cure and charge of my soul, and was like a hen who had hatched a duckling. I had a fine opportunity of studying the *pros* and *cons* of the *Búbú* system. . . . [The *Búbú*] is all but indispensable to the student, and she teaches him not only Hindostani grammar, but the syntaxes of native Life. She keeps house for him, never allowing him to save money, or, if possible, to waste it. She keeps the servants in order. She has an infallible recipe to prevent maternity, especially if her tenure of office depends on such compact. She looks after him in sickness, and is one of the best of nurses, and, as it is not good for man to live alone, she makes him a manner of home.[11]

About forty years later he referred to the blundering techniques of the British soldier in the art of making love to Indian women. Europeans, he wrote, "are contemptuously compared by Hindu women with village cocks; and the result is that no stranger has ever been truly loved by a native girl." And again he wrote, ". . . while thousands of Europeans have cohabited for years with and have had families by 'native women,' they are never loved by them—at least I have never heard of a case." The reason he gave for this sweeping failure—which whether correct or not was a melancholy admission on his own part— was ignorance of the erotic techniques that were taught to Hindu youths as an essential part of their education. The Hindus, he said, were particularly skilled at "Ismác," the art of delaying in the act of love. "The essence of the 'retaining art' is to avoid over-tension of the muscles and to pre-occupy the brain: hence in coition the Hindus will drink sherbet, chew betel-nut and even smoke," for the Hindu woman, he said, "cannot be satisfied, such is their natural coldness, increased doubtless by vegetable diet and unuse of stimulants, with less than twenty minutes."[12] The inference is unmistakable that Burton felt unloved by his native *Búbú*, that the failure caused him anguish, and that he counted himself to blame.

His second amour, more of a madcap adventure than a real love affair, took place in Pangim, Goa, near a British sanatorium where Burton was on sick leave in 1846. He told the story as if it had happened to someone else—an unnamed British lieutenant—but his description of this officer left very little doubt that it was really a self-portrait. He pictures him as "a very clever gentleman who knew everything," who could talk to each man of a multitude in his own language," whose faith "was every man's faith," and who "chaunted the Koran and the circumcised dogs considered him a kind of saint."

Searching for reading matter at the library of the nunnery of Santa Monaca, not far from the sanatorium, the officer, Burton tells us, was overcome at the sight of the Latin teacher, a young nun, "a pretty white girl with large black eyes, a modest smile and a darling of a figure." Pretending to be making inquiries about a place in the nunnery for his sister, he visited the prioress often, meanwhile surreptitiously courting the Latin teacher. Without too great difficulty he persuaded her to flee the convent she hated.

The night of the planned escape he anchored a boat offshore, leaving it in the care of a Portuguese guide, Salvador. Dressed in Muslim garb

with his face blackened, he proceeded cautiously to the nunnery wall
with a hired accomplice named Khudadad. Meanwhile the young nun
had drugged the guards with datura seed mixed in their tobacco, and
waited in the night for the two men to open the gate with a skeleton
key. But the officer, "in the hurry of the moment, took the wrong turning, and found himself in the chamber of the sub-prioress, whose
sleeping form was instantly raised, embraced, and borne off in triumph
by the exulting Khudadad." The lieutenant "lingered for a few moments—crept out of the room, closed the door outside, passed through
the garden, carefully locked the gate, whose key he threw away, and
ran towards the place where he had appointed to meet Khudadad,
and his lovely burthen. But imagine his horror and disgust when, instead of the expected large black eyes and pretty little rose-bud of a
mouth, a pair of rolling yellow balls glared fearfully in his face, and
two big black lips, at first shut with terror, began to shout and scream
and abuse him with all their might."

"Khudadad, we have eaten filth," the officer said, "how are we to
lay this she devil?"

"Cut her throat," replied the ruffian.

"No, that won't do. Pinion her arms, gag her with your handkerchief,
and leave her—we must be off instantly."

And so they fled.

This was Burton at his brandy-after-dinner best. He included the
story in his *Goa and the Blue Mountains* as if he had heard it from
the Portuguese guide, Salvador. But his niece insisted that the lieutenant was indeed her uncle, and at least two other of Burton's biographers, Hugh J. Schonfield and Byron Farwell, count it authentic
biography. The adventure was in character, for the prize was supremely taboo, and therefore a challenge he could not resist. Still one
may recall that he ended the last of his four books on India by pointing
out how easy it was in the East to create "extreme confusion of Fact
and Fiction."[13]

Nowhere are fact and fiction more difficult to unravel in Richard
Burton's life than in the matter of his third love, which, unlike the
others, took on the character of a grand passion. He described his first
encounter with the beauteous Persian girl in some detail in *Scinde; or,
The Unhappy Valley*. Outside Karachi, he wrote, resting beside a
camel-train, there sat "a charming girl with features carved in marble
like a Greek's, the noble, thoughtful Italian brow, eyes deep and
lustrous as an Andalusian's, and the airy, graceful, kind of figure with
which Mohammed, according to our poets, people his man's paradise."
He sat down at once and composed a love letter, which he bribed her

slave boy to deliver to her tent. In tone and style it appropriately echoed the *Arabian Nights*:

> The rosebud of my heart hath opened and bloomed under the rays of those sunny eyes, and the fine linen of my soul receiveth with ecstasy the lustres which pour from that moon-like brow. But, woe is me! the garden lacketh its songster. . . . And he kisseth the shaft which the bow of Fate hath discharged at the bosom of his bliss. And he looketh forward to the grave which is immediately to receive him and his miseries. . . .

She replied coolly, asking if he knew anything of medicine and if he had any European remedies. Burton replied: "I will lay before her ladyship what we men of medicine in Feringistan [meaning, we European doctors in India] consider the Elixir of Life," and immediately began brewing over a slow fire a mixture of gin, powdered white sugar, and Eau de Cologne. The magic potion was duly delivered, but before she could reply she was hustled off by her male duenna, and all he saw was her "latticed face" under the burka, and her body swathed in robes, as she climbed aboard her camel and went off into the night.[14]

Beyond this Burton tells us nothing, and were it not for the wildly romantic account written by his niece, we would know little of what followed. With her well-honed talent for Victorian cliché Georgiana described a full-blown romance:

> The affectionate young soldier-student, separated by thousands of miles from kith and kin, expended the full force of his warm heart and fervid imagination upon his lustrous-eyed, ebon-haired darling; never had he so loved before, never did he so love again. She worshipped him in return; but such rapture was not to last. He would have married her and brought her home to his family, for she was as good as she was beautiful, had not the fell foe that ever lurks in ambush to strike or divide when for awhile we dare to be happy, snatched her from him in the flower of her youth, and the brightest hours of their joy-dream. Her untimely end proved a bitter and enduring sorrow; years after when he told the story, his sister perceived with ready intuition that he could hardly bear to speak of that awful parting, even the gentlest sympathy hurt like the touch on an open wound. From the day of the death of his best beloved he became subject to fits of melancholy.[15]

One could easily discount this as the embroidery of Georgiana's girlish fantasy were it not for the existence of a manuscript of verse in Burton's hand, which includes a long and impassioned outpouring of lament over the murder of a native girl in India. The poem describes the death of the girl by poison, the killing of her murderer by the poet, and the melancholy scene of burying her body. Though very little of Burton's poetry has survived, and that which he chose to publish appeared under a variety of pseudonyms, invariably the poetry is a surer clue than the prose to the turbulent inner man. The poem is remarkable for the intensity of feeling, although the actual narrative details serve only to disguise whatever was truly autobiographical in the episode, and to compound the mystery further. After describing how "the rounded form of her youthful charms, heaved in my circling arms," he wrote:

> Little I thought the hand of death
> So soon would stay that fragrant breath. . . .
> Or that soft warm hand that glorious head
> Be pillowed on the grave's cold stone
> Leaving my hapless self to tread
> Life's weary ways alone, alone. . . .
> Adieu once more fond heart and true
> My first my only love adieu
> The tortures of the poisoned bowl
> Cast the gloom of death around my soul. . . .
> Spirit of my own Shireen Fate heard my vow
> Neer was a maid so fair so loved so lost so 'venged as thou.*

It becomes increasingly clear, as one puts the mosaic fragments together, that the memory of this girl haunted Burton until late in life. The verses quoted at the beginning of this chapter, seemingly of no consequence by themselves, take on in the light of the earlier poem a wholly new significance. Burton wrote them as part of his long, satirical, and frequently impenetrable poem *Stone Talk*, published under the pseudonym Frank Baker in 1865. Here the narrator in the poem, described the "goddess," the object of his passion, as a Pariah's widow. At her death, apparently because of a broken vow, he is changed into stone.

In his last years Burton wrote of the Persians with special affection. "The gifted Iranian race, physically the noblest and most beautiful of all known to me," he wrote, "has exercised upon world history an amount of influence which has not yet been fully recognized," and he called Persian "the richest and most charming of Eastern languages."[16] Eventually he made a pilgrimage back to the Karachi area, revisiting with Isabel many of his old haunts. In the resulting book, *Sind Revisited*, he reprinted his own story of the brief encounter with the Persian girl intact, giving the impression that it had freshly happened, instead of when he was twenty-six. He reprinted also a Beloch

---

* This poem is among the early entries in the remarkable journal of Burton's poetry recently acquired by Mr Quentin Keynes. The watermark on this notebook is 1847. The handwriting corresponds with that of his "Pilpay's Fables" in the Royal Anthropological Institute, which is approximately the same date. Later poems in this notebook show a handwriting somewhat changed, always in the direction of greater illegibility. Shorter, and largely unfinished, they mention other loves, "fair Margaret, the far famed Clifton maid. . . . loved & courted, wooed in vain." The final pages are ripped out altogether, almost certainly by Isabel Burton.

love lyric which had so charmed him that he had translated it for inclusion in *Scinde; or, The Unhappy Valley*, of 1851. It may represent a fragment of autobiography:

> My love is a pigeon, a pea-hen in gait,
> A mist-cloud in lightness, in form a Peria;
> And her locks are like the tendrils of the creeping shrub.
> Burned for her my heart with secret longing,
> As the camel-colt, torn from his dam's side.
> At length when the taste of life was bitter on my palate,
> Came the old minstrel carrying his guitar;
> In one hand was a token from that lovely maid;
> Then my withered heart bloomed as the tree in spring. . . .
> I opened the curtains of her abode,
> And crept in disguised in a beggar's blanket;
> As the tree joys at the prospect of blossom,
> So expanded my heart with delight,
> The torments of months left my heart.[17]

Sind

Existence, too, in India is precarious; who can tell how soon a fever or a bullet may send him to the jackals? Consequently, we are, perhaps, a little over anxious to 'live whilst we may.'

Richard Burton, *Scinde; or, The Unhappy Valley*

*A*PART FROM HIS father, no one man changed the course of Richard Burton's life so irrevocably as Sir Charles Napier. He was the conqueror of the Sind, a little hawk-nosed Scotsman with a Rabelaisian wit and ferocious temper, who in 1843 in two great battles against 60,000 natives had killed 10,000, made nine sovereign princes captive, conquered or conciliated 400 chiefs, and annexed over 50,000 square miles of northern India for the Queen. The Sindians and Belochis, quarrelsome and disunited, armed with matchlocks no better than those made in the sixteenth century, had not been formidable opponents, and Napier sent England news of his success in a single word—the celebrated pun *Peccavi* (I have sinned)—which properly suggested the reality of the violation.

Sir Charles was an acknowledged eccentric. He had outraged his aristocratic family by coming home from a long campaign in Greece with two daughters, born of an alliance with a Greek woman. Devoted to the girls, he had married a woman fifteen years older than himself to raise them. Now in his sixties, he made no secret of the fact that he had accepted command in India only to make enough money to see his daughters properly married. He had been a superior strategist, always conquering with a minimum of British casualties, and he also proved to be a remarkable pacifier, who brought a measure of good government to an area that had been periodically robbed by predatory hill tribes, and misgoverned for generations. He turned Karachi into a usable port, and helped to harness the rampaging Indus River by improving the ancient canal system which drained off irrigation waters into the desert areas. He abolished slavery, did away with brigandage, and did his best to destroy the systems of usury and taxation that enslaved the poor.

He was horrified by the pervasive practice of punishment by mutilation. "As to wives," he wrote, "a husband on the least quarrel whips out his knife and off goes the woman's nose, and she is lucky if her lips and ears don't go also."[1] Thieves invariably had their right hands severed, and it was the custom of the invading Doomkees, a savage hill tribe, to kill the women and cut off both hands of all the children in the villages they pillaged. Under Moslem law murder was legally punished by the relatives of the victim; often this was settled by the payment of fines that were swallowed up in administrative corruption. Napier replaced the Hindu and Moslem legal practices with a police and court system similar to the British, and it was eventually copied throughout India.

Into his diary, the unexpurgated version of which in the British Museum is one of the saltiest documents in Anglo-Indian archives, he poured his rage and lamentation, and daily communed with his tyrannous conscience. Unlike most conquerors he had grave misgivings about his right to conquer. "The whole system of Indian government is constructed for robbery and spoilation, not for conquest, not for good to the multitude, not for justice!" he wrote on April 2, 1846, and deplored all the killing simply "to give commerce an advantage over rivals, and to back the ruling of idiots." He also admitted candidly that he loved winning battles and ruling men. "People say I love war, and so I do, as a man loves gambling though losing. . . ." This conflict between his delight and his guilt over what he called the "hellish work" of war crops up often in his diary. "There is no *intentional* wickedness on my conscience," he wrote on August 4, 1845. In his last period in India he was in constant abdominal pain from the stomach ulcers that eventually killed him, and he wrote to his brother that he longed to be like the cockroaches he had read about, which though experimentally disembowelled by a biologist and stuffed with cotton, were still capable of running about "happy as princes."[2]

Burton was first stationed under Sir Charles Napier in 1844, when the 18th Native Infantry was sent to the Sind. At that time there was talk of ten years' guerrilla warfare, and no one could be certain that the defeated chiefs, the Ameers, would not turn against the conquerors in bloody vengeance as in Afghanistan. It was some months before the old soldier learned of Burton's special linguistic accomplishments and began to use him in intelligence work. Isabel Burton later wrote that her husband had been an intelligence officer under Napier for five years, but it could not have been more than two years and eight months, from January 1844 to September 1846, and during part of this time he was an active field surveyor under Captain Walter Scott of the Bombay Engineers.

Burton had met Scott on board the *Semiramis*, which brought them from Bombay to Karachi. Burton had been sorry to leave Gujerat's tranquil beauty, with its marvelous banyans, pipal trees, and giant figs, which he said dwarfed the English oaks and elms. He had become fond of the villages, walled by luxuriant barriers of caustic milk-bush, with jet-blue smoke from burning dung playing over the landscape. He had become accustomed to the chattering of monkeys and the pervasive smell of curry, and had disliked only the rainy season, which he called "a terribly dull suicidal time." He had left a good mess, many friends, and his "morganatic wife." As they sailed into Karachi harbour, he saw a low line of coast, "sandy as a Scotsman's whiskers, a glaring waste, with visible as well as palpable heat playing over its surface." This was his first glimpse of Little Egypt, "The Unhappy Valley," which he knew to be plagued by heat, dust storms, cholera, and the annual flooding of the still badly tamed Indus River, and though it was some seven years later that he described the journey, in his book *Scinde; or, The Unhappy Valley*, depression even then coloured his narrative.

Captain Scott was going north to supervise the rebuilding of the Indus irrigation system. He was a nephew of the celebrated Scottish novelist and much resembled him in appearance, handsome, with soft blue eyes, yellow hair and a golden beard. Burton found him an admirable conversationalist, with a dry, pawky humour, and an affection for literature and history. "He never said a disagreeable word or did an ungraceful deed," Burton wrote, and it is clear that Scott in turn delighted in Burton's rich endowment and gusty wit. He worked under Scott at intervals for several years. "We never had a diverging thought, much less an unpleasant word," Burton wrote later, "and when he died, at Berlin in 1875, I felt his loss as that of a near relation."[3]

Before being transferred to Scott's staff Burton worked for nine months in the desert cantonment of Gharra, forty miles south of Karachi, mostly doing routine translations in court-martial trials. The area was flat, dusty, and barren, "scarcely affording thorns, salsolae, and fire-plants sufficient to feed a dozen camels." Burton called it "a mild Miltonic hell," where "the world shines and glistens, reeks and swelters, till the face of the earth peels and flakes, cracks and blisters."[4] Farther inland were forests of bamboo, tamarisk, Mimosa and poplars, with masses of sedge, weeds, and grass, which during the dry season burned in vast sheets of flame that trapped British and natives alike. Not for nothing, he discovered, had "the burning jungle" been a favorite theme of Hindu muses. T. E. Lawrence, stationed in Karachi a century later, would write, "We eat dust, and breathe dust, and think dust."[5]

Karachi, the Alexandria of this Young Egypt, destined to become the bustling modern port of Pakistan, was then a settlement of 6,000, mostly Moslems, "a mass of low mud hovels and tall mud houses with flat mud roofs, windowless mud walls, and numerous mud ventilators, surrounded by a tumble-down parapet of mud, built upon a low plat-form of mud-covered rock." The mud, actually clay mixed with straw, was adequate till the rainy season, when it would dissolve "like ice in a London ball room." At times a whole house would come crashing down upon the luckless dwellers. Burton had one foot damaged and barely escaped being buried when, after several days of rain, his hut collapsed around him.

Unlike in Baroda, where the British occupation was older, Burton felt the rancorous hatred of the inhabitants. In Karachi, occupied only since 1839, the boys still shouted curses, and the Sindian fishermen, naked from the waist, with indigo-coloured drawers—and their wives, mostly unveiled, with long coloured pantaloons and embroidered bodices—jeered at the white British faces. Burton found the lack of sanitation worse than in Bombay. The smell of dead fish, putrefying camel corpses, and sewage running in the streets alternated with the faint smell of drugs and spices from the bazaar "like a newly made mummy." Within a hundred yards of the British camp in Gharra, "the corpses of fifty camels are allowed to lie and fester . . . and poison the air," he wrote, "as if a little more death were really wanting." The jackals, "half torpid after their ravenous repast, creep out of their dirty dining-room in the corpse's stomach. In a few days there will be as neat a skeleton as was ever prepared by an enthusiastic medical student."

At first Burton was so wretched he abandoned studying the Sind language and took up Maharati instead, hoping for a transfer. But once appointed to Scott's staff, he returned to the language with zest. Within a year he had Sindi and Persian at his finger-tips, and a smat-tering of Punjabi. He came to bear the 120 degree summer heat, and to love the desert nights, when the mists mellowed the harsh landscape and the sky became "the deepest, purest, and most pellucid blue," with the moon "shedding streams of silver upon the nether world."[6]

Napier dreamed of making the Indus flow "like a child in a go-cart." He ordered the silt to be cleaned from the old canals, tried to eliminate cheating of the native farmers in water fees, and opened up new acreage for cultivation, giving two years free rent and a 14-year lease to natives who moved to the newly irrigated land. This was far-sighted statesmanship, but the British East India Company, which had ex-pected to find Sind a treasure trove, counted the cost excessive. Soon Napier was quarrelling furiously with the company directors, whom he called "a galaxy of donkeys,"[7] and who in turn did their best to see him retired to England as fast as possible.

Burton quickly learned the rudiments of surveying, and found his techniques superior at least to that of the Sindians, who had laid out the canals "with cotton strings and an eye for the rise and fall of the ground." The great Indus, the vagaries of which brought life and death to the area like the Nile to Egypt, was the third river in Burton's life. As a child he had watched the Loire in flood with admiration and fear. At Oxford he had trained in sculls on the Thames, competing among the crew before his expulsion. But the 900-mile-long Indus—extending three-quarters to a mile in width—was the first great river of his life. He called it "a foul and turgid stream, abounding in gyratory currents, tremendous rapids, dangerous drift wood, shifting sandbanks, and violent swells." Taming it became important to him. He learned much local lore teaching the natives to make efficient use of the water, and made himself an expert on the pernicious system of taxation imposed by the Ameers.

Every night he ate with the six officers of the Survey Mess, all young and light-hearted, fond of practical jokes. "Local society pronounced us mad," he wrote, "although I cannot see that we were more whimsical than our neighbours."[8] For a while they took up cock-fighting, and Burton had his own pet bird, a badly-bred barnyard fowl who was a ferocious fighter. When he finally succumbed in battle, Burton buried him ceremoniously outside his cottage, thereby giving rise to the rumour that he had interred a child.

Burton described two of his most complicated practical jokes, which are particularly revealing because they show that he was still angry at professional scholars and clergymen and eager to humiliate them. It was a popular belief among many Christians of his time that the so-called "lost Ten Tribes of Israel" had wandered into central Asia and would one day be rediscovered. When the British conquered an obscure tribe with so-called "Semitic" features in Bráhuistán, the rumour spread that these might be descendants of the celebrated missing Hebrews. Burton, after visiting the tribe, copied an old Hebrew vocabulary and grammar, added "barbaric terminations" and showed it to "sundry scientists" who were electrified with the proof that "the lost was found at last." "The Presidency rang for nine days with the discovery," he wrote, and only the pleadings of Walter Scott prevented him from publishing the complicated spoof.

Similarly at Sehwan, supposed to have been an ancient camp of Alexander the Great, Burton watched with contempt several antiquarians digging at the site. He knew the natives were already faking Greek coins and selling them to the credulous British—as yet archaeology was only a hobby, exacting the derision even of academic people everywhere save in Scandinavia—and he decided to expose the ignorance of his own countrymen. "Antiquarians are everywhere a

simple race," he wrote in his first book.[9] Taking a cheap pottery jar
with copies of Etruscan figures on it, he smashed it, treated it with fire
and acid, and secretly buried it in the site of the diggings. The antiquarians were enchanted, and showed the fragments about as proof
that the Etruscans had originated in the Sind.

Burton ruefully admitted both hoaxes. "I was never forgiven," he
wrote. "But I now repent in sackcloth and ashes," he added when describing what he called these "ugly practical jokes" in 1877, for by then
he had become a serious digger in the Etruscan ruins of Italy and had
gained a healthy respect for the burgeoning young profession.[10] The
shame was real. For at some time during his Indian years, he stopped
such adolescent attacks on scholars and began to forge a career of
serious scholarship in his own right. Two men were largely responsible
for encouraging this leap towards maturity; one was Walter Scott, to
whom he later dedicated one of his books on the Sind; the other was
a young surgeon, Dr John Steinhaeuser, a fine linguist and eager collector of Oriental literature, who first encouraged Burton in his idea
of translating an unexpurgated version of the *Arabian Nights*.

Heartened by their faith in him, Burton added to his collection of
books and manuscripts, began to keep elaborate journals, and to think
seriously about writing books on India. His confidence in having something unique to say was greatly heightened when he began intelligence
missions for Sir Charles Napier. Burton admired and feared his chief,
as did all his staff, and absorbed many of his prejudices, particularly
his favouring military as against civilian rule of native races. He later
wrote about Napier with real affection, but he was also critical of his
weaknesses, noting his "peculiar incontinence of tongue and passionate
recklessness of assertion" which "produced a host of hot and rancorous
enemies," words which could very well be applied to himself.[11]

When Napier began feuding openly with General James Outram,
popular young hero of the Sind war, the quarrel split the British in
India into two factions. Napier poured out his rage in his diary, calling
Outram a "damned scoundrel" and "son of a bitch" who spread "lies
and scurrilities."[12] Burton loyally applauded his chief in writing for the
Karachee Advertiser, a private sheet dedicated to Napier's defense.
Many years later he wrote to Leonard Smithers, "In my youth I served
under Sir Charles Napier, and learned from his career never to be
silent when the Press wants answering."[13]

Napier made no mention of Burton in his diary, but he did obliquely
refer to the fateful mission that meant catastrophe for his able young
lieutenant. It was traditional in India for British intelligence officers
to obtain data from paid native agents. Burton, however, chose to violate precedent by going into disguise. Staining his face with henna
and wearing long false hair and a beard, dressed in expensive native

garb, he appeared in the bazaars of the Sind cities as Mirza Abdullah of Bushire, a rich merchant, a vendor of fine linen, calicoes and muslins, with jewellery "reserved for emergencies." To explain his accent he professed to be half Arab and half Iranian. Sometimes he rented a shop, furnished it with "clammy dates, viscid molasses, tobacco, ginger, rancid oil, and strong-smelling sweetmeats," and sat for days in the market place asking a thousand questions and listening to everything. He conversed with priests and played chess with theological students; he smoked opium and drank bhang with the addicts. He noted that bhang, an intoxicant derived from hemp, affected addicts differently and described its effect upon himself: "You suspect treachery everywhere, and in the simplest action detect objects the most complexedly villainous. Your thoughts become wild and incoherent, your fancy runs frantic; if you are a poet you will acknowledge an admirable frame of mind for writing . . . nonsense-verse."[14]

At night, if he heard sounds of music and dancing, he would enter a house uninvited, his only ticket "a clean turban and a polite bow." By day he had free access to the houses to display his textiles, and soon had a store of private histories, domestic scandals, and details of harem life. "The European official in India seldom, if ever sees anything in its real light," he wrote, "so dense is the veil which the fearfulness, the duplicity, the prejudice and the superstitions of the natives hang before his eyes. And the white man lives a life so distinct from the black, that hundreds of the former serve through what they call their 'term of exile,' without once being present at a circumcision feast, a wedding, or a funeral." But there was more to Burton's disguise than an imaginative approach to intelligence work. He could in a very real sense act out his own fantasies. The elaborate pretence took courage and acting talent, of which he had an abundance, as well as a thirst for the forbidden, which had been with him since childhood. And he was a tremendous success. Mirza Abdullah, he wrote with satisfaction, "secured numberless invitations, was proposed to by several papas, and won, or had to think he won, a few hearts."[15]

He told Napier much that astonished him; one has only to compare Napier's diary for 1844–5 with Burton's Sind books to see the impact of his stories. He seems to have been the first to point out to Sir Charles—who was most reluctant to believe it—that though he had signed the death warrants of several rich convicted murderers, the actual man hanged was usually a poverty-stricken substitute hired in his stead. Burton interviewed one pauper "badal" who had agreed to be executed for a murder he had not committed and asked him why.

"Sain!" came the answer. "I have been a pauper all my life. My belly is empty. My wife and children are half starved. This is fate, but it is beyond my patience. I get two hundred and fifty rupees. With fifty I will buy rich food and fill myself before going out of the world. The rest I will leave to my family. What better can I do, Sain?"[16]

Burton also brought Napier data about domestic crimes that were peculiarly difficult to prosecute. "There is only one crime I cannot put down here," Sir Charles wrote in his diary in 1844, "wife killing! They think that to kill a cat or dog is wrong, but I have hanged at least six for killing a woman; on the slightest quarrel she is chopped to pieces." "Three days ago," said another entry, "a girl was suspected of being unfaithful to her husband. She was seventeen, and he was thirteen; her uncle killed the suspected lover; her father led her to the front of his house. . . . twisted her long hair in his hands, and holds her on tiptoe while her brother hacks off her head! This was all done openly and I will hang them all."

Burton seems also to have brought to Napier evidence of widespread infanticide, particularly among the Ameers, who killed their unwanted daughters. Napier confessed he did not know how to eradicate the vicious practice. "They first give their odalisques, or women, potions to cause miscarriage, and if that fails they chop up the child with a sword. . . . In Cutch they kill daughters who do not marry quickly. . . . I am unable to prevent it."[17] Burton noted that among the Todas, in the Goa hills, where polyandry was the rule, infant daughters were drowned in milk or trampled to death by water buffaloes, and that among the Belochis the girls were killed with opium.[18]

Napier was so impressed by Burton's reports that he sent him on an elaborate tour of the Sind with Captain Walter Scott. Dressed in native costume, to keep off the barking dogs, but not really in disguise, they checked on all the old Ameer forts, and listened for signs of rebellion. They received a mixed reception. One Ameer dined them lavishly and took Burton falcon hunting. Others jeered at them, calling them "crows dressed in parrot's feathers," or "corpses and eaters of corpses." One dancer and prostitute in Sehwan, furious when Burton and Scott ignored her importunities, followed them shrieking, "Infidel Franks! Ye blights upon the land! . . . ye locusts!" Whereupon Burton, who had developed a fine talent for invective, shut her up with some Oriental insults she was astonished to hear from the mouth of an Englishman:

"Thy locks be shaved, dame of all the dogs! May thy nose drop off, eater of the pig! . . . May sweepers deposit their burdens upon thy corpse, O widow woman. . . . female fiend!"

"We leave the lady blowing off her wrath in a long howl," he reported in his journal, adding bitterly, "Everything in this place seems to hate us."[19]

Burton and Scott had only one protection on this journey aside from their personal arms, the reputation of Napier, known throughout the Sind as "the Devil's brother." It was adequate to guarantee their safe return to Karachi, so that Sir Charles was able to write accurately that two years after his conquering the Sind an Englishman could go anywhere without a military escort. Trouble, when it did come in 1846, and with plenty of warning as Burton pointed out, came not from the Sindians but from the fierce neighbouring Sikhs.

Napier and Burton had much in common—defiant honesty, a weakness for vituperation and quarrelling, and ambivalence about the rôle of the military in India—but here the resemblance ended. Burton generally was content to explore and describe, though thievery, lying, and bribery, however endemic in the culture, always enraged him, and he called debauchery debauchery. But Napier felt a burning obligation to change, improve, and above all to Anglicize. Basically he was a simple British soldier [Burton could never have written, "Never have I wronged woman in my life. I have kissed away many a tear but never caused one"][20] who had no real doubts about the superiority of the British way of life. Burton frequently felt defeated in his own negotiations with the Indians, which except with his language teachers were usually infected with intrigue and deception. He came to recognize that Napier's very simplicity gave him special advantages, and he agreed, he wrote, "with Lady Hester Stanhope" that "amongst the English there is no man so attractive to the Orientals, no man who can negotiate with them so effectively, as a good, honest, openhearted and positive naval officer of the old school."[21]

Burton approved of Napier's abolishing slavery, but felt it should have been done more gradually; he had himself heard the lamentations of the old slaves thrust out to starve. He did not approve the death penalty for men who slew their adulterous wives, and Napier came to modify this for imprisonment. But Burton was always realistic rather than compassionate, and he saw nothing wrong in counselling Napier to continue the practice of killing a murderer by shooting him out of a cannon instead of hanging him, because lack of a proper burial to a Moslem meant he would never achieve paradise. So also, as a special deterrent against crime, he recommended burning the corpses of Moslems who had been hanged, and he favoured flogging the poor and fining the rich as more effective punishments in India than imprisonment. If one thinks of Burton as brutal in this regard, however, one has only to read his notes on conventional Oriental punishments, particularly that of flaying alive. "They begin by separating the skin at the soles of the feet," he wrote, "and then tear it upwards by strips till the sufferer expires."[22]

Homosexuality, which though originally forbidden by Mohammed was commonplace among the Moslems, shocked Napier, but Burton wrote of it—at least in later years—with urbanity and detachment: "Le Vice [in Sind] is looked upon at most as a peccadillo, and its name crops up in every jest-book. . . . The Afghans are commercial travellers on a large scale and each caravan is accompanied by a number of boys and lads almost in woman's attire with kohl'd eyes and rouged cheeks, long tresses and henna'd fingers and toes . . . they are called Kuch-i-safari, or travelling wives," and the cause of "perpetual mortification" among the Persian women. Napier was disturbed by rumours that certain homosexual brothels in Karachi were corrupting his troops and asked Burton to investigate. The report of this investigation brought Burton so much slander and humiliation that it is not surprising that he waited forty years before telling something of what happened. Then he wrote of it briefly in his chapter on pederasty in the "Terminal Essay" of his *Arabian Nights*.

It was reported to Napier in 1845, Burton wrote, "that Karachi . . . supported no less than three lupanars or bordels, in which not women but boys and eunuchs, the former demanding nearly a double price, lay for hire. . . . Being then the only British officer who could speak Sindi, I was asked indirectly to make enquiries and to report upon the subject; and I undertook the task on express condition that my report should not be forwarded to the Bombay Government, from whom supporters of the Conqueror's policy could expect scant favour, justice, or mercy." Carefully disguised, he said, "he passed away many an evening in the townlet and visited all the porneia and obtained the fullest details which were duly despatched to the Government House."

Burton was always explicit about what he observed, and this report was apparently no exception. It included the fact that the boys were valued above the eunuchs because "the scrotum of the unmutilated boy could be used as a kind of bridle for directing the movements of the animal."[23] The report did not dismay Napier about Burton, and this is an important fact to be remembered. He did not believe, as many did then and later, that visits to a male bordello automatically meant participation, or that writing about "le vice" proved one to be "vicious." But he immediately destroyed the brothels, noting in his diary that he had improved public morality in the area "by putting down the infamous beasts who, dressed as women, plied their trade in the Meers' time openly," noting that among the chief clients had been the Ameers themselves, whose financial records revealed their deep involvement.[24] He put Burton's report in his secret file, where it lay unnoticed for two years. *

Meanwhile trouble broke out in nearby Punjab, where the belligerent

---

* Sir Charles Napier's own copy of Burton's *Scinde; or, the Unhappy Valley* is now in the Huntington Library. Marginal notes in his hand vary from expressions of approval like "a capital description" to annoyance—"d--d nonsense," and "flippant ass." See I:199, II:125.

Sikhs virtually declared war on the British, who in turn eagerly retaliated with invasion. Burton, who was still technically assigned to the
staff of Captain Walter Scott, told him he could not bear to be a
"carpet soldier" forever, and resigned to rejoin his regiment and see
some fighting. He caught up with the Native 18th at Rohri and went
on the long march to Bahawalpur. But the war was over and Punjab
conquered before Burton could get near the field of battle. On the
dreary return march the officers, bitter at missing a chance for glory
and advancement, began quarrelling with each other, and Burton's
colonel, Henry Corsellis, was among the first to snarl. One evening at
mess Burton was amusing his fellow officers by making doggerel
rhymes on their names. Knowing the temper and touchiness of his
colonel, he passed him by, but the officer demanded a verse for himself. "Very well, Colonel," Burton said, "I will write your epitaph."
Within seconds he produced the following couplet:

> Here lieth the body of Colonel Corsellis;
> The rest of the fellow, I fancy, in hell is.

Corsellis was not amused, and the two men began to quarrel. Burton
does not dwell upon the episode except to say, "It is, perhaps, the part
of my life upon which my mind dwells with least satisfaction."[25]

July 1846 brought cholera to the Sind; 60,000 natives and 400 British
soldiers perished. Burton, struck down in September, became fearfully
ill. When somewhat recovered, he applied for convalescent leave to
the military sanatorium in Ootacamund near Ponnani, in the Neilgherry
Hills on the west coast of India, south of Bombay. He was granted a
two-year leave, a fair indication of his broken health, and set sail from
Bombay on February 20, 1847, "sick and seedy, tired and testy."[26] In
Ootacamund he gradually recovered his strength, only to contract a
new ailment he called rheumatic ophthalmia, which made it impossible for him to read, a misfortune for Burton comparable to deafness
for a musician. Diet, dark rooms, blisters, and a great variety of bad
drugs—one of which, citric ointment, nearly blinded him—served only
to worsen the malady. Finally his eyes improved, and he buried himself
in new languages, this time Telugu and Portuguese, with additional
concentration on Arabic and Persian. Language study served to put
a barrier between himself and dull people, he said, to make him
"independent of society."

He did some sightseeing in the area, accumulating enough material
for a book, later published as *Goa and the Blue Mountains*, and as we
have seen, left hastily after only six months of his two-year leave, probably as a result of the attempted abduction of the pretty nun at the
convent of Santa Monaca. In Bombay he stopped long enough to take

an official examination in Persian, and on October 15, 1847 passed first out of thirty contestants, winning an honorarium of 1,000 rupees from the Court of Directors, and warm praise from the examiners.

In high spirits Burton returned to his old friends on the Sind Survey, where Scott had arranged for a return to his old staff appointment. But there was one fateful change; General Napier had resigned and was leaving for England. He had made the decision in early July, writing in his diary: "I have resigned. My wife has nearly died. Seventeen days and nights have I nursed her. She must not stay. . . . Emily is in bed . . . with four dozen leeches on her head and no sleep but from opium. . . . I am a man smothered with women and children, like a duck with onions."[27]

Still troubled by ophthalmia, Burton found surveying impossible. "My return to the head-quarters of the Survey was a misfortune to my comrades," he wrote, "my eyes forbade regular work, and my friends had to bear my share of the burden." But during what he called the painless intervals, he worked at the same frenetic pace, improving his Sindi and Arabic, memorizing a quarter of the Koran, and embarking on a study of Sufism, a system of Mohammedan mysticism emphasizing ecstasy through contemplation, which was specially popular in Persia. He went through all the rituals of fasting, prayer, and study, and was officially ordained a Master Sufi. Apparently it was sometime during this period that he became enamoured of the mysterious Persian girl whose charms crept into his poetry and whose death, as we have seen, brought despair.

The year 1847 brought, too, evidence of his first creative scholarship. He began translating the charming fables of Pilpay, the Indian Æsop.* He also wrote two technical papers based on his linguistic studies in the Sind, and two papers on the Sindians themselves which were short, tentative experiments in ethnology.[28] There were descriptions of Sindian dress, religion, character, and education, with here and there a hint of the lively, dogmatic Burton to come. "The Beloochee," he wrote, "would rather be able to cut a sheep in two parts than be master of all the sciences ever studied in Baghdad or Bokhara," and the average Sindian is "notoriously cowardly and dishonourable, addicted to intoxication, unclean in his person, and immoral in the extreme." On the "Hindoo females" he wrote more gently that they "appear to be fond of intrigue . . . possess a considerable share of personal beauty, and seldom, if ever, become prostitutes." He provided a glossary of

---

* Curiously this, the first of Burton's translations, a neat 100-page manuscript, survived the burning of Grindlay's warehouse fire in 1861, the burnings of Burton's wife and sister-in-law, the London blitz, and even the post-war flooding of the basement of the Kensington Library. Still unpublished, it may be seen in the Royal Anthropological Institute, London.

common articles of food and clothing which would be useful for British soldiers, and discussed briefly the local intoxicants—alcohol, opium, "maajum" and "tadhal."

The two ethnological papers, the shorter of which was written in collaboration with Surgeon J. E. Stocks, he submitted to the Government Office for possible publication December 31, 1847 and March 2, 1848. Their arrival in Bombay precipitated a crisis which eventually drove Burton from India. For Napier's successor, or one of the officers under him, maliciously pulled out of the secret file the two-year-old report on the Karachi brothels and sent it on to Bombay with the innocuous articles on the Sindian people. With the three articles went a recommendation that Burton be dismissed from the service. Burton did not name his enemy, and one can only guess that it was either Colonel Corsellis or his superior, General Auchmuty. Instead he wrote somewhat cryptically:

But the "Devil's Brother" presently quitted Sind leaving in his office my unfortunate official: this [the Karachi report] found its way with sundry other reports to Bombay and produced the expected result. A friend in the Secretariat informed me that my summary dismissal from the service had been formally proposed by one of Sir Charles Napier's successors, whose decease compels me parcere sepulto. But this excess of outraged modesty was not allowed.[29]

Burton was not cashiered. It would hardly have been good army practice to dismiss a man for obeying orders to carry out an intelligence mission, and someone in Bombay came to his defence. But his reputation in India was ruined all the same, though it was some months before he had evidence of this. Meanwhile the Second Sikh War had broken out in April, 1848; there were heavy British losses, and once more Burton made an effort to get to the scene of the fighting. He wrote to his cousin, Sarah Burton, November 14, 1848:

I keep this letter open for ten or twelve days longer, as that time will decide my fate. A furious affair has broken out in Mooltan and the Punjaub and I have applied to the General commanding to go up with him on his personal staff. A few days more will decide the business—and I am not a little anxious about it, for though still suffering a little from my old complaint—ophthalmia—yet these opportunities are too far between to be lost.[30]

Later in his memoir he wrote what happened:

I applied in the most suppliant terms to accompany the force as interpreter. I had passed examinations in six native languages, besides studying others, Multani included [the language spoken by the enemy Sikhs] and yet General Auchmuty's secretary wrote to me that this could not be, as he had chosen for the post Lieutenant XYZ who had passed [only] in Hindustani. This last misfortune broke my heart. I had been seven years in India, working like a horse, volunteering for every bit of service, and qualifying myself for all contingencies. Rheumatic ophthalmia, which had almost left me when in hopes of marching northward, came on with redoubled force, and no longer had I any hope of curing it except by a change to Europe. Sick, sorry, and almost in tears of rage, I bade adieu to my friends and comrades in Sind.[31]

When the crushing news came, he had not yet mailed the letter to his cousin Sarah. So on November 25, 1848 he added some sealed papers and a postscript that concealed almost everything of what he must have felt: "I am not going up to the siege of Mooltan, as the General with whom I expected to be sent is recalled. Pray be kind enough to send on the enclosed to my father. I was afraid to direct it to him in Italy as it contains papers of some importance."

These "papers of some importance" must have been the most difficult Burton ever wrote. For the wrecking of his military career could not easily be explained to anyone, especially his parents. His mother was ill, and apparently at this time emotionally distraught over the death of her sister.[32] And his father, it will be remembered, was "a highly moral man."

The faint smell of brimstone—provoked and abhorred—would follow Burton everywhere from India, the rumour that "something wrong was known"[33] stayed with him all his life, and none of his hundreds of words affectionately detailing the attractiveness of Oriental women would quite erase it. One should remember, however, that though the practice of homosexuality was probably no less common in England then than now, no one in his time wrote about it save to denounce it as a sin, and even the idea of describing it clinically was for most Englishmen profoundly shocking. Burton did not write on the subject with publication—or even private printing—in mind until 1884. But the documentation for his courageous essay on pederasty in the "Terminal Essay" of the *Arabian Nights* must surely have drawn upon his Indian experience. He seems then to have remembered everything, including a disturbing story he had picked up in Persia, which he included with the rest:

"The detected sodomite is punished with death according to Moslem law," he wrote, "but again comes the difficulty of proof. At Shiraz I have heard of a pious Moslem publicly executing his son."[34]

Burton left the Sind on May 13, 1849. In Bombay he became increasingly ill, till his Indian friends advised him somberly, "It is written that your days are numbered, take our advice and go home to die." Haggard, half-blind, and desperately sick as only a man can be from failure and guilt, he boarded the sixty-year-old teak brig, *Eliza*, with one Indian servant, and set sail for England. Shortly after the ship left Bombay he became certain that he would never reach London alive and wrote a farewell letter to his mother.

Burton Becomes a Writer

You must know that these are the effects of hemp and books, in the regions of the imagination, in the world of authorism—a strange place where men are generous, women constant, the young wise, the old benevolent.

Richard Burton, *Scinde; or, The Unhappy Valley*

*T*IME AND DISTANCE, which often heal sickness arising from guilt and failure, worked some of their magic on the voyage to England, and when Burton arrived in London in the late summer of 1849, with the turbaned Moslem servant who had nursed him on the voyage, he was thin and haggard but otherwise seemingly well. After seeing relatives he went direct to Pisa, where his parents had settled more or less permanently. It had been seven years since he had said farewell in England, and he tells us nothing of his return as a tarnished prodigal. Later, returning from Mecca, he would write obliquely of what it meant to come back to "the turmoil" of European civilization. "The air of cities will suffocate you, and the care-worn and cadaverous countenances of citizens will haunt you like a vision of judgment."[1]

His sister Maria, who had made a distinguished marriage to Lieutenant-General Sir Henry William Stisted in 1845, and had since borne him two daughters, was also in Italy, having chosen to stay with her parents instead of accompanying her husband to India. Maria at once dedicated herself to the rehabilitation of her brother, and accompanied him back to England. Her daughter Georgiana, then not quite four, vividly remembered crossing the Alps in a carriage with her mother, her Uncle Richard, an English maid and "a romantic but surly Asiatic named Allahdad." Her uncle, she wrote, "handsome, tall, and broad-shouldered," was oftener outside the carriage than in it, and now and then gave her bits of snow to eat, telling her it was sugar.

Burton's mother shortly joined them; Allahdad was shipped back to Bombay, and Richard found himself surrounded only by females. He toyed briefly with the idea of going back to Oxford, but the prospect of joining the immature youths at Trinity was no less intolerable than giving himself over to the exacting dons, and he decided instead to try his hand at writing books. Meanwhile, according to Georgiana Stisted, he fell in love with one of his handsome cousins, Elizabeth Stisted, "lively, amiable, and well-dowered." Though she was willing enough to marry, her parents found Richard's prospects dismal and successfully blocked the match. Depressed and bitter—even though, according to his niece, "his affection for his cousin lacked the intensity of his love for the dead girl in Sind,"—Burton crossed the channel to Boulogne, where his mother and sister, alarmed by his low spirits, shortly followed.[2]

For four years—from the age of twenty-nine to thirty-two—Burton lived as the only male with two adoring adult women and two adoring small girls. Edward, now a surgeon-major in Ceylon, came home occasionally on leave, and asthma-ridden Joseph Burton, who seems to have abdicated altogether to his son his position as head of the family, came from Pisa at rare intervals. As Georgiana euphemistically put it, "the keen air disagreed with his complaint." Burton's mother, she reported, had "become quite an invalid, but continued, unlike most invalids, as affectionate and unselfish as of old." There is no more effective combination of virtues to insure maternal tyranny.

Maria, meanwhile, worked at taming her brother, at curbing his "eccentricities in dress" and "roughness of manner." She had her portrait painted with him in 1851, and the French artist, François Jacquand, showed a lean and gaunt young Burton, with improbable black moustaches curving down to his chin. Except for their enormous eyes, neither one resembled the other; Maria looked slight and fragile, with no trace of her brother's fierceness. The canvas captured a certain tenderness between the two, and it is notable that Burton, who ignored her so completely in his writings, could be persuaded to collaborate in this public portrayal of their affection. Georgiana implied in her book that her mother worked hard at getting Richard married, but added that "with characteristic good sense she encouraged the most promising of his love affairs and only the most promising." Under these circumstances nothing could have been less likely than for Richard Burton in these four years to marry anyone. And so it proved.

Meanwhile he was feverishly writing. Recovery of his health brought back all his ambition, but did nothing to curb his corroding hatred of the British East India Company. The first thing he wrote was an impolitic broadside the nature of which we learn indirectly from subsequent writings. Apparently he told the Directors what the Indians really thought of the British—that they are "not brave, nor clever, nor generous, nor civilised, nor anything but surpassing rogues . . . every official takes bribes . . . their manners are utterly offensive, and . . . they are rank infidels." Burton said the Indians privately predicted "a

Bartholomew's Day in the East," and looked forward to the hour when "the foul invader" should be driven out of India—all of which was to be borne out by the mutiny of 1857.[3]

"I need hardly say," Burton admitted, "that the publication was refused with many threats." Had Burton been an enterprising journalist instead of an army captain, and published his criticisms in the British press, he might have won applause, for many thoughtful men in England were critical of "John Company." But he broke a fundamental rule of military service; he attacked his superiors. This was never forgiven him.

Burton went on to write four books on India, totalling 1503 pages, all published in 1851–2, in less than two years. *Goa and the Blue Mountains* was primarily an account of the varied inhabitants of Goa, the Hindus of Malabar, and the mountain-dwelling Todas who practiced polyandry. It was informal, experimental, and unsuccessful. But one does see the sharp observer, fascinated by the bizarre and gifted at communicating its flavour, writing with an exactness tempered with irony that kept him above vulgarity and sensationalism. He wrote of the Malabar women, "It is the custom for modest women of the Tiyar family to expose the whole of the person above the waist, whereas females of loose character are compelled by custom to cover the body." English women, he said, hiring the Tiyar as servants, tried to induce them "to adopt a somewhat less natural costume," but the proposal "has generally been met pretty much in the same spirit which would be displayed were the converse suggested to an Englishwoman."[4]

His *Scinde; or, The Unhappy Valley*, more ambitious than *Goa*, was primarily a travel narrative, drawing upon his journey through northern Sind with Captain Walter Scott. The third, *Sindh, and the Races that inhabit the Valley of the Indus,** was a solid, brilliant ethnological study, written at a time when ethnology was still so young a science that there was no disciplined tradition against which it could be measured and its merits properly evaluated.[5] The fourth book, *Falconry in the Valley of the Indus*, was a short hunting book, with ethnological overtones, valuable today especially for the autobiographical material in the appendix.

The writing of these books, an attempt to rehabilitate his career and reputation, meant a reliving of seven critical years, and as such served also as therapy. Rarely however do we see self-appraisal and regret, and when it appears at all it is cryptic and half-hidden, as when he wrote of British Orientalists in India, clever at ceremony, skilled in languages, who nevertheless turn out to be "diplomatic little children

---

* Burton's spelling was often erratic. He spelled Sind in four different ways.

in the end, which try all things. They had read too much; they had written too much; they were a trifle too clever, and much too confident. Their vanity tempted them to shift their nationality; from Briton to Greek, in order to meet Greek on the roguery field; and lamentably they always failed." Later he wrote sadly, "I am convinced that the natives of India cannot respect a European who mixes with them familiarly, or especially who imitates their customs, manners, and dress. The tight pantaloons [of the British soldier], the authoritative voice, the procurante manner, and the broken Hindostani impose upon them —have a weight which learning and honesty, which wit and courage have not."[6]

The struggle against fakery was always with Burton, the master of disguise, and though he was guilty of some dissimulation about himself, it was never true of his descriptions of native peoples. Here he wrote with exactness. But he seems to have felt the necessity for proof lest he be taken for the prevaricator he so often became with a rapt audience. So we have appendix piling upon appendix, and multitudes of footnotes—in his big book on Sind there are five appendices and 599 notes—as if to show that as a writer if not as a man there must be no doubt of his integrity.

Though he went to some pains to keep his books non-political, he could not avoid an occasional jeer at British imperialism. "Whenever good Madam Britannia is about to break the eighth commandment," he wrote, "she simultaneously displays a lot of piety, much rhapsodising about the bright dawn of Christianity, the finger of Providence, the spread of civilisation, and the infinite benefits conferred upon barbarians by permitting them to become her subjects, and pay their rents to her." And he dared to print the great unspoken fear of all perceptive British officers in the Bombay army, "Everyone knows that if the people of India could be unanimous for a day they might sweep us from their country as dust before a whirlwind."[7]

But Burton was primarily intent on bringing the East to the West, and he was at his best in showing the impact of one culture upon another, whether Moslem upon Hindu, Portuguese Christian upon Indian, or Indian upon British. Some of his greatest stories are of simple cross-cultural incomprehension, like his tale of the British colonel and the drowning Sindian. The colonel, seeing a native struggling in a river, orders the workmen on the bank to save him. When none springs to the rescue, he strikes at them with his whip, instead of properly offering them a rupee, to which, Burton tells us, they would have responded instantly. The Sindians flee the whip, and the colonel is forced to dive in the water himself. Once rescued, the native, instead of thanking him profusely, says, "Sahib, you have preserved me, what are you going to give me?" The Englishman, recoiling in anger, refuses him charity, whereupon the native begins cursing him. The story ends with the now thoroughly outraged officer swinging his whip at the man whose life he has just saved.[8]

Burton described sensitively how the ancient, tenacious Hindu religion had pervaded and changed the newer militant Islam when it invaded India. Hindus who became Moslems, he said, "like such religionists in general, considered it safer to believe too much than too little." Moslem shrines were usually superimposed upon the Hindu shrines, and no one thought of eliminating the old phallic symbols— the Yonis, consisting of natural or artificial holes in the rocks, and the Lingams, carved in stone and placed upon the margins of pools. As yet he lacked the courage to describe Hindu phallic worship in detail. "You look towards me for some explanation of these upright stones, daubed with red. . . . I must place the seal of silence upon my lips, much as I regret to do so." And on this subject he did little more than note that pregnant Hindu women were taken to special shrines and seated upon a particular Lingam with the hope that the fetus, if female, would miraculously be changed into a male.

Burton could be more detached a commentator than most of his fellow officers because he was no longer in any sense a practising Christian, and in fact deplored the Christianization of native peoples. In Goa, which he said had been converted largely by the terrors of the Inquisition, good Hindus and Moslems had become bad Christians, notorious for dishonesty and intoxication. And what the Portuguese fathers had started modern Europeans had not improved upon. The Todas, he wrote, once a noble, unsophisticated people, had become "inveterate, indefatigable beggars . . . morally ruined by collision with Europeans. . . . chastity, sobriety, and temperance fell flat before the strong temptations of rupees, foreign luxuries, and ardent spirits."[9]

Most Burton biographers have been misled into writing that Burton preferred Islam to Christianity; actually he was equally harsh in attacking what he believed to be the superstitions and banalities of both religions. And though for a time he was immersed in Sufism, he was never lost to the mysticism. Instead he watched with lively curiosity the Sufi fanatics who ended their training proclaiming themselves to be God, and he decided that there was an affinity between extreme mysticism and insanity. He noted the similarity in healing techniques between the Hindu saints, who passed their hands over the afflicted parts of the body of the sick, and that of the newly fashionable mesmerists in Europe. Eventually he took up the practice of hypnotism and became skilful in inducing the trance-like state.

Religious relics of every creed amused him, and he delighted in tracing local miracles to what was usually a banal origin. "The miraculous lie," he wrote, "is generally speaking, useful to many who exert all their efforts to adorn and promulgate it: those who know the truth are either sensible enough to keep silence, cunning enough to pretend to believe it, or weak enough to lose reputation and to be considered liars by opposing it." Despite this sophistication, Burton was nevertheless hopelessly enchanted by the folk magic he gently derided. He summarized numerous Indian folk tales in his Sind books, poking fun at their absurdities as if to apologize for his own fascination. Later, with greater maturity of outlook, he translated them in their entirety and published them with manifest affection and no apology whatever.

Burton's style in his Indian books, as in later ones, interposed barriers between himself and his readers. He was chaotic and disorganized, strewing allusions in his path like boulders with no attempt to clear the way by explanation. Often he was simply verbose. He collected and displayed multi-syllable words as if they were his jewels. So in the first few chapters of *Scinde; or, The Unhappy Valley* we get triduan, catalepsed, futilised, graveolent, sesquipedalian, agnomen, confabulate, succedaneum, vaticinating, cachinnatory, and vellication. Nevertheless, as Alan Moorehead has pointed out, Burton "is a natural writer. He feels at ease with his pen just as other men are at ease in their conversation. Similes, witticisms, flights of imagination, scientific speculations and historical theories pour out of him in a bubbling irrepressible stream. The language is Johnsonian, the tone is by turns ironic, boisterous, pedantic, argumentative, and just occasionally downright sardonic."[10]

British reviews of his Indian books were on the whole kind, but unperceptive and patronizing. The influential editor of the *Athenaeum* called *Goa and the Blue Mountains* "at once a very good and a very bad book," and suggested that one third of it should have been burned and the rest rewritten. He dismissed *Scinde; or, The Unhappy Valley* as "smart, rattling, and clever," and objected to the "extreme opinions" in the best book on the Sind. When Burton replied heatedly in his *Falconry in the Valley of the Indus,* the editor became nasty, commenting on Burton's habit of living with the natives in a fashion that was close to libel.[11]

Most editors did not know what they had in Burton. They quoted great chunks of his data, but were also sufficiently frightened or repelled by the nature of much of it that they withheld the praise he justly deserved. The editors were more comfortable with the thin and conventional earlier books on the Sind, like James Burnes' *Narrative of a Visit to the Courte of Sinde at Hyderabad on the Indus* (Edinburgh, 1839), and T. Postans' *Personal Observations on Sindh: the Manners and Customs of its Inhabitants* (London, 1843). But Burton was writing, as W. G. Archer has recently emphasized, with the skill and detachment of the great twentieth century anthropologists, like Malinowski in *The Sexual Life of Savages*, Geoffrey Gorer in *Himalayan Village*, and Verrier Elwin in *The Baiga*, "works which describe with intimate detail the place of sex in village life. In the India of 1845, no one had done this before. Burton discovered Indian sex."[12]

So in his books we learn not only Sindian history, and the distinguishing characteristics of Pathans, Sindians, Jats, Belochi, Khwajehs, Mohanas, and seven castes of Hindus; we learn also about irrigation, taxes, crime, education, intoxicating drugs, and corruption in government. But all this richness is secondary to the primordial ritual—the birth and lactation superstitions and practices, the circumcision and puberty ceremonies, the marriage rites, the punishments for adultery, and the complicated rituals for the dead. Burton even touched delicately on the problems of the marriage bed. In discussing Indian doctors he noted, "Our ignorance of aphrodisiacs is considered the most remarkable phenomenon: there being scarcely a single oriental work on physic that does not devote the greater part of its pages to the consideration of a question which the medical man in the East will hear a dozen times a day."[13] And he described with a light hand Sayyid Hasan Ali's *Lawful Enjoyment of Women*, one of the countless "bride-books" of Asia which though distributed freely among literate betrothed couples in India and China were considered pornographic by Europeans. Burton had read these books with respect as well as excitement. A conviction was born in him—perhaps intensified by failures in his own life, or by sampling the wide variety in the sexual market—that there was in the East a reservoir of experience against which the West, especially England, foolishly barricaded itself with dams of false modesty and shame. One day he would loosen the floodgates.

Burton Looks at Marriage

The first kiss which the bridegroom gives is equal to one hundred and eighty years of worship. It also enables him to escape the torments of the tomb, causes a light to be shed over his grave, and procures the ministering of eighty angels.

Richard Burton, on the benefits of marriage to the Moslem male.[1]

*B*URTON CAME BACK from India with the conviction that celibacy was "an unmitigated evil,"[2] and the next four years saw him involved in what his niece called "a great many *affaires de coeur*." He "made several attempts," she wrote, "to marry a virtuous woman and settle down as a Benedict before he reached his thirtieth year." All his attachments, she said, "were to pretty or handsome women, ugly ones he wouldn't look at; with him love of the beautiful almost took the place of religion." Ugly old women he particularly detested, beginning with his mother's French maid, Eulalie, who, he wrote, "made our hours bitter and our faces yellow."[3]

We have already reported Burton's affection for Elizabeth Stisted. He dedicated his first book to her "in token of gratitude and affection," writing that it "owed its existence to her friendly suggestions." Isabel Burton admitted once that Richard "would have married twice before he married me." She wrote of two of his love affairs in Boulogne, one "a rather strong flirtation with a very handsome and very fast girl, who had a vulgar middle-class sort of mother," and "a very serious flirtation" with her own distant cousin Louisa, who became Mrs Louisa Segrave. Thomas Wright tells us that the latter was a great beauty and that Burton would probably have married her "but for the poorness of his outlook."[4] In his somewhat autobiographical poem *Stone Talk*, written four years after his marriage, Burton devoted one stanza to a description of "Louise," which must have given some pain to Isabel Burton:

> I loved a maid: how deep that love
> The long course of a life may prove.
> What hours of happiness they were,
> Passed in that dearest presence, ere

> Harsh poverty and cursed pride
> Combined to drive me from her side
> And sent me forth to win a name,
> The trinket wealth, the bauble fame!

Georgiana Stisted wrote that the girls of Boulogne fell in love with Richard by the score, and insofar as their mothers permitted, flung themselves at him shamelessly. He was older than most of their callow dancing partners; in looks and bearing he radiated virility, and he was already a legend of exotic experience. But Burton was no favourite with the wealthy English mothers, many of whom, disgruntled that their daughters had not married in their first "coming out," had taken them across the channel to learn French and improve their techniques for snaring a proper suitor. The maternal standards, which effectively eliminated the rebellious, the eccentric, the non-wealthy, and the very intelligent, narrowed the field to the point where the heavily chaperoned girls were in despair, but they were culturally, legally, and often physically trapped in a virtual prison to which their parents held the key. The mothers saw Burton as a mere Bombay army lieutenant, living on half-pay, disturbingly un-English, pursued by obscure rumours of some kind of shameful trouble in India having to do with going native—or worse. Had they read his books, which naturally they did not, their alarm would have only mounted. Above all, they could not forgive his refusal to court them along with their daughters. But Burton, having no patience with ignorance unless it was mitigated by beauty, needlessly offended their vanity. If chatter bored him, he would take up a book or leave the room with scant ceremony. When one mother he disliked asked him his intentions concerning her daughter, he replied, "Alas! madame, strictly dishonourable."[5]

Like many with wilful bad manners and a delight in shocking, he was nevertheless hurt and bewildered when he found himself consequently unloved. He was indignant when members of the most decorous English clique in Boulogne crossed the street to avoid him, and when one matron declared vehemently "she would not and could not sit in the same room with that fellow Burton." He was so thin-skinned, Georgiana wrote, that "we used to say of him, the meanest insect drew blood."[6]

Burton repaid the British matrons in later years in lines dripping acid. But in Boulogne he seems to have made the best of the inanities and snobbery, and having recovered from one disappointment was quickly on the scent for new adventure. If he saw an attractive girl he did not hesitate to strike up an acquaintance, or at least to stare at her. From this there was always an impact, and Burton knew it. But the most extraordinary impact of all his first encounters—when he stared at the girl who was to become his wife—he did not learn about for six years.

Walking along the Boulogne ramparts one day in September 1850 he saw a tall, blue-eyed girl with a queenly manner and long golden-brown hair. Dressed as a schoolgirl like her sister, she seemed younger than her nineteen years, but carried an air of independence that caught his attention. As the two girls were unchaperoned he felt free to stare. It was a fierce, penetrating look, bold, questioning, and demanding of communication. Others in later years, when subjected to the same scrutiny, sought for the exact words to describe it—magnetic eyes, terrible, burning eyes, eyes like a wild beast, the sullen eyes of a stinging serpent—but Isabel wrote simply, "He looked at me as though he read me through and through in a moment, and started a little. I was completely magnetized, and when he had got a little distance away I turned to my sister, and whispered to her, 'That man will marry me.'"

"The vision of my awakening brain . . ." she said, "was five feet eleven inches in height, very broad, thin, muscular; he had very dark hair, black, clearly defined, sagacious eyebrows, a brown weather-beaten complexion, straight Arab features, a determined-looking mouth and chin, nearly covered by an enormous black moustache. . . . He had a fierce, proud, melancholy expression, and when he smiled, he smiled as though it hurt him, and looked with impatient contempt at things generally. He was dressed in a black, short, shaggy coat, and shouldered a short stick as if he was on guard.

The next day they met in the same spot, and he scrawled across the wall with a piece of chalk, "May I speak to you?" and laid the chalk on the wall. Isabel picked it up and wrote underneath, "No, mother will be angry," and walked away. "And mother found it, and *was* angry," she added, "and after that we were stricter prisoners than ever."

It was an extraordinarily wordless beginning for what was to be one of the most articulately documented of the great Victorian romances. Shortly afterward she met him again while walking with her cousin Louisa, who amiably introduced them. When Isabel heard his name for the first time she was galvanized again by a sense of destiny. For years earlier in Stonymoore Wood a friendly gypsy woman belonging to a tribe that had adopted the name of Burton, had cast her horoscope with unusual explicitness and had foretold that Burton would be her married name:

You will cross the sea, and be in the same town with your Destiny and know it not. Every obstacle will rise up against you, and such a combination of circumstances, that it will require all your courage, energy, and intelligence to meet them. . . . You will bear the name of our tribe, and be right proud of it. You will be as we are, but far greater than we. Your life is all wandering, change, and adventure. One soul in two bodies in life or death, never long apart. Show this to the man you take for your husband.

"I could think of no more at the moment," she wrote. "But I stole a look at him, and met his gypsy eyes—those eyes which looked you through, glazed over, and saw something behind, the only man I had ever seen, not a gypsy, with that peculiarity. And again I thrilled through and through. He must have thought me very stupid, for I scarcely spoke a word."

It is clear from Isabel's account—and *all* the details of the courtship are hers—that even though she was nineteen and instantly in love, she was also speechless with fright; and though she blames her mother for forbidding further meetings, the truth filters through her story that it was really she who fled from any meaningful encounter.

I did not try to attract his attention, but after that whenever he came on the usual promenade I would invent any excuse that came ready, to take another turn to watch him, if he were not looking. If I could catch the sound of his deep voice, it seemed to me so soft and sweet, that I remained spellbound, as when I hear gypsy music. I never lost an opportunity of seeing him, when I could not be seen; and I used to turn red and pale, hot and cold, dizzy and faint, sick and trembling, and my knees used nearly to give way under me, my mother sent for the doctor. . . . he prescribed me a pill which I put in the fire.

Richard meanwhile was pursuing her cousin, and Isabel suffered agonies of jealousy. "I was struck with the shaft of Destiny, but I had no hopes (being nothing but an ugly schoolgirl) of taking the wind out of the sails of the dashing creature, with whom he was carrying on a very serious flirtation." He wrote her a casual note, which she cherished in her bosom, but only once did he speak seriously to her and touch her. This was at a dancing party given by her cousin. "There was Richard like a star among rushlights," she said. "That was a Night of nights; he waltzed with me once, and spoke to me several times, and I kept my sash where he put his arms round my waist to waltz, and my gloves which his hands had clasped. I never wore them again."

Isabel's flight from her destiny continued for two years. "I could not push myself forward or attract his notice," she decided, "It would be unmaidenly—unworthy." And when her family finally moved back to London, she elected not to say goodbye. "To see him would be only to give myself more pain, and therefore I did not." She boarded the Channel steamer, describing herself as "suffering, patient, and purified," wrapped herself in a blanket and hid in a lifeboat for the privacy to lament her loss. Burton knew nothing of the torment he had evoked. But Isabel remembered and recorded and relived, in diary, biography and autobiography.[7] The result is a history as remarkable for its dramatization of personal feeling as her husband's writings are remarkable for the absence of it. The great love story is hers, not his, and we can only guess at the extent to which he truly shared.

Isabel Arundell was descended from James Everard Arundell, youngest son of Henry Arundell, Sixth Baron of Wardour (1694–1746). Her ancestors included Sir Thomas Arundell, who had married Margaret, sister of Catherine Howard, fifth wife of Henry VIII. Sir Thomas, Chancellor for a time to the ill-fated queen, was later also beheaded on Tower Hill. His grandson, Thomas Arundell, finding favor with James I, became the first Baron of Wardour.* Though Isabel's father, Henry Raymond Arundell, was "in trade" as a wine merchant on Mount Street, and was not wealthy enough even to provide a proper dowry for his eldest and favourite daughter, Isabel nevertheless brought to her marriage the emphatic sense of identity that pervaded her class. She was goddaughter to the 10th Baron of Wardour and welcome at Wardour castle. Her mother, Eliza Gerard, was sister to Lord Robert Gerard of Garswood. "We children were little gentlemen and ladies," Isabel wrote, "and people of the world from our birth."

Almost equally important, she was a Roman Catholic, and this meant a special identity, for there was little mingling between the Catholic minority among the aristocracy and the large Protestant majority. Thomas Arundel (1353–1414) had as Archbishop of Canterbury sponsored the act for the burning of heretics during the Lollard uprising, and Philip Howard, first Earl of Arundel, (1557–1595), had been sent to the tower suspected of conspiring against Elizabeth I. Though there was apparently no hereditary connection between the Arundels and Arundells, the suspicion of conspiracy that haunted all the great Catholic families had been enough to send Henry Arundell, 3rd Baron of Wardour, to the Tower in 1678, at the time of the anti-Catholic hysteria formented by Titus Oates. Catholic James II had freed Lord Henry and had admitted him to the privy council August 17, 1683.

After the revolution ending the reign of James II in 1688, Catholics had been excluded from English public life for 140 years, until the Catholic Emancipation Act in 1829 reconstituted their privileges. The latter date was only two years before Isabel Arundell's birth, and her parents had vivid memories of the old days of proscription. Moreover,

---

* Baron Arundell fought in the services of Rudolph II, Emperor of Germany. As a reward Rudolph created him a Count of the Holy Roman Empire, decreeing that "every of his children and their descendants for ever, of both sexes, should enjoy that title." Queen Elizabeth I and James I both refused to recognize the validity of this title, but James II acknowledged it. As a result many Arundells used the title of count or countess when travelling on the continent. Thus Isabel Burton felt free to call herself Countess Isabel of Arundell (of Wardour), when at foreign courts. See W. H. Wilkins, *The Romance of Isabel Lady Burton*, I, 4–6.

anti-Catholic feeling still lay close to the surface in England; there was a surge of violence in 1850, the year Richard and Isabel met, when an attempt by the Pope to create English metropolitan titles for Roman Catholic bishops caused a crisis in the government, and mobs smashed Catholic shops and burned effigies of the Pope.

Isabel had been educated from ten to sixteen in the Convent of the Canonesses at New Hall, Chelmsford, and was extremely devout. She would bring to her marriage with Burton a simplicity of intellectual outlook that would alternately amuse and baffle him and a religious conviction so unshakable that he could only retreat from it with mingled outrage and awe. She knew in Boulogne that he was no Catholic, and sadly found evidence in his books, which she read avidly, that he was even anti-Catholic and no proper Christian in any sense. "I asked myself," she wrote, "if I would sacrifice anything and everything for Richard, and the only thing that I found I could not sacrifice for him would be God; for I thought I would as soon, were I a man, foresake my post, when the tide of battle pressed hardest against it, and go over to the enemy, as renounce my God." One suspects, however, that she discovered this flaw in her destiny with something like relief. With her, as with Burton, there was a complicated parental involvement, and any kind of marriage had to mean renunciation of a closer deity and "going over to the enemy."

Isabel's father, "a small, fair, boyish looking man," had been married twice. His first wife had died shortly after the birth of a son, and Isabel, the first child born to his second wife, was named after the first. She was always called Puss, however, and it was a fitting nickname, for she was plump and affectionate, and not unlike a big, blue-eyed Angora cat. "My father adored me and spoiled me absurdly," she wrote. "My mother was equally fond of me, but severe—her spoiling, on principle, went to her stepson." Though Isabel made much of her overflowing affection for her mother, there is good evidence that she feared her and resented her harsh discipline. She described as a nightly childhood terror "saying goodnight to my mother, always with an impression that I might not see her again,"[8] a kind of anxiety that often masks among small daughters a buried wish.

There was nevertheless a close tie between them. Her mother gave her a copy of Disraeli's *Tancred*, March 20, 1854, inscribed "Isabel Arundell from her attached mother." And Isabel in turn faithfully signed her letters to her mother "your fondly attached child." In her last years Isabel described her mother bluntly as "a worldly woman of strong brain, of hasty temper, bigoted, and a Spartan with the elder half of her brood. We trembled before her, but we adored her, and we never got over her death in 1872."[9]

Isabel grew up as the second child with a brother almost four years older—whom her mother obviously preferred—and an almost endless succession of younger children. "They had eleven children great and small," she wrote. "I mean that some only lived to be baptized and died, and some lived a few years, and some grew up." This curious vagueness would seem to indicate that she had seen so much of pregnancy and births and dying—the last baby died in Boulogne when she was twenty—that it may well have been too painful to make a proper counting. Of the eleven children only two sisters outlived her. "Four dear beautiful brothers all died young," she wrote, "by untoward accidents."[10]

In her diary at Boulogne she betrayed her own resistance to the idea of marriage when she described "the vocation of my sex" as "breeding fools and chronicling small beer." Shakespeare had put the phrase "suckling fools and chronicling small beer" into Iago's mouth, and Isabel's paraphrase was a surprisingly bitter statement from one moulded by a society that demanded of its women both pretence and sentimentality. Certainly her fantasies were largely non-maternal. She longed frankly to be a man, to be "a great general or statesman, to have travelled everywhere, to have seen and learnt everything, done everything; in fine, to be the Man of the Day!" At her betrothal she expressed hope in her diary for "a man child," not children, and when even this was denied her in marriage she spoke of it at least to her friends with as much relief as regret.

Isabel tells us nothing of her convent schooling, but only of her delight in being home from school at sixteen, free to roam in the country lanes without an escort. She was happy at Furze Hall, their unpretentious but beautiful country house near Ingatestone in Essex, with its stables, kennels, library and small chapel, though she counted herself ugly and fat, and dismayed her mother by her longings for adventure and a wild life. Against orders she mingled with the gypsies who camped nearby, furnishing them with medicines and defending them against the charge of thieving. Here she confided in Hagar Burton, the *divinatrice* whose horoscope was to play such a curious role in her life. When her family moved to London, so that she might make a proper match, she wept in farewell to her "servants, peasants and humble friends," in farewell as she knew, to her childhood. When her pets were destroyed, she did a little destroying on her own, making a bonfire" of all the things that one does not want desecrated by stranger hands." This burning was a foretaste of things to come.

She dreaded at her first ball being exhibited for marrying like a piece of merchandise, but to her astonishment was counted pretty, original, and altogether attractive. Soon she was "tired proof" and "dancing mad." Delighted with the glitter and gaiety of English Catholic aristoc-

racy, which was small enough to have something of the cohesion and
warmth of a single great family, she had nevertheless a sharp eye for
the techniques of the intriguing mothers, and saw clearly how the
decorum and placidity masked vanity, mendacity and jealousy. To her
mother's annoyance she was critical of potential suitors, counting them
"animated tailors' dummies," and "sexless creatures," and turning up
her nose at men sought after by the daughters of dukes. The season
ended late in July with Isabel still unmarried, and the Arundells, having spent a great deal of money to no purpose, moved to Boulogne,
where their daughters could learn French, and where living was less
dear.

Isabel described her ideal man in her diary at the time, but this
portrait, as reproduced in her autobiography, is so like Richard Burton
that one may be sure she reworked the clay of the original:

> As God took a rib out of Adam and made a woman of it, so do I, out of a
> wild chaos of thought, form a man unto myself. . . . My ideal is about six
> feet in height; he has not an ounce of fat on him; he has broad and muscu-
> lar shoulders, a powerful, deep chest; he is a Hercules of manly strength.
> He has black hair, a brown complexion, a clever forehead, sagacious eye-
> brows, large, black wondrous eyes—those strange eyes you dare not take
> yours from off them—with long lashes. He is a soldier and a *man*; he is
> accustomed to command and to be obeyed. . . . He is a gentleman in every
> sense of the word . . . and of course he is an Englishman. His religion is like
> my own, free, liberal, and generous minded. . . . Such a man only will I wed.
> I love this myth of my girlhood—for myth it is—next to God; and I look to
> the star that Hagar the gypsy said was the star of my destiny. . . . But if I
> find such a man, and afterward discover he is not for me, then I will never
> marry. . . . I will become a sister of charity of St. Vincent de Paul.[11]

Isabel, it can be seen, was a pure romantic; she lived by myth,
knowing it to be myth, and used the myth as a weapon to keep herself inviolable. But having designed an ideal as a bulwark to keep
herself from being pushed into a tawdry marriage, she stumbled upon
her ideal—this tall, dark, well-muscled stranger, this soldier-adventurer
who seemed the very essence of masculinity, and who miraculously
bore the name the very stars had foretold would one day be her own.
"Happy is she," she wrote, "who meets at her first start the man who
is to guide her life, whom she is always to love," and then added perceptively, "Some women grow fastidious in solitude, and find it harder
to be mated than married." We do not know when Isabel Arundell
learned the distinction between mated and married, and whether this
was an expression of her own resistance to marriage or an inadvertent
admission of difficulties within it afterwards. But we do know that this
girl, who at twenty believed that the vocation of woman was "breeding
fools and chronicling small beer," and whose fantasies were always of

what greatness would be hers were she a man and not a woman, was not yet ready for mating. And so Richard Burton remained a fantasy lover for four more years, to be guarded, nursed, dreamed about, and above all manipulated as a defence against marriage with anyone else.

Meanwhile for Richard there were also powerful imponderables at work to keep him from marriage. According to his niece, who could only have been reflecting her mother's memories, the four years at Boulogne resulted in his being tamed into a model son and brother. "The asperities of his early boyhood had all worn away. Marvellously sweet tempered about trifling annoyances, he never grumbled or swore when the household, kept on moderate means, occasionally creaked on its hinges." But he apparently paid penalties for this servitude. "Even when suffering from fits of melancholy . . . he generally succeeded by a heroic effort in concealing much of his depression. And no sooner had his naturally high spirits once more gained the day, than friends and relatives were kept continually amused by his delightful witty sayings, until at last excited by the general hilarity, he became fairly uproarious, and no one could imagine he had ever known sorrow in the world."

Burton, however, described this period in a deadly phrase as "four years' life of European effeminacy."[12] We do not know whether it was primarily his mother's tenacious clinging, his sister's subtle discouragement of his would-be marriages, his memories of the "soft, bending, and relaxed" Eastern women he had known, or simply his failure to convince a pair of British parents that he had a decent future. It is not surprising then that on the single occasion when he mentioned this four-year period he used a phrase—as with so many references to his mother—that hinted of castration.

Many times in Boulogne he escaped into a masculine world. He fenced under one of the great masters of Europe, M. Constantin, and obtained the coveted title of *Maître d'armes*. A fellow officer, Colonel Arthur Schuldham, watched him once enter the ring at Boulogne against a famous French fencer. With a grandiloquent gesture Burton disdained the mask, and kept the crowd gasping as he fought one bout after another—seven in all—each time disarming his masked opponent's sword and receiving himself but a single prod in the neck. The Frenchman, unnerved by the bravado as much as the skill, finally refused to continue, saying his wrist was nearly dislocated.[13]

In 1852, bitter over the popular failure of his Indian books, and no doubt bitter as well over the failure of his love affairs, he turned to writing on a new subject, which he hoped would further his army career. This was his *Complete System of Bayonet Exercise*, a 36-page pamphlet designed to revolutionize bayonet drill in the British army.

It was devoted to perfecting the art of killing men. Though the bayonet had been invented at the end of the 17th century, British soldiers were still taught little beyond fixing and unfixing the blade, and had no valid instruction on how to use the weapon in close combat. Burton's pamphlet was read eagerly by foreign army officers, and the Germans bought it in large quantities. But in Britain Burton was criticized for writing it at all.

Years later, after the Crimean War had demonstrated the ineptness of the British soldier in bayonet use, the War Office realized the value of Burton's pamphlet and reprinted it, with modifications, for general use. By way of thin thanks they sent him a letter from the Treasury with permission to draw one shilling for his service to the crown. This was the only recognition he received for a work that revolutionized writing on the subject.[14] To show his contempt for the thanks, Burton actually went to the War Office to collect his shilling. Having obtained it from the bewildered functionaries, he then gave it to the first beggar he encountered outside the War Office.

"Lord love yer, sir," said the beggar.

"No, my man, I don't exactly expect Him to do *that*," Burton replied wryly. And so the best that he got out of the publication was a story to tell his friends, another story of how the world did not recognize his merits, to his never-ending dismay and delight.

Months before the *Complete System of Bayonet Exercise* was published, Burton returned to an old exploration scheme he had first envisioned in India. This was the penetration of the city of Mecca, forbidden to all non-Moslems under penalty of death. A handful of Europeans had in fact made their way to within the city walls, but only the Swiss Arabist, John L. Burckhart, had written in detail of the sacred city. Burton was determined to penetrate both Mecca and Medina and write about them himself. "Thoroughly tired of 'progress' and of 'civilisation,'" he wrote, "curious to see with my eyes what others are content to 'hear with their ears,' namely, Moslem inner life in a really Mohammedan country; and longing, if truth be told, to set foot on that mysterious spot which no vacation tourist has yet described, measured, sketched, and photographed, I resolved to resume my old character of a Persian wanderer, a 'Darwaysh,' and to make the attempt."[15]

In the autumn of 1852, Burton went to London with a detailed plan, hoping to win permission and patronage. Several members of the Royal Geographical Society who properly valued Burton's Sind books found the Mecca idea exciting. The president, Sir Roderick I. Murchison, and Dr Norton Shaw, who was to be Burton's lifelong friend, accompanied him for a personal interview before the chairman of the Directors of the East India Company, Sir James Hogg, and warmly supported his request for a three-year leave of absence to explore in disguise both the holy cities. Burton hoped also to explore east of Mecca, and to erase the "huge white blot" that constituted eastern and central Arabia on British maps. He planned to cross the peninsula in a direct line either from Medina to Maskat or from Mecca to Makallah.

Hogg, still smarting under the memory of Burton's 1851 attack on the Company's misrule, remembering—as Burton put it—"my impolitic habit of telling political truths," would have granted nothing to what he considered an intolerably impertinent young lieutenant. But since Burton was supported by General Montieth, Colonel William Sykes, and Colonel P. Yorke, he grudgingly granted a single year's leave, not with any official sanction for exploration, but merely "to pursue his Arabic studies in lands where the language is best learned." He warned Burton that all explorations in the area had resulted only in "a string of fatalities." Though this meant a denial of India Office patronage, it still spelled freedom, and since the Royal Geographical Society promised him funds, he was content. The curtailment in time meant haste, however. He had to refurbish his Arabic, master the intricate details of personal and social etiquette, and so recondition his reflexes that he moved, thought, ate, and performed all bodily functions as an Arab rather than as a "Frank."

All his friends with some knowledge of the area knew that Burton would also have to be circumcised. Apparently he had long before accustomed himself to the idea, for his Indian books reveal how he had watched with special curiosity the ceremonies of conversion when a Hindu became a Moslem. He knew the ritual in detail—the bathing, the dressing in black, the joyous street procession where the convert is pelted with money, and finally the circumcision itself. "No evil results are expected from the circumcision of adults," he had written. "The cure, however, is generally protracted for the period of at least six weeks."[16]

Burton grew a beard, shaved his head, and quietly disappeared as Richard Burton in London. By April 3, 1853 he was ready to start. The journey to Mecca meant for Burton an escape from "four years' life of European effeminacy." It meant also a return to the old delights of disguise. And though he clearly counted it an escape from his family as well as from civilization, the break with the former was illusory. For the journey to Mecca, what he frankly called "the mother city of Islam," meant a postponement of his search for a wife, and a reaffirmation of his old love of the forbidden: his mother's continuing triumph.

The Chartered Vagabond

The man wants to wander, and he must do so or he shall die.
                    Richard Burton, *Pilgrimage to El-Medinah and Meccah*

*I*F A MAN turns to disguise as a way of life, it suggests a savage dissatisfaction with himself. Burton's flirtation with disguise was always temporary, and like a good actor he was always in control of the role. He skirted to the edge of imposture, where the disguise envelops the man, but was never lost to it. In later years, after he had abandoned disguise, he wrote of its delights and commented perceptively on imposture itself. "I can scarcely persuade myself that great events are brought about by mere imposture, whose very nature is feebleness: zeal, enthusiasm, fanaticism, which are of their nature strong and aggressive, better explain the abnormal action of man on man. On the other hand it is impossible to ignore the dear delights of fraud and deception, the hourly pleasure taken by some minds in finessing through life, and in playing a part till by habit it becomes a nature."[1]

When Burton assumed a disguise it was always accompanied by danger, and even after he had largely given up the practice, he continued in his explorations a kind of intermittent flirtation with death. In choosing to explore Mecca and Medina he selected shrines held peculiarly inviolate, and protected by a people traditionally given to personal violence. Mohammed in AD 629 had decreed Mecca forbidden to unbelievers. Over the centuries the ban had been rigorously enforced, and many Christians and Jews upon discovery there had been impaled or crucified for their curiosity, two as late as 1845. Although official law in 1853 gave the infidel "a choice thrice offered between circumcision and death," there had been some relaxation, and Burton was confident that any Englishman, if caught and turned over to the law, would be simply expelled. The grave danger was an unofficial knife in the belly at the moment of exposure.

Burton was not, as is sometimes erroneously believed, the first non-Moslem to penetrate Mecca. A good number of other men, either non-Moslem or "temporary converts," had succeeded before him, and Burton did a service to history by summarizing their voyages or citing at length from their accounts in the appendices of his own volumes. As early as 1503 Ludovico de Varthema, an Italian traveller, temporarily embraced Islam, visited Mecca, and corrected the widespread myth that Mohammed's coffin was suspended in mid-air by giant magnets. Joseph Pitts, an Englishman, was captured at sea by Moslem pirates early in the 18th century, forcibly converted, and taken by his master on the pilgrimage. Pitts ate pork in private, counted the Prophet "a bloody impostor," and eventually escaped back to England, where he described his adventures in a lively book. One of the five was a scoundrel, Giovanni Fanati of Ferrar, a deserter from the Italian army who became a convert in Albania to escape a prison sentence. Fanati seduced the favourite wife of a Turkish general, fled to Egypt, then went to Mecca, writing a memoir of his betrayals and plundering with what Burton described as "not candour but sheer insensibility."

The Spanish geologist and botanist, Domingo Badia y Leblich, travelled to Mecca in 1807 as a wealthy Moslem scholar, with a knowledge of Arabic that enabled him to pass the scrutiny of the Arabs perfectly. The last was the Swiss ethnologist Johann Ludwig Burckhardt, the "discoverer" of Petra and explorer of the sources of the Niger, who in 1813 travelled up the Nile as far as Dar Mahass, then crossed the Nubian Desert and the Red Sea to visit Mecca and Medina. Burckhardt died in 1817 in Cairo of a malady he had contracted in Medina. He had not been, as the Moslems said, decapitated in a mosque when someone discovered that he had "the formula of Islam written, in token of abhorrence, on the soles of his feet." His manuscript, by good fortune already mailed on to his London patrons before his death, was published in four volumes, the most detailed and accurate of all the accounts up to his time.[2]

Burton hoped to improve on Burckhardt's feat by entirely crossing the Arabian penninsula, from west to east. He did not know that this meant traversing one of the world's most formidable deserts, largely unexplored even by the Bedouin. One Englishman, G. F. Sadlier, had crossed from east to west in 1818, but so hostile were the terrain and the natives that no other European would manage a crossing in either direction till 1918, when H. St John Philby made his remarkable explorations in the central area. Philby, who mapped what he called "the largest blank spot on the map outside the polar regions," afterwards wrote, in language strangely reminiscent of Richard Burton, of an "insatiable craving within me to penetrate the recesses of that Empty Quarter." He concluded, "I have done enough to set my soul at rest, released from its long bondage."[3]

Burton's primary obsession, however, was penetration into the mysteries of Arab family life. To assure this goal he chose to play the role of combination dervish and doctor. The dervish, he wrote, was "a chartered vagabond," respected for his austerity and granted everywhere the boon of privacy. A man of any age, rank, or creed could assume this monkish role temporarily and travel safely without servants or weapons. "In the hour of imminent danger," Burton said, "he has only to become a maniac, and he is safe," for "a madman in the East, like a notably eccentric character in the west, is allowed to say or do whatever the spirit directs."

To the role of dervish, Burton added what he admitted was the "infinitely seducing" role of doctor, because this was the best way to "see people face to face, and especially the fair sex, of which Europeans, generally speaking, know only the worst specimens." From his youth, he said, he had been "a dabbler in medical and mystical study," and he knew well enough that Eastern medicine consisted largely of magic nostrums, charms, incantations, simple diets, and prescriptions for aphrodisiacs. He equipped his luggage with calomel, bread pills dipped in aloes and cinnamon water, and a magic mirror, believing himself less likely to do real harm than "most of the regularly graduated young surgeons who start to 'finish' themselves upon the frame of the British soldier." He counted his best remedy hypnosis.

From the first day he boarded the steamer *Bengal*, April 14, 1853, with shaven head and long beard, his skin stained with walnut juice, dressed in the flowing robes of Mirza Abdulla (literally Mr Servant of Allah), he played the role with flourish and éclat. The preliminary test came upon debarkation at Alexandria, where the beggars looked sharply at him and then turned away. Only one youth bothered to extend his hand with a whining "Bakhshish," and hearing Burton's contemptuous "Mafish," a retort meaning in effect, "I have left my purse at home," he shrugged and left, convinced, said Burton with satisfaction, "that the sheep-skin covered a real sheep."[4]

Discovering in Egypt that Persians in Mecca were often abused as dissenters, and accused of throwing filth upon the holy Kaaba, he changed his ancestry slightly, returning to his old Indian role of Pathan, an Indian of Afghan parentage. For the first four weeks he stayed in a small garden house at the home of John Larking of Alexandria, who had befriended Burckhardt, and who was one of the few men admitted to Burton's plans. Here he perfected his Arabic and quietly advertised his profession. Within a fortnight he had more patients than he could manage, and had been offered one daughter in marriage.

Burton hardly had the liberties of a modern doctor—no Egyptian would permit a male doctor to examine his wife even if she was dying in childbirth—but he had lively opportunities to satisfy his curiosity about harem life. "In the arts of deceit," he said, "men here have little or no chance against women," but he counted the wives, nevertheless, the best-tempered in the world, and much more amorous than their husbands. A harem, he said pointedly, "often resembles a European home composed of a man, his wife, and his mother." Few men could afford the four wives permitted by Mohammed, but all considered it the ideal number. "If you marry one wife she holds herself your equal, answers you and 'gives herself airs,'" Burton was told; "two are always quarrelling and making a hell of the house; three are no company and two of them always combine against the nicest to make her hours bitter. Four *are* company; they can quarrel and 'make it up' against themselves, and the husband enjoys comparative peace. But the Moslem is bound by law to deal equally with wives. . . ."⁵

In attempting to solve passport problems to get out of Egypt, Burton as Mirza Abdullah suffered indignities and delays he would never have endured as Richard Burton. When one Englishman on the street cursed him roundly because he had accidentally touched his elbow, Burton forgave him "in consideration of the compliment to my disguise." But he learned to call the British in Egypt "model barbarians," and became convinced that all their Moslem servants secretly held them in loathing.

From Alexandria to Cairo he travelled for the first time up the Nile, the attempted conquest of which was later to bring him so much anguish and suffering. One looks in vain in the narrative of this small voyage for any hint of the obsessive preoccupation to come; there is only disillusionment. "To me there was a double dullness in the scenery," he wrote, "it seemed to be Sind over again—the same morning mist and noon-tide glare; the same hot wind and heat clouds, and fiery sunsets, and evening glow; the same pillars of dust and 'devils' of sand sweeping like giants over the plain; the same turbid waters. . . ."

He was unexpectedly lonely, sitting alone smoking, telling his beads upon a mighty rosary, and munching bread and garlic "with a desperate sanctimoniousness." But before the voyage was over, he had made several Moslem friends of whom he was to see much in Cairo. He spent several weeks there studying Arabic grammar and Moslem theology with an old savant, Shaykh Mohammed, from whom he learned, among other things, that note-taking was dangerous. "What evil habit is this?" said the old man in alarm. "Surely thou hast learned it in the land of the Frank. Repent!" So he practiced taking notes surreptitiously, in a tiny, crabbed hand that was virtually indecipherable. And from these Cairo notes there eventually emerged a luminous portrait of the ancient city.

Burton was in Cairo during Ramazan, the Lent-like month of Moslem fasting, when eating, drinking, and "even swallowing our saliva designedly," was forbidden during the daylight hours. The withering June heat turned the city by day into a maelstrom of grumbling and violence; at night the throngs became good-humoured and relaxed, eating cakes and toasted grains, and drinking sugared juices and coffee in the narrow streets. In Burton's pages one sees beggars with crude maps of Mecca collecting coppers to defray the expenses of their pilgrimage, prostitutes "whose only mark of modesty is the Burká, or face-veil," water carriers chanting, "Sweet water, and gladden thy soul O lemonade!" and donkey boys beating their asses with cries of "pander," "Jew," "Christian," and "son of the One-eyed whose portion is eternal punishment." Above all the tumult one hears the melodious voice of the Muezzin calling from the minaret balcony, "Hie ye to devotion! Hie ye to salvation! Devotion is better than sleep!"

Carrying a dim oil lamp, Burton explored the quiet sections of the city by night. "Not a line is straight," he wrote, "the tall dead walls of the Mosque slope over their massy buttresses, and the thin minarets seem about to fall across your path . . . the great gables stand merely by the force of cohesion," all accented by "the graceful bending form of the palm, on whose topmost feathers, quivering in the cool night breeze, the moonbeam glistens." He noted the phallicism in the architecture of the mosque, as in the triangular temple architecture of the Hindus, and called it "an unconscious revival of the forms used from the earliest ages to denote by symbolism the worship of the generative and the creative gods." He claimed no originality for this insight, so unexpected in a nineteenth century British soldier, and freely referred his readers to the French scholar D'Hancarville, who had traced phallic worship and its different modifications among many peoples.[6] This was only one of numerous evidences of his growing erudition, and his insistence on acknowledging his sources.

Burton was enchanted with the Arab's *kayf*, an untranslatable word referring to the voluptuous relaxation following the smoking of hemp, but also to what he described as "the savouring of animal existence; the passive enjoyment of mere sense; the pleasant languour, the dream tranquillity, the airy castle-building, which in Asia stand in lieu of the vigorous, intensive, passionate life of Europe." Arabs, he said, had "a facility for voluptuousness unknown to northern regions, where happiness is placed in the exertion of mental and physical powers . . . where niggard earth commands ceaseless sweat of face, and damp chill air demands perpetual excitement, exercise, or change, or adventure, or dissipation, for want of something better."

In Cairo he continued to practice medicine, and after curing some slave girls from the price-reducing habit of snoring—by hypnosis plus a strong cathartic—he found himself with a brisk business. Still he was lonely, admitting to a desperate desire to talk with English visitors, and writing in his notes, after attending an Armenian marriage, that "after the gloom and sameness of Moslem society, nothing could be more gladdening than the unveiled face of a pretty woman."[7]

In Cairo he became friends with a Russian-born Moslem, Haji Wali, a businessman with a family in Alexandria, who was in Cairo to fight a lawsuit. He was a handsome, middle-aged man with a thin red beard, well-travelled and worldly, who taught Burton much about Egypt. One night in the Caravansarai they met an Albanian Army captain, Ali Agha, a tall, bony, mountaineer who immediately wrenched Burton's pistols away from him for examination. Burton kept his temper. But some days later, when they met again in Haji Wali's room and the Albanian became quarrelsome, Burton flung him backwards, barely saving him from cracking his head on the stone floor. Impressed into amiability by Burton's strength, the captain suggested that they drink together.

Soon they were friends, and Ali Agha was begging the "Indian doctor" for "a little poison that would not lie, to quiet a troublesome enemy." Burton obliged him with five grains of harmless calomel, and the two men went on matching cups of Araki, an Egyptian cognac. Finally Haji Wali, who was a faithful Moslem teetotaler, bolted the room in abhorrence, threatening to call the police. The Albanian rose unsteadily and demanded that Burton join him to search out a troop of dancing girls. Foreseeing a brawl, Burton did his best to dissuade him, but Ali Agha reeled out into the gallery shrieking, "O Egyptians! O ye accursed! O genus of Pharaoh! O race of dogs!"

Putting his shoulder against a door, he burst into a room where two couples were asleep. Awakened by his foul words, the women "retorted with a hot volley of vituperation," and the captain fled downstairs, where he fell over the sleeping form of the night porter. Now thoroughly enraged, and vowing to drink blood, he began beating the porter. At this point Agha's servant was roused, and with Burton's aid managed to drag the shouting Albanian back to his room. "No Welsh undergraduate at Oxford," Burton said, "under similar circumstances, ever gave me more trouble."

By mid-morning, as news of the brawling spread, Burton found he had lost his reputation as a serious Indian doctor. "You had better start on your pilgrimage at once," warned Haji Wali. Together with the old tutor he accompanied Burton to the city gate to say goodbye, and "the chartered vagabond" set forth "in a bad wooden saddle on a worse dromedary," on the 84-mile desert trip to Suez. "I will not deny," he wrote, "having felt a tightening of heart as their honest faces and forms faded in the distance."

Though Burton had tasted much desert life in Sind, he was unprepared for the ferocity of Egypt:

Around like drifted sand-heaps, upon which each puff of wind leaves its trace in solid waves, flayed rocks, the very skeletons of mountains, and hard unbroken plains, over which he who rides is spurred by the idea that the bursting of a water-skin or the pricking of a camel's hoof, would be certain death of torture—a haggard land infested with wild beasts and wilder men— a region whose very fountains murmur the warning words "Drink and away!" . . . Man's heart bounds in his breast at the thought of measuring his puny force with Nature's might, and of emerging triumphant from trial. This explains the Arab's proverb, "Voyaging is victory." In the Desert, even more than upon the ocean, there is present death: hardship is there, and piracies, and shipwreck solitary, not in crowds, where, as the Persians say, "Death is a Festival."

Still, with the sun beating down on him like a blast furnace, and the Simoon, "the poison-wind," caressing him "like a lion with flaming breath," he started out by racing his dromedary with the first Bedouin who challenged him. "This," he wrote, "is a trial of manliness."[8]

Burton found Suez a squalid, filthy town overrun with pilgrims. Loathing the George Inn, he nevertheless described it with the humour that lightens all his travel books. "The walls of our rooms were clammy with dirt, the smoke rafters foul with cobwebs, and the floor, bestrewed with kit, in terrible confusion, was black with hosts of cockroaches, ants, and flies. . . . Now a curious goat, then an inquisitive jackass, would walk stealthily into the room, remark that it was tenanted, and retreat with dignified demeanour."

He planned to carry a change of clothing, a small tent, goat-skin water bag, coarse Persian rug, pillow and blanket, a sheet that could double as a mosquito curtain, and a huge cotton umbrella "brightly yellow, suggesting the idea of an overgrown marigold." Elizabeth Stisted had given him "a housewife," a roll of canvas with needles, thread and buttons. He added a pocket filter to help purify the vile drinking water, pistols, a dagger, a brass inkstand and pen holder, a breast rosary, a money belt, medicine chest, and a carefully made breast-pocket pouch for hiding his notes. He took pencils and paper for sketching, intending to cut his drawings into small pieces and hide them in his empty medicine bottles. Hoping to make geographical observations, he carried a compass and sextant, but was forced to discard the latter early in the journey when it was discovered by his suspicious young servant Mohammed, who almost persuaded his companions that he was a spy. This was a bitter loss, for it meant that in respect to geography he could not much improve on Burckhardt. Equipped with only a compass, he was unable to solve even the mystery of the longitude of Medina, which would remain unknown till the beginning of the twentieth century.

Burton took £80 in gold and silver, secreting part of it in boxes and part on his person. If the Bedouin robbers search a man's luggage and find no money, he said, "they proceed to bodily inspection, and if his waist-belt be empty they are rather disposed to rip open his stomach, in the belief that he must have some peculiarly ingenious way of secreting valuables."

On July 11, 1853 Burton sailed south from Suez for Yenbo on the pilgrim ship *The Golden Wire*, a wretched two-masted, fifty-ton steamer lacking compass, log, chart, or spare ropes. Though it was equipped to hold only sixty passengers, ninety-seven crowded on deck, fighting for standing room among the mountains of luggage. A group of savage, barefoot young Maghrabis from the deserts around Tripoli and Tunis, armed with cut-and-thrust daggers, started fighting for more space. One Syrian, trying to restore order, was fished out of the *mêlée* with his beard half gone, his forehead cut open, and toothmarks in his thigh. Soon five men were bleeding and disabled. The riot was quelled, only to break out again, and this time the Maghrabis, like a swarm of hornets, threatened the poop, where Burton was standing. Seizing a quarter-stave, he laid about him joyously. Finally he pushed a 100lb earthen water jar and its heavy wooden frame down upon the rioters. Drenched and badly bruised, they retreated, consulted briefly, and then sued for peace.

The twelve-day voyage south in the Red Sea was a horror when the sun was high. The pilgrims crouched in a half stupor, suffering the desert wind like a blast from a lime kiln, coming alive only after sunset to cook simple meals of rice and onions in square wooden boxes lined with clay and sand, then singing and telling tales into the night. In wading ashore when the boat stopped at Marsa Mahar, Burton felt a sharp pain in his toe and extracted what he thought was a piece of thorn. It was actually the prickle of a poisonous sea urchin, which resulted in a serious infection. At Yenbo—called Yambu by Burton— he found he could no longer walk without great pain. Ahead of him was an eight day, 120-mile journey to Medina, facing a desert wind "like the breath of a volcano." Undismayed, he ordered a camel with a Shugdug, a litter-like basket ordinarily reserved for children and the aged, swung his big frame into it, and took off with the caravan.

By now he had numerous friends and two servants, a young Indian Moslem, Shaykh Nur, and the cheeky, opportunistic but useful Mohammed, whose parents lived in Mecca, and who had attached himself to Burton hoping for free victuals. They cooked for him, defended him from beggars, and kept his gear in order. The routine dinner was boiled rice, rancid butter, and fried onions, with date paste for dessert. For variety he sampled fried locusts, which tasted, he said, like stale shrimp. His supply of tea, coffee, tobacco, dates and oil was soon almost exhausted, most of it eaten by his servants and friends, whom he questioned systematically but with seeming carelessness. At night he scribbled notes in his small tent, using a guide wire attached to his notebook so that he could write in the dark. One friend, Shaykh Hamid al-Samman, offered him housing in Medina; another, Shaykh Mas'ud, who called Burton "Father of Moustachios," unfolded to him an astonishing amount of Bedouin lore. Burton was enchanted with much that he saw of their nomadic life, which seemed to him to spell freedom, cleanliness, and manliness in comparison with that of the urban Moslem craftsman or shopkeeper. "There *is* degredation, moral and physical, in handiwork compared with the freedom of the Desert," he insisted. "The loom and the file do not conserve courtesy and chivalry like the sword and the spear."[9]

His admiration was severely tested in Pilgrimage Pass, when the caravan was attacked by Bedouin bandits. "They took up comfortable places on the cut-throat eminence," he wrote, "and began firing upon us with perfect convenience to themselves." Though twelve pilgrims and numerous camels were killed in the ambush, he dismissed it laconically as "a questionable affair."

Years later a story became current in London that Burton once failed to crouch while urinating, as was the Moslem custom, and that he was thus detected as an impostor by a young Arab, whom he murdered to save his own life. When Lord Redesdale asked him about this in Damascus in 1871, he answered cryptically, "Well they do say the man died." To Bram Stoker, who asked the same question in 1886, he replied, "The desert has its own laws, and there—supremely of all the East—to kill is a small offence. In any case what could I do? It had to be his life or mine." Still he took pains before he died to brand the story a total fabrication, and "absurd scandal"[10]—as always wanting to confess to the worst and yet to be acquitted.

Approaching Medina, the caravan had to cross a formidable ridge of black basalt, so precipitous that a steep flight of steps had been cut into the stone. The velvet-footed camels picked their way up these steps—the Mudarraj—then threaded through a dark lava defile. Burton noted that the beasts hurried without being beaten and that the pilgrims had become strangely silent.

"Are there robbers in sight?" he asked.

"No," said Mohammed, "they are walking with their eyes, they will presently see their homes." Suddenly they emerged, in full view of the gardens, orchards, and minarets of the holy city two miles below. The pilgrims halted and began prayers of thanksgiving: "O Allah! this is the Harim (sanctuary) of thy Apostle; make it to us a Protection from

Hell Fire, and a Refuge from Eternal Punishment! Open the Gates of Thy Mercy, and let us pass through them to the Land of Joy! . . . Live forever, O Most Excellent of Prophets!—live in the Shadow of Happiness during the Hours of Night and the Times of Day, whilst the Bird of the Tamarisk (the dove) moaneth like the childless Mother. . . ." Deeply stirred by the passion and poetry, Burton wrote, "For some minutes my enthusiasm rose as high as theirs."

Burton spent a month in Medina at the home of Shaykh Hamid. Since his foot was still badly swollen, he toured the numerous shrines astride a donkey, unconcerned about the comic picture he made, his giant frame balancing on a lame, raw-backed little ass with one ear missing. The Prophet's Mosque he found "mean and tawdry, a museum of second-rate art, and an old Curiosity-shop, full of ornaments that are not accessories, and decorated with pauper splendour." He was appalled to learn that the 120 guards were all eunuchs, and astonished to be told that some of these men—"disconnected with humanity"— were nevertheless married. He went to some pains to learn the mechanics of this relationship, but did not publish his findings for many years.

Visiting the burial place of Fatimah, Mohammed's favourite daughter, who was believed a virgin though she had given birth to two sons, he reflected on the ubiquity of the virgin birth idea among the world's religions. He marvelled at the grief Fatimah's shrine invoked, as he watched men "weeping silently like children," then "shrieking like hysteric girls and utterly careless to conceal a grief so coarse and grisly, at the same time so true and real, that I knew not how to behold it."

Though his foot stubbornly refused to heal, he decided to push on to Mecca, and was elated when Shaykh Hamid told him he could accompany a caravan that intended to follow the Darb el Sharki, or inland route rather than the coastal road. No European had ever traversed this road, which was largely waterless, save for a few wells sunk in the eighth century at the order of Zobeida, the wife of Harun al Rashid. It ran south-east from Medina, then south across the Harra lava field, following the high plateau of the Nejd-Hejaz borderland. The caravan started on August 31, 1853, and almost at once Burton was aware of the special ferocity of the landscape. The earth was "scalped" and "flayed," he said, "peopled only with echoes." The occasional wells were guarded by soldiers, who extracted extortionate sums for a nauseous liquid. The route was littered with fresh carcasses of ponies, camels, and asses that had died of heat and exhaustion; beggars cut out the edible portions and cooked them, meanwhile pestering the other pilgrims for coins to buy water.

Burton one day watched a quarrel between a Turk and an Arab in which the Turk bested the Arab with a near lethal blow. That night the Arab crept into the Turk's tent and ripped open his stomach with a dagger. The Turk, still conscious, was wrapped in his blanket and left to die in a half-dug grave. "It is impossible to contemplate such a fate without horror," Burton said, "the torturing thirst of a wound, the burning sun heating the brain to madness, and—worst of all, for they do not wait till death—the attacks of the jackal, the vulture, and the raven of the wild.[11]

Most of the marching was done at night; men fought bitterly over precedence on the trail, and the "huge and doubtful forms of the spongy-footed camels" looked like phantoms in the dim light of the blazing torches. Now and then a thorn tree dragged a Shugduf to the ground, its occupant screaming in terror. In the Pass of Death, a favourite place of ambush, a shot rang out and the dromedary in front of Burton fell with a bullet in its heart. Panic swept through the caravan as several other dromedaries were killed, but a courageous group of Wahhabis swarmed up the hill and put the robbers to flight.

Shortly before entering Mecca the caravan stopped at Al-Zaribah. The men's heads were shaved; all were bathed, perfumed and dressed in the official pilgrim costume, a simple cotton garment with red stripes and fringes. The women replaced their coquettish veils with a hideous mask of dried palm leaves. All were forbidden to kill any living thing— fly, louse, or blade of grass—and warned not to cover their heads under any circumstances.

The caravan threaded into Mecca in the dark; Burton was alerted to their arrival by cries of "The Sanctuary! O the Sanctuary!" accompanied by the sobbing of the women. He spent the night at the home of his servant, Mohammed, and at dawn hastened to the Great Mosque and sacred Kaaba, "navel of the world," set in "the mother of cities."

There at last it lay, the bourn of my long and weary Pilgrimage, realising the plans and hopes of many and many a year. The mirage medium of Fancy invested the huge catafalque and its gloomy pall with peculiar charms. There were no giant fragments of hoar antiquity as in Egypt, no remains of graceful and harmonious beauty as in Greece and Italy; yet the view was strange, unique—and how few have looked upon the celebrated shrine! I may truly say that, of all the worshippers who clung weeping to the curtain, or who pressed their beating hearts to the stone, none felt for the moment a deeper emotion than did the Haji from the far-north. It was as if the poetical legends of the Arab spoke truth, and that the waving wings of angels, not the sweet breeze of morning, were agitating and swelling the black covering of the shrine. But, to confess humbling truth, theirs was the high feeling of religious enthusiasm, mine was the ecstasy of gratified pride.

The Kaaba—the cube—was a square windowless stone building set in the centre of a large courtyard of the Great Mosque, with a single door for entry, seven feet above the ground. It was covered with the

Kiswah, a huge pall of black brocade embroidered with inscriptions from the Koran in gold. Set into the southeast outside corner was the famous Black Stone, said by Moslems to have been white when given to Abraham by the angel Gabriel, and to have become black by the sins of the pilgrims who kissed it. Actually the stone was a pagan idol centuries older than Mohammed, and the Kaaba, which had been rebuilt several times, was probably originally a temple to Saturn. Mohammed had abolished all the idols in Mecca save this one, which he incorporated into the very heart of his religion.

When Burton arrived every inch of space was filled with sweating, sobbing pilgrims. Some were prostrate on the pavement in a religious frenzy; one African was swaying "like a chained and furious elephant," and some were carrying corpses on litters, circumnavigating the cube. Burton marched round the Kaaba seven times, saying the appropriate prayers, and then aided by Mohammed and his friends pushed his way forward through the crowd. "After thus reaching the stone," he said, "despite popular indignation testified by impatient shouts, we monopolised the use of it for at least ten minutes. Whilst kissing it and rubbing hands and forehead upon it I narrowly observed it, and came away persuaded that it is an aerolite."

On his second visit he measured it with a tape, and by careful stepping and pacing managed to take accurate measurements of all that interested him in the Great Mosque. He drank from the sacred well Zemzem, said to have been the same that Hagar drew water from for her son Ishmael, son of Abraham, legendary father of the Arab people. The water caused nausea, diarrhoea and boils, he reported, but it was sold throughout Islam for its magic qualities, and was sprinkled on the eyes of dying men to insure their entry into heaven. Not to be outdone, he secured a bottle for himself; Isabel preserved it even after his death.

Next came the holy march to Mt Arafat, the Mountain of Mercy, where Gabriel was said to have instructed Adam in prayer. It was a bald, ugly 200 foot-high hill, six hours by camel from Mecca. The heat was intolerable, as was the stench from the encampment of 50,000 pilgrims at the base. Burton saw five men die by the roadside as he walked the stony road. "Each man suddenly staggered, fell as if shot, and after a brief convulsion lay still as marble," he wrote. His own feet were blistered, and his shaven head raw with sunburn. That night, retiring to his tent, he was forced to drive away a group of grave-diggers who wanted to bury "a little heap of bodies" within a yard or two of where he chose to sleep.

But all the stench, inconvenience, and visible tragedy he reported without indignation. It was part of the great spectacle, and he refused to let personal fastidiousness deprive him of the excitement and the drama. The next day, listening to the sermon on the top of Mt Arafat, he caught sight of a beautiful Meccan girl with citrine-coloured skin, and a shape like that "the Arabs love, soft, bending, and relaxed, as a woman's figure ought to be." He stared at her a long time, and finally, sensing his admiration, she threw back an inch or two of her head veil, disclosing a dimpled mouth and rounded chin. "She smiled imperceptibly," he wrote, "and turned away. The pilgrim was in ecstasy." Burton tried to pursue the acquaintance, but the moment the sermon ended the crowd became a wild, chaotic swarm rushing down the mountain, and he quickly lost her.

The next day he went to Muna to perform the ritual of hurling seven stones against the Devil Monument, in memory of Abraham who was said to have thrown stones at the devil barring his passage at this spot. The monument was in a narrow defile; thousands of camels and asses struggled against each other, and at one point Burton's donkey fell to the ground and flung his rider beneath a roaring, stamping dromedary. Whipping out his knife, Burton struck at the beast's belly till it lunged forward, and so escaped being badly trampled.

Every Moslem was expected to buy a sheep or camel, drag it to a smooth rock near the Akabah in Muna, and, holding its head in the direction of the Kaaba proceed to cut its throat. This ceremony Burton was content to watch. The meat was given over immediately to beggars, who carved out the choice portions and left the remainder of the carcass. "Literally the land stank," Burton said. "Five or six thousand animals had been slain and cut up in this Devil's Punchbowl. I leave the reader to imagine the rest."

Burton was determined not to leave Mecca without penetrating the inside of the Kaaba, and gave orders to his servant to alert him when the shrine was relatively empty. Nevertheless after returning to Mecca, he was startled when young Mohammed burst into his quarters crying, "Rise, Effendi! dress and follow me!" For an instant fear clutched at his throat. "Now I am suspected," he thought. But the message was simply that the Kaaba was empty, and Burton hastened to the Grand Mosque, where he was hoisted through the single door by two husky guards and lowered into the holy room. Here he was questioned sharply about his identification, but passed the test, as he had so many times on the pilgrimage, without difficulty. "But I will not deny," he wrote, "that looking at the windowless walls, the officials at the door, and the crowd of excited fanatics below—'And the place death, considering who I was,'—my feelings were of the trapped-rat description. . . . perspiration trickled in large drops, and I thought with horror what it must be when filled with a mass of furiously jostling and crushing fanatics." While performing the expected prayers, Burton brazenly sketched a rough floor plan with a pencil on his white Ihram, though he knew that "nothing could preserve him from the ready knives of enraged fanatics if detected."[12]

After this everything was anticlimactic. By now he had taken enough notes to fill two fat volumes. He had mingled with Moslems of every variety, and had enough material on the Bedouin alone to write a classic ethnic portrait. He had paced and measured, and estimated and sketched every important shrine, all at immense personal risk. His six days in Mecca had been rewarding beyond all expectation, but there was nothing left of consequence. He was virtually out of money, and every man he questioned about going east across the desert called it madness and certain death. "I now began to long to leave Mecca;" he wrote, "I had done everything, and seen everything. . . ."

X

Breaking the Guardian Spell

Travellers like poets are mostly an angry race.
Richard Burton, "Narrative of a Trip to Harar"[1]

*D*ESPITE HIS JUBILATION at ending the pilgrimage Burton found himself unexpectedly loath to leave the Arab world and even to shed his disguise. In Jidda, where he stayed ten days awaiting a passage to Suez, it was still dangerous to reveal himself, and he indicated his British identity only to the Vice-Consul.

I was left kicking my heels at the Great Man's Gate for a long time, and heard somebody say, "Let the dirty nigger wait." Long inured to patience, however, I did wait, and when the Consul consented to see me I presented him with a bit of paper, as if it were a money order. On it was written, "Don't recognize me; I am Dick Burton, but I am not safe yet. Give me some money, which will be returned from London, and don't take any notice of me." He, however, frequently afterwards, when it was dark, sent for me, and once safe in his private room, showed me abundance of hospitality.[2]

Before he boarded the *Dwarka*, Burton somehow inadvertently betrayed his origin to his servant Mohammed, who the next day coldly asked for his wages, spent a great deal of Burton's money buying grain, and disappeared with it. Shayk Nur revealed that he had left deeply offended, saying, "Now I understand. Your master is a sahib from India. He hath laughed in our beards."

Burton boarded the ship still in disguise, but emerged from his cabin an Englishman, recognized by none of his former companions. Back in Cairo, however, he could not resist going back to his Arab dress long enough to test it on the English officers at Shepherd's Hotel. He approached a group of them who sat talking and smoking on the veranda, and strode backwards and forwards close to them with the characteristic swinging Bedouin stride. When the flying folds of the burnous brushed against one of the officers, he snapped angrily, "Damn that nigger's impudence! If he does that again I'll kick him."

Whereupon Burton wheeled around and said, "Well, damn it Hawkins, that's a nice way to welcome a fellow after two years' absence."

"By G—d, it's Ruffian Dick," cried Hawkins. And the men crowded about him.

Instead of returning to England, where he was certain to be lionized by the Royal Geographical Society—an open sesame to the great houses of England—Burton chose to stay in Cairo through November 1853, the remaining weeks of his army leave. Here he began to write the account of his pilgrimage, and seems to have found it a necessity during the writing to continue in part living as an Arab. T. E. Lawrence, Burton's twentieth century rival as commentator on Arab life, wrote of his own struggle to live in both worlds. "In my case, the effort for these years to live in the dress of Arabs and to imitate their mental foundation, quitted me of my English self, and let me look at the West and its conventions with new eyes; they destroyed it all for me. At the same time I could not sincerely take on the Arab skin; it was an affectation only. Easily was a man made an infidel, but hardly might he be converted to another faith. I had dropped one form and not taken on the other, and was become like Mohammed's coffin in our legend, with a resultant feeling of intense loneliness in life. . . ." He described his "reasonable mind" looking down on his own body, "wondering what that futile lumber did and why. Sometimes these selves would converse in the void; and then madness was very near, as I believe it would be near the man who could see things through the veils at once of two customs, two educations, two environments."

Burton was never given to this kind of self-revelation, and his *Pilgrimage to El-Medinah and Meccah*, written in Cairo and Bombay over a period of eleven months, was decidedly more detached than the *Seven Pillars of Wisdom*. Where Lawrence was soft and poetic, Burton was brisk and tough-minded; where Lawrence was introspective and selective, Burton displayed a veritable mania for fact-collecting. Both men wrote from notes and journals, but gave the impression of having the gift of total recall. Both were scholars as well as soldiers and adventurers, and talented at describing landscapes and people. But where Lawrence wrote a luminous self-portrait that greatly exposed himself, Burton successfully hid himself and exposed the whole Arab world.

When Lawrence wrote of the Arabs, "Pain was to them a solvent, a cathartic, almost a decoration, to be fairly worn while they survived it," one can be fairly certain, in the light of all that is known of him, that he was then writing of himself. Burton's generalizations were often equally sweeping, but much less projections of his own character, though when he wrote, "Travellers, like poets, are mostly an angry race," the direction of the arrow was unmistakable. With the Arabs themselves Burton was far less involved than Lawrence, and he differed particularly in his attitude towards Arab women. These Lawrence ignored, describing only his horror of the "raddled meat" of the prostitutes, while revealing his admiration for the "clean bodies" of the Arab boys. In the whole Mediterranean world, he wrote, "woman became a machine for muscular exercise, while man's psychic side could be slaked only amongst his peers."

Burton, on the other hand, recorded his pleasure in Arab women whenever he glimpsed a pretty face or figure. "I have often lain awake for hours listening to the conversation of the Bedouin girls," he wrote, "whose accents sounded in my ears rather like music."[3] And he had a solid respect for the sex as such. ". . . women in troubled times," he wrote, "throwing off their accustomed feebleness and frivolity, become helpmates meet for man. . . . Here, between the extremes of fierceness and sensibility, the weaker sex, remedying its great want, power, raises itself by courage, physical as well as moral."[4] He was inexhaustible in ferreting out details of harem life, although much of his livelier information was deleted as "unpleasant garbage" by Egyptologist John Gardiner Wilkinson, who was given the *Pilgrimage* manuscript to edit by Burton's publisher.[5]

Nevertheless, the special lure of the Arab world seems to have been for Burton as for Lawrence essentially masculine. "El Islam," he noted, "seems purposely to have loosened the ties between the sexes in order to strengthen the bonds which connect man and man."[6] And his insatiable appetite for exploration, which the Meccan episode only whetted, in the years following threw him often into the company of soldier-explorers. A few may have been tortured homosexuals of Lawrence's stamp; others were, like himself so far as we know, content with brief encounters with prostitutes or generous native girls. Burton hinted at this kind of adventure in a brief, inexplicit passage in his first book on Africa: "You see, dear L[umsden]," he wrote, "how travelling maketh a man *banal*. It is the natural consequence of being forced to find, in every corner where Fate drops you for a month, a 'friend of the soul,' and a 'moon-faced beauty.' "[7] One result was that Burton, some time during this adventure, contracted syphilis, which probably explains why his attitude toward Egyptian women, heretofore genial, became venomous. Apparently he was not cured before it had entered what was described by his Army physician in Aden as the secondary stage.[8]

Burton gathered notes on homosexuality in the Near East with the same avidity with which he collected information on harem life. Whatever was most forbidden he felt compelled to describe, though over thirty years would pass before his notes on this subject would reach print. He seems to have been diverted in these years from love into

investigation, and the energy that would normally have been chan-
nelled into an affair of passion overflowed like a great river in flood to
cover momentarily a thousand new, unchartered acres. In this respect
Freud's thoughts on Leonardo da Vinci suggest a parallel to Burton.
Leonardo, Freud wrote, "transmuted his passion into inquisitiveness.
He then applied himself to study with that persistence, steadiness, and
profundity which comes from passion. . . ."[9]

When his leave expired, Burton sailed from Cairo to Bombay, wearing on board ship the comfortable free-flowing robe and green turban
of the accredited Haji, which advertised the success of his pilgrimage
to Mecca. James Grant Lumsden, a member of the Bombay Council,
mistook him for a Moslem and exclaimed to a companion, "What a
clever, intellectual face that Arab has!" Burton, his vanity ever close
to the surface, thereupon introduced himself with pleasure, and the two
men became friends. Burton stayed at Lumsden's home to finish writing
his *Pilgrimage*, and found himself for the first time since Napier's departure among powerful friends in India. With Lumsden's aid he won
the patronage of Mountstuart Elphinstone, Governor of Bombay, for
another pilgrimage strikingly similar to the first.

There was a second holy city to which no European had ever been
granted access. This was Harar, a Moslem citadel of learning and missionary activity, the religious capital of Somaliland, and centre of the
East African slave trade. Tradition held that violation of this city by
any infidel meant the end of independence and eventual seizure by the
hated Franks. Even the surrounding tribesmen were fearful of entering
the gates, lest they end their days in the Amir's foul dungeons. "I could
not suppress my curiosity about this mysterious city," Burton said, and
laid careful plans for "breaking the guardian spell."[10] The swiftness
with which this scheme followed his journey to Mecca suggests that his
elation at having penetrated Medina and Mecca was short-lived, illusory, and substitutive. Perhaps in the most primitive sense Mecca was
"the wrong place," and in any case others had been there before him.

What was most surprising, he planned to be exploring in Somaliland
the very months his *Pilgrimage* was to see publication in London,
thereby advertising a seeming contempt for the adulation in England
that was deservedly his own. News of his Arabian exploit had already
reached the British press and caused a sensation. Isabel Arundell had
noted in her diary with mixed admiration and dismay, "Richard has
come back with flying colours from Mecca; but instead of coming
home he has gone to Bombay to rejoin his regiment. I glory in his
glory. God be thanked! But I am alone and unloved." Later, upon reading press accounts of his new plans, she poured out her continuing

melancholy: "Now Richard has gone off to Harar, a deadly expedition or a most dangerous one and I am full of foreboding. Will he never come home? How strange it all is, and how I still trust in Fate!"[11]

When the three volumes of the *Pilgrimage to El-Medinah and Meccah* were finally published in the summer of 1855 and the spring of 1856, the Crimean War was an overwhelming preoccupation to the British press. Nevertheless the Burton volumes were widely reviewed and accorded an admiration never given to his Indian books. "He has produced a book which unites characteristics hardly thought compatible," said the *Athenaeum*, July 28, 1855, "—the solid old Oriental knowledge—the lively familiarity of a contemporary . . . and a wild adventurousness." Burton had in fact written a classic.[12] Aside from *Seven Pillars of Wisdom*, the only other book at all comparable with the *Pilgrimage* is Charles M. Doughty's *Travels in Arabia Deserta*, published in 1888. Doughty was a young geologist and archeologist who spent two years among the Bedouin from 1876 to 1878. A self-consciously devout Christian, he never got to Mecca, and in fact condemned Burton for masquerading as a Moslem, and petulantly refused to read his *Pilgrimage*. He suffered from hardship, exposure, and Arab cruelty, very nearly losing his life. Though his archaic, Elizabethan-era style has a pedantic air, the portrait of Arabia that emerges is memorable. Nevertheless his book lacks Burton's humour, insight into Arab thought, vast knowledge of Eastern manners, and his ethnological sophistication.[13]

Although Burton planned to enter Harar alone and in disguise as a Moslem merchant, he nevertheless sought the aid of several British officers to take part at the same time in the exploration of Somaliland. This was still largely undiscovered country. The missionaries had penetrated to a degree, but an exploration of the coastal areas in 1848 by a Lieutenant Cruttendon had been the only systematic investigation. Burton hoped to go inland from Berbera to Harar, then swing southeast across the peninsula, ending with a thorough study of Zanzibar. He secured three able officers from the British East India service. One was a surveyor and geographer, Lt G. E. Herne, and two were old friends from the Sind Survey, Lt William Stroyan and Assistant Surgeon J. E. Stocks. Stocks, however, died of apoplexy shortly before he was to leave India, and Burton replaced him with a young volunteer he did not know. This was Lt John Hanning Speke of the 46th Regiment, the Bengal Native Infantry.

John Speke was the son of William Speke and Georgina Elizabeth Hanning, a moderately wealthy couple whose estate, Jordans, lay in Somerset near Ilminster. The Spekes were highly respectable; several of John's ancestors had been members of Parliament. He was born on May 4, 1827, the second of four sons. As a child he detested school, preferring, as he said, "birdnesting." At seventeen he had gone to India, followed in a year by his younger brother Edward, and both had fought in the Punjab campaigns.[14] John Speke was a passionate hunter. He hunted not only to kill but also to collect, dissect, and preserve. He carefully shipped back to his parents for safekeeping a sample of every new head and pelt for what he hoped would be a distinguished private museum of natural history. Having exhausted the Indian fauna, he spent his leaves tramping over the Himalayan passes even before they were free of snow, searching for new specimens in Tibet. There, without instruments, he learned the essentials of mapping, and developed, as Burton put it, "an uncommonly acute 'eye for country,' by no means a usual accomplishment even with the professional surveyor."[15] He was a tough, indefatigable walker and a superb shot. If the hunting was good, he was exultant; if bad, he was depressed. His private letters in the archives of the Royal Geographical Society, written in England as well as Africa, are chequered with complaints when a hunt was not up to his expectations. The fact was, as he wrote in a significant admission in his second book, "that I was more of a sportsman and traveller than a soldier, and I only liked my profession when I had the sport of fighting."[16]

Burton was to note with some dismay Speke's taste for eating the embryos of the pregnant female animals he killed. The African natives would find the practice appalling. Speke never admitted to it in his writing, but referred to it obliquely as follows: "On once shooting a pregnant Kudu doe, I directed my native huntsman, a married man, to dissect her womb and expose the embryo; but he shrank from the work with horror, fearing lest the sight of the kid, striking his mind, should have an influence on his wife's future bearing. . . ."[17]

Speke had come to Aden on leave, hoping to shoot as complete a collection of African fauna as in India and Tibet. But the British Resident in Aden flatly forbade his hunting alone, and suggested that he join Burton's party. He was then twenty-seven, six years Burton's junior, with a seemingly pleasant, gentle, placid nature, pliable about trifles, and possessing what Burton described as "an almost childlike simplicity of manner."[18] He was six feet tall, wiry and muscular, with hair, as the natives put it, "the colour of a lion's mane." He was instantly captivated by Burton, and slipped into the role of a quietly adoring younger brother. That he should have taken this role was also satisfactory to Burton; it was like having Edward at his heels again.

There were to be several such young men in Burton's life—usually quiet, handsome, relatively inarticulate men, also restless, footloose and unattached. Some followed Burton on his explorations; some collaborated with him in writing books; several wrote glowing tributes after his death. Speke, however, was no ordinary subordinate; beneath his taciturnity and apparent good nature was a tangle of emotions and a formidable ambition. His involvement with Burton became complicated and ended in tragedy.

In the Somali adventure Speke had the disadvantage of being a newcomer among old friends, and a substitute for Lieutenant Stocks, whom Burton called "the universal favourite." Speke knew no Arabic, and despite his ten years in India had only an indifferent acquaintance with Hindustani; nevertheless Burton gave him an important assignment, the exploration of the Wadi Nogal, said to be a gold-bearing area. Herne and Stroyan he assigned to Berbera, with instructions to explore the maritime mountains and make notes on the slave trade and local commerce. The penetration of Harar he reserved for himself, confident he would return for a rendezvous with his men on the coast by January 15, 1855.[19]

Burton donned his Arab disguise on October 29, 1854, and boarded the little steamer for Zayla. There he spent a month taking notes on Somali customs and preparing for his journey. It was a pleasant time among uncomplicated people. The natives, though impressed by his guns, called them "cowardly weapons with which a poltroon can slay the bravest," and counted skill with the spear, dagger, and war-club a truer test of manhood. Burton eagerly tested himself against their best men. "I soon acquired the reputation of being the strongest man in Zayla," he wrote with satisfaction. "This is perhaps the easiest way of winning respect from a barbarous people, who honour body, and degrade the mind to mere cunning." Though his reporting was usually judicious, occasionally he damned a whole tribe with an epithet. The Danakil, for example, who came to trade in Zayla in a great caravan, he described as "wild as orang-outangs, and the women fit only to flog cattle."

Burton left for Harar with a party of nine, which included two courageous women—he called them Shehrazade and Deenarzade, out of the *Arabian Nights*—who astonished him with their endurance. His chief guide was a former Moslem policeman of dubious character from Aden. Burton called him "End of Time," tolerated him because he was an encyclopaedia of Moslem proverbs, and damned him for his "prodigious rascality . . . infinite intrigue, cowardice, and cupidity." End of Time served as translator with the Somali Bedouin, whom Burton found to be "soft, merry, and affectionate," less bigoted and suspicious than the Arab Bedouin, and also more eloquent. They were capable, however, of atrocities. A Somali warrior, in order to win the coveted ostrich plume that advertised he had destroyed an enemy, thought nothing of spearing a pregnant woman in the hope that he was thereby killing a male child. Burton recounted his horror at hearing of a fight between two slave caravans enroute from Abyssinia to Tajurrah that resulted in the mutilation of "upwards of 100 wretched boys."

The Somali Bedouin found Burton captivating, and offered him adoption in the tribe and wives in abundance. "As a general rule Somali women prefer *amourettes* with strangers," he wrote slyly, "following the well-known Arab proverb, 'The new comer filleth the eye.'" The women, with their big, long eyes, broad brows and brown complexions, reminded him of Egyptian paintings. They were attractive when young, he said, but "when old age comes on they are no exceptions to the hideous decrepitude of the East."[20]

He called them prolific but bad mothers, neither loved nor respected by their children, and of "cold temperament, the result of artificial as well as natural causes." This was a cryptic reference to the barbarous practice of infibulation, which Burton encountered here for the first time. He had long been aware that among Moslems it was the practice to excise the clitoris of young girls, as a counterpart of circumcision among boys. "This rite is supposed by Moslems to have been invented by Sarah," he wrote, "who so mutilated Hagar for jealousy and was afterwards ordered by Allah to have herself circumcised. It is now universal . . . and no Arab would marry a girl 'unpurified' by it."[21] But in Somaliland there was an additional slicing off and crude stitching of the labia with leather or horsehair to ensure virginity. The operation, performed by the old Somali women, caused much suffering and infection among the nine and ten-year-old girls. The stitching remained until the marriage night, and served as a further complication to its normal perils. The bridegroom, Burton said, would "amplify his physical strength by a meat diet," and "when he goes to bed with his newly-wed bride will strain to break through the blockage with his sword of love." Generally he was unsuccessful, Burton reported, and resorted to a knife. After marriage the young husband, if he suspected his wife's fidelity, could "sew up again the aperture of the pudendum; but a woman who is so minded will break the suture with the greatest ease and sew it up again when her desires are satisfied."

Burton described the practice in explicit detail in a special appendix for his *First Footsteps in East Africa*, writing in Latin, as Gibbon did with his racier footnotes, taking advantage of the British notion that anything written in Latin thereby escaped being pornographic. No one had objected when W. G. Browne published in 1799 a slight description of infibulation, with Latin notes, in his *Travels in Africa, Egypt and Syria from the year 1792 to 1798*. Burton's appendix, entitled "Brief Description of Certain Peculiar Customs," did not, however, end with infibulation, but went on to describe techniques of practising adultery, and the special Somali position for the act of love. These were written in a carefree spirit; after describing the wordless signs by which a woman could indicate she was ready to acquiesce in adultery, Burton added lightly, "Si rideat foemina, gaudet Venus"—*i.e.*, "If the woman laughs, Venus rejoices."

The whole thing was too much for Burton's publisher, who at the last moment did some excising of his own. He ordered the appendix to be ripped out and replaced by a single page empty save for the following: "It has been found necessary to omit this Appendix."[*]

Twenty years later Burton returned to the subjects of clitoridectomy and infibulation, giving them a long though still not severely clinical footnote in his *Arabian Nights*. But the lightheartedness was gone. Excision of the clitoris he defended, as many Moslems do today, as "the proper complement of male circumcision evening the sensitiveness of the genitories by reducing it equally in both sexes; an uncircumcised woman has the venereal orgasm much sooner and oftener than a circumcised man, and frequent coitus would injure her health." This was a counterpart of Burton's conviction that women in hot climates were sexually more easily stimulated than men. Burton deplored infibulation, however. "While it diminishes the heat of passion it increases licentiousness and breeds a debauchery of mind far worse than bodily unchastity, because accompanied by a peculiar cold cruelty and a taste for artificial stimulants to 'luxury.' "[23] Burton does not tell us the sources of his information, whether it was folklore from his male informants or first-hand experience with the women.[**]

En route to Harar Burton passed through lion and elephant country, and saw for the first time the marvellous fauna that would send professional hunters like John Speke into ecstasy. Though he did some elephant hunting, and expressed regret at seeing only one lion, which was stalking his party at dusk, he devoted more space to his astonishment at the twelve-foot conical hills of the white ants than to any other animal in Somaliland.

[*] At least one copy, however, which I was fortunate enough to purchase, and which as far as I am aware is unique, was bound with two pages of the offending matter, a fact that escaped even the sharp eyes of Burton's meticulous bibliographer, Norman M. Penzer. The above material is drawn from this source.[22]

[**] Psychoanalyst Marie Bonaparte, who did research on female excision in Egypt in 1941, came to discredit all such folklore and a large measure of the medical lore on the subject, noting that "men of all colors can be deceived by women in this respect." She concluded, on the basis of wide inquiry in the Cairo hospital and her own numerous case studies, that excision was basically an attempt "to feminize or vaginalize" women by reducing the pleasures of clitoridic masturbation. She believed it failed in its purpose, and that it was also cruel and sadistic. See her "Notes on Excision," *Psychoanalysis and the Social Sciences* (1950), II, 67–83.

Burton's white face attracted attention everywhere. He was suspected of being a Turk, a grave danger here where the Turks had a reputation for rapacity and treachery, and he bitterly regretted not having brought a bottle of walnut juice. "They will spoil that white skin of thine at Harar," one native said, and an Arab warned him that "the human head once struck off does not regrow like the rose."²⁴ At Sagharrah Burton's company flatly refused to follow him further, and it was with the greatest difficulty that he persuaded two of the most courageous to accompany him the last twenty miles. At this point he decided that it was less dangerous to enter Harar as an Englishman than as a suspected Turk. Having no papers, however, to establish his true identity, he composed a letter from the Political Agent at Aden to the dreaded Amir at Harar introducing himself and suggesting cordial relations with England. This decision to emerge from disguise, supported by the forgery, may have saved his life.

The first sight of Harar, a long sombre line on a distant hill, contrasting strikingly with the whitewashed holy cities of Arabia, brought acute disappointment. "Nothing conspicuous appeared but two gray minarets of rude shape: many would have grudged exposing three lives to win so paltry a prize." But the thought that "none ever succeeded in entering that pile of stones" revived his excitement and he spurred his mule forward.

Upon entering the city gates, Burton was told to give up his weapons. After disputing heatedly with the guards "in tongues mutually unintelligible," he was finally taken into the presence of Sultan Ahmad bin Sultan Abibakr still bearing his dagger and revolver. The whitewashed room was decorated with old matchlocks and polished leg irons. The Amir, a thin-bearded, yellow-faced youth of about twenty-five, sat on a simple bench, dressed in a flowing red robe trimmed with white fur, his narrow white turban twisted around a tall cone of velvet. A sabre lay barely concealed under one of the pillows. Burton had heard that he was ill, and suspected at once that the Amir was tubercular.

Putting on the boldest manner possible, he said in a confident voice in his best Arabic, "Peace be unto you," and revealed his identity as an Englishman. The Amir answered graciously and smiled.

"The smile, I must own dear Lumsden," Burton wrote, "was a relief." Later he repeated his story to the suspicious Wazir, who accepted Burton's gift to the Amir of a six-barrelled revolver and showed him to his quarters. Burton retired, "worn out by fatigue and profoundly impressed with the *poésie* of our position. I was under the roof of a bigoted prince whose least word was death; amongst a people who detest foreigners; the only European that had ever passed over their inhospitable threshold, and the fated instrument of their future downfall."

Burton was inside Harar, but by no means certain he could get out. Spied upon constantly, unable to take notes, he nevertheless spent ten profitable days, and demonstrated again his capacity for observation and prodigious research in the face of danger. From the local scholars he learned much Harar history, and in turn so impressed the *savants* that they spoke well of him to the Amir. "This is one of the many occasions in which, during a long residence in the East," he wrote, "I have had reason to be grateful to the learned, whose influence over the people when unbiassed by bigotry is decidedly for the good."

Harar, the city of "sanctity, erudition, and fanaticism," was the African centre for Islamic propaganda. Here the Moslem missionaries were trained, and the gospel went forth to the kingdoms beyond the Gibé. Still it was a mean city, only a mile long and half a mile wide, its narrow streets strewn with gigantic rubbish heaps. It was full of "wadads," itinerant friars who had memorized enough of the Koran to impress the ignorant, and who lived by treating illnesses and selling amulets to ward off the evil eye.[25]

Burton lived on a diet of boiled beef, peppered holcus-scones and plantains. He admired the beauty of the unveiled women, dressed in indigo or chocolate-coloured skirts, and carrying light blue sheeting gracefully over their heads. Their eyes were fringed with kohl and their hands and feet stained with henna. But as the days passed and he was still refused permission to leave, he became increasingly apprehensive. Tactfully he sent word that he could send medicine from Aden to aid the ailing Amir, and cure the Vizier's "chronic bronchitis." Finally a messenger from the coast brought to the Amir information that two other Englishmen were in Berbera anxiously awaiting word of their brother in Harar. This prodded the young leader, who was respectful of British power and fearful lest his lucrative slave caravans be cut off. On January 13, 1855 he ordered the gates to be opened for his "dangerous guest," and Burton and his two companions mounted their mules.

"Suddenly my weakness and sickness left me," he wrote, "so potent a drug is joy!—and, as we passed the gates loudly saalaming to the warders, who were crouching over the fire inside, a weight of care and anxiety fell from me like a cloak of lead."

As with Mecca, however, the exaltation at having penetrated and escaped the holy city without damage was followed quickly by languor and disappointment. "I had time, on the top of my mule for musing upon how melancholy a thing is success. Whilst failure inspirits a man, attainment reads the sad prosy lesson that all our glories

'Are shadows, not substantial things,'

"Truly said the sayer, 'disappointment is the salt of life'—a salutary bitter which strengthens the mind for fresh exertion, and gives a double value to the prize."

But "this shade of melancholy soon passed away," he said. "The morning was beautiful. . . . The dew hung in large diamonds from the coffee trees, the spur-fowl crew blithely in the bushes by the way-side:—briefly, never did the face of Nature appear to me so truly lovely."[26]

First Footsteps Towards the Nile

The horses soared up to the very top of the sky and then, plunging headlong down, they set the world on fire. The highest mountains were the first to burn, Ida and Helicon, where the Muses dwell, Parnassus, and the heaven-piercing Olympus. Down their slopes the flame ran to the low-lying valleys and the dark forest lands, until all things everywhere were ablaze. The springs turned into steam; the rivers shrank. It is said that it was then the Nile fled and hid his head, which is still hidden.

"The Story of Phaëthon," as told by Edith Hamilton

*T*HE VILLAGERS AT Sagharrah, who had heard rumours that Burton had been imprisoned, bastinadoed, and slaughtered at Harar, received him with "the joy-cry," and ran to inform his bearers of his miraculous return. The stoical Shehrazade and Deenarzade broke into giggling with pleasure, and even End of Time, kissing his hand, was on the point of tears. Burton stayed a week at Welensi to fatten his thin mules for the return march, and also to compile a vocabulary of the Harari tongue with the help of a Somali who knew Arabic, who had studied at Harar, and who had in addition some sophistication about grammatical forms.

He collected a thousand words, and concluded that the language was closer to Amharic, the official Semitic language of Ethiopia, than to Arabic. This vocabulary, as printed in an appendix to his *First Footsteps in East Africa*, no mere primer for tourists, left out few important words. The Harari equivalents for shame, silence, malice, and revenge are there, along with kiss, love, fame, and dream. He discovered that the word meaning "in love" differed if it applied to a man or to a woman. The anatomical words one comes to expect from Burton are all present, along with circumcision, eunuch, harlot and adultery.

When it was complete, he started for the coast, impatient now to rejoin his comrades, and late for the anticipated rendezvous of January 15, 1855. After crossing the Marar Prairie, he decided to let the majority of his party return at their slow pace and to cut off across the desert. He took a few biscuits, limes, lumps of sugar, and one

water bottle. He was accompanied by three companions, who by way
of preparation drank enough milk to distend their stomachs.

The short cut was pure bravado; the desert was 120 degrees in the
daytime, and Burton's impatience very nearly cost four lives:

> The demon of Thirst rode like Care behind us. . . . the sun parched our
> brains, the mirage mocked us at every turn. . . . Water ever lay before me—
> water lying deep in the shady well—water in the streams bubbling icy from
> the rock—water in pellucid lakes inviting me to plunge and revel in their
> treasures. . . . I opened my eyes to the heat-reeking plain, and a sky of that
> eternal metallic blue so lovely to painter and poet, and so blank and death-
> like to us. . . . A few hours more and the little party would have been food
> for the desert beasts. We were saved by a bird. When we had been thirty-six
> hours without water we could go no further, and we were prepared to die
> the worst of deaths. The short twilight of the tropics was drawing in, I
> looked up and saw a *katta*, or sand-grouse, with its pigeon-like flight, making
> for the nearer hills. These birds must drink at least once a day. . . . I cried
> out, "See, the katta!"

A hundred yards away the bird plunged down, and following to
the spot they found a small spring hedged in with green. "I have never
since shot a *katta*," he wrote.[1]

By riding only at night, prodding their mules till they were bloody,
and by-passing the hostile villages, they were able to reach Berbera
from the Girki Hills in five days, a feat greeted with incredulity by
the natives. Stroyan and Herne gave him "a glad welcome, a dish of
rice, and a glass of strong waters," which made amends, he wrote,
"for past privations and fatigue." The three friends returned to Aden
in the teeth of a wild storm, arriving on February 9, 1855.

Speke joined them about two weeks later, burdened with skins,
feathers, and skulls of animals and birds he had shot—hyenas, gazelles,
antelopes, Egyptian geese, pigeons and teal. He had failed, however,
to reach the chief watercourse in the Nogal area. He blamed his failure
on Mohammed Sumunter—spelled Sammattar by Burton—the "Abban"
or protector who had been hired in Aden as his official guide, saying
the man had cheated him, stolen from him, overcharged him, and
frustrated every serious attempt at exploration. "He was a vile-condi-
tioned man." Speke wrote passionately, "from whom I could never get
one true word. He seemed to me only as an animal in satanical disguise; to have shot him would have given me great relief, for I fairly
despaired of ever producing any good effect upon his mind."[2]

Burton, who until now had seen only Speke's docile, uncomplaining
aspect, was indignant at the Abban and advised prosecution, as Speke
had repeatedly threatened on the expedition. As a result Sumunter was
jailed for two months, fined 200 rupees, and banished with his family
from Aden forever. Burton was clearly torn, however, between his

indignation at Sumunter and his contempt for Speke's bungling innocence. He knew that overcharging foreigners was routine in Africa,
and he had little patience with Speke's language handicap. By Burton's
standards, Speke's Hindustani was wretched, but it was the only
language bridge between Speke's interpreter and the Abban, and it
had failed.

Burton learned later, to his sorrow, that the imprisonment of Sumunter caused intense resentment among the native Somali chiefs.
What he could not know was that Speke in the future would always
return from a major expedition with charges of cheating and fraud
against someone connected with the exploration. Burton himself would
be severely burned in this manner, and John Petherick, British Consul
in Khartoum, would have his reputation ruined.

Speke had kept a diary of his own, which Burton published as an
appendix in his *First Footsteps in East Africa*. The curious way Burton
handled this diary is a clue to his severe disappointment in Speke. The
very title he gave it, "Diary and Observations made by Lieutenant
Speke, when Attempting to Reach the Wady Nogal," exhaled a whiff
of condescension. Then he rephrased the diary in the third person,
though keeping the diary form, as if to insinuate that Speke had no
writing capacity whatever, though actually he was capable of producing a quite graceful narrative. In a final, less-than-subtle thrust, Burton
wrote that though Speke "was delayed, persecuted by his 'protector,'
and threatened with war, danger, and destruction, his life was never
in real peril."[3] Speke was furious when he saw the mangling of his
diary in 1856, but said nothing at the time. It was only later that
Burton learned how deeply he had offended him.

In Aden Burton found letters from England with news that his
mother was dead. We do not know the cause; Georgiana Stisted tells
us only that in moving to the new house in Bath, where her "harmless
and aimable" life ended she had said grimly upon entering it, "I smell
death here." Richard still had the present he had purchased for her in
Mecca; it was a curious, symbolic gift, "a red, sausage-shaped cushion
strung with turquoise rings." Turquoise, he wrote later, if worn in a
ring, was thought to "increase the milk of nursing mothers: hence the
blue beads hung as necklaces to cattle." Eventually he gave the cushion
to his sister.[4]

Instead of returning to London to grieve even briefly with his father
and sister, he chose to remain instead in the grim desert port revising
his journal entries speedily for a new book. One can only guess whether
he paused over his diary entry for that date which also marked his
mother's death, December 18, 1854. His niece wrote sentimentally and

incorrectly that he had been desperately ill with fever on that day, but a careful reading of his narrative makes it clear that though he had in fact been ill he had fully recovered by that date and was arriving in Agjogsi in excellent spirits. "The inhabitants flocked out to stare at us," he wrote, "and the women uttered cries of wonder. I advanced towards the prettiest, and fired my rifle by way of salute over her head."

Still, in recounting in his book the events of December 18, he did write a brief and sombre tale of death. "The cowherds bade us beware of lions: but a day before a girl had been dragged out of her tent, and Moslem burial could be given to only one of her legs." Then he went on in a discussion of native lion lore to say, "The people have a superstition that the king of beasts will not attack a single traveller, because such a person, they say, slew the mother of all the lions."5 So he *did* write of a death, and in fact of the killing of a mother, which was as close as he would ever come, in print, to mentioning the death of his own mother. It will be seen that in the same context he had also mentioned "a single traveller," like himself, as being somehow responsible.

First Footsteps in East Africa, written in haste, was a lesser book than the *Pilgrimage to El-Medinah and Meccah*. The title was misleading. It suggested that Harar was not the main object of Burton's African interest, and that the whole expedition had been tentative and preliminary to something more consequential. The subtitle, "An Exploration of Harar," was the true theme of the book, but before he had finished writing it he was deep in the planning of still another voyage, the significance of which would indeed dwarf the prestige of the Harar adventure to the mere "first footsteps" of a child. Now he looked longingly towards the great fecund river, mother of Egypt, whose head was still hidden, as much a mystery in 1855 as in antiquity when the Greek poets had first sung of how Phaëthon's fiery chariot had blistered the mountains and sent the Nile scurrying into a secret place.

Fifteen months earlier, at Shepherd's Hotel in Cairo, Burton had heard Johann Ludwig Krapf, German missionary to East Africa, speculate about "the White Nile, Killamanjaro and Mts of the Moon." These stories, he wrote to Dr Norton Shaw on November 16, 1853, "reminded one of a de Lunatico," but he indicated nevertheless that he intended to question Krapf on "what really has been done and what remains to be done."6 At Harar he had made inquiries about the Nile, and had heard of a route from Somaliland across the continent to the Atlantic. This he decided to exploit at once, before returning either to London or to India. "My success at Harar has emboldened me," he wrote to

Norton Shaw on February 25, 1855, "and I have applied for a 2nd years leave. . . . There is little doubt of the White Nile being thereabouts. And you will hear with pleasure that there is an open route through Africa to the Atlantic. I heard of it at Harar. . . ." It was a cheerful letter, radiating invincibility. Burton told Shaw he anticipated no trouble except from the British army authorities in Aden: "Our difficulties will be principally amongst that penis-cutting people. Altogether the prospects of the 'Somali Expedition' are bright enough. . . ." This important letter is evidence of a fact long overlooked by Burton biographers, that he intended his second Somali expedition to be more than merely "a new expedition Nile-wards, *via* Harar on a larger and more imposing scale"—as he wrote of it after the failure of the expedition—but actually a determined search for what he spoke of meaningfully in his *First Footsteps to East Africa* as "the Coy Fountains,"[7] long a legendary source of the great river.

The mythology of the Nile is fascinating on many counts, one being the decidedly feminine character of the symbolism. The favourite legend, dating back to antiquity, held that the Nile sprang from two great fountains. A second, almost as tenacious, called the true source two enormous lakes. Arab stories put the beginning of the Nile in snow-covered mountains, or mountains of crystal, where the sun's rays were so hot they burned the unfortunate traveller. One Arab tale said the Nile flowed through the mouths of eighty-five statues of copper, built by Am Kaam, one of the Kings of Egypt, to decorate his palace on the legendary Mount Gumr, south of the equator. Alexander, it was said, misled by his own geographers, mistook the great Indus, flowing from melting mountain snows, as the Nile source, and sat down at once to write the news to his mother, only to erase what he had written when he realized his error. Julius Caesar, according to Lucan, said he would abandon a battle to see "the primal fountains of the Nile."[8]

Alexander and Julius Caesar had both despatched expeditions up the Nile, but these had ended, as had every other expedition up to Burton's time, in the formidable cataracts or in the vast morasses of the Sudd, with heat, malaria, and hostile natives taking their usual severe toll. Over the centuries no one had managed to improve on the map drawn by Ptolemy, showing two great lakes, which were said to have been seen by a Greek merchant named Diogenes in the first century A.D.

In the seventeenth century two Portuguese Jesuits, exploring and proselytizing in the wilderness of Ethiopia, claimed to have seen the Nile rising out of two fountains, or springs. Father Paez, accompanying the Emperor of Ethiopia, whom he had converted, was camped in the province of Sacala on April 21, 1613. "As I was looking round about me with great attention," he wrote, "I discovered two round springs, one of which might be about two feet diameter; the sight filled me with a pleasure which I knew not how to express, when I considered that it was what Cyrus, Cambyses, Alexander, and Julius Caesar had so ardently and so much in vain desired to behold." Father Lobo, visiting the spot in 1622, described the springs as "two holes, each about two feet diameter, a stone's cast distant from each other." The springs he said were bottomless vents of a great subterranean lake, and the natives annually sacrificed a cow at the spot. Samuel Johnson, delighted by the accounts, had translated their stories from the French and had lent his great prestige to their discovery.[9]

A melancholy giant Scot, James Bruce, depressed by the death of his young wife, set off in 1768 to find what had come to be called in England "the coy fountains." He made his way up the Nile as far as Aswan, crossed the desert eastwards to the Red Sea, and then turned back inland to Gondor, at that time the seat of the government of Ethiopia. From there he was directed to the legendary fountains, about seventy miles south of Lake Tana. On November 14, 1770, his guide pointed out the sacred site. "Look at that hillock of green sod," he said, "for in the middle of that watery spot, it is in that that the two fountains of the Nile are to be found." Flinging off his shoes, Bruce ran down he hill, falling twice in his haste. "I after this came to the island of green turf, which was in the form of an altar, apparently the work of art, and I stood in rapture over the principal fountain which rises in the middle of it. It is easier to guess than to describe the situation of my mind at that moment—standing in that spot which had baffled the genius, industry, and inquiry of both ancients and moderns, for the course of near three thousand years. . . . Though a mere private Briton, I triumphed here, in my mind, over kings and their armies."

Bruce, like Burton, was a tall, powerful, virile-looking man, a good scholar and agile linguist. His mother had died when he was three, and at the age of six he had been separated from his stepmother and sent to London, to be cared for by tutors. His third tragic loss came with marriage; his young wife, barely pregnant, died of tuberculosis within three months of the wedding. One suspects that Bruce's search was intimately related to these losses. Certainly the death of Burton's mother was connected with the sudden galvanizing into action of his fantasies of the Nile search. And as one can see from the journals of David Livingstone, the death of his wife was subtly related to his own, compulsive and fruitless looking for the Nile fountains, which ended with his death in Africa.

There is a remarkable passage in James Bruce's account of his discovery of what he thought was the true Nile source; this was his description of the disillusionment that set in quickly afterwards. It is very like Burton's dejection after leaving Harar, though more self-searching. "I found a despondency gaining ground fast upon me," he wrote. "I remembered the magnificent scene in my own native country, where the Tweed, Clyde, and Annan rise in one hill. . . . I began in my sorrow, to treat the inquiry about the source of the Nile as a violent effort of a distempered fancy:—

> What's Hecuba to him, or he to Hecuba,
> That he should weep for her?—

Grief or despondency now rolling upon me like a torrent; relaxed, not refreshed, by unquiet and imperfect sleep, I started from my bed in the utmost agony."[10]

Bruce might have been still more depressed had he realized that his fountains were one source of only the Blue Nile, which, though it contributed six-sevenths of the Nile water would nevertheless be counted only a mighty tributary, secondary to the White Nile, whose true origin lay a thousand miles away. Fearful of this possibility, Bruce refused to call the White Nile by any but its native name, the Abiad. And he ridiculed with all the passion of a man insisting on the chastity of his bride the earlier claims by Fathers Lobo and Paez that they had seen his Coy Fountains.

Bruce's five-volume account of his travels was popular in England. But he was viciously attacked by British geographers, and his reputation suffered further when Samuel Johnson—annoyed at seeing Father Lobo called a liar—accused Bruce of romantic absurdities and incredible fictions. Everyone scoffed at his story of the African natives who cut steaks from the shoulders of live cattle and ate them raw, then stitched up the hide, packed the wound with clay, and set the cattle forth to graze. [Burton would later confirm the story from his own knowledge, though he would describe it somewhat differently, and as part of a religious ceremony.]

French geographers, however, had always counted Bruce's observations sound, and by the time Burton began to take a serious interest in the Nile problem—eighty-five years after Bruce left Ethiopia—the British geographers were finally beginning to concede the validity of his descriptions. The course of the Blue Nile was now fairly well mapped, but the upper White Nile remained shrouded in mystery, and no one could be certain whether the river had one true source or two. Burton revealed his growing preoccupation with the mystery in his *First Footsteps in East Africa*. Here he made clear that he

believed in the discoveries of Fathers Lobo and Paez, whom he counted
accurate as well as courageous. He attacked Bruce for his vanity and
pedantry, but did not deny the basic validity of his discoveries. And
though he tried to give the impression of sardonic amusement at the
whole idea of the "Coy Fountains," it was clear that his plans were
to go west from Harar into the heart of Christian Ethiopia, directly
into Bruce's old territory, where he was certain to have a look for
himself.

It was not easy to get either permission or money. The Crimean War
throughout the winter of 1854–5 had brought nothing but disaster to
British troops and British prestige, and increasing numbers of East
India Company officers were taking leave and volunteering to join the
regular army. Burton, who felt from the beginning that the war was
"an unmitigated evil to England," refused to be diverted from his new
passion, and won the grudging consent of his superiors for an extended
expedition "Nilewards, *via* Harar." He was greatly cheered when a
message came to Aden from the ailing young Amir, who plaintively
asked for medicine, and pledged the safety of any British citizens who
should visit the sacred city.

By mid-April Burton was camped outside Berbera on a rocky ridge
overlooking the Red Sea. With him were Stroyan, Speke, and Herne,
and a force of forty-two men, Egyptian, Nubian, and Arab, well
equipped with camels and supplies. Burton was waiting until surveying instruments he had ordered from London should arrive, and failed
to start inland with a caravan to Ogadayn, as he had hoped. This delay
deprived them of a friendly escort, and left them prey to the disgruntled local chiefs, who were angered at Mohammed Sumunter's
arrest and at Burton's recent decision to refuse to hire an Abban under
any circumstance. They feared, moreover, that the Englishmen were
spies for the British government, which they knew to be hostile to
their flourishing slave trade. Burton, however, knowing that for thirty
years no Englishman had been molested in Berbera, refused to be
apprehensive, and each night posted only two sentries.

At dusk, April 19, 1855, three strangers appeared outside the camp.
Burton questioned them at length after his men had angered them
by firing warning shots, but he let them go. About 2 am he was
awakened by the shouts of his own natives, and "the rush of men
like a stormy wind." Speke described it "as though the world were
coming to an end." Burton and Herne shared a "Rowtie," a large
penthouse-shaped tent; Speke and Stroyan were in smaller tents on
either side. Herne reconnoitred quickly in the dark and reported that
their native guard had fled and that the enemy force was formidable.

Speke joined Herne and Burton inside the Rowtie, aiming as best they could in the dark through the opening, meanwhile dodging the javelins and long heavy daggers thrown at their legs. They had only one revolver apiece, and their sabres. Stroyan was nowhere visible.

When the natives succeeded in partly beating down the tent, the three officers, in danger of being entangled in the folds, stepped outside. Speke, struck at once by several stones, moved back inside the sagging canvas, and Burton cried curtly, "Don't step back or they'll think we are retiring."

Nine years later, when Speke described the fighting, he was still smarting at the memory of Burton's order. "Chagrined by this rebuke at my management in fighting," he said, "I stepped boldly to the front, and fired at close quarters into the first man before me." The three men now plunged forward, swinging their sabres at the naked bodies converging upon them. Speke was felled by a war-club blow across his chest.

In another instant I was on the ground with a dozen Somali on the top of me [he wrote]. The man I had endeavoured to shoot wrenched the pistol out of my hand, and the way the scoundrel handled me sent a creeping shudder all over me. I felt as if my hair stood on end; and, not knowing who my opponents were, I feared that they belonged to a tribe called Eesa, who are notorious, not only for their ferocity in fighting, but for the unmanly mutilations they delight in. Indescribable was my relief when I found that my most dreadful fears were without foundation. The men were in reality feeling whether, after an Arab fashion, I was carrying a dagger between my legs, to rip up a foe after the victim was supposed to be powerless.

Burton meanwhile, fancying he saw the body of Stroyan stretched out on the sand, slashed furiously in that direction, dodging and fending off a dozen Somali war clubs. One of Burton's own men, who had not fled with the rest, now tried to assist him, but Burton, thinking him an enemy, turned to cut him down. He cried out in alarm, and Burton stayed his blow. At that point a spearman hurled a javelin at Burton; it entered one cheek, transfixed his jaw, destroying four back teeth and part of his palate, and emerged on the opposite cheek. Somehow, in the darkness and confusion, Burton managed to escape and make his way to the sea. There, fainting from pain and loss of blood, he was nevertheless able to dispatch a friendly native to a ship anchored in the harbour. He had entertained the captain and crew at dinner only the night before, and luckily had persuaded them to remain till dawn before sailing. Meanwhile, with the javelin still in his jaws, he searched fruitlessly for his three British comrades.

The friendly sailors found Burton and carried him back to the ship, where one of them extracted the javelin and staunched the bleeding.

At dawn Herne joined them, miraculously unhurt save for bruises from the Somali clubs. Eventually Speke too was found. He had been held captive through the night and forced to watch a victory dance around their tents. At one point a Somali had asked him in Hindustani if he was a Moslem or Christian, promising death if he confessed to being "a Nazarene." Speke admitted to being Christian, expecting it to mean the end of him, but the savage only laughed and left him.

Later one of the natives began a game of torture, thrusting a spear into him from all directions as coldly as if he were a sack of cotton. When one spear thrust went entirely through his thigh, Speke— "smelling death," as Burton put it—managed to hurl himself against his assailant with his double-bound fists. Momentarily unbalanced, the native gave way, and Speke fled. "I was almost naked, and quite bare upon the feet, but I ran over the shingly beach towards the sea like wildfire." Bobbing and dodging, he managed to evade the spears hurled in his direction and escaped. Bleeding from eleven spear wounds, he stopped finally to open his bonds with his teeth, and there, by the sea, the sailors found him.

The Englishmen had managed to kill four or five natives, but at heavy cost, for Stroyan was slain. The sailors found him pierced in the heart and abdomen with spears, his head fearfully gashed and his body beaten. Burton was appalled. Though he had been a soldier for thirteen years, this was the first time he had been in any way responsible for the death of a friend. "This was the severest affliction that befell us," he wrote. "We had lived together like brothers."[11]

The war party, meanwhile, had fled with the guns, tobacco, and cloth, leaving the books and heavy equipment. These Burton collected and had put back on the ship, ordering whatever could not be carried to be burned. Then the men sailed back to Aden, sick at heart. The British physician who examined Burton, according to the medical report recently discovered by Gordon Waterfield, declared the wound to be serious, and added, "as he [Burton] has recently suffered from secondary syphilis [he] must immediately proceed to Europe as it would not be proper to allow him to remain in Aden during the approaching hot weather."[12]

Before his departure, Burton urged his superiors to recommend that the British Navy blockade the coast of Somaliland until Stroyan's murderer be given up, and compensation paid for the plunder. He asked for 13,800 rupees, about £1,380. The Aden authorities agreed to the blockade, and used the murder of Stroyan as an excuse to destroy the slave trade at Berbera. Eventually the native who wore the ostrich plume honouring him for Stroyan's death was turned over to the British for punishment. But the Political Resident at Aden,

Lieutenant-Colonel Playfair, refused to exact any compensation for the plunder, and even went so far as to censure Burton for laxity. "The authorities held a Court of Inquiry in my absence," he wrote later, "and facetiously found that we and not they were in fault. Lord Dalhousie, the admirable statesman then governing in general British India, declared that they were right. I have sometimes thought they were."

So the "first footsteps toward the Nile" ended in disaster. He wrote disconsolately in his journal, "If I had 'let well alone,' I should have done well."[13] He pushed the Nile out of his thoughts for the time and decided—perhaps in an act of penance—that as soon as his wounds were healed he would volunteer in Crimea.

Crimea

BURTON WENT TO London from Aden in May 1855. His wound recovered speedily, though an ugly scar on one cheek would stay with him for life, adding a sinister aspect to his face. But his depression was not easily healed. He visited his father in Bath and then went to Boulogne to see his sister. Edward was there, on furlough from Ceylon. He had become a passionate hunter, the crack shot of his regiment, and was eager to talk of his animal conquests —elephants, cheetahs and tigers—tales to dwarf the boar-hunting stories of their father. But Richard, who had hunted tigers in India and killed elephants in Somaliland and had found little of it palatable, could have been neither cheered nor impressed by his brother's prowess.

In normal times Burton would have been feted as a hero, particularly since the first two volumes of his *Pilgrimage to El-Medinah and Meccah* had been published and were now being enthusiastically reviewed. When his jaw had healed sufficiently so that he could speak in public, he read a paper on his Harar exploit before the Royal Geographical Society, June 11, 1855. But the horrors of Crimea dominated British thinking, and accusations of blundering on the part of British generals, particularly from the powerful pen of William Howard Russell of the *Times*, occupied the British press. "The Crimean War seemed to me some opportunity of recovering my spirits," Burton wrote, "and as soon as my health permitted, I applied myself to the ungrateful task of volunteering."[1] This was not meant to be ghoulish; war in that day still had glamour, and even the reports from the front could not deprive it of that patriotic excitement that promised among other things relief from melancholy.

The phrase "ungrateful task" was not mischosen. Prejudice against officers of the Indian service permeated the British officer ranks. The Commander-in-Chief, Lord Raglan, himself the son of a duke, and with little else in his history to account for his rise to top rank, was devoted to the principle that aristocratic breeding was indispensable for an officer. He upheld the system of acquiring commissions by purchase, which permitted aristocrats of wealth to buy commands of regiments over the heads of more efficient officers. Raglan himself—possibly the most inept general in British history to hold top field command—had never before the war commanded a battalion in the field or led troops in battle, and had been for many years in semi-retirement on half-pay. Lord Cardigan, who was to lead the famous charge of the Light Brigade in the wrong direction, had theoretically done a two-year stint in India; actually he had spent only four weeks with the Light Dragoons between 1836 and 1838; the rest of the time he had been enjoying Cairo, Rome and Paris. To go to India was unfashionable, and easy to circumvent by going on half-pay, which meant essentially to be on leave, and usually waiting for the opportunity to purchase a commission from a retiring or advancing incumbent of higher rank. The fatuous Cardigan had paid £35,000 to £40,000 for the lieutenant-colonelcy that put him in command of the Light Brigade.

Raglan had a particular dislike of officers who had served for the British East India Company, and had issued instructions at his assumption of command in 1854 that they were to be discouraged from joining the expeditionary army. Among those who did, not a single officer was given a cavalry command. Thus Raglan rejected at the outset the only experienced fighting officers available. The men he accepted, as Cecil Woodham-Smith has pointed out in her devastating portrayal of the British military leaders in that conflict, had no real experience with war, no education, and no ability.

All of this was bitterly resented by the "Indian" officers. One of Burton's friends, and the colonel he served under in the Crimea, was W. F. Beatson, a tough, seasoned, and imaginative soldier of fortune who had seen fifteen years' service with the Bengal Army and fifteen more commanding cavalry for Indian princes—a man who had been victorious in twenty battles and had won the thanks of the British governors of India fourteen times. He offered his services to Lord Raglan and was turned down. Lord Lucan also refused to use him, and finally General James Scarlett of the Heavy Brigade took him on his staff, where he proved invaluable in several crucial battles. Nevertheless Raglan continued to deny him any official status.[2]

Seeing the appalling lack of cavalry forces, Beatson begged to be allowed to organize a group of irregular cavalrymen among the fierce Moslem horsemen of the Turkish provinces, popularly known as the Bashi Bazouks. They hated the Russians, and were ferocious fighters, but also had a reputation for indiscipline, and for inflicting torture and mutilation. Raglan refused to consider the idea. As Burton put it, "Lord Raglan could not endure the idea of commanding men who kidnapped Bulgarians and roasted Russians. . . . it was contrary to precedent: Irregulars were unknown at Waterloo, and the idea was offensive, because unknown to the good old stock and pipe-clay school."[3]

Burton had missed the first hideous winter of 1854–5 in the Crimea, when cholera, dysentery, and malaria decimated the French and British armies, and then freezing and starvation added to the monstrous suffering and casualty toll. To incompetence in the field was added negligence at home. As Winston Churchill put it in his *History of the English-Speaking Peoples*, "Raglan's men had neither transport nor ambulances, and thousands were lost through cold and starvation because it did not occur to the Government of the greatest engineering country in the world to ease the movement of supplies from the Port of Balaclava to the camp by laying down five miles of light railway."

Raglan said to an aide in the spring, "I could never return to England now. They would stone me to death."[4] But he proceeded on to the folly of June 18, when he sent thousands of raw recruits to their death against the massive fortress of Sebastopol. A few days after this disaster he died, broken-spirited, in his tent. Burton years later wrote a rather compassionate epitaph: "The unfortunate Lord Raglan, with his *courage antique*, his old-fashioned excess of courtesy, and his nervous dread of not prejudicing the *entente cordiale* (!) . . . was exactly the man *not* wanted. . . . A good ordinary man, placed by the folly of his aristocratic friends in extraordinary circumstances, he was fated, temporarily, to ruin the prestige of England."[5]

General James Simpson, who had served for a time in India, now became commander-in-chief. Burton had worked under him briefly at Sakhar in the Sind, and though he held him in contempt, as had General Napier, and described him as "poor old incapable," he nevertheless saw in the appointment some hope for a decent post for himself, and as soon as his jaw was healed he set off for Balaclava, arriving in July 1855. His brother Edward shortly followed him. John Hanning Speke, whose wounds, in Burton's words, "had closed up like cuts in India rubber,"[6] also volunteered, and was assigned to the Turkish Contingent, where he served till the end of the war, February 1856.

Simpson had nothing for Burton, who then applied to General Beatson. The latter, having won the patronage of the War Minister, had at last been given a separate command and permission to raise a contingent of 4,000 Bashi Bazouks and train them at the Dardanelles. Beatson liked Burton and was impressed by his personal history and his knowledge of Turkish. He made him his chief of staff. It was an important post, and Burton was justifiably angered to be denied a suitable elevation in rank. "Every boy captain may be transferred from the line . . ." he wrote bitterly to Dr Norton Shaw, "thereby becoming Major over the head of a Captain of 15 years standing."[7] Beatson was laughed at by the British in Constantinople for his resplendent uniform, which it was said could stand by itself with the weight of its gold braid, but Burton defended this as a legitimate display to impress a people who were accustomed to judge by a show of splendour. He was soon wearing a similarly gaudy uniform of his own.

Burton was appalled, however, by Beatson's failure to discipline his troops. There were no roll-calls, parading, or drilling; and desertions from boredom were commonplace. The Albanians when drunk took to duelling in their characteristic style; each man held a cocked pistol in his right hand and a glass of *raki* in his left. "The first who drained his draught," Burton wrote, "had the right to fire, and generally blazed away with fatal effect." Every rape and theft in Constantinople was likely to be blamed on "Beatson's Horse," as his Bashi-Bazouks came to be called. Burton insisted on daily drill, established a riding school for the infantry officers, and a school of arms for sabre training, and did his best to stop the duelling and thievery. But he could not control Beatson, who was a great brawler, and who quarrelled intemperately with British Consul Skene and Brigadier-General T. G. Neil, when they were sent to check on the outrages of his men. Though himself tactless and hotheaded, Burton was aghast at the style of Beatson's official dispatches, and deplored his failure to conciliate the Constantinople press. When one Beatson letter to a local British dignitary included a formal challenge to a duel—"pistols for two and coffee for one"—Burton simply eliminated it under the pretence of recopying. "My General did not thank me for it," he wrote.

Meanwhile he watched with increasing fury the tactics of the British command, and the needless waste of brave men in assaulting impregnable defences. "Failure," he wrote acidly, "resulted from the normal appointment of thoroughly incapable Commanders. The private soldier was perfectly right, who volunteered before Lord Raglan that he and his comrades were perfectly ready to take Sebastopol by storm, under the command of their own officers, if not interfered with by the *Generals*."[8] He became wildly impatient to take his own Irregulars into action, and finally in late July went to the powerful British ambassador, Lord Stratford de Redcliffe, with a plan to use them for the relief of Kars, a medieval fortress in Armenia manned by a force of 15,000 Turks and commanded by French and British officers, which had been besieged by the Russians for many months and was now threatened with famine. Burton laid out detailed plans, promising "2,640 sabres in perfect readiness to march" and the necessary accompanying carriage for supplies.

Lord Stratford, generally urbane and genial, could give way to calculated rage and contempt when it suited his purposes. Having been warned in advance by the Foreign Office to oppose the idea, he now applied to Burton the same conduct he employed with his secretaries, to whom he frequently applied the epithets of "ass" and "uncouth cub." "He shouted at me in a rage," Burton wrote, " 'You are the most impudent man in the Bombay Army, Sir!' "

Knowing Stratford's reputation, Burton met the ranting with his own calculated good humour. Lord Stratford, on his side, aware of Burton's reputation as an explorer, finally turned amiable and concluded the interview by saying, "Of course you'll dine with us today?" Nevertheless Burton remembered the episode with distaste, and revenged himself later by describing the ambassador as "a weak, stiff-necked and violent old man. . . . a man who had lived his life in the East without learning a word of Turkish, Persian or Arabic. . . . who gained a prodigious name in Europe, chiefly by living out of it."

Kars was not relieved. By November 1855 the starving troops were digging up the carcasses of buried horses and devouring them, and the stronghold finally surrendered to the Russians on November 23.[9] Meanwhile the Bashi-Bazouks sat inactive in camp. In September, after a massive assault on Sebastopol by French and British troops, the Russians evacuated the fortress, leaving only the dying in the hospital. William Howard Russell visited it on September 12. "Of all the pictures of the horrors of war which have ever been presented to the world," he wrote, "the hospital of Sebastopol presents the most horrible, heart-rending, and revolting."[10]

Burton saw none of this. He had spent only one week at the front shortly after his arrival in the Crimea, and did not get a chance to return. Lord Stratford in Constantinople sent for him late in September 1855 to discuss the possibility of his going on an intelligence mission to make contact with Schamyl, "the Bandit of the Caucasus," leader of the Dagestan tribes, who were fighting for independence from Russia. Burton was at first excited by the prospect, but when told that he was expected to travel alone through Russian territory, carrying no promise of money, arms, or troops, he declined the mission. "Without them," he pointed out, "Schamyl will infallibly set me down for a spy, and my chance of returning to Constantinople will be uncommonly small."[11]

When he returned from this interview to his camp at the Dardanelles, he found trouble. In his absence several Bashi-Bazouks had clashed with some French regulars, and the incident, much exaggerated, had resulted in a virtual state of siege. Turkish regulars had surrounded his camp with artillery; three war steamers in the harbour had their guns pointed directly upon his men; the citizens had closed their shops and fled. Beatson and Burton quieted their men without any shots being fired, and the Turkish Military Pasha finally marched his regulars back to their barracks. But the incident sealed Beatson's fate. In the resulting inquiry all the men with whom he had quarrelled now triumphantly trod upon his reputation, and on September 28 he was replaced by Major-General Richard Smith.

Although W. H. Russell defended the Bashi-Bazouks in a dispatch to the *Times*, Burton frankly acknowledged that "the military world declared us to be a band of banditti, an irreclaimable savagery." Fiercely loyal to his chief, he tried to get written statements from his fellow officers testifying to Beatson's talent and ability, but all it gained him was the accusation that he was fomenting mutiny against General Smith. When Beatson finally resigned and returned ignominiously to England, Burton shortly followed him, sailing for London on October 18, 1855. Later he wrote that he was "reported home as a 'brouillon' and turbulent."[12]

Once in London, Burton wrote a letter to the *Times*, on December 6, 1855, asking for "tardy justice" to "a good soldier smarting under undeserved official censure." And he testified for his commander when Beatson brought a civil suit for libel against the chief of his enemies, British Consul Skene. Here Burton himself came under criticism for having supported Beatson against General Smith. The jury awarded the verdict to Consul Skene on technical grounds, agreeing with Foreign Office lawyers that his libel had been "a privileged communication," but added a rider to the verdict declaring they found Skene's charges without foundation. This vindicated Beatson with the press, and restored his reputation with the people.

It is extraordinary that so prolific a writer as Burton never wrote a book on his Crimean experiences, which though covering only four months were so rich in emotion-laden events. Perhaps his commitment to the Army and later to the Foreign Office kept him stifled. All he left was a 23-page memoir called "With Beatson's Horse," published some thirty years later by Francis Hitchman, and reprinted in Isabel Burton's biography. It was a chatty, gossipy piece, with occasional strictures against the imbecility of the whole war. History would agree with Burton that it settled little. For the first time in his writings we see him nationalistic and anti-French. The memoir was nevertheless irreverent; had he published it upon his return to London he might well have been cashiered.

It was a pity that he did not at the time have the freedom of the journalist. We cannot know the contents of the journals he kept during these months; certainly their destruction after his death deprived history of a salty, first-hand impression of the Crimean War written by a man who was gifted at pinioning the inept. Had he written a book, however, it would have been a catalogue of British failures, including his own, and he could not have been eager to document the latter, nor further to incur the wrath of the Indian Army officials by illuminating the former.

Crimea for Burton was an attempt at expiation, an interlude between searchings. It served chiefly to underline the fact that whatever talent he may have had as a staff officer—and here one suspects he let personal loyalty to a particular commander interfere with professional dispassionateness—it was greatly overshadowed by his talents as explorer and scholar. It seems that he tired quickly of war. And it is clear that this man, who was absorbed by every detail of exotic tribal life, including weapons and warfare, had no interest in publishing the details of mass killing, European style.

The Courtship

To me there are three kinds of marriage: first, worldly ambition; that is, marriage for fortune, title, estates, society; secondly, love; that is, the usual pig and cottage; thirdly, which is my ideal of being a companion and wife, a life of travel, adventure, and danger, seeing and learning, with love to glorify it; that is what I seek. *L'amour n'y manquerait pas!*

Isabel Burton—to her diary[1]

*W*HAT A CURSE is a heart! With all to make me happy I pine and hanker for him, my other half, to fill this void, for I feel as if I were not complete. . . . God created me with a warm heart, a vivid imagination, and strong passions. . . . If I could only be sure of dying at forty, and until then preserve youth, health, spirits, and good looks, I should be more cheerful to remain as I am. I cannot separate myself from all thought of Richard. . . . how worthless should I be to any other man."

So Isabel Arundell poured out her anguish in her diary, when her parents vainly urged her to choose a suitor. The extracts singled out for publication by her sister and biographer after her death, unfortunately undated, are remarkable not only for their romanticism but also for their flashes of self-knowledge. "I could not live like a vegetable in the country," she wrote. "I cannot picture myself in a white apron, with a bunch of keys, scolding my maids, counting eggs and butter, with a good and portly husband (I detest fat men!). . . . A dry crust, privations, pain, danger for him I love would be better. Let me go with the husband of my choice to battle, nurse him in his tent, follow him under the fire of ten thousand muskets. I would be his companion through hardship and trouble, nurse him if wounded, work for him in his tent, prepare his meals when faint, his bed when weary, and be his guardian angel of comfort—a felicity too exquisite for words. . . . Why, with spirits, brains, and energies, are women to exist upon worsted work and household accounts? It makes me sick, and I will not do it."

Still, with all this determination and fervour, she lacked the courage to seek out Richard when he came home wounded from Somaliland, and permitted him to go off to Crimea without having dared to send a note of congratulation for his success either in Mecca or Harar. She was content to cherish him like an idol in a secret closet, unobtainable and therefore unthreatening. "How unblessed are those who have no imagination, unless they obtain their wishes in reality!" she wrote, and then added frankly, "I do not obtain, so I seek them in illusion."

There was nevertheless practicality in Isabel. By no means resigned to solitude and lament, she sought vainly to go to Crimea as a nurse, and this was months before Burton volunteered. "I have written again and again to Florence Nightingale," she confided in her diary, "but the superintendent has answered me that I am too young and inexperienced, and will not do." So she enlisted 150 girls in an amateur social welfare club to aid destitute families of the soldiers fighting in Crimea. They collected money—Isabel herself raised a hundred guineas in ten days—doled out food, clothing, and money for lodging, and found employment for the women and schools for the children. "I know the misery of London," she wrote, "and in making my rounds I could give details that would come up to some of the descriptions in *The Mysteries of Paris* or a shilling shocker."

Burton returned from Constantinople in December 1855 shortly before the war ended. Both were in London through the winter. "A gay season that year," Isabel wrote, "everyone being glad that the war was over." Still their paths did not cross. In June 1856 Isabel went to the races at Ascot. She was riding alone slowly in her carriage through a dense crowd when a gypsy woman thrust her way forward and opened the door. It was Hagar Burton, the gypsy who had written her horoscope. "Are you Daisy Burton yet?" the fortune teller asked.

"Would to God I were," she answered fervently.

"Patience," the gypsy answered, her grave eyes alight, "it is just coming."

"I never saw her again," Isabel wrote, "but I was engaged to Richard two months later."

The meeting was appropriately accidental, as the first one had been in Boulogne, and served to heighten for both of them a sense of the intervention of fate. Isabel was walking in the Botanical Gardens with her sister. It was a hot August afternoon. Rounding a clump of shrubbery she found herself looking up at the now deeply scarred face of the man she had danced with four years before. He was walking with her cousin, his old love Louisa, who was now married.

"We immediately stopped and shook hands and asked each other a thousand questions of the four intervening years, and all the old Boulogne memories and feelings which had lain dormant, but not extinct, returned to me."

Isabel was carrying a copy of Disraeli's *Tancred*. When he asked her about it, she replied passionately, "It is the book of my heart." There could have been no more certain way to Burton's own. *Tancred* was the currently fashionable novel of Benjamin Disraeli, at this time an influential member of Parliament—the story of a young Englishman disillusioned with his own nation who went to the Near East searching for a solution to philosophical mysteries in the Semitic world. It had been fashioned in part from Disraeli's own trip to Syria and Palestine, during which, like Burton, he had shared the Arab tents and become enchanted with the nomadic Bedouin life. Burton was already interested in and envious of Disraeli's career. Eventually he wrote a half-admiring, half-hostile pamphlet that revealed a sense of kinship. Both men appeared half alien to other Englishmen, Burton because he had been reared in France, Disraeli for being a Jew, a handicap his baptism into the Church of England as a boy only moderated. Both were able writers, witty, arrogant, and intellectual, and both paid penalties for their superiority.

Isabel tells us that Richard "explained" *Tancred* to her. He could hardly have missed her fascination with the exotic, and her breathless enthusiasm; he must also have seen a new maturity. He asked her pointedly if she came to the Gardens often, and she replied, with an explicitness that was assuredly an invitation, that she came every day from eleven to one. They talked for an hour.

"When I got home," she wrote in her diary, "my mind was full of wonder and presentiment; I felt frightened and agitated."

It was frightening. The illusion had suddenly become reality, the daydream a vital, dangerous presence. This time, however, she did not hide around corners like a peeping child but returned promptly to the Botanical Gardens the following day. Burton was alone waiting for her, writing poetry. Every day for a fortnight thereafter they met at the same spot. Almost at once he outlined his plans for a great new adventure. In October, he said, he was off to Africa with John Hanning Speke and Dr John Steinhaeuser in a daring search for the true source of the great Nile. He had won the support of the Royal Geographical Society and the Foreign Office, with a grant from the latter of £1,000; and the East India Company had given him a two-year leave with pay. He would strike first for the great Sea of Ujiji, painted on the map of the Royal Geographical Society as a great blue slug, a lake of unknown origin, size, and dimension.

Watching her face, radiating adoration, affection and wonder, Burton found a new courage and an old emotion. Perhaps the imminence of his departure hastened the quickening in his blood and made possible an unexpected boldness in both of them. "At the end of a fortnight," Isabel wrote, "he stole his arm round my waist, and laid his cheek against mine and asked me, 'Could you do anything so sickly as to give up civilization? And if I can get the Consulate of Damascus, will you marry me and go and live there? Do not give me an answer now, because it will mean a very serious step for you—no less than giving up your people and all that you are used to, and living the sort of life that Lady Hester Stanhope led. I see the capabilities in you, but you must think it over.'"

Isabel was speechless with elation. "It was just as if the moon had tumbled down and said, 'You have cried for me so long that I have come.'"

Troubled by her silence, he said, "Forgive me, I ought not to have asked so much."

"At last I found voice," she wrote, "and said, 'I do not want to think it over—I have been thinking it over for six years, ever since I first saw you at Boulogne. I have prayed for you every morning and night, I have followed your career minutely, I have read every word you ever wrote, and I would rather have a crust and a tent with *you* than be queen of all the world; and so I say, now, Yes! yes! YES!'"

"I would have suffered six years more for such a day," she continued, "such a moment as this. All past sorrow was forgotten in it. All that has been written or said on the subject of the first kiss is trash compared to the reality. Men might as well undertake to describe Eternity. I then told him all about my six years since I first met him, and all that I suffered. When I got home, I knelt down and prayed, and my whole soul flooded with joy and thanksgiving. . . . I feel that I have at last met the master who can subdue me."[2]

Later she showed him the horoscope given to her by Hagar Burton years before. For all his scientific sophistication Richard Burton was frankly superstitious about occult phenomena. The gypsy prediction that Isabel would marry a Burton deeply impressed him. Years later he wrote to J. Pincherle, who had dedicated to him a Romany version of the *Song of Songs*, "There is an important family of Gypsies in foggy England, who in very remote times adopted our family name. I am yet on very friendly terms with several of these strange people; nay, a certain Hagar Burton, an old fortune-teller (*divinatrice*) took part in a period of my life which in no small degree contributed to determine its course."[3] The horoscope story was only the first in a long series of minor personal miracles, including telepathic communication and hypnotism over long distances, which Isabel was to chronicle in her biography with delectation and faith.

There were those in Burton's own family who held that he was pursued and trapped into a marriage for which he had no enthusiasm. And it is true that he no sooner became engaged than he rushed off on his three-year Nile pursuit. But those plans were well matured months before he met Isabel in the Botanical Gardens, and the choice was between fulfilling what he believed to be his destiny in Africa, or abandoning the Nile search and taking Isabel as his wife to India, where he would have an annual salary of only £350 plus the income from a modest inheritance. If he returned from Africa with the Nile prize, he had every reason to expect a reward from a generous government. Isabel was an aristocrat with no dowry. The post of consul at Damascus would be suitable for one of her rank, even at only £600 annually. Burton was lonely. His mother was dead; his brother had returned to Ceylon, and his sister was occupied with her husband and daughters. He must have found the story of Isabel's six-year adoration captivating and even humbling. He had not been so loved in all his life.

Before he left, Isabel gave him a medal with the Virgin engraved upon it, hanging from a gold chain, to wear upon his journey. "Take the gold chain away," he said, "they will cut my throat for it out there." She replaced it with one of steel; he would wear the medal all his life.

Still his deepest loyalty was chained to a special goddess. He wrote a poem to Fame before he left, weighted with the imagery of the consoling mother, now shadowed in death. He gave a copy to Isabel, and—unknown to her—another copy to her old rival Louisa.[4] It read as follows:

> I wore thine image, Fame,
> Within a heart well fit to be thy shrine;
> Others a thousand boons may gain—
> One wish was mine:
>
> The hope to gain one smile,
> To dwell one moment cradled on thy breast,
> Then close my eyes, bid life farewell,
> And take my rest!
>
> And now I see a glorious hand
> Beckon me out of dark despair,
> Hear a glorious voice command,
> "Up, bravely dare!
>
> "And if to leave a deeper trace
> On earth to thee Time, Fate, deny,
> Drown vain regrets, and have the grace
> Silent to die."
>
> She pointed to a grisly land,
> Where all breathes death—earth, sea, and air;
> Her glorious accents sound once more,
> "Go meet me there."
>
> Mine ear will hear no other sound,
> No other thought my heart will know.
> Is this a sin? "O, pardon, Lord!
> Thou mad'st me so!"[5]

Isabel, in describing the courtship, paints a picture of overwhelming eagerness on her part. Actually there were still as many evidences of hesitation and indecision as of idolatry. She reported that she took Richard home, and that "he fascinated, amused, and pleasantly shocked my mother, but completely magnetized my father and all my brothers and sisters. My father used to say, 'I do not know what it is about that man, but I cannot get him out of my head; I dream about him every night.'" Nevertheless, when she told her mother "in an ecstasy" that she had "found the Man and the Life" she longed for, and that she would never be content with an inferior man, Mrs Arundell made the classic Victorian reply, "He is the *only* man I will never consent to your marrying; I would rather see you in your coffin." And though Isabel was now twenty-five, capable and courageous beyond most of her friends, this was enough to frighten her into secrecy. Fearful about being "sent away," and certain in advance that all of Richard's letters to her would be opened or withheld altogether, she told no one she was actually engaged. Meanwhile she endured silently her mother's snobbish complaints that she never "met" Burton at fashionable parties, and her continuing contempt. "If you marry that man," Mrs Arundell said on one occasion, "you will have sold your birthright not for a mess of pottage, but for Burton ale."[6]

Actually Burton was no longer a mere British East India soldier on half pay with a cloud on his reputation, as in Boulogne days. He was now renowned in scientific circles, a favourite among the best British journalists, and welcome among the great families of England. Monckton Milnes—Lord Houghton—who took pleasure in entertaining men of scholarship, wit, and eccentricity, had become a kind of patron to Burton, helping to win him Foreign Office support for his expedition, and welcoming him often to his famous breakfasts. Isabel did not dare point out now to her mother, as she finally did three years later, that her parents would never meet Richard in society because he found their particular circles fatuous and boring beyond endurance. She had no need to be apologetic to her parents about Richard for any reason save the fact that he was not a Catholic. Here she consoled herself with fantasies of converting him; this presented no obstacle but only a personal challenge. But it was also an excuse for delay. And it is clear that she wanted delay as much as Burton did.

A deep suspicion of marriage crops up more than once in her diary. "I have seen so much of married life," she wrote at the time, "have seen men so unjust, selfish, and provoking; and have always felt I never could receive an injury from any man but him without everlasting resentment." Coupled with this suspicion was a pervasive contempt for the young men she knew, most of whom seemed to her effeminate—

"I always look upon them as members of my own sex," she said. Richard to her seemed worlds apart. "He unites the wild lawless creature and the gentleman," she wrote in her journal. Then she went on, with an ingenuousness now out of fashion, to make a frank and disarming confession:

> I worship ambition. . . . By ambition I mean men who have the will and power to change the face of things. I wish I were a man: if I were, I would be Richard Burton. But as I am a woman, I would be Richard Burton's wife. I love him purely, passionately, and devotedly: there is no void in my heart: it is at rest for ever with him.[7]

Richard had warned Isabel that he might leave precipitately; she did not yet know of his habit of avoiding saying goodbye. One afternoon late in October she told him she was going to the theatre with her family. He seemed agitated, and promised to meet her there if he could, but in any case to return to her home the following day. Watching for him that night, she was certain she saw him across the theatre, and beckoned to him gladly. But he disappeared. She checked her watch and noted that it was 10.30 pm. Now it was her turn to be agitated. During the night she dreamed that he embraced her and said goodbye, "I am going now, my poor girl. My time is up, and I have gone; but I will come again—I shall be back in less than three years. I am your destiny. He put a letter on the table saying, 'That is for your sister—not for you.'"

Wakening, she went into the bedroom of the one brother in whom she had confided, and wept bitterly, saying, "Richard is gone to Africa and I shall not see him for three years."

"Nonsense," the youth replied. "You have only got a nightmare; it was that lobster you had for supper; you told me yourself he was coming tomorrow."

The next day a letter arrived for her sister Blanche, begging her to break the news gently that he had in truth gone to Africa. Isabel figured the time swiftly. "He had left his lodgings in London at 10.30 the previous evening (when I saw him in the theatre), and sailed at two o'clock from Southampton (when I saw him in my room)," she wrote. Certain now of a special magic in this man, she sat down at once and wrote the whole story to him in her first letter.

In his letter to Blanche, Richard had enclosed a letter for Isabel. She put it in a locket on a chain and wore it about her neck. For months afterwards she was troubled with dreams that he had come back from Africa but would not speak to her. Again and again this dream returned, and she often wakened to find the pillow wet with tears. So much anxiety must surely have masked a dread of what he *would* do upon returning, a dread that he would speak to her as only a man can in marriage—and the prospect of the physical confrontation terrified her.

So she lived on, almost content, with the now gloriously heightened fantasy. And when she received only two letters in the first three months of his absence (though she had written him a score), she steeled herself for future disappointments and wrote in her journal a statement showing foresight about what was to be their life-long relationship:

"I must meet this uncertainty with confidence, and not let my love be dependent on any action of his, because he is a strange man and not as other men."

The Impact of Africa

Of the gladdest moments in human life, methinks, is the departure upon a distant journey into unknown lands. Shaking off with one mighty effort the fetters of Habit, the leaden weight of Routine, the cloak of many Cares and the slavery of Home, man feels once more happy. The blood flows with the fast circulation of childhood. . . . Afresh dawns the morn of life. . . .

Richard Burton, Journal entry, December 2, 1856[1]

*M*OST OF THE great Nile adventurers seemed impelled sooner or later to explain the magic lure of African exploration. Departing from Bombay for the African coast, Burton described his feelings in his diary in somewhat contradictory terms as an escape from "Home," but also a return to the excitement of childhood. Only years later would he suggest that the ceaseless searching for the Coy Fountains was kin to madness. Henry Morton Stanley, who solved many African mysteries a generation after Burton, wrote of his "perfect independence" of mind in Africa. "It is not repressed by fear, nor depressed by ridicule and insults . . . but now preens itself, and soars free and unrestrained; which liberty, to a vivid mind, imperceptibly changes the whole man."[2]

David Livingstone, who after the death of his stout little wife in central Africa travelled mostly, and most successfully, alone, living with the simplicity of Robinson Crusoe, tried to explain his lifelong wanderings to Stanley after the celebrated rescue in 1871. "I have lost a great deal of happiness, I know, by these wanderings. It is as if I had been born to exile; but it is God's doing. . . . I am away from the perpetual hurry of civilization, and I think I see far and clear into what is to come; and then I seem to understand why I was led away, here and there, and crossed and baffled over and over again, to wear out my years and strength."[3]

Sir Samuel Baker, who discovered Lake Albert, and for a time believed it to be the "cradle" and only true source of the "entire" Nile, described his feelings the night before reaching the lake as follows: "I hardly slept. For years I had striven to reach the 'sources of the Nile.' In my nightly dreams during that arduous voyage I had always failed, but after so much hard work and perseverance the cup was at my very lips, and I was to *drink* at the mysterious fountain before another sun should set."[4] For all these men the escape into Africa seems to have been a return, if not all the way back to the cradle, at least to childhood. The childish nightmares too were real, for no voyager travelled without the constant possibility of treachery and massacre.

Of all the great explorers, none was more enigmatic and less given to self-revelation than John Hanning Speke. Before his first disastrous venture into Somaliland, he had startled Burton by declaring that "being tired of life he had come to be killed in Africa."[5] Burton dismissed the confession at the time as "a kind of whimsical affectation," but never forgot it. Unlike the other explorers, who always used maternal imagery, Speke referred to the great river as "Father Nile," and on the rare occasions when he used symbolic language concerning his explorations he became curiously violent, with imagery of killing and dissection. Before his second and greatest Nile expedition, he wrote to Dr Norton Shaw, "I have asked Petherick to come here for a few days . . . that we may make arrangements for *ripping* open Africa together, he from the North and I from the South."* Later, in a speech at Taunton in Somerset, he said that he had "hit the Nile on the head in 1857 and in 1863 drove it down to the Mediterranean."[6]

When Burton and Speke came to write about each other in their books, they were so consumed with mutual hatred it is difficult to recapture the climate of their friendship at the beginning of the trip to Lake Tanganyika. Burton described Speke as quiet, gentle and tactful, but added that he had "an immense and abnormal fund of self-esteem, so carefully concealed, however, that none but his intimates suspected its existence. He ever held, not only that he had done his best on all occasions, but also that no living man could do better." Worst of all, said Burton, was his "habit of secreting thoughts and reminiscences till brought to light by a sudden impulse. He would brood, perhaps for years, over a chance word, which a single outspoken sentence of explanation could have satisfactorily settled. The inevitable result was exaggeration of fact into fiction. . . . I had thus with me a companion and not a friend, with whom I was 'strangers yet.' "[7] Privately he confided in his journal that Speke, though "energetic, courageous, and persevering," was nevertheless "crooked-minded and cantankerous," and that he would have done himself a service to have travelled alone.[8]

Speke, on the other hand, complained to Dr Norton Shaw that Bur-

---

* The italics are Speke's.

ton "is one of those who never *can* be wrong, and will not acknowledge
an error, so that when only two were together talking becomes more
of a bore than a pleasure. . . . he used to snub me so unpleasantly when
talking about anything that I often kept my own council." He implied
that Burton had "gone to the devil" in Africa, and later wrote even
more violently of his "blackguard conduct."[9]

Byron Farwell has written that relations between the two men were
bad before they started. "Speke appears to have already hated Burton
but he concealed his feelings and pretended to be Burton's friend
in order to go on the expedition." Actually there is good evidence of
comradeship and mutual affection throughout the first long year in
Africa. They nursed each other through terrible bouts of fever, infection, and blindness. They read Shakespeare together to while away the
tedious night hours. In the beginning Speke brought his journals to
Burton for correction, humbly like a schoolboy. Burton wrote that
he travelled with Speke "as a brother," but as an elder brother one can
be certain.[10]

Speke wrote to Dr Norton Shaw on May 20, 1857, after being with
Burton six months, "Led on from shooting, collecting, mapping, and
ranging the world generally, I feel myself practically wedded with,
and instinctively impelled on to the prosecution of geographical research, the same way as formerly the attainment of sport was the culminating point of my ambition." The word "wedded" is strong and
affirmative, suggesting fascination and captivation. Fourteen months
later he would write to Shaw with great bitterness about Burton's lack
of cooperation, protesting also that there was nothing to shoot in the
African interior except elephants, and complaining of Africa as "one
vast senseless map of sameness."[11] No other fourteen months were so
decisive in the lives of either man. From May 20, 1857 to July 2, 1858
they saw a swing from affection and understanding to a hatred that
had portentous consequences.

The expedition officially started from Bombay, where Burton and
Speke had had to make a special trip to win permission for Speke's
leave from the army. They sailed from there to Zanzibar, arriving
December 20, 1856, and called at once upon the British Resident,
Lieutenant-Colonel Atkins Hamerton, a warm-hearted Irishman, a fine
linguist and Oriental scholar, who for fifteen years had made life tolerable for Europeans on the island with his genial hospitality. He was
now dying and knew it, but refused to go to England. Hamerton
warned them that a drought had brought famine to East Africa and
that exploration was hazardous. By way of accenting his warning he
took them to the local prison and pointed out a captive, heavily ironed

and chained to a gun in such a position that he could neither stand nor lie down. He had been chained in this fashion for ten years. His crime, said Hamerton, was that he had been a drum-beater at the ceremonial murder of a young French explorer, M. Maizan, who had been taken prisoner by the Mazungera. The natives had tied Maizan to a calabash tree, tortured, mutilated, and then beheaded him. Since the executioner had never been caught, the drum-beater was serving his sentence.

The point of the story was not lost on Burton. "Briefly, the gist of the whole was that I had better return to Bombay," he wrote. "But rather than return to Bombay I would have gone to Hades."[12]

With Hamerton's aid Burton and Speke set about preparing for an elaborate two-year expedition. They made tentative explorations along the coast, probing for the best route to the interior. Speke fulfilled an old dream when they hunted hippopotami in the mouth of the Pangani River, but they very nearly met disaster when one bull put two holes in the bottom of their boat with his tusks. At Mombasa they interviewed the only white man in the coastal area, the Christian missionary Johann Rebmann, who together with Johann Krapf in 1848 had been the first Europeans to see the great Mt Kilimanjaro and report snow at its summit. Many English geographers had ridiculed the idea of snow at the equator, but Burton respected Rebmann and learned much from him. Had Burton and Speke gone inland directly from Mombasa, they might well have jointly discovered Lake Victoria, and both lives would have been vastly altered. As it was, Rebmann warned them that the route was impassible because the Masai were plundering the area, so they moved southwards to the mouth of the Pangani. Here both contracted fever. Yellow-skinned, debilitated, and intermittently delirious, they were forced to return to Zanzibar.

Delay followed delay, and it was six months before the expedition started. Burton when in passable health was busy mastering the Kiswahili tongue, and happily taking notes on everything. He was also waiting for his old friend, Dr John Steinhaeuser, who had been granted leave from India to join them. But Steinhaeuser's orders were delayed, and then he became ill and had to abandon the expedition altogether. Had he accompanied them, the breakdown in personal relations that followed might well have been avoided.

Burton took enough notes to fill two volumes totalling a thousand pages. The picture of Zanzibar and the coastal area that eventually emerged was memorable. He described not only the geography, climate, flora and fauna, politics and government, and tribal ethnology, but also the degradation and brutality, callous violence, squalor, and disease. Though the Sultan of Zanzibar in 1845 had declared slave export to be strictly forbidden, the slave trade within his dominions was permitted, and the traffic continued to dominate the island economy as it had for centuries. Twenty to forty thousand slaves were crammed into dhows bound for Zanzibar every year, many of them, as Burton noted, "with 18 inches between the decks," where "one pint of water a head was served out per diem and five wretches were stowed away instead of two." A third of them were kept on the island to replace the number who died annually of disease and malnutrition; the remainder were exported illegally to Arabia, Egypt, Turkey and Persia, where a slave purchased originally at £2 would sell for £20. The British navy was notoriously less efficient here than in the Atlantic in catching smugglers; Burton stated that between 1867 and 1869 the navy intercepted and freed 2,645 slaves, but an estimated 37,000 were carried on to the slave marts of the Near East.

He was inclined to be critical of what he believed to be the excessive sentimentality of the "earnest but also deluded" anti-slavery agitators in England, holding that many slaves were decently treated. He noted that unlike the practice in the New World, if a slaveowner fathered a child he freed it and accepted it as his own, and was forbidden by law to sell the mother. But he did not gloss over the horrors of the Zanzibar slave market, and added a few atrocities of his own, including the story of the Spaniard who "finding his ventures likely to die of dysentery, sewed them up before he sent them to the bazaar." It was a rare slave girl, he noted, who bore children. "Her progeny by another slave may be sold away from her at any moment, and she obviates the pains and penalties of maternity by the easy process of procuring abortion."

Burton had seen nothing in India to match the want of sanitation in Zanzibar. The port stank; the shore was a cesspool; and corpses floated at times upon the water. Tons of cowries were heaped upon the shore waiting for the mollusks to decay away, and piles of copra—coconut meat split to dry in the sun—spread a "nausea-breeding odour." With part of the port sinking gradually into the sea, the tides made periodic inroads into the poorer areas—"a filthy labyrinth, a capricious arabesque of disorderly lanes, and alleys, and impasses, here broad, there narrow; now heaped with offal, then choked with ruins."[13] A rainfall ranging from 85 to 120 inches each year contributed to the general decay and rot. Public wells were as thick with slime as in any English horse trough.

Always the amateur physician, Burton explicitly recorded his impressions of the local diseases. Dysentery, malaria, yellow fever, and hepatitis took a terrible annual toll. He estimated that urinary and genital disease afflicted 75 per cent of the population. Syphilis, he said, was widespread among the slaves, and gonorrhea was "so common it is hardly considered a disease." One detects in his medical notes a growing preoccupation with diseases resulting in sexual impotence.

"Sarcocele and hydrocele, especially of the left testes," he wrote, "according to the Arabs attack all classes, and are attributed to the relaxing climate, to unrestrained sexual indulgence, and sometimes to external injury. These diseases do not always induce impotence or impede procreation. The tunica vaginalis is believed to fill three times. . . . The deposition of serum is enormous; I have heard of six quarts being drawn off. . . . Elephantiasis of the legs and arms, and especially of the scrotum, afflicts, it is calculated, 20 per cent of the inhabitants. . . . The scrotum will often reach the knees."[14]

Burton had no remedies of any value in his medicine chest save morphine and quinine. The value of the latter in warding off malaria was just beginning to be appreciated, but he never took it in large enough quantities to be helpful. He rejoiced that therapeutic bleeding —"that scientific form of sudden death"—was currently out of fashion, and insisted not unsensibly that brandy and beef-tea were better than castor oil, mustard plasters, and diluted prussic acid. Though never easily shocked, Burton found himself looking at many of the Zanzibar Arabs with the indignation of an Old Testament prophet. Contrasting them with the desert Arabs, he denounced them as "weak, effeminate and degenerate," enslaved by "excessive polygamy and unbridled licentiousness." On the Negroes, whether Moslem or heathen, he was even more rancorous.

Burton and Speke sailed from Zanzibar to Kaole, or Wale Point, south of Bagamoyo on June 16, 1857. Here they set forth on a twenty-one month expedition that subjected them to every species of hardship Africa could inflict. Neither was accustomed to travelling with more than a servant or two, except in the ordered discipline of the Indian Army, and here they had to organize a caravan of what became finally 132 men and 30 asses, loaded with cotton cloth, brass wire and beads, food, instruments, and a two-year supply of ammunition. Burton had brought to Africa a 40-foot iron boat that could be dismantled into sections, which he hoped to use exploring the great inland lake. He had christened it *Louisa*—not Isabel, it will be noted—and had sailed in it for a distance up the Pangani River, but now abandoned it, reluctantly, because of its weight. As it was, each man carried a 70-pound load. Many in addition carried weapons, a matchlock musket, a Cutch sabre, a dagger and shield, as well as a private travel kit. Although all were given a sum in advance of the journey and promised wages and a reward for good behaviour upon return, desertions came almost from the beginning. Not surprisingly, desertions were highest among the slaves, even though Burton paid them wages and treated them like free men. Before the two years were over, every man on the expedition had tried to desert save Burton's two Goanese Catholic servants.

Neither leader was prepared for the fears and incomprehension they met with daily among their own bearers. The motivation for their journey seemed mysterious not only to the men they hired, but also to the succession of local chiefs, who, suspecting either sorcery or conquest, exacted exhorbitant fees for passage through their territories. Burton was furious at the blackmail, and regretted that he had not chosen to travel as a simple ivory trader. As the asses died one by one from exhaustion or the tsetse fly—the last one fell to a skulking hyena—Burton learned that in Africa "there is no vehicle but man, and he is so impatient and headstrong, so suspicious and timorous, that he must be humoured in every whim."[15]

At first Burton entrusted his men to the direction of Said bin Salim, a half-caste Arab whom he greatly admired till he discovered that he was stealing from the expedition at every opportunity. He replaced Said with Seedy Mubarak Bombay, an African native, an ex-slave from Uhiao. Bombay was a powerful, ugly man, with incisor teeth sharpened to points, vain, surly and often violent. But he was an intelligent man who, as Burton wrote, "worked on principle and worked like a horse . . . an active servant and an honest man." Bombay, who knew some Hindustani, was the only man on the expedition besides Burton with whom Speke could converse. He was destined in the end—as he aided first Burton and Speke, then Speke and Grant, and finally Stanley—to become the most famous native bearer in all African exploration.

The equipment included a Rowtie tent, beds, chairs, portable table, mosquito netting, and cooking pots, but only a single outfit of clothes for the two leaders, which were soon so worn and torn by thorns they were forced to sew crude substitutes from blankets. They carried scientific books, carpenter's tools, fishing equipment, tea, coffee, sugar and "one dozen brandy (to be followed by 4 dozen more)." They started with a chest of instruments—two chronometers, a lever watch, two prismatic compasses, a bath thermometer, sundial, rain gauge, two sextants, barometer, pedometer, and two boiling thermometers, but by the time they reached Lake Tanganyika all had been lost or destroyed in the frequent fording accidents save the bath thermometer, and Speke and Burton had to calculate altitude as best they could with this, by measuring the boiling point of water. Botanical and zoological collections, and even some of their journals, went downstream along with the tea, coffee, sugar, tools, a prized elephant gun and bullet moulds. Some material was replaced by new porters coming from the coast, and they improvised with great ingenuity, but the instruments could not be replaced, and as a result none of their topographical measurements was quite correct, and some were dismayingly inaccurate.

Burton began the overland journey with deep misgivings. The village where they assembled supplies and bearers was decorated with the skulls of enemies on high poles, and the natives were suspicion itself. When word came that the son of a chief had been drowned when a hippopotamus upset the boat, one half-caste warned Burton darkly, "This is the first calamity which you have brought upon the country by your presence."

"In the solitude and silence of the dark Gurayza," Burton wrote, "I felt myself the plaything of misfortune."[16]

The trail to Kazeh—now Tabora in central Tanzania—paced out by slave caravans since its opening in 1825, went through a dry, red cliff area near the coast, with scrub brush and gnomish baobab trees. It wound in and out of steaming jungle areas, crossing bogs of waist-deep mire interlaced with tree roots, which extended as much as a mile. Leaving what Burton called these "miasmatic putridities," they came upon fine park country where the air was fresh, and the mimosa, gum trees, and thorn bushes shaded herds of antelope and zebra. They saw game of every variety—lions, elephants, gnus, and hyenas—and Speke became increasingly sullen because Burton curtly refused to stop for hunting except to supply the bearers with food. One after another they crossed the three ranges of the Usagara Mountains, which rose in places to 5,700 feet.

Illness paralysed first one leader and then the other. "The new life, the alternations of damp heat and wet cold, the useless fatigue of walking and the sorry labour of waiting and reloading the asses . . . the wear and tear of mind at the prospect of imminent failure, all were beginning to tell heavily upon me," Burton wrote. As his fever worsened, his mouth became full of ulcers. His feet swelled so that he could no longer walk; he was racked with insomnia and depression. Finally came delirium—"a queer conviction of divided identity, never ceasing to be two persons that generally thwarted and opposed each other; the sleepless nights brought with them horrid visions, animals of grisliest form, hag-like women and men with heads protruding from their breasts."

Desertions increased, and the theft of cloth, wire and beads reduced the supplies at an alarming rate. A fire destroyed a prized botanical collection, and mildew threatened to ruin their precious diaries. Both men finally were too ill to police their bearers, as Burton put it, "physically and morally incapacitated for any exertion beyond balancing ourselves upon the donkeys." Next to fever they came to dread the insects most. Pismire ants an inch long, with mandibles powerful enough to destroy lizards and rats, bit the men like red-hot needles and turned the asses mad with torture. The tsetse fly, death to the animals, was capable of drawing blood from a man through a canvas hammock. Marching white ants destroyed their umbrellas and bedding, honeycombing even their crude temporary clay benches. Earwigs, beetles, scorpions, and flies infested the native huts. Mosquitos were everywhere. Burton suspected the latter to be somehow related to fever, insisted on fires at night to keep them away, and religiously used the netting. But he and Speke fell victims to malaria no less easily than their men.

After 134 days and 600 miles, the expedition arrived at Kazeh on November 7, 1857, and Burton saw to his joy a genuine Arab settlement, with clean mud buildings, spacious courtyards and pleasant vegetable gardens. The tall, gaunt, sunken-eyed chief, Snay bin Amir, was one of the wealthiest slave and ivory dealers in Africa. He was also educated and sensitive, with a "wonderful memory, fine perceptions, and passing power of language," as well as brave, honourable and honest. He greeted Burton warmly, and in the best tradition of Arab hospitality ordered two goats and two bullocks to be slaughtered for his use. "Striking indeed," Burton wrote, "was the contrast between the open-handed hospitality and hearty goodwill of this truly noble race and the niggardness of the savage and selfish African—it was heart of flesh after heart of stone."[17]

Alan Moorehead has written of this meeting, "He was back with his own kind again, grave, courteous, bearded men in turbans and long white robes, cultivated men with graceful manners, and never for a moment does it disturb him that the principal preoccupation of their lives was the herding of men, women and children down to the coast, and the sale of such as survived in the slave markets of Mombasa and Zanzibar." Here Moorehead, in one of the rare lapses in his remarkably accurate twin books on the Nile, is somewhat inexact. Burton deplored the slave traffic as calamitous for Africa, and called the Arab traders generally "a flight of locusts over the land." He was perfectly aware that a generation of intensive slave trading in East Africa had decimated the population, destroyed whole villages, and corrupted the Africans themselves into selling and kidnapping each other. The traffic, he wrote, "practically annihilates every better feeling of human nature," and together with the blood feud had made "a howling desert of the land," and "brutalized the souls" of the inhabitants.[18] But in Snay bin Amir he had found a temporary saviour who made the remainder of the harrowing journey possible, who gave generously of his fifteen years of accumulated knowledge of the geography and ethnology of the whole area, and who even helped him compile vocabularies of the three main African dialects in the region he knew best. Burton found it possible, how easily we cannot know, to separate the man from his trade, a trade that Arabs everywhere had condoned for 2,000 years.

There is no doubt, however, that Burton felt a kinship for the Arabs, whereas the Africans fascinated but mostly repelled him. The coastal tribes he called "supersubtle and systematic liars," who "deceive when duller men would tell the truth." The Wanyika he called "a futile race of barbarians, drunken and immoral; cowardly and destructive; boisterous and loquacious; indolent, greedy and thriftless." The Wagago men he described as "idle and debauched, spending their days in unbroken crapulence and drunkenness," "celebrated as thieves," who would "rather die under the stick than level themselves with women by using a hoe."

This sounds like rabid racial hatred, but Burton was first of all an exact observer. There *was* filth, mutilation, ignorance, indolence, drunkenness and violence. The natives did live in huts populated with "a menagerie of hens, pigeons, and rats of peculiar impudence," just like the poor in Ireland, as he was careful to point out. Certain tribes did burn their witches, again, as he noted, like Europeans of a not-too-distant date. Among the Wanyamwezi, he wrote, if a chief fell ill, the head magician tortured members of the chief's family till he either died or recovered. The women were mutilated with impalement, and many preceded their chief to the grave. In several tribes, if an infant cut his upper incisor teeth before the lower, he was killed or sold into slavery. If twins were born, they were often both killed. Among the Wanyamwezi only one was killed; the mother then wrapped a gourd in skins, placed it to sleep beside the survivor, and poured food into it as often as she fed the living child. Burton saw the disregard for life among his own bearers. One bought a slave child, who, it was discovered shortly, could not keep up with the caravan because of sore feet. The owner decided to abandon her, but cut off her head lest she benefit someone else.

Burton recognized that he was seeing the Africans "at their worst," and did his best to record the good along with the bad. He was as quick to denounce lying, treachery, and drunkenness among the Arabs as among the Africans. Where there was beauty he noted it gratefully. The young half-caste girls along the coast, he wrote, "have a pretty piquancy, a little *minois chiffoné*, a coquettishness, a natural grace, and a caressing look, which might become by habit exceedingly prepossessing," and he described the Wasagara women as "remarkable for a splendid development of limb." "Many negro and negroid races," he wrote, possess "an unstudied eloquence which the civilized speaker might envy, and which, like poetry, seems to flourish most in the dawn of civilization."[19]

It is true, as Moorehead says, that Burton in regard to the African was never "kind." But Burton was never kind about any people. He was instead uncompassionate, curious, and clinical. Like almost everyone else in his time he believed the Negro to be inferior to the white, but unlike most he sought for a scientific explanation. Speke believed the Negro to be inferior—"condemned to be the slave of both Shem and Japeth," he wrote—because of the Biblical curse on the sons of Ham, and insofar as he learned to communicate with the natives by interpreters told them so. This explanation Burton dismissed as "beastly humbug."[20] From his own experience of mental torpor in Africa Burton believed that the climate and debilitating tropical diseases explained much of the Negro's lassitude. He wrote, too, that "much of the moral degradation must be attributed to the working, through centuries, of the slave trade." The slave, he said, "must deceive, for fraud and foxship are his force." Like many observers, he was struck by the quickness and intelligence of the African children, which seemed to be replaced, after puberty, by "an apparent incapacity for improvement." Why, he wondered openly, has Africa "few traditions, no annuals, and no ruins."[21] And in answering the question he blamed not only the climate, disease, and the slave trade, but also the sexual freedom—or licence—he saw among the African peoples.

In the beginning Burton described the African not as biologically inferior, but simply a man living in a more primitive society, not unlike that of a European in earlier centuries. He found his fetichism—largely demonology and witchcraft—fascinating, and documented it in several chapters which form a remarkable piece of pioneering ethnology. Fetichism, he said, was the original religion of all peoples, "the infant mind of humanity," and he described it as "the vain terror of our childhood rudely systematized, the earliest dawn of faith, a creation of fear which ignores love."[22]

Despite his perspicacity and detachment, there is, one must admit, a vindictiveness in Burton's accounts of African peoples that does not appear in his description of other races. And here one suspects, as with some kinds of hatred, an element of envy. First there was envy —hardly surprising is so compulsive a worker as Burton—of their capacity to enjoy idleness. "Man in these lands," he wrote almost wistfully, "wanting little, works less. Two great classes, indeed, seem everywhere to make of life one long holiday—the civilized rich, who have all things, and the savage, who possesses almost nothing."[23] Second, Burton's sporadic venom may well have sprung from envy of the African's sexual reputation. The tradition that black men and women are superior in sexual vitality is very ancient—Burton would translate stories in the *Arabian Nights* dating back to the eighth century that underline it—and he lent a ready ear to the immense folklore on the subject. More importantly, he believed it.

This is evident not only from footnotes in the *Nights*, but also from manuscript pages from his *Zanzibar* which were rejected as too indelicate by his publisher, but which accidentally escaped being burned, and were preserved in his private library. Arab women "of the warmest passions," he wrote, "abandon themselves to African slaves, whose attractions are found irresistible. Their embraces are exceedingly prolonged, it is said for the space of an hour, they are capable of performing twice during the night, the tension of the muscles equals their endurance. . . . On the other hand the men . . . neglect their wives for negresses. . . . some cogent reason for the preference must exist. I believe it to be the 'Augustia et concomitas partium.' "[24]

In the privately printed *Arabian Nights* he was equally explicit:

Debauched women prefer negroes on account of the size of their parts. I measured one man in Somali-land who, when quiescent, numbered nearly six inches. This is a characteristic of the negro race and of African animals; *eg* the horse; whereas the pure Arab, man and beast, is below the average of Europe. . . . Moreover, these imposing parts do not increase proportionally during erection; consequently the 'deed of kind' takes a much longer time and adds greatly to the woman's enjoyment. In my time no honest Hindi Moslem would take his women-folk to Zanzibar on account of the huge attractions and enormous temptations there and thereby offered to them.[25]

It will be seen that Burton, with all his note-taking, measuring, and endless questioning, was in every way *involved* with the Africans. Speke, on the other hand, recoiled with distaste from such involvement. Unable because he knew no Arabic to talk to anyone save Burton and Seedy Bombay, he was shut out from many decisions and virtually all of Burton's ethnological research. One can begin to see him, increasingly lonely and suspicious, harbouring a growing conviction that Burton was "going to the devil," and quietly storing "evidence" on the subject to report back in England.

Speke himself held the African in contempt, and would write of his "obstinate fatalism" and "mulish temperament," and insist that he "has as great an antipathy to work as a mad dog has to water." He was shocked by the near nudity of the African women, and on one curious occasion on his second journey, when two thieves "whipped off the clothes" of two women "and ran away with them, allowing their victims to pass me in a state of absolute nudity," he became distraught. "I could stand this thieving no longer," he wrote. "My goats and other things had been taken away without causing me much distress of mind, but now, after this shocking event, I ordered my men to shoot at any thieves that came near them."[26]

Speke at thirty-three was inhibited and prudish. Where Burton sampled every African intoxicant and drug, Speke remained a teetotaller. He deplored both African and Arab polygamy, writing primly that these people "who have so many wives seem to find little enjoyment in that domestic bliss so interesting and beautiful in our English homes," a phrase that stimulated Burton to scrawl "Humbug" in the margin of his copy.[27] Though Speke seems to have enjoyed partying and dancing with European girls,[28] there is no record of a serious love affair. Several letters in the Royal Geographical Society archives hint at a slavish devotion to his mother. In his volume describing his second exploration in Africa there is a passage where he reported that he dreamed every night that Queen Victoria—confused in the dreams with his mother—was calling him home. On this same expedition, when Speke was at the court of King Mutesa in Buganda, the queen mother offered him two of her daughters for wives. He admitted being "staggered at first by this awful proposal," and consulted Bombay, who counselled him to take them, and if he didn't like them to turn them over to one of his men. So, Speke wrote, "I walked off with my two fine specimens of natural history, though I would rather have had princes, that I might have taken them home to be instructed in England." He sent back the younger girl, who was only twelve, and immediately turned the older over to his valet. The girl was indignant at the transfer, and eventually ran away and back to the palace.[29]

Burton, on the other hand, implied slyly in his books and apparently more openly with his friends, that his knowledge of the sexual vitality of Negro women was no mere hearsay. The Wagogo women, he wrote, "are well disposed towards strangers of fair complexion, apparently with the permission of their husbands." Unlike Speke he rejoiced in nudity among the nubile young, whom he found "wholly unconscious of indecorum." In discussing what constitutes modesty in women, he wrote delicately, "It is a question that by no means can be positively answered in the affirmative, that real modesty is less in proportion to the absence of toilette. These 'beautiful domestic animals' graciously smiled when in my best Kinyamwezi I did my devoir to the sex; and the present of a little tobacco always secured for me a seat in the undress circle."[30]

Burton was like a sponge, Speke a stone. For Burton the natives were an intoxicant and a passion. Even when repelled he felt, observed, and recorded with a minuteness Speke found incomprehensible. Perhaps the younger man sensed indignantly, too, that Burton held his own solid British virtues in contempt, and found him after six months to be not only a dull fellow but also an intolerable prig. If so it was Africa first of all that came between them.

XV

Tanganyika

Not *all* shall perish, much of *me*
shall vanquish the grave. . . . men shall know
my daring hand was *first* to show—

> Richard Burton, fragment of a poem scribbled in the
> margin of his Lake Tanganyika journal[1]

ALTHOUGH THE ARABS had been gradually penetrating central Africa as slave and ivory hunters for two generations, astonishingly they had produced no maps. Nor had they improved on the contradictory Portuguese maps dating back to 1591. Information continued to be passed by word of mouth, subject to all the errors imposed by the linguistic complexities of the warring tribes. At Kazeh, Burton and Speke learned for certain what they had heard from the coastal Arabs, that there was not one great slug-like lake in the central area, as had been pictured on missionary J. Erhardt's 1856 map in the Royal Geographical Society, but several lakes, two of great size, one to the west and the other to the north.[2] But whether the westernmost lake was linked to the northern by a river even Snay bin Amir did not know. Burton gambled on the expectation that the southern lake, variously called the Sea of Ujiji and Tanganyika, by virtue of its position, was the true Nile source, and made the fateful decision to go west.

The wholesale desertion of porters, many of whom took their pay at Kazeh, bought slaves and turned back to the coast lest they escape, meant recruitment of virtually a whole new expedition. This took five weeks, from November 8 to December 14, 1857. From Kazeh the explorers went to Msene, described by Burton as a place of "gross debauchery," where they lingered twelve days, with the bearers giving themselves up to dancing, pombe-drinking and related pleasures. Farther on, in Kanjanjeri, Burton was again struck down with fever, this time with such severity that he wrote, "I saw yawning to receive me 'those dark gates across the wild that no man knows.'" The malaria brought paralysis to his legs. Having seen it happen to others in India, he knew that eventually he would recover, and a kind of fatalism set in. "I was easily consoled," he wrote. "Hope, says the Arab, is woman,

Despair is man. If one of us was lost, the other might survive to carry home the results of the exploration."[3]

He could not know, fortunately, that he would not walk for eleven months. At first he rode unsteadily on an ass, and after the last ass died he was carried in a hammock slung on poles, with eight natives supporting his gaunt, giant frame. Both men suffered from inflammation of the eyes, but with Speke the infection in the retina became so bad that by the time they reached western Usagozi he could see almost nothing. Still they went on—the lame man leading the blind—winding among the low conical hills of the Unyamwezi, fording the Ruguvu and Unguwwe Rivers, dogged and persistent, close to but never destroyed by desperation. Finally in early February, 1858 Burton saw in the distance "walls of sky-blue cliff with gilded summits," and knew he was close to the lake. On February 13 they climbed a hill so steep and stony Speke's ass died of exhaustion on the ascent. Reaching the summit, Burton looked expectantly down through the trees.

"What is that streak of light which lies below," he asked.

"I am of the opinion," Seedy Bombay said soberly, "that that is *the* water."

"I gazed in dismay," Burton wrote, "the remains of my blindness, the veil of trees, and a broad ray of sunshine illuminating but one reach of the Lake, had shrunk its fair proportions. Somewhat prematurely I began to lament my folly in having risked life and lost health for so poor a prize, to curse Arab exaggeration, and to propose an immediate return, with a view of exploring the Nyanza, or Northern Lake. Advancing, however, a few yards, the whole scene suddenly burst upon my view, filling me with admiration, wonder, and delight. . . . I felt willing to endure double what I had endured."

Burton was looking down upon the longest—and next to Lake Baikal the deepest—freshwater lake in the world. He stared at its shining green and hazy blue waters "lined by continuous parallels of lofty hills" and guessed instantly and correctly that it was of volcanic origin. They descended to Ujiji, the chief settlement and slave mart on the lake (made famous in 1871 as the meeting place of Stanley and Livingstone). Walking among the beehive-shaped native huts and into the bazaar, they were delighted to find fresh milk, poultry, eggs, tomatoes, Jerusalem artichokes and plantain. The waters were swarming with crocodiles; water buffaloes and elephants abounded in the surrounding bamboo.

The suspicious natives refused all cooperation in the exploration along the shore, and Said bin Salim, who considered the journey at an end, bluntly refused to negotiate. Now Burton's health became worse. "I lay for a fortnight upon the earth," he wrote, "too blind to read or write, except with long intervals, too weak to ride and too ill to converse." Since Speke's eyes were somewhat better, Burton dispatched him with four men, including Bombay, to cross the lake and hire the only sailing craft available, a dhow belonging to an Arab merchant. He hoped then to secure permission to explore the end of the lake, where, they had heard, a large river flowed out to the north. Speke was gone twenty-seven days, during which Burton lay on his cot slowly improving, "*dreaming of things past, visioning things present,*" enjoying the beauty of the lake and what he cryptically called "other advantages, which, probably I might vainly attempt to describe" in this "African Eden."[4]

The younger man returned on March 29, 1858, "thoroughly moist and mildewed," and as Speke himself put it, with "mortifying news." They could hire the dhow, he said, only after a three months delay and upon payment of 500 dollars. Burton, who had been told that the dhow was available at any time, concealed his exasperation badly. "I was sorely disappointed," he wrote. "He had done literally nothing." Though it seemed to Burton further proof of his companion's ineptness as a linguist and negotiator, he could not be angry long, as Speke was suffering from a nasty infection.

It had begun with a bizarre accident one night on the recent journey, when an army of black beetles invaded his tent. Failing to get them out of his bedding, he finally extinguished his candle and went to sleep. He was awakened by a beetle in his ear, digging violently away, he wrote later, "like a rabbit at a hole."

I applied the point of a pen-knife to his back, which did more harm than good; for though a few thrusts kept him quiet, the point also wounded my ear so badly that inflammation set in, severe suppuration took place, and all the facial glands extending from that point down to the point of the shoulder became contorted and drawn aside. . . . It was the most painful thing I ever remember. . . . For many months the tumour made me almost deaf, and ate a hole between that orifice and the nose, so that when I blew it, my ear whistled so audibly that those who heard it laughed. Six or seven months after this accident happened, bits of beetle, a leg, a wing, or parts of its body, came away in the wax.[5]

Speke had, however, brought word that three Arab slave dealers declared it to be true that a large river, the Rusizi, flowed northwards out of the lake. "I went so near its outlet," one Shayk Hamed bin Sulayyaim had said, "I could see and feel the outward drift of the water."[6] Electrified by the news, Burton now set about getting boats by himself. After tedious negotiations, he secured two large canoes, one sixty, the other forty feet in length. They were crudely hollowed trees, badly caulked, which lay lopsided in the water, and which crept along the shore "like the hollowed elders of thirty bygone centuries." Though Burton was already desperately worried about the low state of their supplies, and found Chief Kannena's price for the canoes extortionate, he paid it. "I was resolved at all costs, even if we were reduced to actual want, to visit the mysterious stream."

According to Speke, Burton "was still suffering so severely that anybody seeing him attempt to go would have despaired of his ever returning;" nevertheless he "could not endure being left behind."[7] On April 12, 1858, eight men carried him gingerly to the lake in his hammock and placed him in the forefront of the biggest canoe, where he sat happily as they started off, the Union Jack fluttering above him. The natives paddled rhythmically, accompanied by one man's monotonous melancholy howl, punctuated with a chorus of yells and shouts. Several natives banged on tomtoms and clanged horns incessantly; all observed a strict rule to throw nothing overboard, even offal, lest it attract the crocodiles.

After crossing the lake to the west, they went northwards hugging the coast, which was occupied by the Wabembe, known to be devourers of men, carrion, and vermin. "They prefer man raw," Burton wrote flatly, "whereas the Wadoe of the coast eat him roasted." He looked hard at the Wabembe—"poor devils dark and stunted, timid and degraded . . . less dangerous to the living than to the dead"—and fancied that they looked hard at him in return "in the light of butcher's meat." They stopped at Uvira, a village only two days rowing from the Rusizi River. Here Burton met three Arabs who claimed to have travelled to the lake's northern tip, and questioned them eagerly. He was devastated by the reply. "They unanimously asserted, and every man in the host of bystanders confirmed their words," he wrote, "that the 'Rusizi' enters into, and does not flow out of Tanganyika. I felt sick at heart."

Turning angrily upon Bombay, Burton demanded an explanation of the message Speke had brought back from the shorter lake trip. Bombay replied that Speke "had misunderstood the words of Hamid bin Sulayyaim, who spoke of a river falling into, not issuing *from* the lake." Burton then confronted the native Sayfu, who had also glibly described the river flowing out of the lake; he admitted lamely that he had never sailed far enough north to see it with his own eyes. "Briefly," Burton wrote bitterly, "I had been deceived by a strange coincidence of deceit."[8]

Disappointed and depressed, he was nevertheless determined to see the Rusizi for himself. But his boatmen defiantly refused to paddle further north, fearful of the dreaded Wavira, whose reputation for cannibalism was worse than that of the Wabembe. Bribery, cajolery, and threats all failed. Finally Burton's talented tongue, which he counted on to succeed for him in the most complicated crisis, also failed. It had been covered with ulcers when he left, and was now so swollen and sore he could no longer speak at all.

Dangerously low in supplies, they decided there was nothing to do but return to Ujiji. Neither leader could be *absolutely* certain about the Rusizi, and this uncertainty, magnified and distorted in coming years, was to cause misunderstanding, heartbreak and even egregious error on Burton's part. On the return trip they suffered a wild lake storm that nearly swamped the ungainly canoes. The terrified rowers, moaning for their wives and mothers, managed to make the shore, and Burton settled down in the mud to sleep. He awakened to find the men in wild disorder. His Goanese servant, Valentine, had fired at a drunken marauding native and had instead severely wounded one of their own men. Burton with difficulty kept Chief Kannena from killing his valet on the spot. He paid a generous compensation for the accident, and nursed the wounded man as best he could. But the native died, and Burton himself came to be blamed for the shooting.

The party continued south, sodden in the rain, their guns honeycombed with rust, the grain and flour soaked, the canoes reeking with excrement. Burton sat silent under his mackintosh, constantly watching a little slave girl whom Kanenna had purchased en route to make sure she was not washed overboard. Oddly, the health of both men improved in the terrible 33-day trip. Speke was still deaf, but his eyesight had returned almost to normal. Burton still could not walk, but his hands, till now so paralysed he could not hold a pen, could now write and sketch freely. "Perhaps," he wrote, "mind had also acted upon matter; the object of my mission was now effected, and this thought enabled me to cast off the burden of grinding care with which the imminent prospect of a failure had before sorely laden me."

He had not found the coy fountains, and he would henceforth insist that he had not really been searching for them, except during this period when false stories had "startled me from the proprieties of reason."[9] But he was the first European to discover Tanganyika, "the meeting place of waters," and, as he wrote later, wistfully and privately in his journal, "men shall know, my daring hand was *first* to show—"

He estimated from native reports that the lake was 250 miles long; actually it was 400. The altitude Speke calculated from the crude bath thermometer at 1,800 feet; Burton put it at 1,850. The correct figure was 2,534. Burton was most baffled by native reports that seemed to indicate that all the rivers from north to south flowed into the lake. This, as well as the slightly brackish quality of the water, made him toy with the idea that the lake had no outlet, that the heavy rainfall kept the balance between sweetness and salinity. Here he came very close to being correct. Lake Tanganyika actually overflows into its single outlet only during the rainy season; then the waters pour out through a great swamp in the west to the Lukaga River, an outlet so hidden the natives themselves could not correctly describe it. This mystery would remain unsolved for sixteen years, a fact that greatly complicated Burton's life.

Not till 1875 would he learn that what he had discovered was the source not of the Nile but of the mighty Congo. By then he was past elation, and only wryly quoted David Livingstone's celebrated diary entry, "Who would care to risk being put into a cannibal pot, and be converted into blackman for anything less than the grand old Nile?"[10]

Returning to Ujiji, the explorers discovered that the crafty Said bin Salim, apparently hopeful that they would never return, had "reduced" the supplies they had expected to use for the return voyage almost to zero. They were faced with a return empty-handed through an area where "baggage is life," where no white explorer save the saintly Livingstone could ever live by begging from the Africans. Burton was almost desperate when on May 22 shots announced the arrival of strangers, and a caravan appeared with supplies ordered months earlier, and for which he had long since abandoned hope. Included were precious letters from India, Europe and Zanzibar, including a fat packet from Isabel Arundell, along with sheafs of newspaper and journal clippings she had saved for him. So was broken "a dead silence of eleven months."[11]

"Of course they brought with them evil tidings—the Indian mutiny," Burton wrote. It gave him small satisfaction, in reading of the massacre of English soldiers and civilians in India, to remember that some years earlier in his *Pilgrimage to El-Medinah and Meccah* he had warned of just such a possibility. It is likely, too, that he received at this time the disturbing news that his brother Edward was in India, and he could have no way of knowing if he had survived. Speke's younger brother, also named Edward, was also in India and died of wounds received in the insurrection.

The new supplies had ammunition of the wrong sort and only enough cloth for barter to ensure a return to the coast. Burton was forced to abandon his original plans of exploring the southern two-thirds of Tanganyika, with a return to Zanzibar by way of Lake Nyassa still further south. But at this point, still suffering from paralysis in his legs, he could think of nothing with favour but the minimum mileage back to Zanzibar. On May 26 they took leave of the lake for the last time. "The charm of the scenery was perhaps enhanced by the reflection that my eyes might never look upon it again," Burton wrote.[12]

At Yombo by a fortuitous accident they met porters with additional
bales of cloth and more letters. "As usual they were full of evil news,"
Burton wrote. "My father had died on the 6th of last September, after
a six weeks illness, at Bath, and was buried on the 10th, and I only
knew it on the 18th of June—the following year. Such tidings are
severely felt by the wanderer, who, living long behind the world, is
unable to mark its gradual changes . . . lulls apprehension into a belief
that *his* home has known no loss, and who expects again to meet each
old familiar face ready to smile upon his return, as it was to weep at
his departure."

This was the second time Burton had lost a parent when in a wild,
remote country, beyond the reach of mail, and he must have had the
same disconcerting sensation that ever accompanies belated lament.
The lament seems to have been real, though his affection for his father
had long been tempered by contempt. It is worth noting that he cut
the specific mention of his father out of his African notes when he
published his *Lake Regions of Central Africa*, eliminating again in his
printed pages any evidence of personal affection for his family. Isabel
printed it when she quoted from the journal in her biography. Later
he would describe how an old tree in a forest, an "unwieldy elder, that
has ended his tale of years, falls with a terrible crash, tearing away
with him a little world."[13]

Back in Kazeh Burton chose to stay for several weeks, as his paralysed legs were now finally improving. He hoped to get from his Arab
companions native vocabularies and a detailed account of the tribes to
the north in preparation for a return trip which he and Speke at this
point were both determined to make. Speke was bored, however, by
all the Arab talk he could not understand—so left out of things, Burton
noted, that it turned him "a little sour." Apparently the Arabs in Kazeh
had come to dislike him. As Burton put it privately, he would not have
dared leave him alone in the village, for Speke, like most Anglo-Indians,
"expect civility as their *due* and treat all skins a shade darker than
their own as 'niggers.' "[14]

By now the younger man had made an almost total recovery, and
was eager to do extra exploring before the return. He urged Burton to
try for the northern lake, which the Arabs insisted was bigger even
than Tanganyika and was only sixteen marches away. Burton apparently found the idea appalling. At first Speke described his reaction
with great politeness, "My companion was, most unfortunately, quite
done up, but very graciously consented to wait with the Arabs and
recruit his health, whilst I should proceed alone." Later Speke was
more blunt, writing, "He said we had done enough and he would do
no more."[15]

Actually Speke's relations with Burton had deteriorated so badly he was finding Kazeh unendurable. He complained bitterly in a letter to Dr Norton Shaw:

Burton has always been ill; he won't sit out in the dew, and has a decided objection to the sun. . . . This is a shocking country for sport, there appears to be literally nothing but Elephants, and they from constant hunting are driven clean away from the highways; all I have succeeded in shooting have been a few antelopes and guinea fowls besides hippopotamous near the coast. . . . There is literally nothing to write about in this uninteresting country. Nothing could surpass these tracts, jungles, plains for dull sameness, the people are the same everywhere in fact the country is one vast sense-less map of sameness. . . .[16]

Burton on the other hand was glad to see him go. He wrote formally to the Royal Geographical Society on June 24, 1858, "Captain Speke has volunteered to visit the Ukerewe Lake, of which the Arabs have grand accounts." Later when he came across this letter reproduced in Speke's book, he scrawled in the margin of his own copy, "To get rid of him!" So Burton was betrayed into the greatest mistake of his life. He was betrayed first by his lameness, and second by his incapacity to gauge Speke's real talents, though here it should be remembered that on the two earlier occasions when Speke left Burton to travel alone, he had conspicuously failed in his mission. Third, and probably most important, Burton was betrayed by the fact that he was an eth-nologist first and only secondarily an explorer. Where Speke found the natives "the same everywhere," Burton found an endlessly fascinat-ing diversity.

Speke took off northwards in what proved to be a surprisingly easy march over wide, monotonous plains, with the scrub giving way to ever more fertile vegetation—palms, mangoes, and papyrus—arriving after sixteen days upon the shores of a body of water that looked as vast as the sea. One native, described as the best travelled man in the place, said under Bombay's questioning that he thought the sea "probably extended to the end of the world." No native in the village knew the northern horizon; there seemed to be no communication even between the western shores and the eastern. Speke took the elevation and was elated to find it considerably higher than Tanganyika. At this point, with that flash of intuitive judgment that often accompanies great discovery, he decided that he was standing at the "fountain-head of that mighty stream that floated Father Moses on his first adventurous sail—the Nile," and that quite alone he had "solved a problem which it had been . . . the ambition of the first monarchs of the world to unravel." He decided to name the lake "Nyanza Victoria after our gracious sovereign," and celebrated, characteristically, by shooting something. This time it was some red geese swimming in the lake. A rare specimen—"black all over save for a little white patch beneath the lower mandible," escaped his gun; this he reported with great regret."[17]

After only three days Speke left the lake and rushed back, jubilant and triumphant, to tell Burton of his discovery. One cannot help wondering exactly how he expected Burton to react to the news that he had snatched "the greatest geographical prize since the discovery of America" from his grasp. There are two accounts of that famous breakfast. As Burton put it in his journal:

> At length Jack had been successful. His "flying trip" had led him to the northern water, and he had found its dimensions surpassing our most sanguine expectations. We had scarcely, however, breakfasted before he announced to me the startling fact that "he had discovered the sources of the White Nile." It was an inspiration perhaps. . . . His reasons were weak, were of the category alluded to by the damsel Lucetta, when justifying her penchant in favour of the "lovely gentleman," Sir Proteus—
> "I have no other but a woman's reason—
> I think him so because I think him so"

Speke wrote tersely, "Captain Burton greeted me on arrival at the old house. . . . I expressed my regret that he did not accompany me as I felt quite certain in my mind I had discovered the source of the Nile. This he naturally objected to, even after hearing all my reasons for saying so, and therefore the subject was dropped."

Burton's account continued: "Jack changed his manners to me from this date. . . . After a few days it became evident to me that not a word could be uttered upon the subject of the lake, the Nile, and his *trouvaille* generally without offence. By a tacit agreement it was, therefore, avoided, and I should never have resumed it, had Jack not stultified the results of my expedition by putting forth a claim which no geographer can admit, and which is at the same time so weak and flimsy, that no geographer has yet taken the trouble to contradict it."[18]

The *few days* of argument seem to have been the first decisive testing of each other's strength. Burton learned now, probably to his astonishment, that he was facing not a devoted and bungling younger brother but a tough, ambitious rival who was quite likely back in England to steal the acclaim he felt properly his own. And Speke learned that Burton could not only not bring himself to praise his achievement as anything other than a *trouvaille*, a lucky find, but also that he was certain, back in London, to disparage its significance. Though Burton would in fact admit that a "new light" had been thrown upon "a subject veiled in the glooms of three thousand years— the 'coy sources' of the White Nile," the most that he would concede was that the northern lake was "one of the feeders" of the great river.[19]

It could not be the main supply, he insisted, for one decisive reason. The heavy monsoon came to Lake Victoria and Tanganyika in October and lasted till June, whereas the Nile in the region of Gondokoro was falling fast at the end of January and would rise again at the end of March. This was a circumstance that would puzzle all London geographers. It was one of several arguments Speke would meet upon his return.

Burton apparently insisted now, as he did later, that Speke had seen only a portion of the lake and that the native reports were certain to be exaggerated. There were certainly several lakes that fed the Nile, he said—correctly, as it turned out—and the main source was more likely to be a range of equatorial mountains high enough to be snow-covered like Kenya and Kilimanjaro to the east—as were the Mountains of the Moon—sitting astride the equator, where the rainy season more nearly corresponded with the Nile flooding. Speke held stoutly that the Mountains of the Moon were the crescent-shaped ridges at the north end of Tanganyika. He greatly exaggerated their height and on his map drew them in as a formidable barrier between the lake and what he believed to be the Nile headwaters.[20]

Refusing to be checkmated, Burton placed the Mountains of the Moon on his own map squarely between Speke's Lake Victoria and the known position of the upper Nile. Both men were wrong about legendary mountains, though Burton was closer to the truth. Burton was correct in insisting that Speke was making a far-reaching claim on the basis of evidence that was far from complete. But Speke was right about Lake Victoria, and felt it. One suspects from certain vagaries in Burton's subsequent behavior that from the beginning he felt it too.

Speke wanted to go back to Lake Victoria at once, but Burton refused. "I am a much older man than you, Jack, and I am not getting better," he said. ". . . we will go home, recruit our health, report what we have done, get some more money, return together, and finish our whole journey."[21] There were barely enough supplies to get them safely back to Zanzibar; the monsoon was beginning, and they were nearing the end of their army leave. So they left Kazeh on September 6, 1858, with 132 natives and Arabs. Many were new porters, who demanded double pay since there was no guarantee of a return caravan; some were former deserters. Burton refused to employ the worst of the deserters, or the thieves who had plundered them in the past.

For both men the trip was a four-month nightmare of illness and mutual distrust. At Hanga Speke was attacked by what the natives called "little irons," with stupefying pain in the right breast and spleen. He told Burton he had been awakened by the pain, which was accompanied by "a horrible dream of tigers, leopards, and other beasts, harnessed with a network of iron hooks, dragging him, like the rush of a whirlwind, over the ground." The spasms recurred a second time, accompanied by what Burton described as fits of epileptic description, or hydrophobia. "Again he was haunted by crowds of devils, giants, lion-headed demons, who were wrenching with superhuman force, and stripping the sinews and tendons of his legs down to his ankles." After a third fit, in which he barked like a rabid dog and terrified the natives watching him, he was able to speak, and calling for pen and paper "wrote an incoherent letter of farewell to his family. That was the crisis."

Burton, nursing him as best he could, never left his side. Finally the pains subsided, and Speke murmured, "Dick, the knives are sheathed."

What Speke did not know was that in his delirium he had poured out a torrent of grievance that awakened Burton for the first time to the seething bitterness that lay beneath his placid and disciplined exterior. Now he learned that Speke was still angry over the way Burton had treated his Somaliland diary, and bitter that his animal skins had been sent to Calcutta with Burton's notes instead of his own. He was still smarting, too, over the memory of the fight at Berbera, believing Burton had implied that he was a coward. Most important, he could not forgive Burton for denying his claims about the Nile.

One sees from the description of these outpourings that Speke from the beginning had sought the older man's approval and admiration. Now, confident that he had won the supreme prize, he had to face the fact that Burton could not concede it to him. So one finds that the wretched dilemma was played out in Speke's dreams, where the animals he was most passionate about killing and possessing were in turn destroying him, where giants and demons were immobilizing and castrating him—destroying his legs, the instruments that had carried him to the greatest triumph of his life.[22]

When Speke was well enough to ride in a hammock, they resumed the march, recrossing the mountain ranges, fetid jungles, and stretches of rotting swamp. On January 30, 1859 the men shouted with delight at the sight of the first mango trees. On February 2, Burton wrote, "Jack and I caught sight of the sea. We lifted our caps, and gave 'three times and once more.'" At Konduchi "our entrance was immense. The war-men danced, shot, shouted, the boys crowded; the women lulliloo'd with all their might . . . the crowd stared and laughed until they could stare and laugh no more."[23]

At Konduchi they waited for a craft from Zanzibar, and then, in a final gesture Burton persuaded Speke to visit Kilwa, where one could see the ruins of Quiloa, the legendary port city of 300 mosques, said to have been captured by Vasco da Gama in 1502 and later destroyed in fighting between the Portuguese and Arabs. Burton was enamoured of the Vasco da Gama story, and later would translate the Portuguese poet Camoens' account of his exploits. But his insistence on detouring to Kilwa, in the face of a cholera epidemic in the area, seems good evidence of his increasing reluctance to return to London.

He tried now to persuade Speke to remain with him in Zanzibar, with plans to apply for renewed army leave and fresh funds from the Foreign Office, promising a prompt return to explore thoroughly the whole of Lake Victoria. But Speke, sensing correctly now that this was the only device by which Burton could share in his discovery, would have none of it. "He took pleasure in saying unkind, unpleasant things," Burton recorded, "and said he could not take an interest in any exploration if he did not command it." And so Burton fell into what he called "an utter depression of mind and body," writing that "even the labour of talking was too great."[24]

Colonel Hamerton had died in their absence, and the British Foreign Office had chosen to refill the vacany with Captain Christopher Rigby, Burton's old rival from India, whose hatred he had incurred by beating him roundly in several language examinations. Almost instantly Speke was in Rigby's confidence. Rigby was an intriguing bureaucrat, capable of extraordinary malice, who had already done Burton a great wrong. Before leaving for the interior, Burton had wrapped up his immense manuscript on Zanzibar and entrusted it, along with a second packet of routine meteorological statistics, to a foreign office assistant named Apothecary Frost. The Zanzibar manuscript was clearly addressed to Norton Shaw in London, and it was to be sent by Foreign Office pouch. Because of Hamerton's death it was not sent. Rigby, arriving July 27, 1858, apparently read it, and sent it on to India instead, presumably for army clearance. The Indian army officials, alerted to the few strident criticisms in it of official policy, proceeded to bury it in the strong box of the Bombay Branch of the Royal Asiatic Society.

When Burton learned, apparently upon his return to Zanzibar, that only the least important packet had arrived at the Royal Geographical Society, he was furious. He suspected Rigby, but had no way of proving the deed. Eight years after he had handed it over to Apothecary Frost for mailing, the manuscript was unexpectedly returned to him from India. Only then was he able to unravel the intrigue.[25] But at the moment he could only write, with painful understatement, "Soon the Consulate was no longer bearable to me. I was too conversant with local politics, too well aware of what was going on, to be a pleasant companion." Rigby meanwhile was writing back to London his venomous appraisal of Burton: "Speke is a right good, jolly, resolute fellow. Burton is not fit to hold a candle to him and has done nothing in comparison with what Speke has, but Burton will blow his trumpet very loud and get all the credit of the discoveries. Speke works. Burton lies on his back all day and picks other people's brains."[26]

Burton was faced, too, with the knotty problem of paying and rewarding the Arabs and Africans who had accompanied them, all of whom came forward now with outstretched hands. Colonel Hamerton had promised them a reward from public funds if they cooperated with Burton—Said bin Salim said he personally had been assured a thousand dollars and a gold watch—but Rigby felt no obligation to carry out his predecessor's generous verbal gesture. The £1,000 given by the Foreign Office had long been spent. Burton had bitten into his own private funds to the extent of £1,400, and Speke had promised to draw upon his own capital and share in this expense upon their return to London. Burton insisted that he satisfied all the loyal men. He refused to reward Said bin Salim, saying he had stolen enough to enrich himself handsomely. Several deserters, including some slaves, he refused anything beyond the original $30 advance, saying he could purchase them in the market for less. Speke and Rigby, watching, said nothing, and seemingly acquiesced. So unwittingly Burton laid the groundwork for future trouble.[27]

On March 22, 1859 Burton and Speke boarded the clipper *Dragon of Salem* and sailed for Aden. There Burton met his trusted friend, Dr John Steinhaeuser, who after talking privately with Speke went to Burton in alarm and warned him he would have trouble with Speke in London.[28] Still the two explorers were exchanging formal courtesies, and were to outward appearances friends. But when H.M.S. *Furious* sailed into the Aden harbor en route to London, and they were offered passage, Burton declined. Steinhaeuser had urged him to convalesce a little longer in Aden. Fever still clung to him, Burton wrote, "like the shirt of Nessus."[29] [This was an extraordinary allusion, considering what was to happen. Nessus, it will be remembered, was a centaur shot by Hercules with a poisoned arrow. Hercules' wife steeped her husband's shirt in the blood of the dying centaur, who had tricked her into thinking it would be a love charm, but the shirt poisoned Hercules' flesh, causing such agony he killed himself.]

The two explorers exchanged a brief goodbye. "I shall hurry up, Jack, as soon as I can," Burton said.

And Speke replied, *"Goodbye old fellow; you may be quite sure I shall not go up to the Royal Geographical Society until you come to the fore and we appear together. Make your mind quite easy about that."*

"They were the last words," Burton wrote, "Jack ever spoke to me on earth."[30]

Betrayal and Attack

W HEN SPEKE BOARDED the *Furious* he was immediately taken in hand by Laurence Oliphant, a rich, pampered, well-travelled young Englishman who had met Burton at dinner parties at the home of Monckton Milnes. He was also a reporter for *The Times* and *Blackwood's*, and secretary to Lord Elgin, with whom he was returning from a diplomatic mission to China. At twenty-nine he was already known for several travel books. What was then not so well known about him was that he was a victim of an inordinately possessive mother and an incipient if not already practicing homosexual. Oliphant's eventual marriage at forty-two was literally "a marriage of true minds," and he later stated ingenuously that he "learnt self-control by sleeping with his beloved and beautiful Alice in his arms for twelve years without claiming the rights of a husband." Eventually he exiled himself to a brotherhood cult in Brockton, New York, led by the "bisexual mystic" Thomas Lake Harris, to whom he gave away most of his fortune. He returned to Britain, only to leave again, followed by charges that he had been corrupting the morals of young boys, and spent most of his last years with a second wife in the Near East.[1]

Oliphant now interfered decisively in Speke's life. He persuaded him upon their arrival in London not to wait the extra twelve days for Burton but to go instantly to Sir Roderick Murchison, president of the Royal Geographical Society, and stake out his claim to glory. As Burton later described it, "on board the *Furious* he was exposed to the worst influences, and was persuaded to act in a manner which his own moral sense must have afterwards strongly condemned if indeed it ever pardoned it. . . . The very day after he returned to England, May 9, 1859, Jack called at the Royal Geographical Society and set on foot the scheme of a new exploration."[2]

As Speke put it, "Sir Roderick, I need only say, at once accepted my views; and, knowing my ardent desire to prove to the world, by actual inspection of the exit, that the Victoria N'yanza was the source of the Nile, seized the enlightened view that such a discovery should not be lost to the glory of England and the society of which he was president, and said . . . 'Speke, we must send you there again.' "[3]

Speke lectured before the Society—"much against my inclination," he wrote—and was instantly the young lion of the city. When Burton arrived on May 21, he found "the ground completely cut from under my feet." A whole new expedition had been organized, with £2,500 for financing and with Speke in command. Burton's suggestion that two expeditions be launched, starting at different points on the East African coast, was coldly dismissed. "Everything had been done for, or rather against me," he wrote. "My companion now stood forth in his true colours, an angry rival."⁴

Two days after Burton arrived in England, May 23, 1859, the Royal Geographical Society dutifully presented him with a Founder's medal, but in the presentation speech Sir Roderick Murchison made only the scantiest reference to the discovery of Lake Tanganyika, spending most of his two hour address instead describing in glowing terms Speke's discovery of the Nyanza Victoria. Though stunned by the whole proceeding, Burton made a brief, controlled, and in the circumstances generous gesture to Speke in his acceptance speech: "To Captain J. H. Speke are due those geographical results to which you have alluded in such flattering terms. Whilst I undertook the history and ethnography, the languages and peculiarities of the people, to Captain Speke fell the arduous task of delineating an exact topography, and of laying down our positions by astronomical observations—a labour to which at times even the undaunted Livingstone found himself unequal."⁵

Speke's triumph could hardly have been so total had he not been busy attacking Burton venomously in private. The nature of his accusations became clear years later with the publication of W. H. Wilkins' biography of Isabel Burton, and of Speke's letters to Christopher Rigby in Zanzibar. "I am sure everybody at Zanzibar knows it, that I was the leader and Burton the second of the Expedition," said one characteristic Speke letter. "Had I not been with him, he never could have undergone the journey." Later he wrote to Rigby that he hoped the publication of his story in *Blackwood's* "may have the effect of reforming Burton; at any rate it will check his scribbling mania, and may save his soul the burthen of many lies."

Speke told the editor of *Blackwood's*, a good friend to Oliphant, that he would "die a hundred deaths" rather than have "a foreigner take from Britain the honour of the discovery." The reference to Burton's continental upbringing and generally unEnglish behaviour did not need to be spelled out.⁶ It would have been easy also for Speke to hint darkly of Burton's curiosity about native sexual customs; he would make explicit references to his own sexual purity in his own writings. Speke, however, apparently hinted at something more perverse. W. H. Wilkins, who consulted both Isabel Burton and her sister in preparing his biography, described it as follows: "Speke had spread all sorts of ugly—and I believe untrue—reports about Burton. These coming on top of certain other rumours—also, I believe untrue—which originated in India, were only too readily believed." Here a footnote refers to Burton's study of the homosexual brothels in Karachi.[7]

In an extraordinary repetition of his behaviour after the Somaliland expedition—when he had his Abban sent to jail for cheating him—Speke also proceeded once more to raise the cry of cheating. This time he pointed the finger at Burton. "It is not I," he said in effect, "but Burton who cheats." He pointed to Rigby's investigation in Zanzibar, which he had himself quietly set in motion, of native complaints against Burton for not having given them the reward formally promised by Colonel Hamerton. Rigby, who had himself refused to honour Hamerton's verbal commitment, had formally complained to the India Office that Said bin Salim was demanding a thousand dollars and a gold watch, and said that the British Government was losing prestige over the matter. The charge resulted in a vitriolic correspondence with Burton, who was thunderstruck to find himself rebuked by the India Office on January 14, 1860, and in danger of being held personally liable for the whole sum.[8]

So the vicious counterpoint continued, with Burton denying Speke what the latter most wanted, the admission that the Nyanza Victoria was the true source of the Nile and not simply "a feeder of the White Nile," and Speke in turn robbing Burton of even the secondary glory that was his due as leader of the expedition. Speke went on to accuse Burton, first, of cheating—where he himself was guilty—and second, of homosexual behaviour, something which Speke may unconsciously have been attracted to himself. Such attack is often an essential element in defense against the wish, a means of warding off the intolerable truth about oneself. Speke's history is empty of references to his affection for any woman, save his mother. He continued his close friendship with Oliphant, and spent several weeks with him in France in the spring of 1864, when he was tentatively negotiating with the French government about further explorations.[9]

Burton did not speak out publicly against Speke, whether in speech or writing, until months after his erstwhile companion's personal accusations and innuendoes had done him irreparable harm. Later he wrote of Speke, "No one is so unforgiving, I need hardly say, as the man who injures another." But if one looks closely at Burton's behaviour during these months, one sees a certain acquiescence in the betrayal. His very delay in returning to England invited it. He had toyed with the idea of claiming Tanganyika as the Nile source only to repudiate it. "One wise in his generation," he wrote, "whispered into my ear before returning to England, 'Boldly assert that you have discovered the source of the

Nile—if you are right, tant mieux, if wrong, you will have made your game before the mistake is found out!' "[10] By delaying his return Burton gave Speke an easy chance to seize the maximum glory, possibly because deep in his consciousness he felt the latter deserved it. Had Speke advanced his claim with less certainty, had he acknowledged Burton's role and invited him to share in the next expedition, all England would have applauded. As it was, many rallied in indignation to Burton's side. Soon there were two hostile camps among the scientists and geographers, a division that spread quickly to the press.

Though they had not spoken to each other since Aden, the two men continued to exchange notes, but Burton's salutations changed from "Dear Jack" to "Dear Speke" to "Sir." Finally in November 1859 he wrote to Norton Shaw: "I don't want to have any further private or direct communication with Speke. At the same time I am anxious that no mention of his name by me should be made without his being cognisant of it."[11] Still the notes continued for a time. The Quentin Keynes collection contains several recently discovered letters from Speke to Burton, some with Burton's tentative reply scribbled at the bottom, which indicate that the correspondence became acutely painful, at least for Burton. Speke, on the other hand, whose insensitivity in measuring the effect of his own behaviour on Burton is here glaringly revealed, wrote on February 1, 1860 with what seems to be genuine incomprehension, ". . . you appear *desirous* of shunning me." This insensitivity in Speke was reinforced by his self-righteousness. "I can only say," he wrote to the Under Secretary of State for India on December 1, 1859, "that I never allow enmity to be rankling in my breast."[12]

In addition to the larger betrayal, Speke had infuriated Burton by refusing to pay his share of the personal indebtedness the two men had incurred in Africa. He advanced two reasons, first that he hoped the India Office could be persuaded to pay the amount (Burton was correctly certain it would not); and second, he complained that Burton had never paid him for his personal losses on the Somali expedition. Burton had appropriated both his diary and collections, he said, and had not properly offered him half the royalties for *First Footsteps in East Africa*.[13] Burton, who had also gone in debt on the Somali expedition, and had made no money on the book—all of which was his own writing save the appendix—was outraged at the request for half the royalties, though he was now acutely sensitive to the fact that he had misused Speke's diary. He knew that Speke's family was wealthy, that his companion had considerable funds of his own.

Burton had advanced £1,400 out of his own pocket, and was now asking Speke for £600. "The debt was contracted unconditionally by

you in Africa . . . ," Burton wrote, "Had I known you then as well as
I do now I should have required receipts for what was left a debt
of *honour*. I must be content to pay the penalty of ignorance."[14] This
bitter line, penned at the bottom of Speke's letter of February 1, may
never have been sent, but whatever he wrote abruptly ended the
correspondence. Speke now wrote to Norton Shaw that Burton had
written saying he found it "distasteful" to have any correspondence
with him in regard to money matters, and later, on February 10, asked
Shaw formally to arbitrate between them.[15]

Isabel Arundell was one of several who tried to bring the two men
together. Speke said to her, "I'm so sorry, and I don't know how it all
came about. Dick was so kind to me; nursed me like a woman, taught
me such a lot, and I used to be so found of him; but it would be too
difficult for me to go back now."[16] Meanwhile gossip about Speke's
debt to Burton became widespread. "I hear from my mother that there
was much talk about it in London, rather derogatory to my brother's
honour," wrote Speke's younger brother Benjamin to Norton Shaw.[17]
A week before leaving London on his second Nile expedition, Speke
chose once more to write directly to Burton. He apologized for not
being able to pay the £600 himself, and stated that he had authorized
his brother Benjamin to hand over the sum in whatever fashion Burton
proposed. Burton replied formally, indicating that he too was leaving
England, and directing how the money was to be paid. Speke then
wrote a farewell note; it was conventional enough save for the poig-
nantly revealing first line. "I cannot," he said, "leave England address-
ing you so coldly."[18]

But the gesture, if such it was, seems to have been lost on Burton,
who poured out his bitterness in his journal: ". . . except his shooting
and his rags of Anglo-Hindustani, I have taught him everything he
knows. . . . my reward is, that I and my expenditure, and the cause for
which I have sacrificed everything, are made ridiculous."[19] Eight years
after Speke's death, he permitted a more explicit expression of his
anguish to appear in *Zanzibar*: "The few books—Shakespeare, Euclid,
and so forth—which composed my scanty library, we read together
again and again; he learned from me to sketch the scenery, and he
practiced writing a diary and accounts of adventure, which he used to
bring to me for correction. These reminiscences forcibly suggest to me
the Arab couplet—

> 'I taught him archery day by day—
> when his arm waxed strong, 'twas me he shot.' "

Burton had come home not only to Speke's betrayal but also to a
family tragedy. His brother Edward, who had survived the Indian

mutiny and been given an appointment at Lucknow, was now fur-loughed home with acute mental illness. Georgiana Stisted blamed a head beating he had received from Ceylon natives, who were said to have been enraged at his wanton killing of wild animals on a hunting expedition. Sunstroke in India, she said, had increased the damage.[20] Whatever the exact cause, Edward was now afflicted with a deadly mental torpor. Thomas Wright, Burton's early biographer, wrote that Edward was mute for almost forty years. According to family legend, he broke this catatonic silence only once before his death in 1895, when a physician cousin deliberately tried to anger him into speech by accusing him of not paying an old debt. It was said that Edward raised his head, and with a tortured effort replied, "Cousin, I did pay you, you must remember that I gave you a cheque."[21] It was a curious echo of the "payment-non-payment" theme that plagued his illustrious brother.

There can be little doubt that Edward's illness greatly affected Burton's behaviour in the crisis with John Speke, with whom he had travelled so long "like a brother." What seemed to be passivity in Burton may well have been serious depression. Isabel Burton later found a poem Richard had written in his journal at this time. It said in part:

> I hear the sounds I used to hear
> The laugh of joy, the groan of pain;
> The sounds of childhood sound again.
> Death must be near! . . . .
> The meed for ever deemed so dear,
> Repose upon the breast of Fame;
> (I did but half), while lives my name.
> Come then, Death, near![22]

"I did but half" was truly a "groan of pain," a private admission of defeat and despair. Isabel clearly recognized the hint of suicide in the poem, and it was to her that Burton turned at the time for sustenance and hope.

In the two years and nine months that Burton had been away, he had apparently written to Isabel only four times. In the final twenty months she got no letter whatever. Still she had continued to write long journal-like letters every fortnight. Her mother had taunted her with Burton's neglect, saying that he had either forgotten her or been eaten by jackals. Meanwhile Isabel had toured the continent with her sister Blanche, who had made a fashionable marriage to the wealthy Smyth Pigott. On the surface it had been a lively tour; a Russian general had proposed marriage, as had an American widower who claimed to have £300,000 in California gold. The Emperor of Austria had granted Isabel and the Pigotts a private audience, and she had been pleased to remind him that he had once danced with her mother. But in reality she had been bleakly lonely, elated most of all by the sight of Burton's name chiselled on the leaning tower at Pisa. She had carved her own beneath it.

Back in London she had learned from the newspapers that Burton was in Zanzibar and might return directly to the African interior. "I was getting into despair, and thinking whether I should go and be a Sister of Charity," she wrote, "as the appearance of Speke alone in London was giving me the keenest anxiety," when an envelope addressed to her from Zanzibar arrived. There was no letter, only a short verse:

To Isabel

That brow which rose before my sight,
  As on the palmer's holy shrine;
Those eyes—my life was in their light;
  Those lips my sacramental wine;
That voice whose flow was wont to seem
The music of an exile's dream.

"I knew then it was all right," she wrote.

Still when she read in the press that Burton would arrive in London shortly, the old dread returned. "I feel strange, frightened, sick, stupefied, dying to see him, and yet inclined to run away," she wrote in her diary on May 21, "lest, after all I have suffered and longed for, I should have to bear more."[23]

On May 22, 1859, she was at the home of a friend, and heard a ring at the door.

A voice that thrilled me through and through came up the stairs, saying, "I want Miss Arundell's address." The door opened, I turned around, and judge of my feelings when I beheld Richard! For an instant we both stood dazed. . . . We rushed into each other's arms. I cannot attempt to describe the joy of that moment. He had landed the day before, and come to London, and had called here to know where I was living, where to find me. . . . We went downstairs, and Richard called a cab, and he put me in and told the man to drive about—anywhere. He put his arm round my waist, and I put my head on his shoulder. I felt quite stunned; I could not speak or move, but felt like a person coming to after a fainting fit or a dream; it was acute pain. . . . But it was absolute content, such as I fancy people must feel in the first few moments after the soul has quitted the body. When we were a little recovered, we mutually drew each other's pictures from our respective pockets at the same moment, to show how carefully we had always kept them. . . .

I shall never forget Richard as he was then. He had had twenty-one attacks of fever—had been partially paralyzed and partially blind. He was a mere skeleton, with brown-yellow skin hanging in bags, his eyes protruding, and his lips drawn away from his teeth. . . . Never did I feel the strength of my love as then. He returned poorer, and dispirited by official rows and every species of annoyance; but he was still—had he been ever so unsuccessful, and had every man's hand against him—my earthly god and king, and I could have knelt at his feet and worshipped him. I used to feel so proud of him; I used to like to sit and look at him, and think, "You are mine, and there is no man on earth the least like you."[24]

For Burton such enveloping ardour was antidote and balm for the deepest hurt. Perhaps it was without exaggeration that Isabel wrote, "I think that but for me he would have died."

Still they did not get married. Burton went off to Dover to spend several weeks with his sister, and Mrs Arundell continued to fight the match with every weapon possible, including intercepting and destroying Burton's letters. Her chief arguments were two: "He is not a Christian, and he has no money." Actually Burton had inherited £16,000 from his family's estate, and though he had bitten into this to pay for his Tanganyika venture, there was enough left for a small annual income, provided it wasn't dissipated by further adventure. He talked hopefully about getting a consulship in Damascus. He promised, moreover, to be married in a Catholic church and to give his guarantee in writing that their children would be raised as Catholics.

In October 1859, when her mother was away from London, Isabel wrote her an impassioned letter: "It surprised me that you should consider mine an infatuation, you who worship talent, and my father bravery and adventure, and here they are both united." She quoted from the admiring press which had called Burton "the most interesting figure of the nineteenth century," and then continued, "I would this moment sacrifice and leave *all* to follow his fortunes, even if you all cast me out—if the world tabooed me. . . . If you do not disinherit me, I shall settle my portion on him. . . . The man you would choose I should loathe. . . . And the day he (if ever) gives me up I will go straight into a convent." Like all her letters this too was signed, "Your fondly attached child."[25]

When Mrs Arundell remained adamant, Burton proposed elopement. Though she was twenty-eight, and Richard thirty-eight, Isabel still clung to the hope that she could win her mother's blessing. Burton in annoyance declared they were both "gifted with 'the noble firmness of a mule,'" and went off to the continent. He went first to Paris, where Maria had taken his brother Edward, and then to Vichy, where he took the baths for a touch of gout.

Monckton Milnes had suggested to Burton that when in Paris he visit Fred Hankey, a young Englishman of dubious reputation, who purchased for Milnes many of the books for his great collection of erotica. According to Milnes' biographer, James Pope-Hennessy, Hankey was a sadist and expert in bizarre sexual practices. Edmond and Jules de Goncourt, who visited him in 1862, declared his apartment to be full "of every obscene object possible." Burton, no less curious now than when he was in Cairo, Mecca, or Karachi, sought him out. He wrote back to Milnes on January 22, 1860, "Since we met I saw Hankey. The 'sisters' are a humbug—Swiss women. Cold as frogs and thorough Mountaineers, a breed as unfit for debauchery as exists in this world. I told Hankey so and he remarked philosophically enough that they were sufficiently good for the public of postcards." Hankey had shown him a poem by Milnes which Burton commented on frankly, "I liked very much every portion of it except the name. You are writing for a very very small section who combine the enjoyment of verse with the practice of flagellation. . . . Why not call it the Birchiad?"[26]

Here we see Burton's bi-polarity, first pursuing the innocent—the pious, stubborn, and self-righteous virgin Isabel—and then seeking out the most degraded of men. Hankey, we learn from one journal of the Goncourt brothers, was capable of hiring a room with a window from which he could watch a murderess being hanged, and taking along two prostitutes "pour leur faire des choses" during the hanging. Moreover, this visit of Burton's was no mere single adventure, but the beginning of a friendship. We shall see more of this bi-polarity in Burton's life, a swinging from one pole to its opposite, as if experience with one sent him careening back to the other.

Back in London, Burton continued to pursue Isabel, but in surprising secrecy. Isabel would meet him only in her own home, or in the houses of friends who "allowed and encouraged" their friendship. Burton went often to Boulogne. "Here I can work, but not so in London and Paris," he wrote to Milnes,[27] and it was in Boulogne that most of his two-volume *Lake Regions of Central Africa* was written. Not surprisingly in the circumstances, he dedicated it not to Isabel, but to his sister Maria.

As spring approached, the private rift between Burton and Speke became ever more public. Speke had rushed into print in *Blackwood's* in the autumn of 1859 a series of articles in which he described his own discovery with excitement and conviction, and managed to diminish Burton's role to that of a note-scribbler. But he made errors that left him vulnerable. First, he claimed that his Lake Victoria extended all the way to 4° or 5° north latitude, when there were ample historical documents to show that an Egyptian expedition up the river twenty years earlier had reached 3°22′ north latitude without discovering a lake.[28] Second, he decided in a quite arbitrary fashion that the River Kivira, which he had never seen but which according to natives flowed into Lake Victoria from the west, must actually flow out of the lake and was in all probability the Nile itself. Burton, who had also learned of this river from Bombay and the Arabs in Kazeh, was certain it was not.[29]

Finally, Speke made the mistake of continuing to claim that the relatively low ridges near Lake Tanganyika were the Mountains of the Moon. Burton, who took very seriously the mythology about their being snow-covered, put those mountains farther north and east. Actually they were north and west—the great Ruénzori—which were not to be discovered until 1889, when the clouds rolled back for Henry Stanley and he saw their snow-covered summits virtually astride the equator, 18,000 feet high.

In the beginning Burton pointedly ignored all Speke's claims. In a meeting of the Royal Geographical Society on June 13, 1859, he spoke only on the economics of the area he had visited, leaving it to his friend James M'Queen, whom he had thoroughly briefed, to dispute his rival. In a letter to *The Times*, October 8, 1859, he presented his version of Central African geography, which subtly undermined the importance of Speke's Lake Victoria. There were four great lakes in Central Africa, he said, "disposed in an irregular crescent or semi-circle, the arc of which fronts westward, while its chord faces the Indian Ocean." The southernmost was Lake Nyassa, recently discovered by David Livingstone, which flowed south. The second was Chama Lake, described though not seen by the Portuguese traveller Lacerda in 1798—later to be named Bangweulu.[30] The third was Tanganyika, and the fourth the Nyanza Victoria. But Burton pointedly made no speculation about the Nile.

Speke, increasingly irate, wrote to Norton Shaw in November:

> I cannot help thinking what a green thing it was of Burton not remarking that when at Kazeh we were due south of Gondokoro with a Sea according to everybodies [sic] account stretching clean up to it. It is a devil of a bore having to go all over the same stale ground again and I would not attempt doing it on any account if I did not feel quite certain of being able to connect *my* lake with the Nile. For there is no shooting in the country or any other inducement save and except the connection of the Nile and the Lake. We ought never to have gone Westward from Kazeh and the distance that took us to Ujiji and back would have landed us at Gondokoro.[31]

Speke was three to four hundred miles wrong when he said the Nyanza Victoria stretched "clean up" to Gondokoro, as he discovered with great suffering in 1861. Burton was right when he insisted that Speke greatly exaggerated the size of his lake, but he was guilty in the other direction, shrinking it to a lake of virtually no consequence, when his own lengthy conversations with the Arabs at Kazeh had told him otherwise. When Burton published his *Lake Regions in Central Africa* in the early summer of 1860, the ambivalence in his attitude, the desire to be generous counterbalanced by the impulse to anger and denial, was evident to any thoughtful reader. His arguments were confused and somewhat contradictory. And while he made no claim that his own Lake Tanganyika could be the Nile source, neither did he rule it out.

If the public was confused over exactly where Burton stood about the Nile, it knew exactly where he stood about John Speke. He had struck out bluntly in his preface:

> The history of our companionship is simply this:— As he had suffered with me in purse and person at Berberah, in 1855, I thought it but just to offer him the opportunity of renewing an attempt to penetrate Africa. I had no other reasons. I could not expect much from his assistance; he was not a linguist—French and Arabic being equally unknown to him—nor a man of science, nor an accurate astronomical observer. . . . he was unfit for any other but a subordinate capacity. Can I then feel otherwise than indignant, when I find that, after preceding me from Aden to England, with the spontaneous offer, on his part, of not appearing before the Society that originated the Expedition until my return, he had lost no time in taking measures to secure for himself the right of working the field I had opened. . . .[32]

In an appendix to his volumes Burton printed in full the correspondence between himself and Colonel Rigby over the problem of payment to the Arab porters, an act that revealed much of Speke's secretive participation. After this, the friends of both men knew the depth of the chasm between them. The *Lake Regions of Central Africa* was not off the press, however, until after Speke had left for his second expedition, in April 1860, and he did not learn of Burton's attack until he was back in Africa.

Speke had first selected as his companion for the journey an Anglo-Indian officer named Edmund Smyth, describing him enthusiastically to Norton Shaw as "a first rate sportsman . . . and a chap who won't go to the devil, full of pluck and straight-head foremost. . . . a man of precisely my habits, and one entirely after my own heart."[33] As it turned out, it was not Smyth but James Augustus Grant, a handsome, quiet, self-effacing officer formerly of Speke's Indian regiment, who was finally selected. Speke wrote to Shaw on April 15, 1860, "Mother thinks no end of our friend Grant and is immensely pleased with the idea of my having such a good companion." Grant, ideally passive, would later write of their relationship, ". . . not a shade of jealousy or distrust, or even ill-temper, ever came between us during our wanderings and intercourse."[34]

Speke was in Kazeh with Grant in February 1861 when he learned, apparently from Rigby, about what Burton had said of him in his *Lake Regions*. He wrote to his publisher, William Blackwood, in a fury: "I can't stand it no longer, so I have let fly at Burton's eye. . . . Old Grant says the man ought to be hung, an opinion I must say I long ago arrived at. What a vile dastardly wretch not to have taken it out with me at home, when we were there so many months together. But as he has taken up the pen instead of a pistol, we will now have it out so—"[35] What he wrote to Burton privately we do not know. It would be three years before the British public saw his next public attack, in *What Led to the Discovery of the Source of the Nile*.

While Speke and Grant were still in England, busily preparing for the expedition, Burton apparently found life in London increasingly intolerable. There were now to be two great expeditions; he was a member of neither. David Livingstone, who had been feted by the Queen in 1858 for his great discoveries in south and central Africa, had been given a grant of £5,000 to return to the Lake Nyassa area, and had already departed. His book, *Travels and Researches in South Africa*, was a best seller. Speke and Grant would shortly be off with a grant of £2,500. Burton, superior as a linguist, ethnologist, and observer to all three, was going nowhere. Thanks to Isabel Arundell's concern about her hostile mother, he was not even getting married. Sometime in April, apparently just after the *Lake Regions* was in the press, and just before Speke's departure, Burton abruptly left England.

Isabel, who was more sensitive to his corroding exacerbation than either of them realized, described his departure with her usual touch of comic mysticism:

One day in April, 1860, I was walking out with two friends, and a tightening of my heart came over me that I had known before. I went home, and said to my sister, "I am not going to see Richard for some time." She said, "Why, you will see him tomorrow!" "No, I shall not," I said; "I don't know what is the matter." A tap came at the door, and a note with a well-known writing was put into my hand. I knew my fate, and with a deep-drawn breath I opened it. He had left—could not bear the pain of saying goodbye; would be absent for nine months, on a journey to see Salt Lake City. He would then come back, and see whether I had made up my mind to choose between him or my mother, to marry me if I *would*; and if I had not the courage to risk it, he would go back to India, and thence to other explorations, and return no more. I was to take nine months to think about it.

The shock of recognizing the absurdity of her continuing delay sent her reeling. "I was for a long time in bed," she wrote, "and delirious."[36]

Salt Lake City

Man is by nature polygamic whereas woman as a rule is monogamic and poly-androus only when tired of her lover. For the man, as has been truly said, loves the woman, but the love of the woman is for the love of the man.

Richard Burton, *Arabian Nights*

*B*URTON COULD BE very secretive, as Isabel was to learn to her sorrow even after their marriage. He did not confide in her his plans to go to the Mormon Mecca in the desert fastnesses of the Far West, nor apparently did he tell her who was partly responsible for the idea. We learn something of the latter from eighteen manuscript pages now in the British Museum, the only fragments preserved from the burning of Burton's diaries. These pages are from two different journals, one designed for publication, the other intimate.[1] They were written on the S.S. *Canada* beginning on April 21, 1860. Here Burton relates that a friend with whom he had been drinking "off and on for 15 years" begged him to "come with me and drink through America." "I'll drink mint-juleps, brandy-smashes, whisky-skies, gin-sling, cock-tail sherry, cobblers, rum-salads, streaks of lightning, morning-glory," he wrote, "and it'll be a most interesting experiment—I want to see whether after a life of 3 or 4 months, I can drink and eat myself to the level of the aborigines—like you."

"So I replied in the affirmative," Burton wrote. He does not identify this friend, nor describe him further except to say that "generally he exists upon bottles, flasks . . . demijohns, corbozes, graybeards. . . ." The diary fragments do not mention his being on board ship, nor does *The City of the Saints*, Burton's lavishly detailed account of his stage-coach ride from St Joseph, Missouri to San Francisco. The Mormon press, which welcomed Burton cordially on his arrival, made no mention of another officer on the coach save an American, Lieutenant James J. Dana, travelling with his wife and daughter.[2] Still there is a gap in Burton's story from early May until August 4, 1860, about which we know almost nothing save that he visited Secretary of War John B. Floyd in Washington to obtain letters of introduction to the military leaders in the western territories, and that he heard Massachusetts

Senator Charles Sumner speak. Much later, in another book, he tells us that he had wandered through "every state of the Anglo-American Republic." And a casual reference in his *Zanzibar*, written twelve years after his American journey, finally identifies his companion as his good friend from Aden, Lieutenant John Steinhaeuser. "We wandered together over the United States," Burton wrote, with no further details.[3] It seems likely that Steinhaeuser joined him somewhere in America and went back to Aden before Burton left "the United States" for Mormon and Indian territory. Why Burton chose not to mention him in *The City of the Saints* remains a mystery. Isabel, who must have known that they travelled together, chose not to mention the fact either.

Though Burton's belated identification was casual, his relationship to Steinhaeuser was not. He dedicated *Zanzibar* to Steinhaeuser's memory, and wrote with special candour:

> No unkind thought, much less unfriendly word, ever broke our fair companionship. . . . He was one of the very few who, through evil as well as through good report, disdained to abate an iota of his friendship, and whose regard was never warmer than when all the little world looked its coldest. . . . he died suddenly of apoplexy at Berne, when crossing Switzerland to revisit his native land. At that time I was wandering about the Brazil, and I well remember dreaming, on what proved to be the date of his death, that a tooth suddenly fell to the ground, followed by a crash of blood. Such a friend, indeed, becomes part of oneself. I still feel a pang as my hand traces these lines.[4]

Such a revelation of emotional involvement is extremely rare in Burton's books. But there is evidence in his letters, and particularly in the eighteen pages of diary written aboard the S.S. *Canada*, that Burton was intensely involved even if only momentarily not only with primitive peoples, as we have seen in Africa, but with practically everyone who crossed his path. Here in the intimate journal fragments, written in a script so illegible it was almost a code, we see his responsiveness to strangers, and his frequent fluctuation from interest and quick affection to momentary hatred.

He expressed delight when awakening the first morning on board ship to see "a beautiful face opposite me . . . a lovely glow upon her." It was the reflection of the stewardess in the cabin mirror. He detested the ship's captain instantly. "The Capt. is a d—d d—h of a d—l. . . . I think he is a liar." Later, when he suspected the Captain of making fun of him, he wrote, "I *hate* that man." He described the May Day dance on deck, where he won the "sweetest" of the girls by a lucky toss, only to lose her to the Captain. "I could have cried with vexation," he wrote, "but I hope that I appeared calm." He quickly became acquainted with a Mr R—, whom he described as "a very handsome

Burton's diary enroute to Salt Lake City. This is one of eighteen pages, the only known surviving extracts from Burton's forty-year collection of daily journals.

man though middle-aged and very polite." By May 3 he was already at odds with him, writing, "*I wish this journey was over.* Only imagine that wretch R is a widower with 3 children, one nearly grown up— how could I have thought him handsome. I refused to walk with him this morning and I thought he looked disappointed."

Most surprising is the diary revelation of his sensitivity to ridicule. When he dressed for the May Day dance in a new poplin jacket, and the stewardess noted that it was the same material as the gown she had been married in, Burton's evening was ruined. "My poplin *did* look so ridiculous," he wrote, like any blushing adolescent. Later, when they landed in Nova Scotia and visited Halifax, he commented on the civility of the people as follows: "Accustomed as a steamer passenger and tourist to the jeers and mockery of every woman and child . . . I could not detect in a single countenance an expression of contempt."

There is no reference to Isabel Arundell in the diary fragments but much evidence of melancholy. "What a misanthrope I am," he wrote. Later, quoting what he called the "copy-book wisdom, 'Man must eat to live not live to eat,'" he added, "A salad, a youngster may have something better to do, after 40 a man should eat and live, after 60 he hasn't any pleasure in life but to eat. As for the other excitements, 'twixt 60 and 70 its all dead weight."

Three months later, when Burton boarded the stagecoach at St Joseph, Missouri to begin the dusty trip across the great plains, his depression had long since vanished. *The City of the Saints*, whose tone must certainly reflect the journal entries, is one of his most cheerful books. This journey was the speediest of all Burton's explorations; he spent three weeks on the coach to Salt Lake City, arriving on August 28, 1860; he spent another three weeks among the Mormons and then was off to California. He left San Francisco by steamer for Mexico and Panama on November 15, 1860. Yet in a hundred days in the west he amassed enough material to fill 700 pages. Not content with this, he edited a new edition of a celebrated guide-book to the west, Randolph B. Marcy's *The Prairie Traveller, A Hand-book for overland expeditions*, adding footnotes on the basis of his own experience.[5]

On this expedition Burton was travelling a well-rutted road; he was simply one more in a series of distinguished visitors curious about the polygamous empire ruled over by Brigham Young. The French botanist Jules Remy, travelling with the British naturalist Julius Brenchley, had visited it in 1855, and they had together written a perceptive book. William Chandless had written a friendly account in 1857. Editor Horace Greeley had filled many columns of his *New York Tribune* describing his Mormon interviews in 1859. Burton came in 1860; Mark Twain would follow in 1861, Fritz Hugh Ludlow, 1864, and Ralph Waldo Emerson, 1871, all save Emerson writing about the experience. But none wrote as sagacious and thorough a study as Burton.

The Mormons were considered a thorny problem in America, where their polygamy was universally deplored. The federal government had almost entered into a war against a Mormon citizen army in 1857, and now kept a contingent of troops stationed near Salt Lake City. Mormon history almost from the beginning had been punctuated by persecution, bloodshed, and massacre. Ever since the murder of the Mormon founder, Joseph Smith, in Illinois in 1844, and the subsequent dramatic exodus of the whole society from the temple city of Nauvoo on the Mississippi River to Great Salt Lake, the sect had flourished beyond the wildest predictions. Brigham Young had become virtual sovereign over an immense area extending from the Rockies to the Sierra Nevada, and from Oregon Territory south to the Colorado River. Active proselyters, the Mormons had persuaded 30,000 converts in Britain and Scandinavia to emigrate to Deseret Territory between 1840 and 1860. *The Times*, September 4, 1855, had estimated the total number of

Mormons in Great Britain as between 30,000 and 40,000, describing the religion as "the most singular phenomenon of modern times," a conglomeration of "Judaism, Mohammedism, socialism, despotism, and the grossest superstition."

Burton was interested in the American Indian almost as much as in the Mormons. His account is interlarded with lively descriptions of Indian ethnology, including a clinical essay on the art of scalping, a comparison of African and Indian totemism, and a detailed account of Indian sign language, which of course he added instantly to his linguistic collection. Along with detailed descriptions of the Sioux and Dakota villages are botanical and geological notes, and ironic asides on the nature of man. His comparisons with the ethnology of other native peoples make for a richness and sophistication rare in overland journey accounts.

The red man, not red at all as he pointed out, reminded him of "a Tartar or an Afghan after a summer march," or the Mongolians he had seen in northern India. The Indian rode his horse "like the Abyssinian eunuch, as if born upon and bred to become part of the animal." Independence Rock he found had a surprising resemblance to Jiwe la Mkoa, the Round Rock in eastern Unyamwezi, and Devil's Gate was very like the Brèche de Roland in the Pyrenees. The Sioux practice of "cutting, or more generally biting off, the nose-tip" of an adulterous woman did not surprise him; he had seen the same practice in Hindustan.[6]

Characteristically, Burton preferred the red man who had been least touched by the white. Though he himself delighted in burying his identity in an alien culture, the spectacle of others crossing over into a different society always troubled him, whether it was the Hindu in Goa who had become Christian, the African who wore the white man's clothes, or the mountain man in the Rockies, who, Burton wrote, "betrays a remarkable aptitude for facile descent into savagery." The Indians closest to the emigrant routes had become, he said, beggars, liars, horse-stealers, and prostitutes. "I do not believe that an Indian of the plains ever became a Christian," he wrote. "He must first be humanised, then civilised, and lastly Christianised; and, as has been said before, I doubt his surviving the operation." He refused to romanticize the mountain men, calling them superstitious, indolent, and transcendental liars. Still he could report with sympathetic understanding, "I have heard of a man riding eighty miles—forty into camp and forty out—in order to enjoy the sweet delights of a lie." Seeing that the Indians, despite the U.S. Bureau of Indian Affairs, were still bribed and cheated by the white traders, and that poverty, disease, and debauchery were rapidly thinning the tribes, he predicted correctly that the Indians would soon be scattered to the most inhospitable regions of America, "as the grey rat in Europe expelled the black rat."

When the stagecoach emerged from the Wasatch Mountain canyon and stopped for a view of the great Mormon valley below, Burton was truly awed. "This lovely panorama of green and azure and gold," he wrote, "this land, fresh as it were from the hands of God. . . . Switzerland and Italy lay side by side. . . . and then bounding the far horizon, like a band of burnished silver, the Great Salt Lake, that still innocent Dead Sea." Among the Mormon immigrants looking out over the same scene, like the Hajis of Mecca and Medina, he witnessed laughter and tears, psalm-singing and hysterics. "It is indeed no wonder," he wrote, "that the children dance, that strong men cheer and shout, and that nervous women broken with fatigue and hope deferred, scream and faint; that the ignorant should fondly believe that the 'Spirit of God pervades the very atmosphere,' and that Zion on the tops of the mountains is nearer heaven than other parts of earth."[7]

Burton was formally welcomed by the Mormon *Deseret News*, August 29, 1860, and treated with great respect throughout the city. During his three week sojourn he sampled everything permitted; he talked to Mormons and gentiles; he attended Mormon services and dances; he looked at prices in the stores, wandered through the cemeteries, and read a prodigious amount of Mormon and anti-Mormon literature[8]—Burton is unique among scholars writing on Mormonism in providing a long bibliography and telling the books he has *not* read—and he interviewed Brigham Young.

Stories of his brawling and drunkenness in the Mormon capital, published in 1930 by the nephew of Lt James J. Dana, who with his wife and daughter accompanied Burton in the stagecoach west, are patently apocryphal,[9] although Burton made no secret of his affection for whisky—tested in the West, he said, by the distance a man could walk after tasting it. The editor of the *Deseret News* bade him a courteous farewell, writing on October 3, 1860, "As far as we have heard, Capt. Burton has been one of the few gentlemen who have passed through Utah without leaving behind him a disagreeable *Souvenir*. The Captain has seen Utah without goggles; we wish him a safe journey."

Polygamy, of course, excited Burton most, and he found it amusing to compare the Mormon harems with the varieties he had seen in Africa and the Near East.

The Mormon household has been described by its enemies as a hell of envy, hatred, and malice, a den of murder and suicide. The same has been said of the Moslem harem. Both, I believe, suffer from the assertions of prejudice or ignorance. The temper of the new is so far superior to that of the old country, that, incredible as the statement may appear, rival wives do dwell together in amity; and do quote the proverb "the more the merrier" . . . . I believe that many a "happy English home" is far stormier despite the presence of monogamy.

The Mormon women were not depressed and degraded, as many believed, he wrote, but "exceedingly pretty and attractive, especially Miss —." "I looked in vain for the outhouse-harems in which certain romancers concerning things Mormon had informed me that wives are kept, like any other stock. I presently found this but one of a multitude of delusions." With what was probably a gentle jab at Isabel, he noted that the beauty of the English women—"a sex which is early taught and soon learns to consider itself creation's cream"—improved in Utah.

Burton reported the conventional Mormon "physiological" defence of polygamy, that it abolished prostitution, concubinage, celibacy, and infanticide. "The old maid is, as she ought to be," he said, "an unknown entity." Mormons insisted, he went on, that "all sensuality in the married state is strictly forbidden beyond the requisite for ensuring progeny," and pointed out slyly that this made polygamy, for the males at least, "a positive necessity."

He examined the phenomenon of the ready acceptance of polygamy by Mormon women, which many found inexplicable, and which Burton was certain could not be explained merely by "promises of Paradise" or "threats of annihilation." He described on the one hand a certain type of British and American woman, "petted and spoiled," "set upon an uncomfortable and unnatural eminence . . . aggravated by a highly nervous temperament, small cerebellum, constitutional frigidity, and extreme delicacy of fibre," and contrasted her with the Mormon wife, supreme in her domesticity and motherhood, surrounded by other women and masses of children, preferring the society of women to men in any case. To annotate this he quoted in full the proud defence of polygamy by Mrs Belinda Pratt, who held that "nature has constituted the female differently from the male; and for a different purpose," namely, motherhood, that she needs "relief at regular periods, in order that her system may be kept pure and healthy." Mrs Pratt shared her husband with six other wives; there were altogether twenty-five children. Burton admitted that Belinda Pratt showed "little heart or natural affection," but applauded "the soundness of her physiology," implying that many women were attracted to Mormonism because for them it meant less sex than monogamous marriage.[10]

Though Burton was later accused of defending polygamy—this with special indignation by Isabel—he understood what was wrong with the average polygamous marriage in the city of the Saints. "The choice egotism of the heart called Love . . . subsides into a calm and unimpassioned domestic attachment: romance and reverence are transferred, with the true Mormon concentration, from Love and Liberty to Religion and the Church. The consent of the first wife to a rival is seldom refused, and a *ménage à trois*, in the Mormon sense of the phrase, is fatal to the development of that tender tie which must be confined to two. In its stead there is household comfort, affection, circumspect friendship, and domestic discipline." The result, he said, was a pervasive atmosphere in Salt Lake City which could best be described as "gloom."

Moslem polygamy, on the other hand, he believed to be based on a reverence for the body. Moslems "do their best to countermine the ascetic ideas inherent in Christianity, are not ashamed of the sensual appetite but rather the reverse." While readily admitting that polygamy would be "a sore trial" to Europeans, he insisted that "in the East, where the sex is far more delicate, where a girl is brought up in polygamy, where religious reasons separate her from her husband, during pregnancy and lactation, for three successive years . . . the case assumes a very different aspect and the load, if burden it be, falls comparatively light."[11]

Mormon polygamy, he pointed out, was essentially Puritanical. The leaders decried sensuality in all its aspects, and set extreme penalties for adultery—three to twenty years in prison, with fines ranging from $300 to $1,000. "I reached this place about a week ago, and am living in the odour of sanctity," he wrote to Norton Shaw on September 7, 1860, "—a pretty strong one it is, too! prophets, apostles, *et hoc genus omne*."[12] He noted in his volume that "a suspicion of immorality is more hateful than a reputation of bloodshed," and concluded that "in point of mere morality the Mormon community is perhaps purer than any other of equal numbers."

When Burton asked formally for an interview with Brigham Young, he presented a personal introduction from Alfred Cumming, the federally appointed governor of the territory, who was on good terms with the Mormon leader. Ushered into Young's study in the Beehive House, Burton was astonished by his youthful appearance; though fifty-nine, he appeared to be about forty-five. With his marvellous eye for detail Burton came away from the interview with a total recall of face, hands, hair, clothes, mannerisms, and an astute judgment of his character. "The first impression left upon my mind by this short *séance*," he wrote, "was that the Prophet is no common man, and that he has none of the weakness and vanity which characterise the common uncommon man." He was impressed by the absence of bigotry, dogmatism, and fanaticism, by his cold, "somewhat bloodless" manner, by his sense of power. "There is a total absence of pretension in his manner, and he has been so long used to power that he cares nothing for its display. The arts by which he rules the heterogeneous mass of conflicting elements are indomitable will, profound secrecy, and uncommon astuteness."[13]

Brigham Young in his turn seems to have found Burton impressive, and later escorted him about the city. When Burton asked if he could be admitted to the Mormon fold, Young replied with a twinkle, "I think you've done that sort of thing once before, Captain." They ascended the hill north of the city, where Young pointed out the chief buildings below, including the houses of his leading men and his own gabled Lion House, in which he kept many of his wives. At this point Burton complained facetiously that he had come all the way to Salt Lake City without a wife only to find that all the ladies had been captured by Mormon men. He waved his right hand toward the lake, saying mournfully, "Water, water, everywhere"—and then his left towards the city—"and not a drop to drink." Brigham Young laughed heartily, and they parted, apparently with great mutual respect.[14]

In contrasting Brigham Young with Joseph Smith, the founder of Mormonism, Burton described the former as "the St Paul of the New Dispensation: true and sincere," giving "point and energy, and consistency to the somewhat disjointed, turbulent, and unforeseeing fanaticism of Mr Joseph Smith."[15] Burton found the character of the latter more elusive. Smith, who had been killed by a mob in 1844, was dismissed by most non-Mormon writers of the time as a charlatan: Remy, for example, called him "a mere impostor and speculator," but Burton took a more subtle and compassionate approach. Having himself played impostor many times, Burton knew the pleasure of disguise and pretence. But he had stepped facilely into and out of his disguises; there was always purpose and control, as with an actor. Though admitting the "dear delights" of "finessing through life," and "playing a part till by habit it becomes a nature," Burton felt that mere imposture alone could not explain the phenomenon of Joseph Smith. He chose to characterize him rather as "a man of rude genius, of high courage, of invincible perseverance, fired by zeal, of great tact, of religious fervour, of extraordinary firmness, and of remarkable talent in governing men."

Burton made no attempt to explain the writing of *The Book of Mormon*, said to have been a translation from golden plates temporarily loaned to Joseph Smith by an angel, but did not fall into the error, then almost universal among non-Mormon scholars, of supporting the theory that it was a remake of an old manuscript by one Solomon Spaulding. Reconciling Mormon and non-Mormon views on Joseph Smith he rightly saw to be hopeless. "The Mormons declare that if they knew their prophet to be an impostor, they could still love, respect, and follow him in this life to the next. The Gentiles, I can see, would not accept him, even if he were proposed to them by a spirit from the other world."[16]

The *Athenaeum*, reviewing *The City of the Saints* on November 30,

1861, complained, "Captain Burton is one of the best travellers we have. One would like him better if he had a little more faith and a little less credulity." Actually Burton was one of the least credulous observers of the Mormon scene. He looked at it with immense curiosity and absolutely without reproach. That he defended the Mormons against the grossest charges hurled at them—scouting the stories of Danite atrocities and judiciously giving the Mormon as well as the non-Mormon versions of the Mountain Meadows massacre*—did not, however, make him their champion. On the contrary, he disparaged their secularism and levelling materialism, and wrote ironically of their "mysticism and marvel-love." When he pointed out to Mormon leaders that their religion was essentially an agglomeration of Jewish mysticism, millennialism, transcendentalism, and freemasonry, plus certain Moslem practices, they replied that their religion embraced all truth, "come whence it may." "The mind of man," he concluded, "most loves those errors and delusions into which it has become self-persuaded, and is most fanatic concerning the irrationalities and supernaturalities to which it has bowed its own reason."[17]

On September 20, 1860, Burton left Zion for the Pacific coast. "The road is full of Indians and other scoundrels," he wrote to Dr Norton Shaw, "but I've had my hair cropped so short that my scalp is not worth having." At American Fork he met Porter Rockwell, the celebrated former bodyguard of Joseph Smith, whose reputation for assassination had assumed mythical proportions. They swapped stories, and tested each other's capacity for "squar" tumblers of whisky—variously designated in the West as Jersey lightning, strychnine, and tarantula-juice. Rockwell advised him to shun the direct route west, not because of Indians but rather because of the white desperadoes who infested the route, which, he said, was about as fit for travelling as "h—ll for a powder magazine."

The journey was not without adventure. The stagecoach driver sighted Indian fires, and fearing an ambush, hurried on to Egan's Station, which they found reduced to a chimney stack and a few charred posts. It had been fired by the "Gosh-Yutas" in revenge for the killing of seventeen of their tribe the week before. Wolves had torn up the Indian corpses, and mutilated remains projected above the snow. Although there was far more violence and excitement in Carson City

* The Mormons at this time blamed the Indians for the massacre of 120 immigrants en route to California in 1857. Non-Mormon accounts, indicating that several fanatical Mormon leaders in the southern part of the territory had, in fact, planned the massacre and carried it out with the aid of Indians, were later shown to have been accurate. See Juanita Brooks' definitive study, *The Mountain Meadows Massacre* (Stanford University Press, 1950).

than in Salt Lake City—"My informants declared that in and about Carson a dead man for breakfast was the rule"—Burton lingered only three days and then went on to San Francisco.

He returned to England by way of Panama. Almost nothing of this portion of the journey is reported; Burton seemed eager to get back to England. Certainly the Mormon scene did not weaken his interest in marriage; on the contrary, the cleanliness and domesticity delighted him, for he contrasted it frequently with the slovenliness of the non-Mormon stagecoach stations. The sight of Christian men living contentedly with several attractive women, often English women at that, may even have helped to crystallize his determination to pursue his courtship with at least one.

The First Seven Months

I have undertaken a very peculiar man; I have asked a difficult mission of God, and that is to give me that man's body and soul.

Isabel Burton, in her devotional book, 1861

DURING RICHARD'S ABSENCE, Isabel had been systematically grooming herself for a wild and strenuous life. She had spent the summer at a farmhouse learning to cook, clean, care for chickens and horses, even milking cows. Back in London she had implored her friend, Dr George Bird, to teach her to fence. "Why?" he had asked in astonishment. "To defend Richard," she had replied, "when he and I are attacked in the wilderness together."

Learning of his arrival in London, she rushed back from the country, where she had been spending the Christmas holidays at the Yorkshire castle of Sir Clifford and Lady Constable. As Isabel described it, the question of their marriage was now settled very quickly:

As soon as we met, and had our talk, he said, "I have waited for five years. The first three were inevitable . . . but the last two were not. Our lives are being spoiled by the unjust prejudices of your mother, and it is for you to consider whether you have not already done your duty in sacrificing two of the best years of your life out of respect to her. If *once* you *really* let me go, mind, I shall never come back, because I shall know that you have not got the strength of character which *my* wife must have. Now, you must make up your mind to choose between your mother and me. If you choose me, we marry, and I stay; if not, I go back to India, and on other explorations, and I return no more. Is your answer ready?"
I said, "Quite. I marry you this day three weeks, let who will say nay."[1]

Isabel's father approved, as did her brothers and sisters, all of them no doubt acutely conscious that Isabel was now a spinsterish twenty-nine. But Mrs Arundell only said nastily that she would never attend the ceremony nor grant permission to her daughters to do so. Burton would later write with bitterness of "the abominable egotism and cruelty of the English mother, who disappoints her daughter's womanly cravings in order to keep her at home for her own comfort."[2]

Fearful that any shock would precipitate a paralytic stroke in her mother, Isabel decided finally to marry Richard in an almost secret ceremony and to inform her parents "at a suitable time." She prepared herself for the marriage with much prayer and meditation, confining in her devotional book sentiments Richard might well have found alarming: "I have undertaken a very peculiar man; I have asked a difficult mission of God, and that is to give me that man's body and soul. It is a grand mission; and after ten years and a half of prayer God has given it to me." By way of consecrating her success, she drew up a remarkable covenant: Rules for My Guidance as a Wife. There were seventeen altogether, several of which suggest that her infatuation was by no means as blind as her mother feared. "Let him find in the wife what he and many other men fancy is only to be found in a mistress," she wrote. "Keep pace with the times, that he may not weary of you. . . . Hide his faults from *every one*. . . . Never permit any one to speak disrespectfully of him before you. . . . Never answer when he finds fault; and never reproach him when he is in the wrong, *especially when he tells you of it*. . . . Never ask him *not* to do anything. . . . Do not bother him with religious talk. . . . cultivate your own good health, spirits, and nerves, to counteract his naturally melancholy turn. . . . let nothing ever be at a standstill; nothing would weary him like stagnation."[3]

At 9 am on January 22, 1861, the day of the marriage, a cab drew up outside the Arundell house in London. "I went downstairs with a beating heart," Isabel wrote, "after I had knelt in my own room, and said a fervent prayer that they might bless me, and if they did, I would take it as a sign. I was so nervous, I could hardly stand. When I went in, mother kissed me and said, 'Good-bye child, God bless you.' I went to my father's bedside, and knelt down and said good-bye. 'God bless you, my darling,' he said, and put his hand out of the bed and laid it on my head. I was too much overcome to speak, and one or two tears ran down my cheeks, and I remember as I passed down I kissed the door outside."[4]

Instead of going to visit friends in the country, as she had indicated to her parents, she went to the home of Dr George Bird and his sister Alice—who had promised "to throw a mantle of respectability over the marriage"—changed into a fawn-coloured dress, a black lace cloak and white bonnet, and went off with them to the Bavarian Catholic Church in Warwick Street. "Richard was waiting on the doorstep for me," she wrote, "and as we went in he took holy water, and made a *very large* sign of the Cross." He was informally dressed in a rough shooting coat, his niece tells us, "and with a cigar in his mouth, bravado to hide his deadly nervousness."[5] There were eight in the wedding party, including the Registrar—essential in the case of mixed marriages—and the priest, Dr Hearne, Vicar-General, who performed the ceremony.

Afterwards at the wedding breakfast, when Burton was describing the fight at Berbera which left the scar on his cheek, Dr Bird tried clumsily to bait him. "Now, Burton, tell me; how do you feel when you have killed a man?"

"Oh, quite jolly, doctor!" came the drawled reply, "How do you?"

Isabel was able to keep the secret of their marriage from her mother for only a fortnight. Then two of her aunts reported that she had been seen "going into a bachelor lodging." Mrs Arundell wrote in agony to her husband, who was visiting in the country, "that a dreadful misfortune had happened in the family." Henry Arundell, weary of the pretence, wired back, "She is married to Dick Burton and thank God for it." Then he sent her the graceful letter Burton had mailed him on the date of the marriage:

> My dear Father
>
> I have committed a highway robbery by marrying your daughter Isabel at Warwick St Chapel and before the registrar—the details she is writing to her mother.
>
> It only remains for me to say that I have no ties nor liasons of any kind, that the marriage was perfectly legal and "respectable." I want no money with Isabel; I can work, and it will by my care that Time shall bring you nothing to regret.
>
> I am
>
> Yours sincerely
Richard F. Burton

Isabel wrote that her mother now acquiesced, "received Richard in the nicest way," and asked their pardon "for flying in the face of God and opposing what she now knew to be His will. . . . It was not long before . . . she loved him as much as her own sons."[6] Georgiana Stisted was certain she knew better. Mrs Arundell "never forgave her son-in-law," she wrote. "Almost the last time I saw her she exclaimed, in answer to some remark from her daughter, 'Dick is no relation of mine.'"[7]

Burton's possessive sister and her daughter were no less dismayed at the marriage than Mrs Arundell. Georgiana—who never married—in writing her passionately defensive biography of her uncle, seemed to be drawing from a bottomless well of indignation. "Looking back at this match," she wrote, "it is clear that Burton committed as serious an imprudence as when he sent Speke alone to search for the Victoria Nyanza." She attacked Isabel's "fatal want of tact and judgment," "flimsy conventual education," "very excitable brain" and "deficiency in reasoning faculties." Georgiana found her Catholicism particularly intolerable because she was always bubbling over about it. "Though a Romanist, she need not have ranged herself with the extreme or Jesuitical party, nor allowed her mind to sink into depths of superstition almost incredible in Burton's wife. He often looked, oh! so sad and weary when hearing for the twentieth time how a leaden image had tumbled out of her pocket during a long ride, and then miraculously returned to its despairing owner." To Mrs Lynn Linton Georgiana wrote of Richard's "vain and bigoted wife," saying that "Dick Burton's chance of any great fortune in life vanished when he married Isabel Arundell."[8]

Nevertheless in the beginning both families discreetly kept their dismay private, and feted the couple properly. It was not the snobbish relatives on either side, however, but Burton's good friends who turned the marriage into a triumph. Monckton Milnes gave a party with Isabel as "bride of the evening," and invited Lord Palmerston, the Prime Minister. Monckton Milnes, as Henry Adams put it, was "the first wit in London and a maker of men—of a great many men. A word from him went far. An invitation to his breakfast table went farther. Behind his almost Falstaffian mask and laugh of Silenus, he carried a fine, broad and high intelligence which no one questioned. . . . he went everywhere, knew everybody, talked of everything and had the ear of Ministers. . . . He was a voracious reader, a strong critic, an art connoisseur in certain directions, but above all he was a man of the world by profession and loved the contacts—perhaps the collisions—of society."

The Milnes party, as Isabel described it in sweet triumph, "settled the question of our position. Lord Palmerston gave me his arm, and he introduced Richard and me to all the people we had not previously known, and my relatives clustered around us as well. I was allowed to put my name down for a Drawing-room. And Lady Russell, now the Dowager, presented me at Court 'on my marriage.'" This started the Burtons on a round of parties at the great houses of London. Happily, too, Burton's *Lake Regions of Central Africa*, which had sold badly at first, was now avidly purchased. Its sale was aided by the cumulative effect of many favourable reviews. All of this contributed to Isabel's description of the first seven months of their marriage as "uninterrupted bliss."[9]

Isabel went into her marriage with three ambitions concerning Richard: to make him powerful, respectable, and Catholic. She confided in her diary: "Some understand Ambition as Title, Wealth, Estates; I understand it as Fame, Name, Power."[10] Power was impossible without position. Burton had seen his inheritance of £16,000 shrink as a result of his explorations and unfortunate investments to £4,000. He now sought a Foreign Office post, hoping to be sent to Damascus. But the most that pressure from his and Isabel's friends could secure was the consulship of Fernando Po, a disease-ridden Spanish island off the coast of West Africa, used by the British navy as a base for suppressing the slave trade. Burton described the offer in a letter to Milnes on March 20, 1861 as a "governmental crumb," which he would accept in hopes one day of getting a "governmental loaf."[11]

Hoping to keep secure his Indian army pension, Burton asked that he be permitted to continue on half pay, as Rigby did at Zanzibar. He had not reckoned with his India Office enemies, who remembered his critical memorandum of 1848, who disapproved of his quarrel with Rigby, and who were now furious at his recent publication of letters that made several of them look like fools. En route to Africa in December 1856, Burton had picked up warnings of trouble in Jidda, and had strongly urged increasing British naval strength in the Red Sea to protect British subjects in the area, as well as to put down the slave trade. Instead of sending the letter to his superiors in Bombay, he had mailed it to the Royal Geographical Society. As a result he had been officially rebuked for his "want of discretion, and due respect for the authorities" to whom he was technically subordinate. Twenty months later almost every Christian in Jidda was massacred, including the British consul.

In his *Lake Regions of Central Africa* Burton published both his warning letter, and the carping letter of censure, as well as press accounts of the massacre. The India Office retaliated now by cutting him off the Indian list altogether. Thus Isabel learned for the first time what she was to learn over and again, that her husband would pay heavily for his disregard of protocol and his eagerness to publish every hot-tempered exchange with officialdom. Several Burton biographers have held that it was the old Karachi brothel study that cost him his pay and pension, but they ignore his habit of baiting his superiors. This habit was not promising for a career with the Foreign Office, where discretion if not sycophancy was the first key to advancement.

Making Burton respectable was a far more difficult undertaking than making him powerful. Here one suspects that Isabel, with her cheerful, child-like capacity for self-delusion and fantasy, had no suspicion whatever that she had taken on the labours of Sisyphus. She knew that he belonged to three clubs, the sedate Garrick, the Bohemian Arundel Club, and the Beefsteak, which attracted newspapermen like George Augustus Sala of the *Illustrated London News*, Sir Francis Burnand of *Punch*, Edmund Yates of the *World*, William Russell of *The Times*, and

Carlo Pellegrini, who made wicked caricatures for *Vanity Fair*, including one of Burton. Later Burton would organize the Cannibal Club, a frankly crack-brained offshoot of the Royal Geographical Society. In all these clubs there was prestige, and a tolerance of eccentricity.

The society Burton sought most, however, during his first seven months of marriage, was that of Monckton Milnes, and it was to his London house and to his manor "Fryston" in the country that he went with the greatest eagerness. He made Milnes a gift of his passport to Mecca, and dedicated to him *The City of the Saints*. Milnes, who was twelve years older than Burton, responded with affection and hospitality—he wrote admiringly of *The City of the Saints* for the *Edinburgh Review*—and admitted him to his most intimate circle of friends.

Monckton Milnes had made Fryston the English Mecca for poets, wits, and eccentrics as well as politicians and journalists. He welcomed those artists and men of letters rigidly excluded by Lady Palmerston—Thomas Carlyle, Algernon Swinburne, William Thackeray, Coventry Patmore, Aubrey de Vere—and gave them free use of one of the great private libraries of the world, containing his collection of poetry, fiction, biography, memoirs and literary criticism in four languages. At Fryston, Isabel wrote, "we met all that was worth meeting of rank and fashion, beauty and wit, and *especially* all the most talented people in the world. . . . I can remember Vambéry telling us Hungarian tales and I can remember Richard cross-legged on a cushion, reciting and reading 'Omar el Khayyam' alternately in Persian and English, and chanting the call to prayer, 'Allahhu Akbar.' "[12] Milnes delighted in bringing together wildly improbable dinner companions, like Burton and the Archbishop of York. Carlyle described him as the "Perpetual President of the Heaven and Hell Amalgamation Society."

Isabel probably did not know that Monckton Milnes's library contained also the greatest collection of erotic literature in England, including many works on flagellation and school punishments. He owned not only the complete published works of the Marquis de Sade, but also many of his manuscripts. Much of the pornographic material came from Fred Hankey in Paris, part of it smuggled in in diplomatic bags. Whether Hankey introduced Milnes to anything besides erotic books is not clear, and his biographer, James Pope-Hennessy, does not venture to speculate on it, writing only that Milnes "was incapable of passionate love," but also "incapable of real evil," that he was "given to occasional black moods, writing in his commonplace book on one occasion, 'There are moments when I feel that nothing is real but evil, nothing true but pain.' "[13] In his marriage he seemed to enjoy comfort, stability, and affection. He had three children, and his wife apparently radiated a light-hearted innocence and "irresistible zest for living."

Only her closest friends knew that she suffered from headaches and melancholia.

Monckton Milnes kept Burton's letters over the years, and it is from this collection, now in Trinity College, Cambridge, that we learn something of Burton's at least peripheral involvement with a small group of men who found excitement in practices that would have horrified Isabel. We have seen that Burton first met Fred Hankey at Milnes' suggestion in the summer of 1859. Burton's curiosity about this sadist continued for many years. "Remember me with love to . . . Bellamy and Hankey," he wrote to Milnes from Fernando Po, April 26, 1862, ". . . when shall we all meet again." "Anything of Hankey?" he asked on March 29, 1863, "Any news of Fred Hankey?" in 1871, and finally in 1873 he wrote, "Fred Hankey must nearly have been burnt out." Burton even dedicated the eighth volume of the *Arabian Nights* to Hankey's memory, writing:

My dear Fred,

If there be such a thing as "continuation," you will see these lines in the far Spirit-land and you will find that your old friend has not forgotten you and Annie.

When Edmond and Jules de Goncourt visited Hankey in the spring of 1862, they described him as about thirty years old, lean, tall, yellow-skinned, with a languid, effeminate manner, looking like "an emaciated and ecstatic young priest attending on a bishop in an old painting . . . exquisitely polite . . . noticeable for an especial sweetness or gentleness of manner." But the sweetness was dispelled when he held out an unbound volume telling them that the human skin for binding it, *"un peau de jeune fille,"* was still being tanned, a lengthy process taking six months. "It was not an interesting skin," he added, as it had not been stripped from a living victim, and added happily that he had a friend, Dr Barth, who promised to bring him *"un peau comme ça . . . pendant la vie."*[14]

"Doctor Barth" was clearly an error for Richard Burton, who had promised to bring Hankey a skin from the annual human sacrifices in the African kingdom of Dahomey, which he planned to visit in 1863. Later, as we shall see, though he saw enough fresh corpses to sicken him, he avoided making good his promise, writing to Monckton Milnes on March 24, 1864, "Poor old Hankey, I did so want to get him a human hide . . . and I failed."[15]

Much of this was bravado on Burton's part, and a Rabelaisian delight in shocking; much of it stemmed from his insistence on collecting every conceivable specimen of human behaviour for his own writings. There is no evidence that Burton had any continued involvement in sado-masochistic practices. He found Sade's works revolting. "I shall have nothing to do with . . . Justine," he wrote when a friend suggested his translating the work. "The French of Dr Sade is monstrous enough and a few pages choke me off, but what bile would it be in brutal Anglo Saxon?"[16] Still he took something more than a bibliophile's interest in flagellation, and he had a lifelong and intense interest in mutilation—specifically male and female castration. Thomas Wright tells us that a story circulated in special circles in London that Burton had been caught in a Turkish harem, apparently during the Crimean War, "and allowed to escape only after suffering the usual indescribable penalty." "As this was the solitary story that really annoyed Burton," he continued, "we think it our duty to say that conclusive documentary evidence exists proving that whether or not he ever broke into a harem, he most certainly underwent no deprivation."[17]

Of all the friends to whom Monckton Milnes introduced the Burtons in these months, none was more excited by Richard than Algernon Charles Swinburne. The twenty-four-year-old poet, whose talent was just beginning to be recognised, would have been drawn to Burton in any case. He was fascinated by the Near East; he shared Burton's contempt for European religions, and in erudition was a near match for the older man. As it turned out, he was also electrified by Burton's vitality and Satanic aura. Henry Adams, who was also invited to several of the famous Milnes breakfasts in April 1861, described Swinburne in his *Education* as small and volatile, with violent red hair—"a tropical bird, high-crested, long-beaked, quick-moving, with rapid utterance and screams of humour, quite unlike any English lark or nightingale. One could hardly call him a crimson macaw among owls, and yet no ordinary contrast availed. . . . The idea that one has actually met a real genius dawns slowly on a Boston mind, but it made entry at last."

Burton, who counted himself an incipient poet, was flattered by Swinburne's admiration, and no doubt immediately sensitive to his effeminate nature. Isabel must have guessed at once, as most women did, that he was totally uninterested in her sex. But she could not know what Burton apparently learned quickly, that Swinburne was obsessed with flagellation. Like many other English schoolboys, Swinburne had discovered when at Eton, where his tutor prepared the flogging room with scents, that being caned could be sexually exciting. "*This* I call real delicate torment," he wrote. "Once, before giving me a swishing that I had the marks of for more than a month . . . he let me saturate my face with eau-de-Cologne. . . . but he was a stunning tutor."[18] According to Sir Edmund Gosse, Swinburne's friend and biographer, the young poet's mania for flagellation was stimulated by his reading of Sade's works in 1861 at the home of Monckton Milnes. Swinburne went as far as to say that the day would come when statues would be erected to Sade on the walls of every city, and sacrifices would be offered up at their bases. And it was in this summer that he began to frequent an establishment in St John's Wood, where two women "consented to chastise" gentlemen for large sums.[19]

Swinburne's friends and biographers blame Milnes for introducing the poet to Sade, and Burton for introducing him to brandy. Apparently, however, Burton saw Swinburne only twice in this critical summer of 1861, first at a bachelor breakfast on June 5, and later for three or four days in August with Isabel at Fryston. It is absurd to lay at his door the blame for Swinburne's chronic alcoholism of fifteen years, which nearly destroyed him. But the summer did see the beginning of an enduring friendship. On Burton's periodic returns to England he invariably sought Swinburne out, and their drinking bouts became famous. Luke Ionides once spent an evening with them which ended with Burton picking up the slight poet under one arm and carrying him kicking down a flight of stairs. Swinburne, too glazed with drink to find the steps of the hansom cab, complained that their steps were getting "higher and higher each year."[20]

As the friendship deepened, on at least one occasion something more than drinking was involved. On July 11, 1865, just after the Burtons left for Santos, Brazil where Burton was appointed consul, Swinburne wrote to Milnes:

> As my tempter and favourite audience has gone to Santos I may hope to be a good boy again, after such a "jolly good swishing" as Rodin alone can administer. The Rugby purists (I am told) tax Eaton generally with Maenadism during June and July, so perhaps some old school habits return upon us unawares—to be fitly expiated by old school punishment. That once I remember and admit. The Captain was too many for me; and I may have shaken the thyrsus in your face. But after this half I mean to be no end good. . . .[21]

Cecil Y. Lang, editor of the Swinburne letters, writes, "For roughly a decade and a half Swinburne was a chronic alcoholic. He was also a masochist. (Whether he was overtly homosexual, as a persistent oral tradition maintains, I do not know.)"[22] In the summer of 1861 Isabel did not know either. Her biography and letters, and Burton's letters, all indicate that until Richard's death—when she and Swinburne quarrelled—the relations between the poet and Burton's wife were superficially cordial. Once, however, she protested to Monckton Milnes about Swinburne's excessive drinking. Milnes wrote a note scolding the poet, to which Swinburne replied:

> As to anything you may have fished (how I say not) out of Mrs Burton to the discredit of my "temperance, soberness and chastity" as the Catechism

puts it—how can she who believes in the excellence of "Richard" fail to disbelieve in the virtues of any other man? *En moi vous voyez les Malheurs de la Vertu; en lui Les Prospérités du Vice.* In effect it is not given to all his juniors to *tenir tête à Burton. . . .*[23]

Isabel may well have sensed in the summer of 1861 that the real rivals for her husband's affection were likely to be men and not women. Some three years later she would read in one of Richard's West African books a paragraph that must have been disturbing. Describing the natives of Abeokuta, he wrote:

The male figure here, as all the world over, is notably superior, as amongst the lower animals, to that of the female. The latter is a system of soft, curved, and rounded lines, graceful, but meaningless and monotonous. The former far excels it in variety of form and in sinew. In these lands, where all figures are semi-nude, the exceeding difference between the sexes strikes the eye at once. There will be a score of fine male figures to one female, and there she is, as everywhere else, as inferior as is the Venus de Medici to the Apollo Belvidere.[24]

Isabel's biographer, W. H. Wilkins, wrote that marriage "steadied" Burton, that it "gave him someone to work for and some one to love, and it did more than anything else to give the lie to the rumours against him which were floating about."[25] And it appears that Burton found satisfaction in Isabel's enveloping ardour and struggled to reciprocate it. He was not given to flattery, and she cherished all her life the few examples of his open praise. One she recorded with special pleasure. She was charmingly dressed and about to descend to a ballroom, the first party in her own drawing room. Richard looked at her critically and then said to her mother, *"La jeune fille n'a rien à craindre."*[26]

She wrote that Richard's character "expanded with me in the privacy of our domestic life," and that he became "quite another man the moment anyone else entered the room." Shortly after their marriage they were visiting her family in Worthing, and Burton went off to spend the day with his cousin, Samuel Burton, at Brighton. Taking the last train back he fell asleep, waking up twenty miles beyond the proper stop. Instead of waiting till morning, he simply inquired the direction, checked his pocket compass and set out on a long trot across the country, reaching Isabel, who was frantic at the delay, at one in the morning. Such memories prompted her to write, "This was a large oasis of seven months in my life, and even if I had no other it would have been worth living for."[27]

Burton learned, too, in these seven months, something of the nature of his own rivals, chief of them being the Catholic church. It quickly became apparent that Isabel's determination to capture Richard's soul would mean a quiet, undeclared chess game that would go on through thirty years of married life. Burton handed her a pawn now and then—by wearing her medal of the Virgin about his neck, by giving her money to have masses said upon the death of one of her brothers, by weeping quietly at one midnight mass, and by his affectionate talk of a Catholic padre in India—all of which made her hopes for ultimate victory soar. She would have us believe that he treated her intense piety with gentleness, and made no objection to her building a private altar in each of their various homes. Actually he made no attempt in his books to curb his expressions of contempt for the church, and it is questionable how much he spared her in private talk. To Monckton Milnes he would write of the "monstrous humbug" of the Christian missionaries in Africa, and in 1863 he publicly praised Darwin's *Origin of Species*, then causing consternation throughout England, as "the best and wisest book of this, or, perhaps, of any age."[28] But it is from Burton's private comments in his letters to Milnes that we discover the special mixture of irony and amusement that characterised his attitude towards his wife's faith. Describing a holiday with Isabel in Madeira in 1862, he wrote, "My wife is too frantic with running about the churches and chapels and convents and other places of idolatrous abominations to do anything else. . . . her only danger was of being burned for a Saint."[29]

When they were first married, he was nettled by Isabel's going off to confession. His sense of rivalry challenged, he determined to ferret out for himself his wife's innermost thoughts, one of the supreme secrets for this passionately inquisitive man. Foiled by the defences of a woman schooled from childhood in pretence, he turned to hypnosis. Isabel herself described it:

Richard was a great mesmeriser. He always preferred women, and especially of the blue-eyed yellow-haired type. I need not say that he began with me as soon as we were married; but I did not like it, and used to resist it, but when once he had complete control, no passes or contact were necessary; he used simply to say, "Sleep," and I did. He could also do this at a distance, but with more difficulty if water were between us, and if he tried to mesemerise anybody else and I was anywhere in the neighbourhood, I absorbed it, and they took nothing. . . . He used to mesmerise me freely, but he never allowed any one else, nor did I, to mesmerise me. Once mesmerised, he had only to say, "Talk," and I used to tell him everything I knew, only I used to implore him to forbid me to tell him other people's secrets, and as a matter of honour he did, but all my own used to come out freely; only he never took a mean advantage of what he learnt in that way, and he used laughingly to tell everybody, "It is the only way to get a woman to tell you the truth."

Burton wanted all Isabel's secrets, perhaps especially her sexual feelings. And she may have welcomed the hypnosis as a chance to communicate these feelings without embarrassment. But the game being one-sided, and provocative of resentment on her part, it was probably profitless for mutual understanding. Wilfrid Blunt wrote that Burton used to boast of his hypnotic domination over his wife. "I have heard him say that at the distance of many hundred miles he could will her to do anything he chose as completely as if he were with her in the same room."[30]

Once when the Burtons were house guests of John Russell, Lord Amberley, Lady Amberley's sister Blanche Stanley begged Richard to put her in a trance. At first he refused, saying it made his wife angry if he hypnotised another woman, but finally agreed, provided it was kept secret. As was to be expected, Isabel found out. Lord Amberley wrote in his journal:

> Mrs Burton was in a state of rage (as was natural). . . . We heard this morning that there had been an awful row after we had gone to bed between Burton & his wife, because she was so angry at his mesmerizing without her. She said he would now be doing it with women who were not so nice. He was angry at this & affected to think it folly, that he had himself said that if any man mesmerized her he would kill the man & her too, a threat that I daresay he is quite capable of executing.[31]

By this time for both Richard and Isabel hypnosis had apparently taken on the significance of seduction.

Burton knew from the beginning of his courtship that he had two formidable rivals, Isabel's mother and the Catholic church, and he was aware how they were intertwined. Actually he was as intent on winning her away from the church as she was to salvage his soul. From the first moment of their marriage he made extraordinary demands upon her intellect—she must read, she must learn, she must copy and proofread his difficult and often scarifying manuscripts; she must manage his business details. Isabel has been called a goose by more than one writer who failed to see her lively intelligence, zest for adventure, capacity for adaptation, and even talent for writing.

But throughout their marriage her allegiance to the church strengthened rather than diminished. It was a fortification upon which he hammered with exasperation and perhaps envy, for he had no similar fortress in his own life. The church was her refuge against his desertions and cruelty. It was a steel cord he could not snap, binding her to her past. And the private altar she built in each house symbolized, one suspects, not only the closeness of her ties with her parents as well as God, but also an inability to give herself wholly to her husband.

It is the rare biographer who has been willing to speculate on this aspect of their marriage. Their friend Ouida wrote, "In the eyes of women he had the unpardonable fault: he loved his wife." There is evidence from Burton's poetry that he went into the marriage with as high hopes as she for fulfilment and affection, and there are many suggestions of domestic tenderness. They soon had nicknames for each other; she called him Jemmy, and he called her Zoo or Zookins, or Puss, like her family. It is hard not to believe that Isabel was writing from a richness of experience with marital intimacy when she said, "I always think that a man is one character to his wife, another to his family, another to *her* family, and fourth to his mistress or an *amourette* . . . if he have one—and so on, ad infinitum; but I think the wife, if they are happy and love each other, gets the pearl out of all the oyster shells."

Yet, after seven months of marriage Richard went off to be consul at Fernando Po, and flatly refused to let his wife accompany him even as far as the Madeira or Canary Islands, familiar tourist spots for Europeans. He did not return for eighteen months, and then only because Isabel wept copiously at the Foreign Office and won him a generous leave. Though he never tired of emphasizing that Fernando Po was a pesthole with a fearful mortality rate, there were many white women, wives of traders and missionaries, all along the West African coast.

"I am surprised at the combined folly and brutality of civilized husbands," he would write ironically, "who, anxious to be widowers, poison, cut the throats or smash the skulls of their better-halves. The thing can be as neatly and quietly, safely and respectably, effected by a few months of African air at Zanzibar or Fernando Po," though at the time of his marriage he had written to *The Times* that Zanzibar was a healthy place, "where Europeans have lived successfully for many years."[32] The mortality rate at Fernando Po was appalling—78 out of 250 Spanish soldiers died in a yellow fever epidemic on the island in March 1862—and Burton had some anxiety about preserving his own life as well as his wife's. Nevertheless, the length and uncompromising nature of the first separation are suspicious. They suggest that the "uninterrupted bliss" of the first seven months of marriage was something of a fiction for him as for her. They may well have uncovered sexual failure, and to have roused, in Burton at least, fantasies of separation and death.

Burton referred fleetingly in *The City of the Saints*, written during the first seven months, to the "constitutional frigidity" of certain kinds of British women, and in comparing white wives unfavourably with American Indian wives he used the metaphor: "porcelain where pottery is wanted." Shortly before leaving for Fernando Po, he wrote to Monckton Milnes, "My wife is fretting herself into a fever, which greatly increases the pleasure of my departure."[33] Nevertheless the parting was wretched. Isabel tells us that her husband permitted her

to go aboard the ship provided she "would not cry and unman him."
"I went below and unpacked his things and settled his cabin, and saw
to the arrangement of his luggage. My whole life was in that goodbye,
and I found myself on board the tug, which flew faster and faster from
the steamer. I saw a white handkerchief go up to his face."

Burton himself admitted to depression. "A heart-wrench—and all is
over," he wrote. "Unhappily I am not one of those independents who
can say, '*Ce n'est que le premier pas qui coute.*'" The first nightfall on
board, which he described as "the saddest time that the veteran wanderer knows," brought to his mind the lament of the Persian poet Saadi:

> So yearns at eve's soft tide the heart
> Which the wide wolds and waters part
> From all dear scenes to which the soul
> Turns as the lodestone seeks its pole.

After landing at Fernando Po, "the very abomination of desolation,"
he wrote that he felt "uncommonly suicidal."[34]

In Burton's finest poem, the *Kasidah*, which was written at least in
part during this period, one sees haunting evidence of his torment, the
hints of impotence, the revulsion against "tame" women:[35]

Hardly we learn to wield the blade before the wrist grows stiff and cold:
Hardly we learn to ply the pen ere Thought and Fancy faint with cold:
Hardly we find the path of love, to sink the Self, forget the "I"
When sad suspicion grips the heart, when Man *the* Man begins to die. . . .

Sips from the maiden's lips the dew; brushes the bloom from virgin brow
Such is his fleshly bliss that strives the Maker through the Made to know
I've tried them all, I find them all so same and tame, so drear, so dry
My gorge ariseth at the thought; I commune with myself and cry:—

Better the myriad toils and pains that make the man to manhood true,
This be the rule that guideth life; these be the laws for me and you:
With ignorance wage eternal war, to know thyself forever strain,
Thine ignorance of thine ignorance is thy fiercest foe, thy deadliest bane.

As we have seen, Burton recognized that he had a "mania" for discovery. He had sought discovery through disguise, and discovery
without disguise, and now discovery in marriage. But there was no real
satiety. And so he was off again to add to his store of secret data, still
hungry for knowledge, and now increasingly desperate since knowledge
at best could serve only as a poor substitute for the satisfactions of love.

The Desperate Quest

Little islands are all large prisons: one cannot look at the sea without wishing for the wings of a swallow.

Richard Burton, *Wanderings in West Africa*

*B*URTON HAD NO intention of remaining chained at Fernando Po taking meterological observations. To be isolated on this island was like being "a caged hawk," he wrote, "a Prometheus with the Demon Despair gnawing at my heart."[1] After living there only one week he was off exploring the delta of the Niger. He returned in October, only to set off immediately for Abeokuta, the capital of Nigeria, where he spent three weeks. In November 1861 he was exploring the Brass and Bonny Rivers; in December he was back in southern Nigeria, where he led a small expedition to climb the still unscaled Mt Victoria, one of the highest peaks in the Cameroon Mountains. "To be first in such matters is everything, to be second nothing," he wrote with satisfaction after reaching the top. One of the lesser peaks he named Mt Isabel.

Back in Fernando Po in February 1862, he stayed six weeks, and then went up the Gabon River looking for gorillas and cannibals. After a four-month leave in London and Madeira he was back for fifteen more months, during which he canoed up the Congo river as far as the Yalalla rapids, and made two trips to Dahomey, the African kingdom celebrated for its human sacrifices and Amazon army. During all these trips he had accumulated notes enough to fill four two-volume studies totalling 2,500 pages, *Wanderings in West Africa, Abeokuta and the Camaroons Mountains, Two Trips to Gorilla Land and the Cataracts of the Congo,* and *A Mission to Gelele, King of Dahome.* He also found time to compile a collection of native proverbs, his 450-page *Wit and Wisdom in West Africa.* The writing of almost 3,000 pages in three years provides one of the most extraordinary records of industry and observation in the annals of the British Foreign Office. He had become its great serendipitist. If he was drinking heavily, as several of his biographers intimate—based no doubt on his own admission that he drank a flask of brandy a day at Fernando Po—it did not noticeably damage his capacity for work.

Yet except for the collection of proverbs, the books do represent a series of studies in disenchantment. Burton avowed in *Abeokuta and the Camaroons* that his intention was "to paint black, black" without "fictitious feeling and unreal romance."[2] Here, far more than in his *Lake Regions of Central Africa*, one sees him making wholly cynical and sometimes bigoted judgments. Panoramas of great scenic beauty roused in him only a kind of anguish—"brooding over them all," he wrote, "darkening sun and sky, and clothing earth with sombre hues, is the sadness of a stranger-land." He recognized that his depression was related to nostalgia, which he called "a disease as yet imperfectly recognized," and described his own private remedy as "constant occupation of mind if not of body."

Perhaps to his surprise, he discovered that he missed his wife. "There is no place where a wife is so much wanted as in the Tropics," he wrote wistfully, "but then comes the rub—how to keep the wife alive."[3] Isabel was very much alive, and wretched at being left in England with her parents—as she put it, "neither maid, nor wife, nor widow." Stoutly determined to make the marriage real, she finally put an end to her months of loneliness by going to the Foreign Office and begging in tears for a respite for Richard from Africa. The sympathetic Sir Henry Layard at once ordered a four-months leave.

Burton landed at Liverpool in December 1862. "The cold is awful, rain & frost, no snow yet," he wrote to young vice-consul Frank Wilson at Fernando Po. "At the F.O. they had the impudence to congratulate me upon my return home—Speechless I pointed at the window, through which appeared a peasoup fog defiling the face of earth & heaven and when voice returned I faintly asked what they *could* mean. To make matters more pleasant I shall be dragged to 'midnight mass' the day after tomorrow."[4]

He spent a month partying with relatives, Monckton Milnes, and other friends. In January he helped James Hunt organize the Anthropological Society of London, which he hoped would become an organ for publication of many of his ethnological studies that ordinary publishers would be certain to expurgate. He called it "a refuge for Destitute Truth," permitting "a liberty of thought and a freedom of speech unknown to any other society in Great Britain."[5] Starting with eleven members, this society grew into an organization comprising some of the most imaginative explorers in Great Britain of the nature of man. As with the birth of many other sciences, the methodology was primitive, and some of the fledgling anthropologists used their early studies only to reinforce their racial prejudices. James Hunt, in the first article published by the society, asserted that Negro cranial sutures closed earlier than those of the white man, and therefore his brain was smaller. Burton, long puzzled by his own observation that the Negro child, though as quick if not quicker in learning than the white child, seemed to stop developing in adolescence, accepted Hunt's "measurements" as a valid explanation, even though the latter had based his theory on the examination of only two skulls.

After five or six weeks in England, Burton realized he would never finish his African books while immersed in the social whirl Isabel loved, and decided to seek the solitude of the Madeira and Canary Islands. This time he let his wife accompany him, and they spent two months in and about Madeira and Teneriffe. Here Burton learned that it was possible to mould Isabel into a tough, adaptable traveller. The first test came three days out from Liverpool, when a storm staved in the door of the main cabin and saloon, filled the hold with seven feet of water, and washed the quartermaster overboard to his death. Isabel, fleeing the saloon, where bird cages, kittens, and parcels were floating about in the water among the screaming women, made her way to the cabin of the captain, who had generously turned over his own quarters to the Burtons that they might have some privacy. Seasick and terrified, she was unable even to protest when a drunken naval officer pushed his way in and sank in a stupor on the floor. Burton, who had been helping man the pumps, came to the cabin, picked up the officer and booted him out of the door, and then turned to say cheerfully to his prostrate and weeping wife, "The Captain says we can't live more than two hours in such a sea as this."

Isabel moaned feebly, "Oh thank God it will be over so soon."

"I shall never forget how angry he was with me," she wrote.[6] So, according to her account, she trained herself not to be seasick and not to weep. She had long since learned to fear her husband's temper. "It is very dangerous to say anything to B, he is so *hot tempered*," she had written to Norton Shaw on December 1, 1862, "and makes himself *so* disagreeable to anyone if he takes a dislike. . . ."[7]

In Madeira and Teneriffe Burton discovered that Isabel was resilient and good-humoured, that she could be silent when he was writing, and that she could be counted upon to let him alone for long periods as she wandered enthusiastically about the Catholic churches, convents and shrines. He wrote obliquely to Monckton Milnes about "proposing a little orgie" the nature of which he did not elaborate upon. Apparently it never materialized. "I was looked at as Sathana might be," he wrote. "The priests of course monopolize all that sort of thing." And it is quite possible that he did not mind the failure, and that he was only keeping up old appearances of wickedness, which with Monckton Milnes he felt he must do at all costs.

They spent a month among the peasants, and Burton found himself admitting even to Milnes that "Teneriffe has been delightful."[8] Isabel demonstrated that she could cook, market, clean and wash. When Burton finished his *Abeokuta and the Cameroons*, he found it in his heart to write the following dedication: "To my best friend, My Wife, these pages are lovingly inscribed." Beneath this was a Latin quatrain from one of the elegies of Tibullus, which the *London Review*, in describing the book on January 16, 1864, translated as follows:

> O, I could live with thee in the wild wood
> Where human foot hath never worn a way;
> With thee, my city, and my solitude,
> Light of my night, sweet rest from cares by day.

Isabel wrote in the margin of her own copy: "Thank you, sweet love!"[9]

During Burton's final fifteen months at Fernando Po, Isabel visited him again at Teneriffe, though it is not clear how often. Much of his initial hatred of West Africa now disappeared; the first chapter of his book on Dahomey was, remarkably enough, entitled "I Fall in Love with Fernando Po." He had moved his headquarters from the deadly, mosquito-ridden coastal area to an elevation of 800 feet, where he lived with a retinue of Negro servants, almost, as he admitted, like a slave-holder in the United States.

Like most Europeans of his time he was completely insensible to African art, and failed to mention even the remarkable bronzes of Benin. Englishmen in these years collected only the native sculpture they counted pornographic. "I could have carried off a donkey's load," Burton wrote drily, "had I been aware of the rapidly rising value of Phallic specimens amongst the collectors of Europe."[10]

Burton still found the sight of the Negro in the white man's dress unendurable, though he detested the clothes himself, saying that wearing them in Africa was "like living in a poultice." Giving Negroes permission to dine on board ship in the main cabin he called "a political as well as a social mistake."[11] And when a Negro in Fernando Po addressed him too familiarly with a clap on his shoulder, Burton pitched him out of his office. A visit to Sierra Leone, the long established British colony of free Negroes, praised by many as the most civilized area in West Africa, filled him with more consternation than admiration. Thanks to British aid and education, Negroes in Freetown sat on juries and took part in the local government. But after hearing local Englishmen complain that they had been fined £50 in the local courts for "raising a stick to an insolent servant," Burton wrote of this jury system as "a machinery for tyranny" where the worst of the Aku criminals were invariably found innocent and most of the innocent whites guilty. He favoured instead a white jury for white men, and a black jury for blacks.

There were many mulattoes in Sierra Leone, some of whom had been educated in England. These Burton trusted least. "The uneasy idea that he is despised," he wrote, "fills him [the mulatto] with ineffable bile and bitterness." And he echoed a curious myth common also in the United States at the time, that mulattoes were inclined to be sterile. Of all the Negroes in Sierra Leone he admired only the Moslems. "The dignity of El Islam everywhere displays itself," he wrote, "it is the majesty of the monotheist who ignores the degrading doctrines of original sin." And he implied that they alone in the colony kept their women honest. The Sierra Leone Christian he attacked as "an inveterate thief." "He drinks, he gambles, he intrigues, he over-dresses himself. . . . The women have become as vicious as those of Egypt, the basest of kingdoms."[12] Burton later paid for his intemperate strictures when a distinguished Sierra Leone lawyer, William Rainy, a mulatto who had been educated in London, wrote an angry pamphlet, *The Censor Censured, or the Calumnies of Captain Burton on the Africans of Sierra Leone Refuted.* In addition Rainy, acting as legal counsel in a lawsuit involving three natives, saw to it that Burton was forced to pay out of his own pocket for some administrative carelessness.[13]

Burton disliked the Christian missionary in West Africa almost as much as the Christianized African. He condemned him for teaching English instead of the native languages, for breaking up the polygamous marriages—Livingstone cut off from communion all natives who would not give up their extra wives—for insisting on clothing the native nakedness, and for adding to the already multitudinous native fears a new fear about hell. He accused Jesuit missionaries of flogging their converts, and participating actively in the slave-trade. He noted sardonically that the same missionaries who objected to the native's use of magic teeth, bones and wizard's mats, recommended in their stead relics, medals and consecrated palm leaves. And he took special pleasure in pointing out that in Africa evil spirits were white and ugly, as they were black and ugly in Europe.[14]

These fulminations won him no praise in England. The missionary societies were outraged, and many journals that would otherwise have lauded his books deplored his carping and lack of compassion. The editor of the *Spectator*, reviewing his *Gorilla Land*, November 27, 1875, complained that Burton was "aggressive, dogmatic, and dictatorial," adding that his readers felt "partly bored and partly bullied."

Burton was in fact contradictory and arbitrary. He deplored the lack of chastity among the Christianized natives of Sierra Leone, but did not condemn the natives in the Gabon country for offering their wives or daughters to the European guest as a gesture of hospitality. He blistered the natives of Sierra Leone, but held the Gold Coast natives to be superior to the Europeans in the area. He was appalled at the treatment of slaves on the Bonny River, where the native master had been known to nail his slave's hands to a water-cask for thievery, or to blind him by peppering his eyes with coarsely powdered cayenne, but the only remedy he suggested was to export these slaves to the Americas, where he believed they would be treated better.

Still, at his best, Burton could be unpatronizing and judicious. And his irony, heatly honed, frequently made for memorable lines. "The African will say," he wrote, " 'The white man is an old ape,' and doubt that he is human. . . . Thus we observe, that whilst the Caucasian doubts the humanity of the Hamite, the latter repays the compliment in kind."[15] He went to great pains to compile from the writings of French and English missionaries, and from his own notes, a book of 2,268 Negro aphorisms, many of which, he noted, "for brevity and elegance . . . may claim an equal rank with those of any other nation in ancient or modern times." These he published in 1865 as *Wit and Wisdom from West Africa*, with the African phonetic transcriptions, giving examples from the Wolof, Kanuri, Oji (Ashanti), Ga (Accra), Yoruba, Efun (Dahome), Isubu, Dualla, Efik, and Fan tongues. They furnished striking evidence of cumulative folk wisdom, and many had a special freshness of expression: *When the mouth stumbles, it is worse than the foot — Running about gives no scholars — The Child hates him who gives it all it wants — Frowning and fierceness prove not manliness — 'I have forgotten thy name' is better than 'I know thee not.'* Some had a special poignancy: *A bad person is better than an empty house — Thought breaks the heart.*

Burton at this time was surprisingly anti-imperialist. When in London in 1865 he was called before a Parliamentary Select Committee for questioning on the West African settlements. There he urged Britain to get out of the area, abandoning her consulships at Badagri, Lagos and Palma, and retain only a single consulship protected by a steamer.[16] He saw West Africa at a dismal period in its history, demoralized by three centuries of slave traffic, which was still being conducted in defiance of the British blockade, and despite the fact that the American Civil War had broken out. Like many Tory Englishmen, Burton was convinced that the South would succeed, and expected the slave trade to be a continuing problem. "When do you expect the Northern States to sue for peace?" he wrote to Milnes on December 1, 1861.[17]

Burton faced up only partially to the European and Arab responsibility for the barbarous exploitation and systematic inhumanity that had corrupted the native African into kidnapping and selling his neighbours on a major scale, wrecked his tribal economy, decimated his communities, and had whetted his appetite for cruelty. The cruelty Burton did see, and he documented it with an almost loving eye for detail. The extraordinary lengths he went to to expose this cruelty for all the world to shudder at reveal an important facet of Burton's own character. He seemed bent on searching out the worst in Africa, as if by exposing it he could exorcise his own preoccupation with cruelty. So he was not content to describe only the casual rather indiscriminate executions of Benin, dramatic as they were, but planned four special expeditions, first to the country of the gorilla, symbol of much animal atrocity folklore, second to the Fan, a tribe renowned for their cannibal feasts, and finally two visits to Dahomey, whose name spelled human sacrifice and ritual murder on an appalling scale.

Gorillas were largely a mystery to Europeans and Americans before 1850, but in the 1860s, especially after the publication of Paul du Chaillu's *Explorations and Adventures in Equatorial Africa* in 1861, hunting the great ape became fashionable. Burton, who was a friend to Chaillu and had defended him when his account of African gorillas had been denounced in London as fictitious,[18] set out for the Gabon country to see the beasts for himself in 1862. He had seen Chaillu's mounted gorilla specimens in the United States in 1860, but noting their mutilation had resolved to bring back a specimen intact. He knew that gorilla brains were held to be an aphrodisiac by natives, and that stories of the rape of native women by gorillas were endemic in the Gabon territory.

But his own trip was largely a failure. He saw only one gorilla, which he did not kill. In his books on the subject he was able to do little but correct the wilder observations of Chaillu. "The Gorilla is a poor devil ape, not a 'hellish dream-creature, half man half beast,' " he wrote. "He is not the king of the African forest. . . . His tremendous roar does not shake the jungle; it is a hollow apish cry . . . explosive like the puff of a steam-engine, which, in rage, becomes a sharp and snappish bark. . . . the gorilla, on the seaboard at least, is essentially a coward; nor can we be surprised at his want of pluck, considering the troubles and circumstances under which he spends his harassed days."[19] Though he had hoped to send a gorilla to the British Museum, the best he could do was to send the carcass of a chimpanzee brought in by the natives. He wrote to Monckton Milnes, April 26, 1862, "The skin has been sent home and I have also transmitted the head and penis in a keg of rum for Professor Burke. Will you kindly let him know this. I promised him a gorilla's brain and will do my best to keep my word, but it may be some time before that can be done."[20]

Visiting the Fan, celebrated for their cannibal feasts, meant going still further up the Gabon River beyond the area inhabited by the

Mpongwe, who had aided in the gorilla search. Burton was astonished to find the Fans "finely made, light-coloured people, of decidely mild aspect." They lived, he said, "in a chronic state of ten-days war," with the fighting ending in the capture of two or three warriors and a feast. The eating was a secret religious rite, he discovered, to which only men were admitted. After the feast, they broke all the cooking pots. Though Burton was inclined to minimize the Fan feasting as no more exceptional except in the matter of secrecy than similar ceremonies in the areas of the Niger and Brass rivers, he did not dismiss the subject lightly. The widespread nature of the practice of cannibalism, he wrote, showed it to be an almost routine step in man's religious development.

Of the cruelty of the African in general he wrote, "Cruelty seems to be with him a necessary way of life, and all his highest enjoyments are connected with causing pain and inflicting death. His religious rites— a strong contrast with those of the modern Hindoo—are ever causelessly bloody." "I can hardly believe," he concluded perceptively, "this abnormal cruelty to be the mere result of uncivilization; it appears to me the effect of an arrested development, which leaves to man all the ferocity of the carnivor, the unreflecting cruelty of the child."[21]

It can be seen from Burton's books on West Africa that documenting this cruelty had become more important to him than exploration. Since the upper Congo was still unmapped, he thought seriously of ascending the river beyond the lower rapids and Isanglia, which had been reached by Captain J. K. Tuckey, R.N., in 1816. The expedition had cost Tuckey and sixteen European companions their lives, and no one since had even reached Isanglia. Burton wrote lightly to Milnes on May 31, 1863—in the letter that gives this biography its title—of going "some thousand miles" up the Congo. But as we have seen in the same letter, he had begun to ask himself "Why?" and to ponder on the nature of his own demon. More importantly, he had neither equipment nor permission from the Foreign Office for a major expedition.

He travelled the first thirty-eight miles by launch, then transferred to canoes for another forty to forty-five miles, then made the final last few miles to the Yalalla cataracts on foot. With this he seems to have been content. In August 1863 he had received permission from the Foreign Office to visit the King of Dahomey, and he was very intent on arriving in time for the ritual massacres that came at New Year. It was now late September, and he turned back. So Burton ended his explorations of the Congo still unaware that five years earlier, when he stood on the shores of Lake Tanganyika, he had seen the easternmost source of the mightiest river in Africa.

Of all the kingdoms in West Africa, none had so sinister a name as Dahomey. Europeans greedily accepted stories of 2,000 sacrificial victims with the death of every Dahomey king, and a lake of blood big enough to paddle a canoe in. Burton had asked official permission to visit Dahomey as soon as he won his appointment to Fernando Po, but it was denied. He had gone anyway, in secret, spending five days in the capital, Agbome, in late May, 1863. "I have been here 3 days and am generally disappointed," he had written to Monckton Milnes on May 31, continuing with the blend of mockery and bravado that characterized many of his letters, "Not a man killed, or a fellow tortured. The canoe floating in blood is a myth of myths. Poor Hankey must still wait for his peau de femme. . . . The victims are between 100 and 200 a year instead of thousands. At Benin . . . they crucified a fellow in honour of my coming—here nothing! And this is the blood-stained land of Dahome!!"[22]

Determined to return for a longer visit, Burton had applied again to Lord John Russell, pointing out that the aggressive King Gelele was engaging in continual warfare with Abeokuta and selling all his captives as slaves. Russell had finally agreed that Burton should pay an official visit to protest against the slave traffic and the annual human sacrifices. As soon, therefore, as he had returned from his voyage up the Congo, he made preparation for an extended stay.

Dahomey had emerged as an African state in the 17th century, and had become famous in the 19th under King Gezo (1818–58), who had moulded his Amazon army into a serious fighting force. Upon Gezo's death, his son, Gelele, following ancient tradition, had slain 500 natives to be his father's servants in the nether world, and had since periodically added to the entourage. Many Europeans had visited the kingdom, and at least seven Englishmen had published accounts of their journeys.[23] Burton, in addition to his fascination with cruelty, brought to Dahomey a disciplined questioning intelligence that would not be matched until the 1930s, when the American anthropologist Melville J. Herskovits settled down for a two year study.

Burton started from Fernando Po in November 1863, accompanied by a Royal Navy surgeon, John Cruikshank, a native Wesleyan missionary, the Reverend Peter W. Bernasko, and a considerable native escort. Gelele greeted the party with gun salutes, dancing and toasts in rum drunk from the skulls of recent Abeokuta captives. He was an impressive king, Burton said, with a tall, muscular, agile body, dressed in a white body cloth, purple-flowered silk shorts, and scarlet sandals embroidered in gold. An immense circle of wives stood behind his throne, and behind them a circle of female warriors. Everywhere were enormous cheerful umbrellas, the colour symbolizing rank. If the king so much as sneezed, the women flung themselves prostrate and touched their foreheads to the earth.

Burton had brought as official presents a forty-foot circular crimson tent, a silver pipe, two silver belts, and a coat of mail and gauntlets. But Gelele, who had told a Royal Navy officer visiting Dahomey in 1862 that he would be pleased to receive a coach and horses, was visibly disappointed. Burton added his own personal gifts, cloth, liqueurs and whisky. On his first visit, he confided to Monckton Milnes, he had presented the king with "three very dégagé coloured prints of white women in a state of Eve-ical toilette. This charmed him and he inquired whether such articles are to be procured alive. I told (Heaven forgive me) a fearful fib and said that in my country the women are of a farouche chastity."[24]

Gelele treated Burton with courteous deference, but for six weeks refused to grant him a private audience to hear his message from the British Government. Burton moved into a rude clay hut and settled down to note-taking. The king's physician, who boasted eighty wives, begged Burton rather plaintively for aphrodisiacs, and in exchange gave him much information. The Amazon army he found to be very different from the warrior maidens of antique legend who were said to have fought in the seige of Troy, to have tangled with Hercules and Bacchus, with Alexander the Great, and Pompey. "I was looking forward with prodigious curiosity to see 5,000 African adult virgins, never yet having met with a single specimen," he wrote to Milnes. "I found that most of them were women taken in adultery and given to the king as food for powder instead of being killed. They were mostly elderly and all of them hideous. The officers were decidedly chosen for the size of their bottoms."[25]

Nevertheless, they made a colourful display, some dressed in red, with white loin cloths and black horsetail headdresses, others in chocolate and dark blue. They carried drums, duck-guns, muskets, blunderbusses and immense, razor-like knives. Instead of 5,000, Burton counted 2,500, of which only 1,700 constituted the actual fighting force. All were official wives of the king, and those who were caught in adultery were either killed with their paramours or sold into slavery. Nevertheless, Burton noted, "so difficult is chastity in the tropics," 150 were pregnant. "They maneuvre," he continued, "with the precision of a flock of sheep, and they are too light to stand a charge of the poorest troops in Europe. . . . An equal number of British charwomen, armed with the British broomstick, would . . . clear them off in a very few hours." But he knew from his visit to Abeokuta that in that kingdom they had the reputation of being tough fighters, trained to attack barefoot through thorny acacia bush defences, and he gallantly blamed their recent defeats on the stupidity of their male officers.

Burton was particularly fascinated by the insistence of the Amazons

that they were "no longer females but males," and went on to speculate about their sexuality in a fashion—as anthropologist Melville
Herskovits has pointed out—remarkably like that of a modern psychoanalyst:

> The regimen in which these women are compelled to live, doubtless in-
> creases their ferocity in fight. It is the essence of training every animal, from
> a game cock to a pugilist, and a married she-soldier would be useful only
> as a mother of men. . . . all the passions are sisters. I believe that bloodshed
> causes these women to remember, not to forget LOVE; at the same time
> that it gratifies the less barbarous, but, with barbarians, equally animal feel-
> ing. Seeing the host of women who find a morbid pleasure in attending the
> maimed and dying, I must think that it is a tribute paid to sexuality by
> those who object to the ordinary means.[26]

On another occasion he wrote, "They are bound, like the female priests
of Grewhe, under penalty of death, to chastity and celibacy, and this
naturally communicates a certain amount of ferocity to their minds—
'horrors' are, with the eunuch, their succedaneum for love."[27] One
wonders whether Burton, contemplating his own self-imposed celibacy,
turned similar insight in upon himself.

As always in Africa, Burton made inquiries about circumcision,
excision, and skin mutilation, and Dahomey provided material on all
three. Circumcision was deferred till the youths were almost twenty,
he wrote, and many died of infection. Cicatrization of adolescent girls
ranged from a few cuts on the forehead to elaborate designs on the
cheek, base of the spine and legs.*

Burton was more explicit than Herskovits about the mutilation of
the female genitalia, which in Dahomey consisted not of excision but
of elongation. He dared not describe it in his published volumes on
Dahomey, but wrote extensively of the practice in a letter to Milnes,
and included a remarkably explicit discussion in a paper for the Anthropological Society of London. "The parts in question," he wrote,
"locally called '*Tu*,' must from the earliest years be manipulated by professional old women, as is the bosom amongst the embryo prostitutes
of China. If this be neglected, lady friends will deride and denigrate
the mother, declaring that she has neglected her child's education. . . .
men are said to enjoy handling the long projections. . . . It is popularly
said, 'There can be no pleasurable Venus without '*Tu*.' "[28]

As the days neared for the human sacrifices, there was a palpable

---

* Herskovits, almost a hundred years later, found this practice virtually un-
changed. The cutting was done in the presence of the girl's fiancé, he wrote, with
as many as eighty slashes on the inside of each thigh. The rationalization had not
changed—an alleged increase in sexual pleasure. "It is said that if a woman does
not have these cuts," he wrote, "she will never be able to hold a man's love."
Dahomey, I, 293.

increase in tension in Agbome. Burton, who had seen twenty of the intended victims tied up in rude sheds, earnestly interceded for them, and insisted that no executions take place in his presence. Gelele complied to the extent of freeing ten. The "customs" began with parades, dancing and ceremonial drinking. Burton was astonished at the elaborate preparations, intricate etiquette and exact timing. The king himself led the ritual decapitation dances, which became ever more frenzied, and insisted at one point that Burton and Cruikshank join him. Burton admitted to doing a *pas de seul* which won great applause, and finally a *pas de deux* with the king which brought him a thunderous ovation. The king then toasted him, drinking from a fresh skull, and solemnly presented Burton with two skulls for himself.

Burton was the first traveller to point out the specifically religious nature of the "customs," which were usually described by Europeans as a mere prelude to a new series of raids on Abeokuta. The executions, he said, were specifically for the purpose of carrying messages to the dead. "The king, wishing to send a message to his father, summons a captive, carefully primes him with the subject of his errand . . . and strikes off his head. If an important word be casually omitted he repeats the operation, a process which I venture to call a postscript."[29] All the victims were intoxicated at the moment of death, he said, "the object being to send them to the other world in the best of tempers." Then forsaking the grisly humour, he pointed out that the practice "originates from filial piety, it is sanctioned by long use and custom, and is strenuously upheld by a powerful and interested priesthood." It could no more be abolished outright, he concluded, than a European monarch could abolish prayers for the dead. He estimated the total annual slaughter at 500.

In deference to Burton, the victims in 1863 were all executed at night, the first group being slaughtered on New Year's Eve. Burton was told that the king had cut off the head of the first male victim, and that his ministers had executed the remainder. Going to the palace after the first of what he called "the evil nights," Burton counted nine naked male corpses. All had been mutilated after death, "in respect," he wrote delicately, "to the royal wives." Later he saw twelve heads, each in front of a small totem, and later two more victims, a total altogether of twenty-three. Female criminals in similar numbers, he wrote, "are executed by officers of their own sex, within the palace walls, not in the presence of men." Reminded, no doubt of the guillotining of the French mother in his own childhood, he went on to say, "Dahome is therefore one point more civilized than Great Britain, where they still, wondrous to relate, 'hang away' even women, in public. . . . We can hardly find fault with putting criminals to death when in the Year of Grace 1864 we hung four murderers upon the same gibbet before 100,000 gaping souls at Liverpool, when we strung up five pirates in front of Newgate, when . . . our last Christian king but one killed a starving mother of seventeen, with an infant at her breast, for lifting a yard of linen from a shop counter." Four days later he saw the nine corpses still suspended, and covered with buzzards. Upon detailed inquiry, he learned that in five days eighty victims had been killed.

When finally he was granted a private interview with Gelele, he protested indignantly at the barbarous happenings, and threatened reprisals on the part of the British government for Gelele's part in the slave traffic. He told the king that what Dahomey needed was not deaths but births, that the slaughter was revolting, and the spectacle and smell of decayed and mutilated corpses too disgusting to be borne. The king, he said, "who had never heard so much truth before in all his life," was visibly annoyed but controlled his temper to reply that he slew only criminals and war captives, and that unless he sold his captives he must slay them, which the British would like even less.

Burton, feeling now "a sense of hopelessness . . . like talking to the winds," bade Gelele farewell. The king shook his hand and said, "You are a good man, but too angry."

Back in Fernando Po, Burton wrote a passionate indictment. Dahomey, he said, was "a mixture of horrors and meanness . . . mingled puerility and brutality, of ferocity and politeness." The Dahomans "are a mongrel breed, and a bad. They are Cretan liars, *cretins* at learning, cowardly and therefore cruel and bloodthirsty; gamblers, and consequently cheaters; brutal, noisy, boisterous, unvenerative, and disobedient, dispas-bitten things, who deem it a 'duty to the gods to be drunk,' a 'flatulent, self-conceited herd of barbarians,' who endeavour to humiliate all those with whom they deal; in fact a slave race—vermin with a soul apiece."[30]

September Tragedy, 1864

Speke you must take up tenderly, for his geography is fashioned very slenderly. Burton you must take up gingerly, for he is fashioned after a hedgehog, his prickles are hardening every year, and though anything but poisonous, they are apt to hurt the bare hand and are meant to do so.

"Dishonour est at Nilo," *Saturday Review*, London July 2, 1864

SPEKE AND BURTON had both left England in April 1860, Burton for America and Speke for Africa with James Grant. By the beginning of April 1863, Speke and Grant were eighteen months overdue, and many feared them dead. John Petherick, ivory trader and British consul at Khartoum, had agreed to carry supplies for the last leg of Speke's expedition as far up the Nile as Gondokoro, and a generous subscription in London had supplied him with £1,000 for the purpose. By now it was believed that both Petherick and his wife were dead. The wealthy sportsman-explorer Samuel Baker, accompanied by his beautiful Hungarian wife had started up the Nile, partly in search of Speke and Grant, partly in their own pursuit of the coy fountains. Then in mid-April the Secretaries of the Royal Geographical Society were electrified to get a wire from Alexandria, "Inform Sir Roderick Murchison that all is well, that we are in the latitude 14° 30' upon the Nile, and that the Nile is settled." It was signed John Hanning Speke.

Speke and Grant had made a monumental voyage of discovery, travelling the old Burton-Speke trail with two hundred bearers to Kazeh, then north to the virgin Uganda, and finally down the whole terrible length of the Nile to the Mediterranean. From the beginning they had been exasperated by desertions, petty thievery and exorbitant demands for *hongo*. Both men blamed the desertions on Burton because he had failed to reward the Zanzibar bearers properly on the first journey, but the trouble continued with new porters.

In the kingdom of Karagwe Speke found the shooting excellent, and killed elephants, rhinoceroses, giraffes, buffaloes, zebra, lions, hyenas, and a great variety of antelopes. King Rumanika was hospitable, and Speke found his wives a wondrous curiosity. Constantly eating under threat of being beaten, they had become gigantic, virtually immobile barrels of flesh. Speke persuaded one to let him measure her, and recorded her chest at 4 feet 4 inches, her thigh at 2 feet 7 inches, and her calf at one foot 8 inches. Beside her sat her sixteen-year-old daughter, quite naked, sucking at a milk-pot. Normally disturbed by nudity, Speke seems to have felt no embarrassment. "I got up a bit of a flirtation with Missy," he wrote, "and induced her to rise and shake hands with me. Her features were lovely, but her body was as round as a ball."[1]

Grant developed a nasty leg infection which kept him bedridden in Karagwe. When after two months of waiting vainly for it to heal, he and Speke learned from natives that a white man had appeared in the area to the north, Speke became impatient. Instead of having the natives carry Grant in a hammock, as had been done with Burton, he pushed on alone to Buganda. Certain that the white man was Petherick coming up from Gondokoro, he wrote that the rumours "drove us half wild with delight." It seems likely, however, that he was fearful lest Petherick beat him to the spot where he was certain Lake Victoria poured into the Nile. Buganda he found to be an isolated island with a special civilization, where the natives lived in beautifully made conical houses, sailed in 70-foot war canoes, and displayed basketware of great artistry. But the twenty-year-old king, Mutesa, was a butcher to rival Gelele of Dahomey. Speke learned that at his "coronation" he had burned alive thirty of his brothers, and that almost daily he singled out members of his harem of 300 women for execution. Uncertain of his own fate, he was quick to impress the king with his skill at shooting birds on the wing. Mutesa permitted him to live, keeping him captive but still treating him as an honoured visitor. There was no word of Petherick, but Speke felt certain he was in the area and dispatched a letter with north-bound natives inviting him to come without delay and to bring a load of presents for the king.[2]

The queen mother took great interest in Speke, begged him for medicine to cure her stomach pains, and as we have already noted gave him two of her daughters for wives. When he sent the twelve-year-old back, and passed the other on to his valet, she pressed him to take a third. "It frightened me from visiting her for ages after," he said.

Mutesa's palace was not far from Lake Victoria, and here Speke obtained exact information about the great river that flowed out of it to the north. When Grant appeared, limping but finally mobile after a separation of three months, Speke wrung from Mutesa permission to leave his kingdom. They started north on July 17, 1862 and two days later Speke made a fateful decision. Fond as he professed to be of his lieutenant, he chose now to send Grant off on the trail to Bunyoro, ostensibly "to communicate quickly with Petherick," while he turned east to Urondogani and the Nile. Making his way through huge grass and jungle vegetation, he came finally, on July 28, 1862, to the spot where his Lake Victoria emptied into the river. Here he saw a waterfall about twelve feet high and 600 to 700 yards broad. Hippopotami and crocodiles lay sleeping in the water below; Wasoga and Waganda fisherman dangled rods from the rocks, hoping to catch the passenger-fish that leapt at the falls by the thousand. "We were well rewarded . . ." he wrote. "I saw that old Father Nile without any doubt rises in the Victoria Nyanza, and, as I had foretold, that lake is the great source of the holy river which cradled the first expounder of our religious belief."

Struggling to communicate his excitement, he told his men they should shave their heads and bathe in the sacred waters, "the cradle of Moses," but Bombay only looked at him with some amusement to reply, "We don't look on those things in the same fanciful manner you do."[3] Speke named the spot, somewhat unimaginatively but perhaps not without method, Ripon Falls, after Lord Ripon, then president of the Royal Geographical Society.

Speke never explained in print why he cheated Grant out of this sight, but once in England he would be hounded by reproaches. Geographer James Macqueen would accuse him of treating Grant as "a cipher," and Burton, too, would mention the event accusingly. The act was contrary to British notions of sportsmanship; it was unnecessary to protect his reputation for being first, since that would be guaranteed to him as leader. For many it would cast a new light on his shabby treatment of Burton after the first expedition. Speke had to push aside all rivals, especially rivals who were in some fashion brothers, particularly older brothers—he referred to his elder brother contemptuously as "an *idle* country squire"[4]—whether by six years as with Burton, or by three weeks as with Grant.

As far as we know from the writings of both men, Grant accepted the decision with an almost feminine passivity and pushed on to Bunyoro without protest. Nor did he ever make any open complaint. A subtle evidence of bitterness appears, however, in his diary entry of July 19, 1862, two days after Speke's peremptory order to go west. Here Grant described in detail a quarrel between two of his porters which turned out to be a striking personal parable. "Manua, who had charge of our cattle, came crying and bleeding from a jagged cut on the back of his head," he wrote. "A Seedee twice his size had struck him with a bludgeon for refusing to give up his hut." The native complained, "It is not the wound that pains me, but here, here," and violently beat upon his heart. "Poor little fellow," Grant commented. "He felt his honour at stake, and swore he would take the other's life; but nothing further occurred."[5] So it must have been with Grant himself.

After a month of separation, Speke rejoined Grant in Bunyoro, and the two men spent six weeks at the court of King Kamrasi, again in a state of partial imprisonment. They still had 70 men and 4 women of the original expedition. Once more they heard about a white man in the area, but no Petherick appeared, and their hopes of rescue appeared bleak.* Finally they freed themselves and again started north. In Bunyoro they had learned of a lake to the west, the Lûta Nzigé, "dead locust,"—later called Lake Albert—into which the Nile poured, and from which it poured out again at no great distance. Though it was clear to both men that this might be a second important source of the Nile, and that if it were by some unhappy circumstance connected with Tanganyika the whole purpose of their expedition would be nullified, Speke elected not to follow the Nile west to have a look at it but instead took a short cut directly north. His decision against making this ten-day journey was a curious repetition of Burton's failure to go on to the Victoria Nyanza, and it was to give Burton a wholly unexpected weapon. Speke was already so confused about the smaller rivers he had crossed that he decided Lake Victoria must have at least four outlets which combined to form the Nile, thus betraying an innocence of hydrography that would subject him to ridicule among the more scientific geographers at home.

When they met the Nile again farther north and tried to use it as a highway, they were forced back onto the land by cataracts and hostile natives. On they went through increasingly desolate and famine-ridden country, arriving in Gondokoro on February 13, 1863.

Here it was not Petherick but Samuel Baker who rushed forward to greet them. After the initial excitement Baker asked somewhat plaintively, "Does not one leaf of the laurel remain for me?" Whereupon Speke generously handed over a map of the Lûta Nzigé which he had made from native accounts.[6] Baker, who was no fool, realized after studying it that so long as the dimensions of this lake remained unknown he still had a chance for the Nile prize. Speke, already regretting that he had not sought out the lake himself, predicted correctly that the armchair geographers in London would give him a bad time over it.

Meanwhile, where was Petherick? Speke asked it of Baker; he would ask it again in London, in his speeches, and in his book, *Journal of the Discovery of the Source of the Nile* (1863), until the whole British press would feel his fury at not having been rescued. Actually there were four boats and abundant supplies awaiting Speke at Gondokoro,

---

* Actually there had been a white man in the area, the Italian explorer Giovanni Miani, who had penetrated the wild area south of Gondokoro and then turned back, leaving only his name carved on a tree by the Nile as evidence that he had been in Uganda at all.

which Petherick had sent up the Nile many months before. But Petherick and his wife, who were seventy miles west on an ivory-trading expedition, did not arrive for five days. When they explained their own delay Speke was hostile and disbelieving.

Petherick described how he had sent supplies up the river according to his promise, and how shipwreck had delayed his own arrival for a whole year. Since the Nile was navigable only two months out of the year, he and his wife had arrived but a few weeks earlier. Finding Speke's supplies intact, they had assumed, since the explorers were a year overdue, that they had either perished or had returned to Zanzibar. There had been no word of Speke or Grant from Moslem traders who had been up the Nile from Gondokoro. Moreover, as Petherick pointed out delicately, the Royal Geographical Society had explicitly stated that he and his wife were not expected to remain at Gondokoro beyond June 1862, and had never asked him to go beyond this point. Speke in reply made no secret of the fact that he felt cheated and abandoned.

Once in London Speke was overwhelmed with public adulation close to idolatry. Nevertheless he took the trouble to pursue Petherick with a pathological intensity. Privately he accused Petherick of selling stores which really belonged to him. Publicly, with no justification, he accused Petherick of participating in the slave trade. When Petherick finally arrived in London, he was thunderstruck to find his consulship revoked and himself the victim of concentrated public slander. At once he prepared to sue Speke for libel.[7]

Speke lashed out also at Burton. In his first speech to the Royal Geographical Society, June 23, 1863, he said, "Had I been alone on the first expedition, I should have settled the Nile in 1859 by travelling from Unyanyembi to Uganda with an Indian merchant . . . but my proposal having been negatived by the chief of the expedition, who was sick at the time and tired with the journey, I returned to England."[8] The vainglory did him no credit.

At a dinner in his honour at Taunton in late December 1863, though he said somewhat defensively, "I have been accused in the public press as being ungenerous," he went on to attack Burton again. On January 14, he wrote in a letter to the *Athenaeum*, "I don't wish to say anything about Captain Burton. I taught him, at his own request, the geography of the countries we traversed, and since he has turned my words against me."[9] The suspicion grew among members of the Royal Geographical Society that Speke at the zenith of his success, was acting the cad. When the publication of his *Journal of the Discovery of the Source of the Nile* revealed that he had cheated Grant out of even seeing the Nile source, the suspicion became conviction.

Burton, still in Fernando Po, tells us that indirect efforts were made to mend his old friendship with Speke. "His brilliant march led me to express, despite all the differences which had sprung up between us, the most favourable opinion of his leadership," Burton wrote. "Again, however, either old fancied injuries still rankled in his heart or he could not forgive the man he had injured. . . . the malignant tongues of 'friends' urged him on to a renewal of hostilities, and the way to reconciliation was for ever barred."[10] Speke's speeches had in fact led to open warfare between the two men, with Burton in his letters from Fernando Po now openly championing Tanganyika as the true "head source" of the Nile.

Speke as a reward for his achievement had been permitted to incorporate the phrase "Honour est a Nilo" in his coat of arms, and Viscount Strangford, writing anonymously in the *Saturday Review* of July 2, 1864, maliciously entitled his piece "Dishonour est a Nilo" and let fly at both antagonists. "Burton and Speke," he wrote, "are so blind with rage and bitterness that they fight like untrained street boys. Had Burton acquired a continental tact and self control rather than a curious infelicity in the manner of displaying and misplacing his cleverness . . . the world might have rung with his name." Still Strangford in the end came down strongly on Burton's side. "So far as it is possible to see the points at issue through the haze of sneer and wrath with which they are encompassed, we believe him to be mainly in the right."

Geographer Charles Beke swung into Burton's camp, and James Macqueen, author of *A Geographical Survey of Africa*, wrote a series of anti-Speke articles in the *Morning Advertiser*. Particularly damaging was his documentation of Speke's apparent carelessness in taking altitude measurements, noting at one point that Speke had actually made the Nile run uphill for one 90-mile length.[11] Macqueen also insinuated that Speke had cavorted naked with the fat queen of Rumanika, had taken part in drunken orgies with the mother of King Mutesa, had been a willing lecher with the native girls, and had even had an affair with Petherick's cook.

Macqueen's articles were malicious and libellous, and Speke, who had gone to great pains to document his sexual purity, found himself now the butt of sniggering all over London. But instead of suing Macqueen for libel, he suffered in silence. During the spring of 1864 he went off to Paris to negotiate with the French government about possible explorations. Accompanying him was Laurence Oliphant.[12] No companion could have been more intent on exacerbating the feud, or more certain to agitate the uncertainty Speke felt about his own masculinity.

Meanwhile another star entered the Nile drama. David Livingstone

Richard Burton. A heretofore unpublished photograph, 1854.
Courtesy of Quentin Keynes

Richard Burton, 1848.

Richard Burton and his sister, Lady Maria Stisted, from a painting
by Jacquand, 1851.

Richard Burton as Haji Abdullah,
en route to Mecca, 1853.

Burton's drawing of El-Medinah, from the *Pilgrimage to El-Medinah and Meccah*,

Mganga, or medicine man.   The porter.   The Kirangozi, or guide.

Muinyi Kidogo.   Mother and child.

Burton's drawings for his *Lake Regions of Central Africa*, 1860.

Head Dresses of Wanyamwezi.

Richard and Isabel Burton at
the time of their marriage.
Portraits by Louis Desanges, 1861.

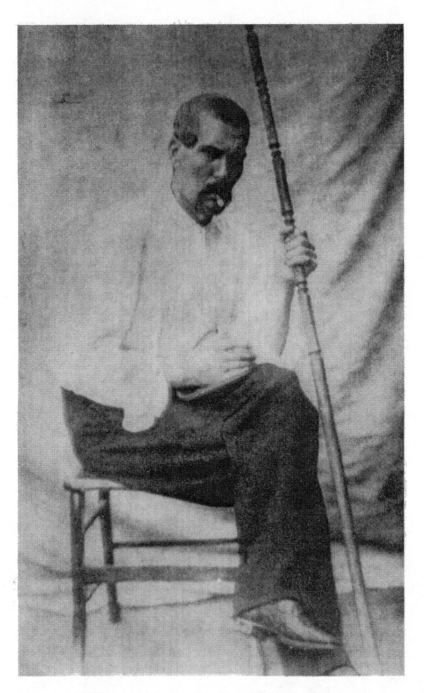

Richard Burton in his tent in Africa. From Isabel Burton's biography.
Probable date, 1862.

David Livingstone, 1864.

John Hanning Speke and James A. Grant, 1863.

Isabel Burton in 1869.

Richard Burton, portrait by Sir Frederick Leighton, 1872. Courtesy of the National Portrait Gallery.

Richard Burton at fifty-eight, from a painting by Madame Gutmansthal de Benvenuti, Trieste, 1879.

John Payne, rival translator of *The Arabian Nights*.

Foster Fitzgerald Arbuthnot, Burton's collaborator.

Richard Burton from *Vanity Fair*,
October 24, 1885.

Richard Burton in fencing
costume, 1889. From a painting by Albert Letchford.

Sir Richard Burton, at
sixty-nine, 1890.

Sir Richard and Lady Burton, Trieste, 1890. Photograph by Dr. F. Grenfell Baker.

Burton's mausoleum at Mortlake, as originally constructed.

had returned to London in July 1864, after a six year exploration in
the Lake Nyassa and Zambezi River areas. Disconsolate over his wife's
recent death in the jungle, for which he felt considerable guilt, he
vowed never to return. Almost instantly he was drawn into the Nile
controversy. Livingstone had never met Burton, but disapproved of his
writings and preferred Speke, with whom he had exchanged friendly
letters. Nevertheless Livingstone now elected to lend his immense prestige to Burton. Speke had been so intent on destroying any argument
in favour of Tanganyika as the head-source of the Nile that he had
claimed that the river at the south end of Tanganyika, which neither
he nor Burton had seen but which according to native reports flowed
into the lake, actually flowed out of it southwards into Lake Nyassa.[13]
His only reason for reversing the flow of this river had been a semantic
one; he had learned, he said, that when an African native said a river
flowed into a lake he meant actually that it flowed outwards, and vice
versa. This foolish tactic cost him Livingstone's championship. For
though Livingstone had never been to Tanganyika, he did know the
Nyassa water system and insisted that no large river entered Lake
Nyassa from the Tanganyika area.

The British people loved Livingstone. He was patient, robust, opti-
mistic and resolute, a simple Scot cast in a heroic mould. He was the
only African explorer to travel alone for long periods and survive. The
natives, who called him "the good one," fed him, doctored him, and let
him live. Though a speech defect made him an inept speaker, crowds
nevertheless swarmed to him in London, warmed by his shrewd and
pawky humour, his palpable sincerity. They stared at his ineptly func-
tioning shoulder, torn by a lion early in his missionary years, and
listened with indignation to his terrible tales of the slave trade. They
loved him the more because he was uncomfortable with praise and
troubled lest people think he explored Africa for the adulation of men
rather than the love of God. Unlike Burton he had faith in the Negro's
educability, industry, and capacity for moral improvement through
Christianity.

Burton came to London from Fernando Po in August 1864, one
month after Livingstone, and for the first time the three African explorers were in the city together. Someone suggested that it would be
a capital idea for Burton to debate publicly with Speke before the
British Association for the Advancement of Science in their annual
meeting at Bath, with Livingstone acting as a kind of unofficial referee.
Confronted with the invitation, Burton at first hesitated. Then Laurence
Oliphant, once more falling into what Isabel called "his habit of sunder-
ing friends," told Burton that Speke had said, "If Burton appears on
the platform at Bath I will kick him."

"Well," said Burton, "that settles it. By God, he shall kick me"; and so to Bath he went.[14]

By now the enmity was at such heat that Burton, in preparing his case, even repudiated information he had himself collected from the Arabs in Kazeh. Speke's Lake Victoria, he decided, was not a lake but a lake region, and he drew a map which virtually obliterated it altogether.[15] Lake Tanganyika appeared instead as the true source of the Nile, flowing into the Lŭta Nzigé, and thence directly south to Gondokoro. Completely reversing his earlier position, he held that the Rusizi flowed north *out* of Tanganyika. There were Arabs who said it flowed in, and Arabs who said it flowed out, he argued. Who could be sure who was right, considering that at the time of his own visit Speke had been deaf and blind and he paralytic. So Burton became guilty of the same kind of irresponsible geography-writing as Speke. This symbolic manipulation of influents and effluents became a kind of desperate game where reason fled and checkmating became the only goal.

How much Speke knew in advance of the details of Burton's argument we cannot be sure. He had withheld from Burton the knowledge that the thermometer used on the first exploration for measuring altitude was grossly inaccurate, and that Tanganyika was probably a thousand feet higher than he had estimated.[16] But he must have suspected that Burton had deduced this in any case. He knew that Burton was formidable in debate, with enormous resources of language and history at his command, and that he himself—ironically enough, considering his name—spoke haltingly. He knew that though Sir Roderick Murchison, Francis Galton, and others were on his side, Livingstone, Macqueen and Beke were all against him, and Petherick was about to sue him for libel. Even Grant, who had ostensibly remained faithful, had taken pains to stay out of the controversy, even declining his invitation to attend the debate. Speke could not easily have dislodged from his mind the cruel editorial in the *Westminster Review* of April, 1864: "But Grant will have little to regret, and Burton will be more than avenged, should Tanganyika and not Nyanza prove to be the head of the Nile."

And so the tragedy of this courageous young man, for whom success at thirty-seven had brought only guilt, confusion and hatred, moved on inexorably to its climax. Burton walked into the preliminary session at Bath on September 15 with Isabel on his arm. Almost at once they encountered Speke. Burton was shocked by the ageing in his face, but could not bring himself to greet him. Speke looked at Richard and his wife for a fleeting instant, his face questioning, perplexed and full of yearning. Then his look hardened and he strode past them. During the meeting he became increasingly and obviously nervous. Finally he exclaimed half aloud, "I cannot stand this any longer," and stood up. The man standing nearest him said, "Shall you want your chair again, sir? May I have it? Shall you come back?"

He answered, "I hope not," and left the hall.[17]

The next day when Burton walked to the debate platform, he noticed a crowd in the adjoining room, including the most distinguished members of the Council. Seeing a special stiffening in several faces, he did not enter. Nor was he invited. He stood for an uncomfortable twenty-five minutes while a note was passed about among the group. Finally a friend came out and whispered to him its contents, and the chairman announced to the audience—as Burton wrote it—"Captain Speke lost his life on the yesterday, at 4 pm, whilst shooting over a cousin's grounds. He had been missed in the field and his kinsmen found him lying upon the heath, shot through the body close to the heart. He lived only a few minutes and his last words were a request not to be moved."

A persistent legend puts it that Burton reeled back and sank into a chair saying, "By God, he's killed himself." When called upon to speak, he abandoned his prepared speech and spoke haltingly, and in a voice that frequently trembled, of conditions in Dahomey. After a few moments he sat down.[18]

Speke, after leaving Bath on the previous day, had gone to Neston Park, near Box in Wiltshire, the home of his uncle, John Fuller. As at so many other times of great emotional stress in his life, he went out shooting birds. Accompanying him on the partridge hunt were his cousin, George Fuller, the gamekeeper, Daniel Davis, and a surgeon, Thomas Fitzherbert Snow. Speke carried a Lancaster breech-loader shotgun with no safety catch. They spread out, as usual, and before long Speke fired both barrels of his gun. Later, about four o'clock, Fuller, not far distant from Speke, heard a third blast. He saw the explorer, who was standing on a two-foot stone wall, fall heavily to the ground. Rushing forward he found him bleeding from a great hole in his chest. Speke whispered only, "Don't move me." Fuller called to Davis, the gamekeeper, for help, and then ran for the surgeon, who was a considerable distance away. Davis remained behind helplessly to watch Speke die. It took about fifteen minutes. The date was September 15, the anniversary of the death of his brother Edward in the Indian Mutiny six years before.

Later the surgeon surmised that Speke had mounted the wall and then drawn the gun up after him. In some fashion it had gone off accidentally while he was holding the muzzle close to his chest. One barrel had been discharged; the other had its hammer at half-cock. The coroner recommended to the jury at the inquest that they rule the death an accident, and they did. *The Times* obituary of September 19 speculated that "one of the hammers must have struck against a stone or hitched in a bough, and the blow just lifted the hammer, and then allowed it to fall back upon the pin of the cartridge." Still the editor was puzzled. "Speke was the last man who could have been expected to succumb to so poor a peril as this," he wrote. "He was a veteran sportsman. . . . firearms must have been to him familiar as the pen to the writer, or the brush to the painter. Perhaps it was the great familiarity which produced the momentary incaution." This was a decent camouflage hiding the question everyone was asking.

It is now generally recognized that suicide is a supreme act of hate, often directed against someone one has loved. If one knows the intimate life of the victim, it is sometimes possible to see clearly the design of murder, which is turned inward at the end.[19] Since the most closely affected people are likely to feel a burden of guilt for not having prevented the deed by some manifestation of compassion or affection, there is enormous unspoken resentment against the dead. Hence suicides are covered up, when at all possible, with elaborate fabrications designed to protect the living. We do not know what happened at the stone wall, for the person closest to the tragedy was Speke's cousin, who, even if he was certain it was suicide, would have had strong motives to protect his distinguished relative's reputation, and also to conceal and thereby diminish his own sense of outrage. We cannot on the evidence assert that it was deliberate suicide, which is, however, strongly suggested by the fact that the gun was held against his chest. But even if it was an "accident," this fatal gesture of carelessness alien to twenty years of strict conditioning against such carelessness would indicate a strong preconscious inclination to suicide. Speke may well have feared that Burton would "destroy" him in the debate; by his own act of self-destruction he would seal Burton's mouth forever, thus destroying *him*.

Although Burton wrote shortly afterward to *The Times*, "The sad event . . . must seal my mouth concerning many things," he nevertheless found himself compelled to speak out in his own defence. Thomas Wright tells us that even at Bath "Burton expressed his opinion, and afterwards circulated it, that Speke had committed suicide in order to avoid 'the exposure of his misstatements in regard to the Nile sources.'"[20] Five days after the tragedy Burton wrote to Frank Wilson at Fernando Po, "Captain Speke came to a bad end, but no one knows anything about it." Later, bitter at the blame that came his way, he confided to Wilson again, "Nothing is known of Speke's death. I saw him at 1.30 pm and at 4 pm he was dead. The charitable say that he shot himself, the uncharitable say that I shot him."[21]

Even eight years later, in his *Zanzibar*, when Burton described

Speke's death more cautiously as "an unaccountable accident," he nevertheless went on to say, "The calamity had been the more unexpected as he was ever remarkable for the caution with which he handled his weapon. I ever make a point of ascertaining a fellow-traveller's habit in that matter, and I observed that even when our canoe was shaken and upthrown by the hippopotamus he never allowed his gun to look at him or at others."[22]

Speke's death brought consternation and guilt to others as well as Burton. Grant wrote, ". . . had I gone hither and been with my friend, this calamity might have been averted. . . . I reproached myself for having silently born all the taunts and doubts thrown upon his great discovery.[23] He dedicated the book he was writing, *A Walk Across Africa*, to Speke's memory, and said nothing but good of him within its pages and ever after.

But Burton would not be silenced. He was angered enough to speak out publicly in his own defence, first of all by *The Times* obituary, which said in part:

Captain Speke and Captain Burton can no longer be pitted against each other for the gladiatorial exhibition. It must be very hard for Captain Burton, who has won so many laurels, to reflect that he was once slumbering under the shadow of the very highest prize of all while another, and less experienced hand reached over and plucked the fruit. . . . In fact, poor Burton was ill and Speke was well. Speke was shooting Egyptian geese and catching perch in the lake while Burton lay in his hammock. Moreover, Speke had the happy sagacity to guess the vast importance of the discovery on which he had lighted. Burton was very near gaining the blue riband of the Geographers, but did not gain it. He may well be content, however, with his other achievements. In all future time Captain Speke, whose loss we deplore, must be remembered as the discoverer of the Source of the Nile.

Though admitting that his mouth was sealed about Speke himself, Burton protested that the Nile source was not settled, and that it could not be as long as the connection between his own Tanganyika and the Lŭta Nzigé remained unresolved.[24] In this he was right. Later, on November 14, he delivered before the Royal Geographical Society the speech he had intended to give at Bath. And he rushed this speech into print before the year's end in a thin volume called *The Nile Basin*, which included also a reprint of Macqueen's libellous articles from the *Morning Advertiser*.

"Be it distinctly understood that . . . I do not stand forth as an enemy of the departed," Burton wrote in the preface, "that no man can better appreciate the noble qualities of energy, courage, and perseverance which he so eminently possessed than I do who knew him for so many years, and who travelled with him as a brother, until the unfortunate rivalry respecting the Nile Sources arose like the ghost of discord between us, and was fanned to a flame by the enmity and the ambition of 'friends.' " This disclaimer fooled no one. Reviewers universally deplored *The Nile Basin* as a tasteless attack. *Blackwood's* called Burton an unscrupulous and jealous rival, saying his journey to Tanganyika was "a mere holiday pastime" in comparison with Speke's second expedition.[25]

Enmeshed in the web of justification, attack, and further justification, Burton would not be gagged. "Why should 'the very controversy be allowed to slumber' because the gallant Speke was the victim of a fatal mishap?" he asked in the *Athenaeum* of January 14, 1865. And he continued to distort and belittle. No one apparently except his wife knew that he suffered a private grief. "He wept long and bitterly," she said, "and I was for many a day trying to comfort him."[26]

In February 1869 a remarkable story appeared in *Fraser's Magazine*, ostensibly written by Isabel Burton. It described how in the winter following Speke's death the couple had been invited to the studio of sculptor Edgar G. Papworth, who was making a bust of the dead explorer. Papworth, pointing to the death mask on the floor, asked Burton for suggestions. "I only took the cast after death," he said, "and never knew him alive; but you who lived with him so long can surely give me some hints." Whereupon Burton, who had learned something of sculpturing in Italy as a boy, took up the tool and worked at the clay for a few moments. Speke's face emerged in astonishing fidelity.

Following this account there was printed a poem of twenty-three six-line stanzas which was in every way extraordinary. It began with Richard Burton's contemplation of Speke's death mask in the studio, and evolved into a deeply intimate elegy, rich in oblique allusions that only Burton himself could have fashioned or understood. It had the same iambic tetrameter line and the same rhyming scheme as his old unpublished poem of lament for the dead Persian girl of his Indian days, and was similar in quality to his *Kasidah*. No one seems to have suspected that it was almost certainly Burton's poem rather than his wife's. That he should have persuaded Isabel to publish it as her own in *Fraser's Magazine* is a great curiosity. One can conjecture only that he wrote the elegy and wanted it in the public record, but could not bear to sign it himself because it laid bare a piece of his inner life.[27]

The elegy begins with the discovery of the death mask:

> A molded mask at my feet I found,
>   With the drawn-down mouth and the deepen'd eye,
> More lifeless still than the marbles 'round—
>   Very death amid life's mimicry:
> I raised it, and Thought fled afar from me
>   To the Afric land by the Zingian Sea. . . .

Then follows vivid reminiscences of their illnesses in Africa:

> Where Fever, yellow-skinned, bony, gaunt,
>   With the long blue nails and the lip livid white;
> With the blood-stain'd orbs that could ever haunt
>   Our brains by day and our eyes by night;
> In her grave-clothes mouldy with the graveyard taint
>   Came round our sleeping mats—came and went. . . .

The poem goes on to a definition of friendship between man and man, followed shortly by a remarkable stanza that is as close as Burton ever came to describing his own marriage:

> On the guarded tablet was writ by Fate,
>   A double self for each man ere born,
> Who shall love his love and shall hate his hate,
>   Who shall praise his praise and shall scorn his scorn,
> Enduring, aye to the bitter end,
>   And man's other man shall be called a friend. . . .
>
> 'Twixt man and woman use oft hath bred
>   The habits that feebly affection feign,
> While the common board and the genial bed
>   And Time's welding force links a length of chain;
> Till, where Love was not, it hath sometimes proved
>   This has loved and lived, that has lived and loved.

Having thus intimated that love had finally come to a marriage that had begun without much love on his part, Burton went on to define at least poetically the difference between a true friendship between men and his relations with Speke:

> But 'twixt man and man it may not so hap;
>   Each man is his own and his proper sphere:
> At some point, perchance, may the lines o'erlap;
>   The far rest is far as the near is near—
> Save when the orbs are of friend and friend
>   And the circle's limits perforce must blend.
>
> But the one sole point at which he and I
>   Could touch, was the contact of vulgar minds;
> 'Twas interest's forcible, feeble tie,
>   Which binds, but with lasting bonds ne'er binds;
> And our objects fated to disagree,
>   What way went I, and what way went he?
>
> Yet were we comrades for years and years,
>   And endured in its troth our companionship
> Through a life of chances, of hopes, and fears;
>   Nor a word of harshness e'er passed the lip,
> Nor a thought unkind dwelt in either heart,
>   Till we chanced—by what chance did it hap?—to part.

Eight years after Speke's death Burton included this poem, with Isabel's introduction, in his *Zanzibar*, where he wrote significantly of his relations with Speke. With this poem he ended the chapter and the volume. So ended, it would seem, the chapter on Speke in Burton's own life.

There was a sequel, however. If Speke was dead, the Nile controversy certainly was not. Almost every year after 1864 explorers drew new lines into the white spaces on the map of Africa, in the end forcing Burton into ever greater silence and retreat. Samuel Baker reached the Lŭta Nzigé in March 1864, and was convinced that he had found the Nile's western source, and the only source from which "the whole Nile" flowed. Because of unfriendly natives he did not circumnavigate the lake, which he called Lake Albert, but greatly exaggerated its size, and his account increased Burton's hope that there was a connection with Tanganyika. Then in 1871 Livingstone and Henry Stanley dealt Burton a body blow. Exploring Tanganyika together, after their celebrated meeting at Ujiji, they established unmistakably that the Rusizi River flowed into and not out of the lake. Still they missed the outlet to the west, lost in a great swamp.

Livingstone, who had by now become even more obsessed by the Nile mystery than Burton, Speke, or Baker, clung to the theory that Lake Tanganyika somehow flowed into the Lualaba and thence northwards to the Nile. "He has heard of the existence of four fountains," Stanley wrote, "two of which give birth to a river flowing north . . . the Lualaba, and two to a river flowing south, which is the Zambezi. He has repeatedly heard of these fountains from the natives. Several times he has been within 100 and 200 miles of them, but something always interposed to prevent his going to see them. . . . they rise on either side of a mound . . . which contains no stones." Long after Stanley left him, Livingstone kept searching. On April 25, 1873 the natives of Chitambos, on the Lulimala, found him dead, kneeling before his bed as in prayer. Three or four days earlier he had asked them, "Did they know of a hill on which four fountains rise?" He had been asking it to the end.[28]

In 1874 Burton's friend, Lieutenant V. L. Cameron, finally discovered that Tanganyika overflowed in the wet season into the sluggish Lukaga, and on into the Lualaba. Then Stanley in 1875 circumnavigated Lake Victoria, showing Speke to have been wholly right in his conviction that it was one immense lake. Burton now frankly acknowledged his error about Lake Victoria before the Royal Geographical Society, November 29, 1875, but still clung stubbornly to his hope that a water passage existed between Tanganyika and Baker's Lake Albert.[29] In 1876 he speculated in his *Two Trips to Gorilla Land* that Tanganyika had two outlets, one to the west, which overflowed in the rainy season, and one to the north. He did not, however, like Livingstone and Stanley, believe that the Lualaba was the upper Nile, predicting correctly that it would prove to be the northeastern branch of the Congo.[30] Finally Stanley, in the greatest of his explorations, decided in 1876 to prove conclusively that Livingstone was right in his theory that the Lualaba led to the Nile. But after following the river north for a great distance, he discovered that it swung west in a great arc, and realized to his consternation that he was following not the upper Nile but the formidable Congo, and that instead of arriving in the Mediterranean he must perforce go all the way down the Congo's terrible course to the Atlantic.

After Stanley reached the ocean, and publicized his voyage, Burton was faced finally with the certain knowledge that his own lake had proved to be "the head-reservoir not of the Nile, but of the mighty Congo." He now wrote a letter to the *Athenaeum* pointing out that in 1858 neither he nor Speke had been aware that they looked out upon the greatest watershed of the continent, dividing "the Giant of Egypt and the Giant of Angola." "We were," he continued, "allowed by fate to see the Nile small." Only in the sense that the smallest tributaries of the River Kagera—the main stream feeding Lake Victoria—did in fact arise in the 6,000-foot mountains north of Lake Tanganyika, and that he did see, if not the rivulets themselves at least the mountains in which they sprang, was Burton right. But this was stretching a point to absurdity, and served only to underline once more the intensity of his hunger for the one prize he could not share under any circumstances.

Burton waited until 1881 to make a written public admission of complete defeat. "I am compelled formally to abandon a favourite theory," he wrote, "that the Tanganyika drained to the Nile basin via the Lŭta-Nzigé." He went on to list the explorations that had proved him to be in error, commenting finally not on Speke's death but on how the search for the Nile sources had cost Livingstone his life. "There is a time to leave the Dark Continent," he concluded sombrely, "and that is when the *idée fixe* begins to develop itself. 'Madness comes from Africa' . . . ."[31]

The Taming

I have domesticated and tamed Richard a little, and it would not do to give him an excuse for becoming a wandering vagabond again. He requires a comfortable home, and a tight hand upon his purse-strings.

Isabel Burton to her mother, September 2, 1866[1]

*T*HE YEAR OF Speke's death was decisive for Burton. It marked an end not only to their complicated private involvement, but also to Burton's life as a serious explorer. For a time his curiosity about exotic peoples seemed utterly destroyed. He turned increasingly to poetry on the one hand, and on the other to the practical problems of making a decent living for himself and his wife. For the first time one sees in him a dependence upon Isabel, though in his verse one sees also a certain resentment against her and against marriage. Journalist Justin McCarthy, who knew Burton both before and after his marriage, insisted that Isabel's tenderness and devotion resulted in his becoming kindly and considerate, patient of other men's opinions and surprisingly tolerant of their motives.[2] Whether this mellowing resulted from Isabel's devotion, or whether it evolved more from his own personal anguish as a result of the whole complex of Speke's death, his brother's madness, and his own sense of guilt and failure, one cannot say. In any case, Isabel's taming was neither sudden nor total. Burton's explorations did not end altogether, and his preoccupation with people did not die but rather altered in emphasis and direction.

Still one must admit that Burton's final acquiescence in conventional married life with Isabel coincided in time with the end of his career both as an explorer and as an ethnologist. In 1864 all his great original works were behind him save for two books largely written but still unpublished—his lost manuscript on Zanzibar, discovered and published in 1872, and his *Gorilla Land and the Cataracts of the Congo*, most of which he had written in 1862 but would not publish till 1876. Though his reputation as an explorer should have been solidly established—no one could rightfully deny him Mecca, Harar and Tanganyika—his fame was seriously clouded by Speke's suicide and the continuing Nile controversy. Only a few men in England who were beginning to call themselves "anthropologists" recognized that Burton deserved equal fame as a student of native societies. In addition to his four books on India, his celebrated *Pilgrimage*, and his *The City of the Saints*, he had written altogether nine studies on Africa totalling thirteen volumes—4,606 pages. It is probable that at this time he knew more about Africa than anyone in England. Moreover, at forty-three, he was one of the great linguists of Europe.

Still there seemed to be no proper place for him. No post at Cambridge or at Oxford was offered him; nor would it have been had there been a vacant chair in anthropology or in African studies—which there was not—simply because he lacked the necessary scholastic degrees. In the Foreign Office no one seems to have felt that Burton should be specially rewarded either for his explorations or for his fantastic accumulation of data on native peoples. In diplomatic circles in England erudition was more likely to be considered a handicap than an aid in the governing of men.

The role of consul was lowly, then as now. According to the *British Consul's Manual* of 1856, the most important of the consul's duties "consist in his being present, if possible, at the shipwreck of any of his countrymen's vessels, and in seeing that the abuses and plunder on wrecked ships, which generally occur, are not permitted." Of secondary significance were "all matters relating to manufactures, arts, sciences, commerce, and navigation." Actually, as Burton knew well enough, his only real duty lay in expediting British trade and keeping British nationals out of trouble. Beyond that little was expected of him. A preoccupation with native rituals concerning birth, lactation, sex and death was accounted eccentric or even sinister.

Moreover, promotions to posts of real consequence such as ministers were almost certain to be made on the basis of aristocratic birth rather than merit. Only the consulate posts such as Damascus or Tripoli or Teheran offered a challenge to Burton, and even these were best served —by Foreign Office standards—by mediocre and timid men. Burton found it difficult to make importunities to the Foreign Office for advancement or transfer, counting all such overtures demeaning. He was hopeful that his books would speak for him. The Foreign Office being what it was, these books did him no special service.

Isabel on the other hand, who had no inhibitions about asking favours, wrote several times directly to Lord Russell begging for a better consulate for Richard. Russell replied with mild exasperation October 6, 1863: "I know the climate in which your husband is working so zealously and so well is an unhealthy one, but it is not true to say that he is the smallest of consuls in the worst part of the world. . . . However, if I find a vacancy of a post with an equal salary and a better position, I will not forget his services."³ Russell made good his promise in September 1864, and transferred Burton to Santos, Brazil, though still at £700 a year. Burton wrote cheerfully of the transfer to Frank Wilson in Fernando Po, September 21, 1864, "I want so see S. America. Plenty of travel there," adding affectionately, "Do *knock about*."⁴

Before leaving for Brazil the Burtons had a holiday in Ireland and another in Portugal. The London Anthropological Society honoured him with a farewell dinner, and as a great concession this all male group gave Isabel permission to listen to the proceedings, hidden discreetly behind a screen. There were innumerable parties, where, as she put it, "we met an immense quantity of distinguished people." Though she professed to be in mortal terror at these gatherings lest Richard offend the wrong people, it is clear that she took a secret relish—like his mother—in his playing the role of *gamin*, or "dirty Frenchman" as she sometimes called him to his face. "He adored shocking dense people," she wrote, "and seeing their funny faces and stolid belief, and never cared about what harm it would do him in a worldly sense. I have frequently sat at the dinner-table of such people, praying him by signs not to go on, but he was in a very ecstasy of glee; he said it was so funny always to be believed when you were chaffing, and so curious never to be believed when you were telling the truth."⁵

Lord Redesdale remembered one of Burton's more brutal tales and related it in his memoirs. They were discussing swords at a smoker, he said, and Burton interrupted with what seemed to be a true reminiscence:

Ah it has always been a matter of regret to me that I never quite succeeded in cutting a man in two. I very nearly did once. I was alone in the desert and saw that I was being pursued by three men; my horse was tired and they were gaining upon me. As the leading man came up with me I drew my sword and dealt him a furious blow on the shoulder, cutting him slantwise right down to the waist; unfortunately I did not cut through the last bit of skin, so the horse galloped off with half the man's body hanging over the saddle.

Still Burton made clear with a wink, Lord Redesdale said, that it was only a tall tale. And Lovett Cameron, one of Burton's best friends, noted that "his witty remarks were not calculated to really hurt any man but himself."⁶

Shortly before leaving England for Brazil Burton published without his wife's knowledge 200 copies of a 121-page satirical poem called *Stone Talk*, signing it Frank Baker, a pseudonym adapted from his own second name and the maiden name of his mother. Burton labelled it privately in the margin of his own copy (now in the Royal Anthropological Institute) "a pestilent lampoon." Certainly nothing else he wrote portrayed such disillusionment, gall and spleen. He gave a copy to

Isabel indicating that he had purchased it, and she tells us that she read it "with peals of laughter," till something in his expression gave the secret away. "You wrote it yourself, Jemmy," she said accusingly, "and *nobody* else." Having gained his admission, Isabel read it again and was appalled.

The poem was a long obscure dialogue between a drunken scholar, Dr Polyglott, and a paving stone in a London street, which in the dim lamp light assumed the features of an East Indian. The dialogue was between Burton and himself—one part sardonic, bitter, depressed and cold as stone, the other lively, protesting, witty, and warm-hearted. The poem was also a social and political lampoon. Burton attacked Britain's heroes in India—Clive, Hastings, Dalhousie and Napier—as bandits bringing "death and doom" to a lovely land, and summed up the Crimean War in a bitter couplet:

> A hundred thousand souls had died—
> To gratify two despots pride.

He freely paraded his atheism and enthusiastic Darwinism, describing man as a "little vermin spawned of mud," poking fun at Genesis, and calling Adam "an hermaphrodite." There were poignant recollections of his old loves, including a glowing description of Isabel's cousin, Louisa, which we have quoted in an earlier chapter, followed by expressions of disillusionment with "the corseted woman" in general, and of marriage in particular.

> A pinched wretch, encased, enrolled
>   Like rotten mummy in its fold
> Of linen swaddlings. I prefer
>   A camel-load of flesh to her—
> Th' obesest Mooress that e'er trod
>   Of Atlas hills the verdant sod. . . .

> Your happy hearth is oft a hell
>   Where Temper, Spite, and Disgust dwell,
> And Ennui sheds her baleful gloom
>   Making the place a living tomb. . . .

Burton sent copies of the poem to leading journals, and his own copy shows many pencilled marginal changes, as if he had hoped for a second printing. But Isabel took the poem to Monckton Milnes, expressing fear that it would damage Richard with the Foreign Office if the authorship became known. Milnes advised her to buy up the copies and destroy them, which she did.[7] Whether Richard knew of her action she does not say. But the episode demonstrated that he could, and would, inflict hurt—and that she could, and would, destroy.

Burton took off for Brazil in advance of his wife, leaving her to "pay, pack, and follow," as so often in their marriage. Before sailing, Isabel spent a week in retreat at the Convent of the Assumption in London. Here she poured out her anguish in her devotional book: "I am to bear *all* joyfully, as an atonement to save Richard. . . . I have bought bitter experiences, but much has, I hope, been forgiven me."⁸ Fortified and cheerful, she sailed from England in August 1865, determined to establish a real home for the first time in her marriage.

Santos, 230 miles south of Rio de Janeiro, now a great coffee port, was then little more than a village surrounded by a mangrove swamp, nine miles inland from the sea, infested with insects, and as fever-ridden as Fernando Po. "I do hate Santos," Isabel wrote her mother on December 15. "The climate is beastly, the people fluffy. The stinks, the vermin, the food, the niggers are all of a piece. There are no walks; and if you go one way, you sink knee-deep in mangrove swamps; another you are covered with sand-flies." Other letters reveal that her tie with her mother was still strong. "I got the same crying fit about you, dear mother, last week, as I did at Lisbon," she wrote on March 9, 1866, "starting up in the night and screaming out that you were dead; I find I do it whenever I am overfatigued and weak. The chance of losing you is what weighs most on my mind, and it is therefore my nightmare when I am not strong."

She was soon ill with fever, and Richard, alarmed by her delirium, which he treated vainly with hypnosis, decided to move to a less hostile area. At São Paulo, fifty miles west and 2,500 feet above sea level, there was a temperate climate and less malaria. Here Isabel found an abandoned convent, dilapidated but spacious, with extravagant views of the surrounding country. Enchanted by the site, she set about with three servants papering, painting, and covering up the rat holes in the floor. She worked fiercely. "Only fancy, the Brazilians are dreadfully shocked at me for working!" she wrote to her mother. There was a forty-foot study for Burton, a chapel, and several bedrooms. "I have had their hard, lumbering, buggy beds removed," she said, "and have put up our own little iron English bedsteads with spring mattresses. I slept in my own cosy little bed from Montagu Place last night for the first time since it left my room there (now Dilly's); I kissed it with delight and jumped in it. I also bought one in London for Richard."⁹ The chapel she painted herself, white with a blue border, and the domed ceiling blue and gilt. It was soon in demand for christenings, as Isabel, speaking imperfect Portuguese, welcomed in the neighbourhood.

She found a horse that ran like the wind, and rode him everywhere, often carrying her servant Chico, a dwarf, behind her saddle. In the wilds she rode straddle the horse like a man, regretting that São Paulo was too civilized for such behaviour. Once she caused a sensation by bringing home four squawking live geese tied to the pommel of her saddle. Burton, hearing the noise, ran out on to the balcony. He laughed and shook his fist and said, "Oh, you delightful blackguard—how like you!"

At first Burton was happy in Brazil. He enjoyed watching the exhilaration of his wife in her new freedom; he taught her fencing, the art of Indian clubs, and the more difficult art of copying his manuscripts. He seems even to have enjoyed being tamed a little, and since he alternated living in Santos and São Paulo he did not feel enchained. He took his work seriously, sending in long reports on cotton, geography and general trade. Intermittently he and Isabel went to Rio de Janeiro, and Petropolis, summer residence of the diplomatic corps, where they participated in lively parties.

The emperor, Dom Pedro II, was an educated, sensitive ruler, who since his crowning in 1841 had brought stability to Brazil. A fine linguist who knew both Arabic and Sanscrit, he found Burton fascinating and treated him with the courtesy befitting his reputation and scholarship. Ignoring protocol, Dom Pedro gave him many interviews, attended two of his public lectures, and at one dinner gave him and Isabel precedence even over the ministers, an act that roused no little jealousy among Burton's superiors in office. The empress gave Isabel a diamond bracelet. So it was not surprising that when they returned to Santos and São Paulo they found life tedious.

Burton toyed with a grammar of the Tupy-Guarani language, which was never published. More importantly he began a work that was to occupy him fitfully for many years, a translation of the complete works of Portugal's foremost poet, Camoens. And he took time out to translate a volume of Hindu folk tales. Though most of his Indian manuscripts had been burned in the Grindlay warehouse fire in London shortly after his marriage, he had begun replacing them and he singled out the *Vétála-pancha-Vinshati, or Twenty-five Tales of a Demon*,[10] part of the collection of folk literature known as the *Kathā Sarit Sāgara*, written originally in Sanscrit and dating back to the 11th century. Working with the 1799 Hindu version of Lalualal, Burton adapted eleven of the twenty-five tales. He was the first to bring to an English audience these ironic, amoral stories of fantasy and magic, precursors of the *Arabian Nights* and the *Decameron*.

The tales are told by a vampire, who is captured by Vikram, the legendary Hindu equivalent of King Arthur and Harun al Rashid. Among the provocative titles were the following: "In Which a Man Deceives a Woman," "On the Relative Villainy of Men and Women,"

"Of a Woman who Told the Truth," and "Showing that a Man's Wife Belongs not to his Body but to his Head." The last was a story of a woman who in an accidental act of magic affixes the head of her husband on to the body of a former suitor, whose head in turn is fastened to the body of her husband. The question becomes: "To which does she belong, the head or the body of her husband?" The problem remained unresolved, as it may well have, in a more subtle sense, in Burton's own marriage.

Burton would publish these tales in 1870 in London under the title *Vikram and the Vampire, or Tales of Hindu Devilry.* The book would lose money, and its failure would delay Burton's plans to translate an unexpurgated version of the *Arabian Nights.* It is curious that out of all the Hindu and Arabic literature he could have translated, he chose first that particular sequence of stories in which the storyteller—normally a vagrant hero like himself—is here pictured as a monster feeding on corpses and sucking the blood of the living.

Burton inserted a special message in his very first tale, "The Vampire's first story." Here, in a paragraph that was entirely his own, he described a minister's son who married a woman exactly like Isabel Arundell:

The minister's son especially hated talented, intellectual, and strong minded women. . . . Amongst womankind he admired—theoretically, as became a philosopher—the small, plump, laughing, chattering, unintellectual, and material-minded. And therefore—excuse the digression, Raja Vikram—he married an old maid, tall, yellow, strictly proper, cold-mannered, a conversationalist, who prided herself upon spirituality. But more wonderful still, after he did marry her, he actually loved her—what an incomprehensible being is man in these matters![11]

This was the closest Burton would ever come to a personal declaration, in print, that somewhat to his surprise he loved his wife.

Perpetually short of funds, Burton speculated in Brazil in cotton and coffee, and in lead, gold and diamond mines. The Foreign Office had strict rules against consuls participating in trade, and at one point he was almost called home in disgrace. Only the intercession of his fellow "anthropologist," Lord Stanley, head of the Foreign Office, saved him.[12] The mining schemes, which only lost him money, carried him ever more often into the Brazilian wilderness, and he took to drinking heavily. It was from his own experience that he wrote, " 'Brandy,' said Dr Johnson, 'is the drink of heroes,' and here men drink their Cachaça heroically; the effect is 'liver,' dropsy, and death."[13]

After what he called "eighteen dull months" at Santos, he asked for a three-months leave to make an extensive trip to the rich province of Minas Geraes, ostensibly to study the mineral resources and to advise on the best route for a railroad. But Burton was also seeking out an old love—a great river. The Rio São Francisco presented no mystery like the Nile. There were scattered ranches along its banks; it was neither as civilized as the Indus nor as savage as the Congo. But it had one long cataract-ridden stretch from Sabara to the great Falls of Paulo Affonso that no man had ever ridden down successfully in either boat or raft. This Burton was determined to do.

Isabel begged to accompany him, and Richard, who wrote with admiration that she would not have hesitated to travel anywhere, decided to risk taking her. They went on horseback, alternating between the hospitality of the great ranches and the wretched overnight stations, where they slept in hammocks to avoid the vermin. They descended the great gold mine at Morro Velho lowered in a crude basket, suspended by a chain of dubious reputation. "We had seen the poor smashed negroes brought up," Isabel wrote, "and it did break the next day, but *our time was not yet come.*" Burton described the mine as "distinctly Dantesque." "The heavy gloom, the fitful glare, and the savage chant, with the wall hanging like the stone of Cisyphus, like the sword of Damocles, suggested a sort of material Swedenborgian hell."[14]

At Morro Velho Isabel sprained her ankle. After waiting ten days for it to heal, they tried the river together from Sabara to Santo Antonio da Roca, a stretch that included two rapids. But Isabel was clearly too lame for the whole voyage, and it is likely that both of them looked upon the accident with relief. After several weeks of rest, she made the 15-day trip back to Rio with several servants. As she wrote to her mother frankly upon arrival, the city seemed a kind of paradise. Her boots were in shreds, her dress had "forty slits in it," her skin was the colour of mahogany, and she had grown "fat, and coarse, and vulgar."[15]

Burton meanwhile took off with three natives on the 1,500-mile trip in a raft made of two 33-foot canoes lashed together. "I confess to having felt an unusual sense of loneliness as the kindly faces faded in the distance," he wrote, adding with some wonder, "What made me think of the Nile story . . . of the white man paddled by dark Amazons adorned with barbaric gold?" Though he kept a careful journal when riding on what he called "the bosom of this glorious stream," it is clear that the river was a disappointment when matched against his fantasies. The diamond diggings he inspected on the way were also unrewarding. Only the falls themselves, the Brazilian Niagara, an incredible "Quebrada" 260 feet high, kindled the excitement for which he hungered. Leaving the canoes as they neared the falls, he descended to a table of jutting rock, and clinging to a tree trunk peered spellbound into the "hell of waters boiling below."

And the marvellous disorder is a well-directed anarchy: the course and sway, the wrestling and writhing, all tend to set free the prisoner from the prison of walls. . . . The general effect . . . is the "realized" idea of power, of power tremendous, inexorable, irresistible. The eye is spellbound by the contrast of this impetuous motion, this wrathful, maddened haste to escape, with the frail stedfastness of the bits of rainbow, hovering above. . . . The fancy is electrified by the aspect of this Durga of Nature, this evil working good, this life-in-death, this creation and construction by destruction. . . . I sat over the "Quebrada" till convinced it was not possible to become "one with the waters:" what at first seemed grand and sublime at last had a feeling of awe too intense to be in any way enjoyable, and I left the place that the confusion and emotion might pass away.

Later he wrote, "My task was done. I won its reward, and the strength passed away from me."[16]

Isabel waited for her husband in Rio for more than four months. Wilfrid Scawen Blunt, a young Foreign Office attaché destined for a career as poet, publicist and writer on the Near East, met her during this period. He described her as "a very sociable, and very talkative woman, clever, but at the same time foolish, overflowing with stories of which her husband was always the hero. Her devotion to him was very real, and she was indeed entirely under his domination, an hypnotic domination Burton used to boast of."[17] Actually at the time she was ridden with anxiety. "I fear Richard is ill, or taken prisonor or has his money stolen . . . ," she wrote to her mother. "I am not afraid of anything except the wild Indians, fever, ague, and a vicious fish which can easily be avoided." She met every steamer as it arrived from Bahia, writing later, "I used to make a fool of myself by crying when I did not find him. . . . At last the first steamer that I did *not* go to meet, he arrived in, and was quite angry to find that I was not on board to meet him."[18]

The river trip solved nothing. The two volumes Burton wrote to describe the journey were pedestrian—the *Athenaeum* would call them "a mere compilation"—and he must have known it. Promotion and transfer seemed as far away as ever. In April 1868 he fell ill of what Isabel described as liver congestion, almost certainly the result of his heavy drinking. The hepatitis was complicated by a lung infection that nearly cost him his life. A doctor from Rio gave him the usual incredible remedies of the time. "He put twelve leeches on and cupped him on the right breast, lanced him in thirty-eight places, and put on a powerful blister on the whole of that side," Isabel said. "He lost an immense deal of black clotted blood. . . . The agony was fearful, and poor Richard could not move hand or foot, nor speak, swallow, or breathe without a paroxysm of pain."

"He seemed to be dying, and I knew not what to do," she continued. Finally she took some scapulars (white cloths worn over the shoulder and chest by devout Catholics) and holy water from her chapel. "The doctor has tried all his remedies," she said to Richard with some trepidation; "now let me try one of mine." "I put some holy water on his head, and knelt down and said some prayers, and put on the blessed scapulars. . . . He was quite still for about an hour, and then he said in a whisper, 'Zoo, I think I'm a little better'. . . . He has never had a *bad* paroxysm since."[19]

To the end of her life Isabel cherished the memory of this day as a private miracle. And Burton did recover, though he remained thin and grey, looking more like sixty than forty-seven, and his voice remained hoarse for months. He must have been touched by her prayers, and her eight weeks' vigil, but they did not induce him to become a Catholic, or to become less hostile to the church in his books. Less than a year later he would write ironically of the Jesuits in Paraguay, "They crushed out the man that he might better become an angel, and they forced him to be a slave that he might wax fit for the kingdom of heaven."[20]

Later in London, when in her husband's absence Isabel was seeing through the press *The Highlands of Brazil*, she was angered by his strictures against the church she held sacred. He had attacked the religious schools in Brazil as "fifty years behind the world," and had written that the church in Brazil "still grants dispensations to commit incest for a consideration."[21] His light-hearted defense of polygamy in the same book also offended her deeply. So, without Richard's knowledge, she wrote and published a spirited protesting preface. Insisting that she had not altered one word of the text, she wrote that nevertheless she wished to "point the finger of indignation particularly at what misrepresents our Holy Roman Catholic Church, and at what upholds that unnatural and repulsive law, Polygamy, which the Author is careful not to practice himself, but from a high moral pedestal he preaches to the ignorant as a means of population in young countries." She concluded with a slap at the book itself, warning the reader "to steer through these anthropological sand-banks and hidden rocks as best he or she may."

The preface vastly amused the reviewers. And Burton realized, perhaps with real shock, that in teaching his wife to fence and throw Indian clubs and ride astride a horse like a man he had also given her the courage to slap him soundly in print. He withstood the shock, as did their marriage, which may even have benefited from it.

Burton had not yet completely recovered from his illness of April 1868 when he decided abruptly to resign his Santos consulship. "Richard told me," Isabel wrote, "that he could not stand it any longer, and he asked me to go to England and see if I could not induce them to give him another post." The decision was a wrench for Isabel; it meant an end to life in São Paulo, "the only home I had ever really had quietly with him." But she accepted it, sold everything, said goodbye to her many friends, and sailed for England on July 24, 1868, loaded with manuscripts which her husband had given her with orders to seek out a publisher.* Moreover, once again he was fleeing from her, even if by sending her away; she would not see him for over a year.

Burton had obtained sick leave from the Foreign Office, which he intended to spend in Buenos Aires. But after Isabel's departure, though still gaunt and "shuddering," he set off for Montevideo and the River Parana, eager to have a look at the battlefields where Paraguay had been waging war against Brazil, Argentina and Uruguay since October 1864. Whether he went with official orders is far from clear.

The war had begun in a dispute between the Brazilian government and Paraguay's capricious dictator, Francisco Solano Lopez. The Brazilian army had invaded Paraguay; Lopez had retaliated by marching across Argentina territory to invade Brazil. Argentina and Uruguay had then united with Brazil to attack Paraguay. Burton described the war as "an obscure nationality eaten up . . . by its neighbours," an "unflinching struggle . . . against overwhelming odds, to the very verge of racial annihilation." He described Paraguay as having "the bulldog tenacity and semi-compulsory heroism of a red-skin Sparta" defending

---

* She had Burton's two-volume *The Highlands of Brazil*, the Hindu tales, *Vikram and Vampire*, a manuscript on Uruguay (still unpublished, now in the Huntington Library), and two translations of Brazilian stories, one of which she had done herself, *Iracéma, The Honey-lips, a Legend of Brazil*, by J. De Alencar, and the other a translation she and Richard had worked on together, *Manuel De Moraes, A Chronicle of the Seventeenth Century*, by J. M. Pereira Da Silva. (The latter two were published together in 1886.) In addition she carried the manuscript for Burton's *Lacerda's Journey to Cazembe*, the adventures of a Portuguese explorer in central Africa, which her husband had translated and annotated, and his *Guide-book, A Pictorial Pilgrimage to Mecca and Medina, Including Some of the More Remarkable Incidents in the Life of Mohammed, the Arab Lawgiver*, a 58-page booklet, summarizing his celebrated expedition to Mecca. This latter pamphlet is now among the rarest of all Burton's publications. She also had Burton's "Lowlands of Brazil," a manuscript which Norman Penzer described as "unfinished," which was never printed. A letter from Burton to Albert Tootal, March 5, 1871, now in the Edwards Metcalf collection, indicates however, that it was in fact ready for the press. Burton had hoped to give Isabel the manuscript story of a lively tale of cannibalism on the Brazilian coast, *The Captivity of Hans Stade of Hesse, in A.D. 1547–1555 Among the Wilds of Eastern Brazil*, which was being translated by Albert Tootal, and which he expected to edit and annotate. But it was not yet finished, so he carried it out himself in 1869 and published it in 1874.

her western frontier "with a stubbornness of purpose, a savage valour, and an enduring desperation rare in the annals of mankind." He was in fact describing one of the most bloodthirsty wars in all history.

Burton took notes like an old soldier, interested in weapons and knowing how they should be used tactically. He contrasted the Brown Bess and old flintlock muskets of the Paraguayan soldiers with the Spencer and Enfield rifles of the Allies, and the Paraguayan punts on the rivers pitted against Allied ironclads. He held that Lopez had made the same mistake as the Confederates in the American Civil War, trying to fight along extended lines.* Though Burton made some pretence, as Brazilian consul, of being on the Allied side, he was nevertheless openly critical of the role of Argentina in prolonging the "disastrous and by no means honourable war."²² He predicted, correctly, that unless Lopez was killed the whole male population of Paraguay was likely to disappear. The war ended in 1870 with four-fifths of the population dead—221,000 left, out of 1,337,000—and only 28,700 male survivors.

Burton was astonished at the semi-barbarism of the Paraguayans, which he called "a palaeozoic humanity," and blamed their backwardness on the isolation imposed by the Jesuits before their expulsion in 1769. Isabel must have been pained to read his description of the Jesuit period as "a deadening, brutalizing, religious despotism," resulting in a culture "whose history may be summed up in absolute submission, fanaticism, blind obedience, heroic and barbarous devotion to the tyrant that rules it, combined with crass ignorance, hatred of, and contempt for, the foreigner."²³ His notes included descriptions of Montevideo, Buenos Aires, Rozario, Corrientes, Humaita and the Gran Chaco, and included interviews with generals and statesmen, including Bartolomé Mitre, Argentine president between 1862 and 1868. Mitre, who was a scholar as well as soldier and politician, received Burton like an old acquaintance. Domingo Faustine Sarmiento, then president of Argentina, also received Burton. Though he never met Lopez, who was by then fleeing northwards, Burton wrote a terse little portrait, which included local gossip about his celebrated Irish mistress, Madame Lynch.

Burton's first visit to the battlefields lasted from August 15 to September 5, 1868. Then he went back to Buenos Aires, disreputable in dress, haggard and thin, and still drinking. Wilfrid Blunt, stationed

---

* He became so interested in the problems of fighting on horseback that he designed a gun which could be fired from a horse without lifting it to one's shoulder, an Albini rifle cut short with the stock changed to a saw handle. Back in London Burton got a gunsmith to make up a sample and patented it. But it failed to sell.

in Buenos Aires, saw him upon his return. Later in his memoirs he wrote a vivid portrait:

> Burton was at that time at the lowest point I fancy of his whole career, and in point of respectability at his very worst. His consular life at Santos, without any interesting work to his hand or proper vent for his energies, had thrown him into a habit of drink he afterwards cured himself of, and he seldom went to bed sober. . . .
>
> His dress and appearance were those suggesting a released convict . . . a rusty black coat with a crumpled black silk stock, his throat destitute of collar, a costume which his muscular frame and immense chest made singularly and incongruously hideous, above it a countenance the most sinister I have ever seen, dark, cruel, treacherous, with eyes like a wild beast's. He reminded me of a black leopard, caged, but unforgiving. . . .
>
> My talks with Burton were of a most intimate kind, religion, philosophy, travel, politics. . . . In his talk he affected an extreme brutality, and if one could have believed the whole of what he said, he had indulged in every vice and committed every crime. I soon found, however, that most of these recitals were indulged in *pour épater le bourgeois* and that his inhumanity was more pretended than real. Even the ferocity of his countenance gave place at times to more agreeable expressions, and I can just understand the infatuated fancy of his wife that in spite of his ugliness he was the most beautiful man alive. . . .
>
> I came at last to look upon him as less dangerous than he seemed, and even in certain aspects of his mind, a "sheep in wolf's clothing." The clothing, however, was a very complete disguise, and as I have said he was not a man to play with, sitting alone with him far into the night. . . . a grim being to be with at the end of his second bottle, with a gaucho's navaja handy to his hand. . . .[24]

Blunt tells us that Burton was frequently in the company of the "Tichborne Claimant," a mysterious character who claimed to be the lost heir to a baronetcy and substantial estates in England, and who turned out later to be one of the most celebrated impostors in English history. Since the Tichborne fortune was intimately bound up with that of the Arundells, Burton was intrigued by his story, and for a time believed in him. Later he became disillusioned, and gave the "Claimant" no aid when subpoenaed to testify on his behalf in London.[25]

According to Blunt, Burton was talking enthusiastically of exploring Patagonia and the western Pampas, and of climbing the highest mountains in the Andes, including the Aconcagua, "then a virgin peak." But Blunt counted Burton "physically a broken man," and said that the expedition was treated as a joke by Burton's friends. If Blunt's portrait is valid, it would seem incredible that this broken, dispirited, drunken man, compulsively intent on establishing a reputation for blackguardism and vice, and talking wildly of climbing virgin peaks, could have travelled anywhere without collapsing or could have written anything whatsoever of note. But he did manage by some miracle of self will to get himself out of Buenos Aires and across northern Argentina to Cordoba, then on to Mendoza. Following a dangerous, bandit-ridden route over the Andes by way of Uspallata Pass, he crossed into Chili. According to Luke Ionides,[26] Burton was badly wounded and killed four men on this journey, but since neither Richard nor Isabel mentions the excitement, it may be laid to one of Burton's "chaffing" evenings, when only the truth was disbelieved.

Of the whole arduous cross-continental journey we know almost nothing, save that he travelled with William Constable Maxwell and a Major Ignacio Rickard, and that he spent Christmas Day 1868 fleeing from hostile natives in the mountains. Apparently he climbed no virgin peaks and counted himself lucky to be out of the Andes alive.[27] If he kept a journal, it never appeared as a book, which makes one suspect that he had even stopped note-taking, evidence of the gravest apathy. The ethnologist in Burton seemed dead; so far as he was concerned the exotic and enormously varied Indians of South America simply did not exist. The aborigines of the New World, he wrote contemptuously later, "were savages that can interest only in Fenimore Cooper."[28]

He was no longer in touch even with his wife. One day in February 1869, he was sitting in a cafe in Lima when an acquaintance approached and congratulated him on his new good fortune. Burton could have done nothing but stare. Word had reached the British Embassy in Lima that he had received the consulate at Damascus.[29] No one save Isabel could know what this meant to Richard Burton. It was the fulfilment of an old dream. No one but Burton could know how much it was also a rescue. He sailed immediately for Buenos Aires via the Straits of Magellan.

Lord Stanley, spurred by Isabel's pleadings, and no doubt also by an appreciation of Burton's fitness for the post, had overridden the many objections of Burton's enemies—among them Christian missionaries—and had appointed him to Damascus three months earlier, December 1868, asking him to "proceed immediately to his post." Isabel had written many letters, and must have suffered agonies waiting for an answer, having no idea of her husband's whereabouts. Lord Stanley meanwhile went out of office with a change of government, as Gladstone became Prime Minister, and was succeeded by Lord Clarendon. Isabel wrote again to Buenos Aires, this time with real apprehension, "The new Government have tried to upset some of the appointments made by the last. There is no little jealousy about yours. Others wanted it even at £700 a year and were refused. Lord Stanley thinks, and so do I, that you may as well be on the ground as soon as possible."[30]

Burton caught up with all this mail in Buenos Aires in March 1869.

Instead of returning immediately to London, however, he did a surprising thing. He made a second trip to the Paraguayan battlefields, between April 4 and April 18, this time visiting the capital, Asuncion, newly captured by the invading Allied armies. He took careful notes, enough for eighty pages of print, and so went back to England—eight months late for his post—with the makings of a complete book on the Paraguayan War. Though somewhat disorganized, and in parts carelessly written, it was one of Burton's better books. As published in 1870 after Lopez's death, it provided more accurate information and perceptive analysis of the subject than anything the British public had seen up to that time. By tarrying in Paraguay he risked censure and even the loss of the Damascus post that his wife had won for him. But there was something important to be regained in Paraguay—his self respect.

Damascus

Our lives were wild, romantic, and solemn.

Isabel Burton, on their stay in Damascus.[1]

*W*HEN BURTON DISEMBARKED at Southampton on June 1, 1869, he looked haggard and disreputable, and Isabel rushed him off to the haberdasher before letting him see anyone in London. Then, neatly scrubbed and clothed, he went to the Foreign Office where Lord Clarendon told him that in Constantinople his appointment was looked at askance by the Moslems because of his Mecca adventure. Burton pledged himself to act "with unusual prudence," and Clarendon was satisfied. Though Burton had regained much of his health, his hepatitis was still troubling him, and he begged for an extra six weeks of sick leave. This Clarendon granted, knowing that the leisure would give Burton a chance to transform his notes on the Paraguayan war into a useful book.

Byron Farwell has intimated that Burton's repeated requests for leave were evidence of serious truancy from his consular duties. Apparently the Foreign Office was now willing to give Burton a long rein it would not have permitted lesser men. If he was difficult, he was also enormously productive, and did far more on sick leave at half pay than most men on regular hours in the best of health.

Burton went first to Boulogne with Isabel, then alone to meet Swinburne in Vichy. Remembering their drinking bouts of the past, Isabel soon took off for Vichy herself. Swinburne wrote of her coming to Alice Swinburne on August 10, 1869, "I rather grudge Mrs Burton's arrival here on Monday, though we are excellent friends, and I daresay I shall see none the less of him. . . . I feel now as if I knew for the first time what it was to have an elder brother. He is the most cordial, helpful, sympathetic friend to me it is possible to have: and it is a treat at last to have him to myself instead of having as in London to share him with all the world. . . ."

When he wrote this, Swinburne had been with Burton almost four weeks, alternating between sight-seeing expeditions and collapses. They had climbed 5,000 feet to the top of the Puy de Dome, a hike so strenuous, Swinburne wrote to Whistler on August 6, that "even Burton who was born of iron avowed himself tired and sleepy at the end of the day." Years later in an elegy to Burton, Swinburne recalled his own terror on the high, fog-shrouded ledges:

> Foot following foot along the sheer strait ledge
> Where space was none to bear the wild goat's feet
> Till blind we sat on the outer footless edge
> Where darkling death seemed fain to share the seat.[2]

To his mother, Lady Jane Henrietta Swinburne, he wrote on August 13, 1869:

If you had seen *him*, when the heat and the climb and the *bothers* of travelling were too much for me—in the *very* hot weather—nursing, helping, waiting on me—going out to get me books to read in bed—and always thoughtful, kind, ready, and so bright and fresh that nothing but a lizard (I suppose that is the most insensible thing going) could have resisted the influence—I feel sure you *would* like him (you remember you said you didn't) and then, love him, as I do: I have been now nearly a month alone with him—and I tell you this, he is so good, so true, kind, noble, and brave, that I never expect to see his like again—but him I do hope to see again. . . .[3]

Swinburne at this time was writing great poetry. But much of it had a perverse quality quite apart from its exuberant paganism, which scandalized the British public. The publication of his *Poems and Ballads* in 1866 had brought both public and private abuse. The *Saturday Review* of August 4, 1866 had called him "an unclean fiery imp from the pit . . . the libidinous laureate of a pack of satyrs." *Punch* had called him Mr Swineburne. On January 11, 1867 he had written to Burton in Brazil, "One anonymous letter from Dublin threatened me if I did not suppress my book within six weeks from that date, with castration. The writer, 'when I least expected, would waylay me, slip my head in a bag, and remove the obnoxious organs; he had seen the gamekeeper do it with cats.' "[4]

This "fiery, unquiet spirit," as Edward Fitzgerald described him, looked upon Richard Burton with real idolatry. Though they saw little of each other after this month, only at occasional dinners in London, his affection and admiration never died. He dedicated the second series of his *Poems and Ballads* in 1878 to Burton, who in 1884 in turn dedicated his translation of Camoens' *The Lusiads* to Swinburne. Upon Burton's death he wrote two elegies, one of which said in part:

> A wider soul than the world was wide
> Whose praise made love of him one with pride . . .
> Who rode life's lists as a god might ride.[5]

In Vichy in 1869 Burton apparently saw with apprehension the morass of alcoholism into which the poet was sinking, and tried his hand at rehabilitation. But where Burton in a remarkable act of will managed to stop his own heavy drinking, Swinburne did not. His alcoholism continued, according to his friend and biographer Edmund Gosse, "until he was taken to Putney, in 1879, then completely overmastered by it, and rendered unfit for decent society."[6] He was saved from death by malnutrition by Theodore Watts-Dunton, who became his companion, nurse, and confidant for the remainder of Swinburne's life, which surprisingly lasted another thirty years.

Isabel described her own stay in Vichy with chronic cheerfulness, noting that their friends there included not only Swinburne but also the painter, Sir Frederick Leighton, and the opera singer, Adelaide Kemble Sartoris. "They were happy days. We made excursions in the day and in the evenings the conversation, I need not say was brilliant. . . . Swinburne recited poetry, Mrs Sartoris sang to us."[7] After Swinburne returned to London, the Burtons toured the French Alps and then crossed the mountains to Turin, where Richard left for Damascus. Isabel returned to London to pack; it took her two and a half months.

Burton went to Syria with high expectations, counting on the desert to succeed where the green forests of Brazil had failed to restore his old zest and taste for involvement. Never in his whole career was his involvement so absolute as in his two years in Damascus. Syria was then under Turkish rule, and Damascus, which styled itself the oldest city in the world, was a hotbed of Moslem fanaticism. There were a multitude of sects: the Moslems were split into four orthodox schools, to say nothing of the schismatics—Shiahs, Dervishes, Sufis, Persians, and Bedouins. There were Sephardim and Ashkenazim Jews, the latter broken up into Parushim, Khasidim and Khabad sects. The Christians were divided into Maronite Catholic, Greek Catholic, Greek Schismatic, Armenian Catholic, Armenian Schismatic, Syrian Catholic, Jacobite, Latin Catholic, Copt, Abyssinian, Chaldean Catholic, and Chaldean Schismatic, as well as various Protestants. The esoteric Druses lived in the nearby mountains.

The city was surrounded by a wall with thirteen gates, all securely locked at night. Within the gates Christians, Jews and Moslems were segregated from each other by inner walls. Intrigue, assassination and massacre were endemic. Burton came to describe government in the Near East as "despotism tempered by assassination."[8] In July 1860 one terrible day the Moslems in Damascus had slain 3,000 Christians and left their quarter a charred ruin.

Burton was expected to look after the welfare of the thirty-odd citizens under British protection, and numerous tourists and merchants, to encourage trade, and to keep Sir Henry Elliot, British ambassador to the Porte at Constantinople, informed about Turkish intrigues. All his dispatches, however, had to go first to the Consul-General at Beirut, S. Jackson Eldridge, who took his duties so lightly he never once visited the Syrian capital. "Eldridge does nothing and is very proud of what he does," Burton wrote contemptuously in his journal.[9]

Before long Burton had made friends with every Sheikh and religious leader in the area, and had gained some insight into the religious and political intrigues. A true romantic, despite his veneer of cynicism, he also took it upon himself to right the wrongs of the oppressed. Occasionally he tried out his old disguise, like Harun al Rashid, testing the temper of the people at night, his excitement heightened by his having for the first time in his life real political power. The Turkish Wali governing Syria in 1869, Mohammed Rashid Pasha, was a corrupt ruler who became so notorious for maladministration and extortion that even in this venal period of the decaying Ottoman Empire he was recalled to Constantinople in chains in 1871 and later conveniently assassinated. The last thing he wanted in Damascus was an inquisitive British consul who could speak Arabic like an Arab, and who had a reputation for being a gifted spy. Burton soon documented the Wali's venality, and secretly urged the Foreign Office to agitate with the Turkish government for his recall. What Burton did not know was that he had an enemy, too, in the British ambassador, who seems to have feared losing his own post to Burton, and who from the beginning undermined his authority with the Turks. Even before Burton's arrival Elliot had gratuitously informed Rashid Pasha that the new consul had been warned to be "extremely careful to avoid doing anything calculated to give offence."[10]

In his first year Burton avoided incidents and made himself popular. The richness of detail about his life comes not from Burton, who wrote very little of his life in Damascus, but from Isabel, who published a lively, ingenuous two-volume account. "I have written this book without consulting my husband," she wrote with satisfaction.[11] Her *Inner Life of Syria*, which would have been more exactly titled *My Inner Life in Syria*, was much more than a gossipy "woman's view of the Near East"; it was a treasure of detail about their improbable life together.

Isabel arrived in Damascus from London on December 31, 1869 with a mountain of luggage and five dogs. She had come expecting, as she wrote in her diary the day she left England, to find in Damascus "my Pearl, the Garden of Eden, the Promised Land, my beautiful white City with her swelling domes and tapering minarets, her glittering golden crescents set in green of every shade." But upon arrival she saw only barren yellow mountains, ugly shrubbery, wild dogs, and offal in the streets. In the first stages of cultural shock she felt "six times farther away from home than when living in Brazil." Unwilling to be locked up at night within the Damascus gates, Burton insisted on taking a house on a river in the Kurdish village of Salihiyay, on the foothills of the mountains to the north. It was a spacious house, with a garden full of apricot, lemon and orange trees. There was a fountain in the patio, and the flat roof was laden with potted flowers.

To the five dogs—a St Bernard, two brindled bull-terriers, two Yarboroughs—the Burtons added a Kurdish pup, a camel, a white donkey, three goats, a pet lamb, a Persian cat, as well as chickens, turkeys, geese, ducks, guinea fowls, and pigeons. Later a Moslem leader gave them a panther cub that had been trapped in the desert, which soon became their favourite. "He used to sleep by our bedside," Isabel wrote. "He had bold bad black eyes that seemed to say, 'Be afraid of me.'" For a time she spent most of her days keeping the pets from eating each other.

More than all the animals Isabel loved her horses. They kept a stable of twelve, where Richard gave her full command, and her servants soon learned to fear the lash of her tongue if they were caught abusing them. "I know everything they say, and think, and feel; and they know also what I say to them," she insisted. She kept only three-quarter and half-breds; purebreds, she said, would have led to whisperings of corruption. Both she and Richard were offered bribes, as was every diplomat in the Near East, Burton once as much as £20,000. "When you refuse a good thing they are amazed," Isabel wrote. "Although I am a woman, jewellery is no temptation to me. . . . I have refused enough to enable me to wear as many as any woman in London; but when they brought me horses, it was quite another sensation; and I had to screw up my courage hard—and bolt."[12]

The Burtons gave precedent-breaking receptions to which they invited natives of every tongue, race and creed. They had to adhere, however, to the custom of segregating men from women, serving lemonade, sherbet, chiboques, *narghilehs* and cigarettes in separate rooms. In return they were invited to weddings, funerals, circumcisions, and dervish dances. Isabel delighted in the surprising beauty and luxuriance of the homes of the wealthy, hidden as they were behind deliberately deceptive façades of filth and decay. Her best friend was the notorious Jane Digby El Mezrab, formerly Lady Ellenborough, who had run away from her husband, the Governor General of India, picked up at different times half a dozen other "husbands" on the continent, and finally ended up in Syria married to a Bedouin chief. Jane Digby was now sixty-one, still beautiful, and a talented painter, sculptor and linguist. Burton said she was the cleverest woman he ever met.

Accompanying Richard on his expeditions into the mountains, Isabel rode dressed as a man, and admitted to being "very much amused and very much pleased" when she was taken for Burton's son. "It all *sounds* indecent," she wrote apologetically, "but all Arab clothes are so baggy and draping that it little matters whether you are dressed as a man or woman." Sometimes, forgetting her male attire, she would enter a harem and send the women screaming to their quarters. Where younger wives looked upon her freedom with astonishment and envy, the older women watched her with thinly disguised contempt. "This is neither man nor woman, nor anything else," they said. "Allah preserve us from this manner of pestilence!"

Often they questioned her about her childlessness. "Thou has never had a child, O lady! Let us hope that Allah may be merciful, and remove thy reproach. . . . And does not the Sidi Beg . . . want to put thee away, and take a second wife? Dost thou not, Ya Sitti, feel insecure of thy place?"

To which she would reply, "The English husband would not put his wife away for anything. I feel quite secure of my place. The Sidi Beg may marry another after my death, but not before."[13]

One missionary in Damascus noted that Burton was fond of his five-year-old son but took some pains to hide it, playing with him in the wild, abandoned fashion that the boy loved only when he thought them both unobserved. Ouida insisted that Richard regretted their failure to have children but that Isabel did not. To one friend Isabel wrote, "Yes, I have twelve nephews and nieces, five boys and seven girls . . . quite enough. Thank God we have none." But the devotion she lavished on her animals, an ardour that extended to every starving dog and badly beaten donkey, suggests rather that she felt her deprivation keenly. When their dogs died it was always a calamity. And when their half-grown panther was poisoned by a peasant she was almost undone. "I sat down on the ground, and took him in my arms like a child," she wrote. "He put his head on my shoulder, and his paws round my waist, and he died in about half an hour. Richard and I were terribly grieved." Once, visiting a Bedouin encampment where an epidemic was decimating the tribe, she distributed quinine and Warburg's drops. When these remedies failed, she saw in despair that the children were still dying. "I gave the only benefit in my power," she wrote, "I baptised them."[14]

Isabel regularly nursed the sick in her own village outside Damascus, sometimes as many as fifty a day, handing out calomel and other pills, binding up the sabre cuts of the villagers after a brawl, and fearlessly entering areas where cholera was raging to dispense meagre supplies of opium. One cannot help wondering if Richard, in watching her, remembered a reflection he had written in Africa, "Seeing the host of women who find a morbid pleasure in attending the maimed and dying, I must think that it is a tribute paid to sexuality by those who object to the ordinary means."[15] One suspects in any case that sexual intimacy in their marriage had become extremely rare. Burton complained in one article written during this period that "man in hot and enervating climates coming to maturity early," loses "the powers which he is tempted by moral as well as physical agencies to abuse," going on to say that without polygamy no man could raise a large family.[16] But Isabel was right when she indicated that Burton would never put her away. When he was ill he accepted her nursing gratefully, as from his mother, and she was proud to describe herself as his "best friend."

In Damascus Burton found a new passion, archaeology, and he came to lavish upon the ancient dead all the inquisitiveness he had devoted to the living in India and Africa. He spent weeks in the Syrian mountains, searching for skulls, bones and inscriptions, mapping ruins and correcting geographical errors on the local maps. He described Syria as a "luxuriance of ruin." "There is not a large ruin in the country which does not prove upon examination to be the composition of ruins more ancient still. . . . That speechless past has begun to speak; the lost is no longer the utterly lost; the gone is not gone forever."[17]

Isabel often went with him, though she had no love for digging and was sometimes ill with exhaustion. She insisted to Richard that she adored it all, but he did mention once, with some guilt, seeing her on an arduous trip "jogging along, weeping in her saddle." They visited the two most famous Syrian ruins, the temples at Baalbek and Palmyra, and afterwards Burton tried vainly to raise money in Damascus and London to preserve especially the great pillars from collapsing into still greater ruin.

E. H. Palmer, a gifted Orientalist from Trinity College, Cambridge, and Charles F. Tyrwhitt-Drake, a young archaeologist sent out by the Palestine Exploration Fund, joined them on several expeditions, giving Burton the advantage of their professional knowledge. Tyrwhitt-Drake, a tall, attractive red-head in his twenties, was fond of the Burtons, and when he ran out of money they took him in for a long period almost as an adopted son. When he died three years later of an illness in Palestine, they grieved as if he had been their own.[18]

To escape Damascus's enervating summer heat, the three of them moved to Bludan, a Greek Orthodox village clinging like a wasp's nest to the eastern flank of the mountain overlooking the valley leading from Damascus to Baalbek. Here they lived 5,000 feet above the sea in a primitive stone house with a view of six mountain ranges. "We made our own bread, we bought butter and milk from the Bedawi," Isabel wrote. "We woke at dawn . . . and took long walks over the mountains with our guns." On the longer expeditions Burton always travelled with a large escort. Isabel kept behind her husband at a respectful distance, as befitted a son, cheerfully ate the soured milk, raw onions, and eggs fried in clarified butter, and learned not to fear the "jackals gambolling in the moonlight, sounding in a distant pack like the war cry of the Bedawi."

I can never forget some of those lovely nights in the desert . . . mules, donkeys, camels, horses, and mares picketed about, screaming, kicking, and holloaing; the stacked loads, the big fires, the black tents, the Turkish soldiers, the picturesque figures in every garb, and the wild and fierce-looking men in wonderful costumes lying here and there, singing and dancing barbarous dances . . . Richard reciting the Arabian Nights, or poor Palmer chanting Arab poetry, or Charley Drake practising magic to astonish the Mogharibehs. . . .

I have seen the gravest and most reverend Shayks rolling on the ground and screaming with delight, in spite of their Oriental gravity, and they seemed as if they could never let my husband go again.

The Bedouins called him "Brother of the Lion," she said, and made up a song in his honour:

> Mashalla! Mashallah! At last we have seen a man!
> Behold our Consul in our Shaykh! . . .
> Let us follow them all over the earth![19]

Where Isabel saw their lives as "wild, romantic, and solemn," the Turkish Wali saw only spying and intrigue. News that Burton had sacked every man on his staff caught taking bribes served only to heighten his uneasiness. Until August 1870, however, he had no specific reason to send a complaint to Constantinople. Burton was in Bludan on August 26 when a messenger came with news that a collection of small incidents had sent the Christian community in Damascus into a panic. A Catholic had been beaten by a Moslem when he tried to collect a debt; he had complained to the Catholic Patriarch, who had had the debtor imprisoned, causing great indignation among the Moslems. Two young Jews, ten and twelve years old, had been caught scribbling signs of the cross in a privy attached to a Moslem mosque. The act, considered blasphemy by both Christians and Moslems, was said to have been similar to those that preceded the massacre of 1860. Discontented Turkish militiamen had been heard to threaten Christians with a repetition of the massacre, and the rumour had spread that August 27 would be the day of slaughter. Many Christians were fleeing the city.

Upon hearing this Burton ordered his horses to be saddled and weapons cleaned, and said to his wife:

We have never before been in a Damascus riot, but if it takes place it will be like the famous affair of 1860. I shall not take you into Damascus, because I intend to protect Damascus, and you must protect Bludan and Zebedani. I shall take half the men, and I shall leave you half. You shall go down into the plain with me to-night, and we shall shake hands like two brothers and part; tears or any display of affection will tell the secret to our men.

Isabel hoisted the Union Jack on the roof, locked up her pretty Syrian maid; collected every available weapon, gave each man a gun, revolver and bowie knife, and stationed them strategically about the house. Two stood on the roof with Burton's elephant guns; Isabel herself manned the terrace, armed with soda water bottles filled with gunpowder and equipped with fuses, ready to hurl them down on the village below. Then she sent word to the Christians in the village to join her in her fortress.

Richard meanwhile galloped into Damascus and informed the city council members that a massacre was imminent. "Which of you is to be hanged if this is not prevented?" he said bluntly. "It will cost you Syria, and unless you take measures at once, I shall telegraph to Constantinople."

"What would you have us do?" they asked.

"Post a guard of soldiers in every street; order a patrol all night. I will go the rounds with Holo Pasha. Let the soldiers be harangued in the barracks. . . . Issue an order that no Jew or Christian shall leave the house till all is quiet."

"All these measures were taken by ten o'clock," Isabel wrote, "and continued for three days. Not a drop of blood was shed, and the frightened Christians who had fled to the mountains began to come back."[20]

There is small glory in preventing violence, and Isabel's narrative radiates a bravado that is somewhat comic. But henceforth the Christians of the city looked upon Burton as a hero, and most of the missionaries swung to his support. A few remained resentful; as one missionary put it, "Burton could not refrain from saying things to frighten old women of both sexes, and to make the servant maids stare. . . . he could not put up with stupidity in others."[21]

Many respected Moslems also applauded Burton's intervention, but the Wali found it insupportable. The local Jews, too, were offended, particularly when Burton called in for questioning the boys who had been scribbling crosses in the Moslem latrine. A flood of false stories spread through the Jewish quarter, among them one that Burton had had the boys tortured, another that Isabel had torn the diamonds from the head of a Jewish woman at a party and stamped on them, saying they were made out of the blood of the poor.[22]

Burton, whose ambivalent feelings about Jews we shall examine in some detail later, had become extremely hostile to three Jewish money-lenders who were technically under the protection of the British consulate. When a debtor in Syria could not pay, his creditor could send him to prison, and if the creditor was under British protection, he had the legal right to demand that the consul assist him in the act. The record of previous British consuls in this matter, according to the Christian missionaries, had not been savoury. When one moneylender, who Burton said "had ruined and sucked dry forty-one villages," approached him with a request to assist him in collecting £60,000 in debts, he had coldly refused. "I was not sent here as a bailiff, to tap the peasant on the shoulder in such cases as yours," he said. He posted a notice on the consulate door that he would not assist in prosecution for debt, and regularly visited the prison to see if any British-protected subjects "had immured pauper Christians and Moslems on their own responsibility." If he found them he had them freed.

The moneylenders retaliated by sending letters to leading Jews in London accusing Burton and his wife of antisemitism. Sir Moses Montefiore, Jewish philanthropist, who had won many civil rights for Jews in the Near East, protested to the Foreign Office, as did Sir Francis Goldsmid, Chief Rabbi of London. The latter wrote, "I hear that the lady to whom Captain Burton is married is believed to be a bigoted Roman Catholic, and to be likely to influence him against the Jews."

Isabel was already in trouble in London. Sir Henry Elliot had maliciously passed along a story that in a fit of temper in a Damascus street she had struck a young Moslem in the face with her riding whip. Actually the youth had spat at her and tried to pull her off her horse. Later she made friends with him and took him into her house as a servant. But this explanation did not follow the story to London. A still wilder story circulated that Isabel had killed two men and wounded a third because they failed to salute her.[23]

Furious at the charges, Burton blamed the moneylenders, and vainly tried to get permission for Isabel to defend herself officially. Most Jews in Damascus, he wrote to the Foreign Office, were "hard-working, inoffensive, and of commercial integrity, with a fair sprinkling of pious, charitable, and innocent people," but he refused to assist the few usurers "in ruining villages and in imprisoning destitute debtors upon trumped up charges." Consul-General Eldridge, who thought Burton was tilting at windmills, pointed out wearily that this "had always been a part of the Turkish system of Government."[24]

In April 1871 the Burtons decided to visit Palestine for Easter. "The Holy Land," under strong Turkish rule, was at this time the scene of intense rivalry among religious sects, all competing for the sacred shrines. Burton and Tyrwhitt-Drake, who took the overland route to Jerusalem, looked upon the journey as an archaeological expedition, but for Isabel, who went by sea, it was the great pilgrimage of her life. "I sit on a mound, gazing at these holy places," she wrote, "and I think over them; and then I kneel on the grass, and I pray and weep, and weep and pray, not because I am sad, but because I cannot stay my tears. . . . I cannot tell you how strange it is to see, to think, and to pray by, touch, the very scenes and monuments of which you learned at your mother's knee."

But touring the sacred places with her iconoclast husband and his sceptical companions—Tyrwhitt-Drake and the French orientalist Clermont-Ganneau—she often found painful. "No one doubts the sites except the English," she wrote in exasperation. "I have seen every kind of Christian kneeling at our Saviour's tomb, except my countrymen, and they remain outside in the church, gazing at the chapel which encloses it, and staring at the people kneeling three times as they approach it, as if they were watching some wild Hindoo practice." Nowhere in all her writings does one feel so much rage against the scientific world, and sorrow that her husband had so enthuiastically embraced it. Her Catholic faith colours almost every journal entry; it intervenes, supervenes, and intimidates. "We shall weep for ourselves," she wrote, "for all those who betray Him still, for the insults of the wicked, for the uselessness of His sufferings to the many, for the revolted children, for those who betray Him in secret, or abandon Him like the disciples."[25]

Exploring the quarries outside Jerusalem on Mount Bezetha, Isabel entered one of the old caves by herself to rest, and fell asleep of exhaustion. "I dreamt a wonderful dream," she wrote, "perhaps I ought not to detail it, but an inner voice bids me do so—a long vivid dream, which I committed to paper." The commitment to paper turned out in her book to occupy fifty pages. Including it was an ingenuous and even arrogant gesture, but Isabel, who insisted that she learned much from her own dreams was right in recognizing that this one was important. Here she truly laid bare her "inner life."

She found herself in heaven, she wrote, standing before a resplendant Jesus, "trembling and abashed at my own nothingness." "I dreamt that He put His hand upon my head, and blessed me, and I felt as if a flood of grace and happiness flowed over my soul, and took away all the pain and disquiet." Given a mandate to redress all the wrongs of the world, she took off in the company of an angel, flying from one place to another. There was contempt and hatred in her dream, as well as ecstasy. "The most pitiable and the most foolish thing that I saw was the condition of men of science. . . . They appeared like small objects—midges—studying a little section, a little particle of this huge mosaic, Creation, and very ill comprehending even that." She hanged three men for high treason [*"whom I have since recognised,"* she wrote], and ordered every man guilty of cruelty to women, children, and animals to be flogged. She married all the disagreeable "Mrs Grundys" to "a certain class of feminine men who seem to have sprung up more thickly of late" and banished them to Pitcairn's Island.

She built, she recalled, a splendid palace in Jerusalem and brought the Pope to live in it, and saw to it that all the Jews were instantly converted. She flew over the battlefields of the Franco-Prussian War, then raging in Europe, where she detected "Lucifer and his Court directing the French forces." Part of her dream was a plea for justice for Richard before the throne of Queen Victoria, a plea given in such detail that she felt obliged to state stoutly in her book, "I did not compose any part of my dream for the public." She asked the Queen to restore her husband's military privileges, appoint him Envoy Extraordinary to some Eastern Court, and make him a knight. "I shall cry like an angel for justice till it comes," she told the Queen. "I shall cry for it, Madam, till I die!"[26] After two hours of dreaming she was awakened by a goatherd, who had found her in the cave and shaken her, fearing her to be dead.

The one thing Isabel did not reveal was Richard's reaction either to her dream or to her publication of it. He believed dreams to be important, but not for mystical reasons. He sensed that they were a kind of communication, and he tried vainly to read this complicated and most obscure of all languages. He could hardly have objected to the pages that were a paean in his praise, but he was perhaps too perceptive to have missed altogether her rage, contempt, and longing for power.

The Burtons encountered an ugly incident in Nazareth on May 5, 1871, when a begging Copt tried to enter Isabel's tent when she was still in bed. Thrown out by her servants, he retaliated by hurling stones. The servants began to beat him, only to be set upon in turn by several men emerging from the nearby Greek Orthodox Church. Burton and Tyrwhitt-Drake tried vainly to stop the fighting and were themselves stoned. Finally, seeing one of his servants being trampled, Burton pulled a pistol from his belt and fired a shot in the air. English and American pilgrims camped nearby came running, and the Greeks fled.

Burton was furious at the injuries to his servants. His own arm was severely lamed, and he may have been further angered by a suspicion that the Copt had been intent on raping his wife. He went to the local police and insisted on the imprisonment of several Greeks. The Greek

Orthodox Bishop in Nazareth, who believed Burton to be hostile to his own sect, chose to turn the brawl into a damaging political incident. Several Greeks swore before the police that Burton had fired into a crowd of innocent children, that he had entered the church, torn down pictures and shot a priest, and that Isabel had entered the church in her nightgown, torn down whatever she could and jumped on the debris. Burton made the error of delaying his report to Ambassador Elliot in Constantinople, who in turn delayed several weeks before sending it on to London. Meanwhile the wildly fabricated Greek stories arrived at the Foreign Office, causing consternation. Though the subsequent trials in Nazareth ended nine months later in complete vindication for the Burtons, and a three-month jail sentence for three Greeks, the verdict came too late to undo the damage. The Turkish Wali in Damascus clamoured for Burton's recall, and Elliot, instead of supporting Burton, wrote to Lord Granville damagingly, ". . . his presence tends to unsettle the public mind." On May 25, 1871 Granville wrote to Elliot telling him he was at liberty to inform the Turkish government that Burton would be given another post. As Byron Farwell put it, ". . . it is certain that Sir Henry Elliot, more than any other single person, was responsible for Burton's downfall."[27]

Rumours now began to circulate in Damascus that the British Consul was about to be recalled. But Granville had written only of transfer, not recall, and Rashid Pasha apparently feared that Burton would be retained in Damascus for many months. At this point, if Burton's evidence is correct, the Wali began to plan his assassination. When Burton asked his formal permission to visit the Druses, a sect in the mountains known to be hostile to Turkish rule, the Wali duly granted his request, May 24, 1871. Then he altered Burton's letter, which was to be sent on to Constantinople, making it appear that he was implicated in some kind of treason against the Turkish government. The Wali also wrote an accusatory letter to Isabel, who had remained home somewhat ill. Greatly alarmed by this, and by inquisitive questions about the date and route of her husband's return, she sent a warning to Richard by a servant—a coded message hidden in a medicine bottle.

Taking her alarm seriously, Burton and Tyrwhitt-Drake sent their men on ahead, hid their horses in a cave in the mountains, and watched the trail from the rocky crest. "After a few hours," Burton wrote, "we saw a hundred horsemen and two hundred dromedary riders beating the country, looking for someone in the plains." They questioned Burton's dragoman, Azar, threatened to kill him, and when he refused to divulge his master's whereabouts, plundered his own village. "So we rode into Damascus," Burton said, "escaping by peculiar good fortune a hundred horsemen and two hundred dromedary riders, sent on purpose to murder *me*. I was never more flattered in my life, than to think that it would take three hundred men to kill *me*. The felon act, however, failed."[28]

Burton returned to Damascus on June 7, 1871; on June 14 he received a wire from London saying that the Turkish government had made serious complaints about him, and ordering him not to leave his Damascus post under any circumstance. He defended himself vigorously—though he did not find out about the altered letter until later—and called Rashid Pasha's rule "a dangerous and unscrupulous autocracy."[29] He might still have stayed in Damascus until a post with similar prestige and pay could be found for him had he heeded the London warnings and behaved with circumspection. Instead he entered a calamitous involvement into which he was led by his wife.

Isabel's confessor in Damascus was a Franciscan priest of Spanish descent, Fray Emanuel Förner, who had become the hero and confessor of several hundred members of an esoteric Muslim sect known as Shazlis, or Shadili, who had been secretly converted to Christianity in the spring of 1870. They were now experiencing what Isabel described as miracles, including visitations from Jesus and Mary. Burton, perennially curious about mysticism of any sort, had spent several evenings in disguise with the Shazlis, watching their evangelistic fervour. Fray Förner had begged Isabel to get British protection for the group, which was certain to be persecuted by the Moslems once news of the mass conversion became known, even though the Turkish government had recently promised religious freedom to all its subjects. In the beginning Burton had flatly refused. But on returning from Palestine, they found that the Damascus authorities had discovered the proportions of Fray Förner's success—there were exaggerated estimates of 25,000 ready for baptism—and had sentenced twelve Shazlis to death, ostensibly for having evaded military conscription. After much protest on Burton's part, the sentence was modified to banishment to Tripoli. Fray Förner had meanwhile died under mysterious circumstances.

The Shazlis now turned to Burton as a kind of saviour. And Isabel, fresh from her Palestine pilgrimage, was caught in a kind of hysterical enthusiasm, visioning herself as "godmother" at the baptism of somewhere between 400 and 4,000 eager new Catholic converts. There seems little doubt that she persuaded her husband into an act of folly. He seriously entertained the idea of buying a tract of land and settling the converted Shazlis upon it, free from any kind of land taxation. "The village was to *belong to him*," Isabel wrote emphatically. Richard was to be a security for their safety, and Patriarch Valerga of Jerusalem was to come and baptise them. Burton did in fact send a letter to Earl Granville telling him about the mass conversion, the persecutions and banishment, and suggested the possibility of a separate settlement out-

side Damascus, under British protection. He urged Granville to write
to the Patriarch of Jerusalem. The jubilant Isabel believed that her
husband, too, was now close to baptism. "This was the time that Richard
was nearest making a public declaration of Catholicity," she wrote.

When Granville received the letter, he was convinced finally that
Ambassador Elliot was right, that Burton instead of being the ideal
consul—a patient, self-effacing, analytical observer—was indeed playing the role of powerful local sheikh. He did, however, pass the information about the Shazlis to the Jerusalem patriarch, who naïvely tried
to negotiate on their behalf with the Turkish authorities. The resulting
explosion of protest finished Burton in Damascus.[30]

Richard, Isabel and Tyrwhitt-Drake were in Bludan on August 16,
1871 when a grimy messenger from Damascus brought word that
Thomas Jago, the vice-consul in Beirut, had arrived with orders to take
over the consulate. Henceforth Damascus would be represented only
by a vice-consul, at greatly reduced pay. Unbelieving, Burton mounted
his horse and together with Tyrwhitt-Drake galloped down the mountain into Damascus. Here he read Granville's chilling dispatch: "I
regret to have now to inform you that the complaints which I have
received from the Turkish Government in regard to your recent conduct and proceedings render it impossible that I should allow you to
continue to perform any consular functions in Syria."

Burton scribbled a note to Isabel and sent it back with Tyrwhitt-
Drake. "Don't be frightened—I am recalled. Pay, pack, and follow at
convenience." Then he set off at once for Beirut. In his diary he wrote
as follows:

August 18th.—Left Damascus for ever; started at three a.m. in the dark,
with a big lantern; all my men crying; alone in *coupé* of diligence, thanks
to the pigs. Excitement of seeing all for the last time. All seemed sorry; a
few groans. The sight of Bludan mountains in the distance at sunrise, where
I have left my wife. *Ever again?* Felt soft. Dismissal ignominious, at the
age of fifty, without a month's notice, or wages, or character.

Back in Bludan Isabel read the note. "I was not frightened," she
wrote, "but I do not like to remember what I thought or what I felt."
That night she was disturbed by dreams in which someone seemed to
be pulling at her, saying, "Your husband wants you—get up and go to
him!" When the dream was repeated three times, she took it as a command, dressed herself, saddled her horse and against the protests of her
servants rode off into the night, hoping to intercept the coach to Beirut.
After five hours of hard riding, she sighted it at the half-way station.
The coachman had his whip in hand, ready to leave. Racing her exhausted horse in front of the coach, she raised her arms and stopped it.

In Beirut she found Richard walking alone. "Not even a Kawwass was sent to attend on him, and to see him out with a show of honour and respect. . . . The jackals are always ready to slight a dead lion. But *I* was there (thank God!) in my place, and he was so surprised and glad when he saw me! I was well rewarded for my hard ride, for when he saw me his whole face was illuminated, and he said, 'Thank you, *bon sang ne peut mentir.*'"

"Everybody called on us, and everybody regretted," she wrote—all save Consul-General Eldridge, who cut them dead. Later Eldridge said, "If Burton had only walked *my* way, he would have lived and died here." Within a month after Burton's sailing, Rashid Pasha had been taken to Constantinople in chains. But it was too late to save Burton.

Isabel went sadly back to Damascus to pack. Messages of regret poured in from Moslem, Christian and Jew, many of which she carefully saved to take to London. For a time it seemed that every poor wretch she had succoured with Warburg's drops and quinine came to give her thanks. She was haunted by the fear that she had herself been responsible for Richard's recall by insisting on his intervention with the Shazlis. Later in London she went to the Foreign Office and demanded an official explanation. After being told "thirteen different reasons by thirteen different officials" she confronted Granville himself and came away convinced that her fears were true. "Lord Granville *had not understood* Richard's letter about wanting to have the Shazlis baptised, and feared that it might result in a *Jehad* or religious war. . . . *That was the real cause of the recall.* . . . It broke his career, it shattered his life, it embittered him on religion; he got neither Teheran, nor Morocco, nor Constantinople."[31]

But in Damascus she could know only that Richard was gone, that he would never be an enlightened sheikh ruling over a city of new converts, that she would never be a godmother to anyone in Syria. Before leaving she did a curious thing. Haunted by the memory of a young Bedouin boy she had treated briefly for fever, she rode off in the desert to his tribe and sought him out. The boy was dying.

"Would you like to see Allah," she asked him.

"Yes," he said, "I should. Can I?"

"Are you sorry for all the times you have been naughty and said bad words?"

"Yes," he said. "If I get well, I will do better, and be kinder to grandmother."

"I thought that was enough," Isabel wrote. "I parted his thick matted hair, and, kneeling, I baptized him from the flask of water I always carried at my side."[32] It was as close as she could come for the moment to her dream of baptizing Richard himself.

"*This Desperately Learned Man*"

I, too, 'am a neglected book gnawed by the moth,' 'a stream dammed up with mud,' by Phalaris clapped, for nothing in particular, into the belly of a brazen bull.

Burton compares himself to Ovid in exile, 1872[1]

*B*ACK IN LONDON Burton went directly to the home of his sister, Maria Stisted. "Never had we known him so wretched, so unnerved," her daughter wrote later, "his hand shook, his temper was strangely irritable, all that appreciation of fun and humour which rendered him such a cheery companion to old and young had vanished. He could settle to nothing; he was restless, but would not leave the house; ailing, but would take no advice. . . ." A visit to "poor Edward"— as he referred to his brother in his letters—still in the Surrey County Lunatic Asylum served to deepen his melancholy.

Maria Stisted and her daughter were quick to blame his recall upon Isabel. "He knew that thanks to his wife's imprudence and passion for proselyting," Georgiana wrote, "all further promotion was hopeless— Morocco, Constantinople would never be for him; his career was blighted."[2] In his first impulsive gesture of rage and flight he left her without funds, and she had to borrow money from her wealthy uncle, Lord Gerard, to get to London. Upon her arrival she found Richard in one room in a very small hotel. She was appalled by his apathy. "He had made no defence—had treated the whole thing *de haut en bas*," that is with utter contempt.[3] During these several weeks though Burton had not stopped working, he had retreated wholly into the past. By accident his lost manuscript on Zanzibar had reappeared from India, and he had been revising it for publication. This meant a reliving of his old Nile failure and for the first time he wrote a serious appraisal of Speke's character and death. The first paragraph of the book was coloured by futility and despair.

I could not have believed, before Experience taught me how sad and solemn is the moment when a man sits down to think over and to write out the tale of what was before the last Decade began. How many thoughts and memories crowd upon the mind! How many ghosts and phantoms start up from the brain—the shreds of hopes destroyed and of aims made futile; of ends accomplished and prizes won; the failures and the successes alike half forgotten! How many loves and friendships have waxed cold in the presence of new ties! How many graves have closed over their dead during those short ten years—that epitome of the past!

> "And when the lesson strikes the head,
> The weary heart grows cold."

Burton was just finishing his 1,034-page *Zanzibar* when Isabel arrived from Damascus, October 14, 1871. He signed the preface the next day, and with this gesture seems to have put behind him the trauma of the Nile. In any case Isabel, with her mountainous luggage and beautiful Syrian maid, Khamoor, whom she could not bring herself to leave behind and was now treating almost like a daughter, brought him back emphatically to the present. Isabel had also brought a fat packet of letters from their Damascus friends protesting against his dismissal, praising the honesty and independence of his consulship, and urging his reinstatement. The day following her arrival he wrote a long letter defending his actions, and asking Lord Granville's permission to see the correspondence that had led to his dismissal.

Isabel meanwhile hounded her friends in the Foreign Office for explanations, and begged for an official apology. Wives and husbands alike were subjected to her energetic bombardment. Laura Friswell Myall, then only nine, never forgot Isabel's visits to her mother. "It seemed to me that this beautiful woman came and talked for whole days at a time, and it was all about 'Dear Richard and the Government.'" She quoted a letter Isabel had written to her mother, "Yes, they are making a complete Aunt Sally of the poor fellow, and he can't stand up for himself. You and Mr Friswell will say he deserves it for his polygamous opinions; but he married only *one* wife, and he is a *domestic* man at home, and a *homesick* man away."

"I was very sympathetic," Laura Myall remembered, "and felt as if I could kill the Government."[4]

After the Turkish Wali in Damascus was replaced by a liberal ruler, Subhi Pasha, still more letters came to England praising Burton. Many Moslems who felt that he had somehow been responsible for the hated Rashid Pasha's downfall joined in large prayer sessions begging for his return. Protestant missionaries wrote that though strongly prejudiced against him in the beginning, they had come to admire his "manly, vigorous, upright course." Eight Moslem divines and merchants signed a letter that said, "And we saw no bad in him, and he loved the Mohammedans and those who were under him. And there never came from him anything but truth, and he always walked with justice and hated none but the liars." The British press now swung behind Burton, and the Foreign Office in defence issued in March 1872 a white paper, *The Case of Captain Burton, late H.B.M.'s Consul at Damascus,* which included the official correspondence, including Burton's own defence and many of the private letters of protest. It was an explanation, not an apology.

Meanwhile Lord Granville offered Burton the consulship of Pára in northern Brazil, but he turned it down as too small, too obvious a demotion. When the post of Teheran, which was open, was given to someone else, he rightly counted it a slap in his face. "Why," he would ask his friends in posing a bitter riddle, "are the Egyptian donkeyboys so favourable to the English?" The answer, "Because we hire more asses than any other nation."[5]

During these months of waiting, Burton spent much time in the British Museum writing a diatribe against the Jews. In *The Highlands of Brazil* he had written, "Had I a choice of race, there is none to which I would more willingly belong than the Jewish. . . ."[6] And he had long been an admirer of Disraeli. But now, like many men who have difficulty with particular Jews and jump easily to an indictment of the whole people, his rage became generalized. Since, however, Burton ascribed to the Jews special virtues he knew himself to possess in abundance, what emerged was not a stereotyped antisemitic tract but a study in identification and ambivalence.

Among all Jews, he wrote, one finds those who are "fierce-eyed, dark-browed, and hollow-cheeked, with piercing acuteness of glance, and an almost reckless look of purpose." He attributed to the Jews immense passion, pugnacity, love of mysticism, symbolism, and the occult arts, as well as "abnormal powers of lying" and "excessive optimism." The Jews, he said, are bold and resolute, persistent and heroic, but also subtle and unscrupulous. They may be guilty "of greed and craft, and even ferocity, but rarely weakness and never imbecility." In the Near East, he continued, the two great branches of Jews were notably dissimilar. The Sephardim, though intellectual and scholarly, he counted cowardly and effeminate. The Ashkenazim, on the other hand, bringing from the North a manliness of bearing, a stoutness of spirit, and a physical hardness, are, he wrote, "in a word 'men,' the Sephardim are not." Burton, as we shall see, had come increasingly to count himself dual-natured, with feminine and masculine counterparts striving for mastery. He had also come to equate scholarship with femininity.

The Jews in Burton's eyes possessed, however, something he lacked, an emphatic sense of identity. They have in addition, he wrote, "an indestructible and irrepressible life-Power without which they would have utterly perished," "a vigour, a vital force," a "prodigious superiority of vital power." By contrast Burton felt himself, at least in defeat, to be "soft" and empty. "Gentiles," he wrote, "have a natural alacrity in sinking—look how heavy I can be—but . . . the Chosen People have as natural a tendency toward buoyancy."

Then Burton went on to ask why, with all his virtues, the Jew had been persecuted remorselessly throughout the ages, and he fell back upon medieval antisemitic mythology. The Jew, he said, was guilty of ritual murder, and he listed a score or so of such murders attributed to Jews from 1010 to 1840. He gave no historical documentation but a simple listing, such as had been passed down from one antisemitic tract to another over the generations.* Even the modern, civilized Jew, Burton continued, was capable of "a terrible destructiveness," he was "a sleeping lion . . . ready to awake upon the first occasion," made ready for murder by the long history of defeat and subjugation of his own people. Stripped to its essentials Burton's argument was as follows: The Jew is persecuted, therefore he becomes capable of murder, and has in the past murdered, therefore it is right to persecute him. So too Burton—so often called "a lion" by his wife—seems to have felt unconsciously about himself: I am persecuted; I am capable even of murder; therefore it is right to persecute me. So one begins to have some intimation of the guilt that immobilized him, and to understand why he made no attempt to defend himself before the Foreign Office until he was goaded to do so by his wife.

After finishing "The Jew," Burton, like many another author whose murderous impulses in defeat are assuaged by literary attack, put the manuscript upon the shelf. Twice he took it down and made some attempt to publish it, but never did. After his death Isabel indicated her intention to publish it, along with other manuscripts, but died before she could carry it out. It was finally published by her biographer, W. H. Wilkins, in 1898, when the Dreyfus excitement was at its height and antisemitism was raging throughout Europe.[7]

As the weeks of Burton's unemployment dragged into months, he became embarrassingly short of money. Being a great trencherman and gourmet, he felt the denial keenly, noting in his journal one night that he had longed to buy some oysters in a market but had strode resolutely past them. "They were three shillings a dozen—awful, forbidden luxury!"[8] Only their families knew of their penury, and Lord Gerard quietly saved them from public humiliation or serious debt by inviting

---

* The list included the alleged murder of the two-year-old Simon of Trent, who had been canonized by the Roman Catholic Church. In October 1965 Pope Paul VI, on the basis of a careful new investigation of the ancient evidence, officially exonerated the Jewish elders of Trent, who had been executed for this alleged ritual murder, declared them to have been innocent, and forbade Catholics to pray to this saint.

them to spend several months at his estate at Garswood. By this time, December 1871, they had between them exactly £15. On the journey to Garswood one of their precious gold coins rolled out of Isabel's purse and slid between the boards of the railway carriage and the door. She sought hopelessly to recover it. "I sat on the floor and cried," she wrote, "and he sat down by me with his arm round my waist, trying to comfort me."

Still they managed to have good times together, and continued to go to fashionable parties. Lord Houghton and Lord Strangford were warm hosts, as was Lady Marian Alford. They met the Prince of Wales, Disraeli, and Gladstone, and later Disraeli himself invited the Burtons to dine. Knowing Burton's dislike of old, ugly women—"There is no difference except civilization between a very old woman and an ape," he had written—the Disraelis laid a trap for him. Seating herself close to a low mirror, Mrs Disraeli, who was both old and plain, pointed to her reflection and said to Burton, "There must be an ape in the glass. Do you not see it?"

Recognizing the allusion Burton adroitly saved himself. "Yes, madame," he said quickly, "I see myself."[9]

In the spring of 1872 a British mining speculator offered to pay Burton's expenses to Iceland if he would explore the sulphur resources of the area. He promised him an addition £2,000 if the deposits proved profitable. Burton took off at once for Reykjavik, landing on June 8, and staying three months. Though his report was favourable, his hopes for the exploitation of the deposits which he mapped seem to have failed. An anonymous letter signed "Brimstone" in the *Mining Journal* later accused him of incompetence. "I have the greatest respect for Captain Burton as a traveller, but none whatever as an inspector of mining properties." Burton took pleasure in replying as follows:

"I have no idea who Mr 'Brimstone' is, but I must say that he deserves a touch of his own metal, hot withal."[10]

In the end Burton had nothing to show for his summer's work but his usual two-volume study. This time, as with his volumes on Brazil, it was tedious and pedantic. Though *Ultima Thule* seemed to have everything—Icelandic history, geography, geology, population statistics, taxation problems, fishing industry economics, and a discussion of the island's political relations with Denmark—one has the impression that for the first time in his life Burton was writing simply to keep himself afloat. Having seen the Himalayas and the Andes, he refused to exult over the Icelandic mountains, and he called the geysers a gross humbug. The natives he said were unwashed and generally unfriendly. As on every expedition he had started out with wistful fantasies: "Fair visions of girls who kiss the stranger on the mouth, who relieve him of his terminal garments, and who place a brandy bottle under his pillow and a bowl of milk or cream by his side, where are ye?" he wrote. Instead the Icelandic women reminded him of "the chilly women of the north who live only by the head" and who "gorgonize us into stony statues."[11]

While Burton was in Iceland, the consulship of Trieste became vacant, and Lord Granville wrote to Isabel asking her to urge her husband to take it. Though Trieste, then the port of the Austro-Hungarian empire, was not unimportant, the pay of £600 a year was clearly a down-grading from Damascus with its £1,000. Burton accepted, telling his wife he would stick on as long as there was ever a hope of getting Morocco, but fearing that his career was broken. Ouida insisted that Burton hated the foreign service and knew he did not belong in it, that he went back to it only for his wife's sake.

Back in London Burton remained long enough for an operation to remove a small tumour on his back, the result of an old blow, and on October 24, 1872, sailed alone for Trieste. Isabel followed him, after packing, taking the overland route. Burton's voyage took longer than he expected, and Isabel, without knowing of his whereabouts, caught up with him in Venice. Burton was in the steamer salon, writing, waiting for departure to Trieste, when he looked up to discover his wife, accompanied by the British consul at Venice.

"Hallo!" he said, "what the devil are *you* doing here."

"Ditto," she replied somewhat tartly.

Later the story was repeated by the consul and changed by others. As it came back finally to the Burtons, it was related as follows: Burton and his wife had been wandering separately over Europe and met by accident in the Piazza at Venice. Shaking hands "like a pair of brothers" they then walked off to their hotel and sat down in the lounge to work on their respective books as if such an occurrence was routine.[12] They *had* come to live "like a pair of brothers" and both of them used the phrase, apparently not caring that it suggested an absence of the essential intimacy in marriage. Still they had become indispensable to each other. "I am a spoilt twin and she is the missing fragment," Burton once said cryptically.[13] And though he continued to escape from this "woman of the north" for long periods—five months in 1875, seven months in 1877–8, and six months in 1880—it is clear that his dependence upon her deepened as he became older.

The post at Trieste was a Foreign Office sinecure. "Here is six hundred a year for doing nothing and you are just the man to do it," Lord Derby had said to Burton's predecessor, Charles Lever. Though small, Trieste was a cosmopolitan city of Austrians, Italians, Slavs, Greeks, and Jews. The Burtons had an airy flat of ten rooms at the top of a hotel, which they gradually extended till the suite occupied twenty-seven rooms altogether. Later, having received several legacies, they had money enough to buy a "palazzo."

The first quarters, as described by a reporter for the *World* in 1877, were divided into the Cross and the Crescent. The former, including a room with an altar, held Isabel's cherished religious collections; the latter, which housed Burton's library of 8,000 volumes, was bright with Oriental hangings, gold and silver trays, Bedouin rugs, Persian enamels, and divans covered with Damascus fabrics. The corners were piled with guns, boar-spears, swords of every shape and make, and numerous scientific instruments. There were gods everywhere, the reporter noted, the elephant-nosed Gupati sitting side by side with Vishnu. The bedrooms by contrast were furnished "in Spartan simplicity with little iron bedsteads covered with bearskins."

Burton used a separate table for every book, and when tired of one moved on to another. The *World* reporter counted eleven such tables, covered with manuscripts and writing materials. "You see," Burton said to him, "that my wife and I are like an elder and younger brother living *en garçon*. We divide the work. I take all the hard and scientific part and make her do all the rest. When we have worked all day, and said all we have to say to each other, we want relaxation. To that end we have formed a little 'Mess,' with fifteen friends at the table d'hôte of the Hôtel de la Ville, where we get a good dinner and a pint of the country wine made on the hillside for a florin and a half. By this plan we escape the bore of housekeeping and are relieved from the curse of domesticity, which we both hate."[14]

Since Burton suffered fearfully from insomnia, Isabel rose every morning between three and four to make him tea. After breakfasting at five, on bread, tea, and fruit, he worked on his books still lunch. Then they went fencing for an hour, or in late summer swam in the Adriatic. Only then would Burton go off to the consulate. To escape the summer heat they went often to Opçina, a Slav village 1,000 feet above the sea with a magnificent view of the Carnic Alps. On their long walks in the mountains Burton always carried an iron walking stick as heavy as a gun to keep his muscles in trim—it was no wonder, as Edwin de Leon noted, that "a blow from his fist was like a kick from a horse."[15]

The Foreign Office at first was generous about leave, and they made frequent trips to Venice, with occasional visits to Rome, London, and their favourite spas in Germany. Though Burton felt himself to be in a genteel prison, Isabel came to speak of Trieste as "my much loved home," and "my beloved Trieste." She entertained her women friends regularly on Fridays. Burton was often impatient with their chatter, and once interrupted their tea when he walked suddenly into the room, slapped a manuscript on the tea table and stalked out without a word. "Twittering with curiosity," as Seton Dearden put it, several of the ladies "bent over the manuscript lying among the teacups. It was entitled *A History of Farting*."[16]

Burton called his daily writing "raising the platform of his knowledge." In the eight years following the Damascus failure—1872 to 1880—he published eight new works comprising thirteen volumes totalling over 5,000 pages, as well as more than 800 pages of magazine articles. Though none of these works matched the distinguished performances of the days before his marriage, they do provide illumination on what was happening to their tormented and still restlessly inquiring author.

The two best books published during this period were written from notes he had made long before in Africa, *Zanzibar* (1872), and *Two Trips to Gorilla Land and the Cataracts of the Congo* (1876). Two translations came out of his Brazilian years: *Lands of the Cazembe*, a translation of the Portuguese explorer Lacerda's *Journey to Cazembe in 1798* (1873), and *The Captivity of Hans Stade of Hesse*, (1874), translated by Albert Tootal, for which Burton wrote a 94-page preface. *Unexplored Syria*, based on his Damascus years, was disappointing. It was a mere pot-pourri, large portions of which were written by his wife and Charles Tyrwhitt-Drake during his absence in Iceland. Burton refused to document his own failure. Except for a compilation of Syrian proverbs, he put in almost nothing about living people, concentrating instead on his diggings among the dead. Disgruntled reviewers, with small interest in archaeology, missed the fact that some of it, however, was original and important.

When in Syria Burton had heard of John L. Burckhardt's discovery in 1812 of four black basalt stones covered with mysterious characters embedded in a wall in the town of Hama. Suspecting them to be significant, he hired a local artist to make impressions. Since the stones were caked with the mud of centuries, the rubbings were faulty, but native suspicion prevented his getting the stones cleaned. Even the inexact reproductions of these rubbings, published in his *Unexplored Syria*, served, however, to alert British scientists, and after Burton left Syria Dr William Wright obtained permission from the new Turkish Wali—himself an art collector and scholar—to dismantle the wall, cut out the stones and clean them. Accurate casts were made and sent to London, and the stones were sent to the museum in Constantinople. Burton and Wright were much ridiculed for believing the stones to be Hittite in origin, but their theory was later proved to be correct by A. H. Sayce, who established that the Hittites had once had an exten-

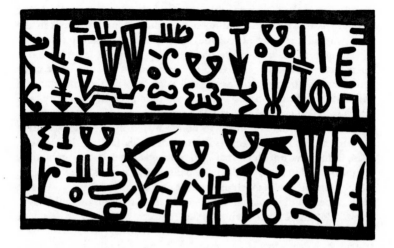

Burton's copy of one of the "Hamath stones."

sive empire, and that the "Hamath stones" represented the same culture as the impressive sculptures of Kara-Bel in west Asia Minor. Burton tried in vain to decipher the Hittite inscriptions; they would not yield up their secrets until the second decade of the twentieth century.[17]

Burton also publicized in *Unexplored Syria* the story of the discovery of a greater landmark in archaeology, the Moabite Stone. This was an inscribed slab of basalt, discovered in 1868 by a missionary in the Arab village of Dhiban on the eastern shore of the Dead Sea. Charles Simon Clermont-Ganneau—the Orientalist at the French consulate at Jerusalem who explored with Burton and Tyrwhitt-Drake on their Easter visit in 1871—had made plans to copy the inscription scientifically. But before he could get to the stone the Arabs had smashed it and distributed the pieces to local Arabs as talismens to ward off crop blight. Clermont-Ganneau recovered two large pieces and eighteen fragments, and fitted them together. In 1870 he published photographs and a translation, which rocked the scholarly world in a manner comparable to the twentieth century discovery of the Dead Sea scrolls.

The stone—eventually placed in the Louvre—was the first archaeological discovery of the record of an event which was also told in the Bible. It recounted the triumphs of Mesha, King of Moab, over Omri, King of Israel, in the ninth century B.C., a story which had also been described in the Book of Kings, with the notable difference that in the Biblican account the Hebrews had triumphed. Burton underlined the significance of the discovery with unconcealed relish. "It is evident that in the Book of Kings we tread upon enchanted ground, whereas in the stele, we find a chapter of realistic, local, and contemporary chronicle. The former offers, in a single chapter, a 'prophet,' a miracle, and a phenomenon so inexplicable as to be quasi-miraculous; the latter deals throughout with the world as we still know it. And the unprejudiced will find no difficulty in answering the question, Which is history, and which is the romance of history?"[18]

In Trieste Burton continued to be fascinated by archaeology. First he dug on the Istrian Penninsula, reporting his findings in October, 1874, in the new British journal *Anthropologia*; later he was invited by Count Gozzadini to dig in the necropolis on his property near Bologna. At this time there was much excitement over the mysterious pre-Roman civilizations, with wholesale pillaging of the Etruscan and Villanovan tombs. But there were some Italian scholars who tried to excavate properly and to record their discoveries as scientists. Burton soon made friends with Professors L. Calori and Ariodante Fabretti, and G. Capellini, rector of the University of Bologna, and in 1876 he published their findings in a guidebook, *Etruscan Bologna*. Like these scholars Burton tried to solve the mystery of the Etruscan language (which still awaits a Rosetta stone), and failed.

He was struck with what he called the "modesty" and "respectability" of the funereal statuary and reliefs, and recognized that the Etruscans had derived much from the Near East and had contributed greatly to the Romans. Still it was extraordinary that in writing about this ancient people, whose abundant and wonderful art radiates so much exuberant gaiety, vitality and innocent phallicism, he should have written so sterile and lifeless a book. It would seem that Burton, finding that he could not reach a people by way of their language, himself became tongue-tied. He had in any case become "a stream damned up with mud."

The book was badly reviewed in England, though after its publication archaeologists like A. H. Sayce, Arthur Evans, and Heinrich Schliemann, the discoverer of Troy, sought out Burton in Trieste. The *Scotsman*, the *Standard* and *John Bull* called the book shallow, superficial, and inaccurate. Even the normally friendly *Athenaeum* admitted it to be a failure. Only the *Gazette* defended him: "But it is indeed a novelty to see this hard student, *this desperately learned man*, charged with shallowness, with inaccuracy, and hasty incompleteness. . . . It will be amusing to follow the pigmies in their task of assailing the learned modern Gulliver."[19]

Isabel's book *The Inner Life of Syria, Palestine, and the Holy Land*, was published the same year as *Etruscan Bologna*, 1876. The critics loved it, and it sold well. So, in addition to his professional failure, Burton had to face the fact that his wife had now become a rival, winning praise even from his old enemy, the editor of the *Edinburgh Review* for her "vivid, clever, and brilliant sketches." Insofar as he looked upon her maturing talent as his own creation, he could take pride in being largely responsible. Insofar as her triumph underlined his own failure, however, it could serve only to complicate their marriage.

One day in the presence of a friend Isabel could not refrain from teasing Richard about her own success. "You are like an iron machine," she said, "and I do all the wit and sparkle."

"Oh, I dare say," he replied tartly, "the sparkle of a superannuated glow-worm."[20] It was a cruel metaphor—the glow-worm's light being notoriously cold—and the fact that Isabel retold it may well be evidence of how much it hurt her.

Discouraged by the reviews, as well as by his failure to unlock the secrets of the languages of the ancient dead, Burton abandoned archaeology. For a time he occupied himself with the history of the gypsies—the supreme wanderers—for whom he felt a special affinity. His 150-page essay on the subject of their origin was marred, however, by his testy quarreling with a French scholar, Paul Bataillard, who claimed to have been the first to discover that the gypsies came originally from India. On the basis of what he had written on the subject in 1851, Burton claimed the honour for himself.[21]

In 1875, after another effort to win him a transfer had failed, Burton asked for six months leave to go back to India. Isabel was jubilant when he promised to take her. The journey, which began on December 31, 1875, was a significant excursion into his own past, for during the journey he began to write his autobiography. At Jidda he looked for old acquaintances; at Aden he tried to find all the Arabs who had accompanied him into Somaliland. He even secured passage for himself and his wife to India on a ship laden with pilgrims going back from Mecca, as if he were hoping to recapture the sounds and smells of his own pilgrim ship in the Red Sea. For Isabel the voyage on this ship was an incredible experience:

Imagine eight hundred Moslems, ranging, in point of colour, from every shade, from lemon or *café au lait* to black as polished as your stove; races from every part of the world, covering every square inch of deck and every part of the hold fore and aft . . . men, women and babies, unwashed, smelling of cocoa-nut oil; the tedium of the long days, the air stagnant and heavy, tainted with the reek of this oil; unwashed bodies, sea-sick, covered with sores, the dead and dying, cooking their messes, and—save to cook or fetch water, or kneeling up to prayer—never moving out of the small space or position which they assumed at the beginning of the voyage. . . . They die not of disease but of privation, fatigue, hunger, thirst, and opium—die of vermin and misery. . . . No one would believe the scene unless they saw the dirt and smelt the horrible effluvia that arises from them.[22]

While Burton scribbled at his memoirs, an inkpot in one hand and pen in the other, Isabel staggered about the rolling deck distributing sherbet, food, and medicines, treating dysentery and fever. "During my short snatches of sleep I dreamt of the horrors," she wrote. "Several came to me daily to wash, clean, anoint, and tie up their feet, covered with sores and worms." In the first twelve days aboard ship twenty-three died. Richard seems never to have discouraged such ministrations, wherever they travelled, though once in Aden when he discovered her nursing a Negro whom she thought to be dying and saw that he was only drunk, he became violently angry.

In addition to his memoir describing his life up to the end of his army career in 1847, Burton also wrote a book about the trip itself. *Sind Revisited* was not a new book, however, but largely a reprint of his old *Scinde; or, The Unhappy Valley*, with interpolations about the changes wrought by the passing of thirty-two years. Old memories and new impressions were intertwined, usually with no attempt to label them in terms of time. Now and then he stepped out of the memories and admitted to his feelings of the moment. So, in visiting his old headquarters of the Sind Survey, scene of the happy "mess" and the careless years of his youth, he wrote, "Were I a woman, my first act would be to 'sit down and have a good cry!'" Karachi, he said, had become "externally at least, mighty respectable and dull"—no doubt like himself. At one point he wrote, "How very unpleasant to meet one's Self, one's Dead Self, thirty years younger!"[23]

Isabel also kept a journal on this trip, later publishing her impressions in her second book, *AEI, Arabia, Egypt, India*. Here for the first time she described a new activity which occupied her time and contained her passion. In Trieste, instead of nursing the sick as in Syria, she had organized a Society for the Prevention of Cruelty to Animals. She had given prizes for conspicuous acts of kindness, had threatened and cajoled the worst malefactors until every donkey owner in Trieste knew of her preoccupation. In India she was elated to find organizations of the same kind as her own, and visited an immense hospital for sick and maimed animals in Bombay. Once while driving alone in Bombay she saw a native wringing a bullock's tail to make it move faster. "I flew out of my carriage, and all the blacks huddled up together like a covey of partridges in a fright . . . I pounced upon my man, as I thought, and had him transferred to a policeman." Later, fearful that she might have seized the wrong man, she let him off without charges "if he would promise to pull no more cow's tails." She added somewhat ruefully in her account of the episode, "If my husband did not keep me in order, I should always be in the 'lock-up' for assault, for these sights make me forget that I am a lady."[24]

One would think that a woman so intent on stopping the abuse of dumb animals must feel herself abused. Isabel would have us believe, however, that her Richard was gentleness itself:

> He was not only the best husband that ever lived, but the pleasantest man to live with, and the easiest. . . . I have very seldom seen him in a rage, except, as I say, at anything cruel or unjust, ungentlemanly or immoral. . . . we never had a quarrel in our lives, nor even cross words. . . . if I ever saw him a little put out about anything, and felt myself getting irritable, I used to go out of the room on some excuse till it had passed. . . . I remember once slamming the door when I went out, and I heard him roaring with laughter. . . .
> I am glad to say there was only *one* will in the house, and that was his. . . . I was only too lucky to have met my master.[25]

A woman who never quarrels with a husband who is capable of very great rage, and who slams the door but once in her marriage, is certain to be harbouring a reservoir of revengeful feelings about "the best husband that ever lived," though they may be buried so deep she has no intimation of their presence. When Isabel returned from India, she resumed work with her Society for the Prevention of Cruelty to Animals with renewed fervour. She plastered the walls of Trieste with handbills promising new prizes for gentle behaviour and begging for an end to cruelty. One such handbill was an imaginary letter from the cab horses and bullocks of Trieste to their masters. It was not exactly a letter from Isabel to Richard Burton, but the overtones were suggestive:

> Man! God made me for your benefit, but He also recommended me to your mercy. The only wish that I have is to love and serve and obey your will. Do not, therefore, break my heart with ill-treatment. I have intelligence, memory, affection, and gratitude, only I do not know how to speak. I want to understand you, but I am often so terrified by you that I no longer know what it is that you want me to do. My head throbs from the blows you give me on my tender nose. . . . Treat me well, and you will see that I shall be able to do double my work. . . . We shall both be proud and happy because we shall have done our duty. . . .

It was signed, "The most Broken-down Horse, in the name of all the ill-treated horses and bullocks of Trieste."[26]

The Dual Man

But he is not intentionally irreverent. . . . he speaks the things that others think and hide.

Burton describes himself in the guise of Haji Abdu
Preface to *The Kasidah*

*W*HEN BURTON IN his later years ruefully resorted to spectacles for reading, he was fascinated to discover that his eyes measured differently, the right eye requiring a number 50 convex lens, and the left number 14. "I always told you that I was a dual man," he said to his wife, "and I believe that that particular mania when I am delirious is perfectly correct."[1] Here he was harking back to the fearful illnesses in Africa and Brazil, when in the most acute stage he felt as if he had split into two persons. For many years he lived with the conviction that he had a dual nature, seeing with two different sets of eyes, perpetually at war with himself. At its most obvious the war waged between the man of action and the scholar, the swordsman-soldier and the poet, the bawdy brawler and libertine versus the tormented searcher for the secrets of sexual vitality. In writing about Disraeli after his death in 1881, Burton likened him to Lord Byron, whom he also much admired, noting that both had "that exceeding sensitiveness, that womanly (not effeminate) softness of heart which finds safety in self-concealment from the coarse, hard, and cruel world that girds it."[2]

Burton took infinite trouble to hide what he felt to be the poetic or "womanly" side of his nature. He published his finest poem, *The Kasidah of Haji Abdu El-Yezdi, a Lay of the Higher Law*, under a pseudonym in 1880 in a private edition limited to 200 copies. Unlike most of his writings the *Kasidah* was honed and polished, and a skilful rendering of his own philosophy. Still he published this song of brooding melancholy as the work of an old Persian friend from Darabghird, who had supposedly given the manuscript to him for translation in India. Burton even hid his identity as the alleged translator and editor, signing only the initials F.B., indicating his old pseudonym, Frank Baker, which he had used for *Stone Talk*. He added to the deception by analysing the poem in notes at the end with presumed serious detachment, and by adding footnotes to explain certain Moslem metaphors. He never publicly admitted being the author.

Edward Fitzgerald had published anonymously in 1856 his first version of *The Rubaiyat of Omar Khayyam*; it had been greatly admired by Swinburne, Rossetti, Lord Houghton, and Burton himself, and thanks initially to the shrewdly managed publicity of Schütz Wilson had become one of the best known poems in the English language. Burton secretly hoped to see this history repeated with his own *Kasidah*, and asked one of his friends to bring it to Wilson's attention.

"I showed the *Lay* to Shütz Wilson," the friend wrote in reply. "He seemed absorbed in the idea of *Omar*, and said, 'Oh! I am the cause of its going through five editions.' I told him this was even more striking than Omar, but he didn't seem able to take in the new idea!"[3]

The *Kasidah*, printed twenty-four years after the *Rubaiyat*, did not catch fire. Only one hundred copies were sold, and the remainder apparently were distributed among Burton's friends, many of whom must have believed that he was indeed only the translator or adaptor, as Fitzgerald had been. There were few reviews. "We feel pretty sure that the ingenious writer is perpetuating a mystification," said *The Scotsman* of February 8, 1881, the reviewer going on to speculate that the author was a Mrs Harris.[4] Burton must have been outraged to see his poem dismissed as the work of an obscure woman, and this may have crystallized his determination to keep his authorship secret. "The Kasidah is mine after a fashion," he admitted privately in a letter to Leonard Smithers on August 2, 1888, "but I do not own it before the world, simply because it is tentative and only half of the whole."[5]

When Isabel republished the *Kasidah* in her biography of her husband, she was anxious to dispel any notion that he had composed it in imitation of Fitzgerald's magical verses, and insisted that he had written it in 1853 on his return from Mecca, three years before the *Rubaiyat* appeared. But there is abundant internal evidence, as well as the many references to ageing and decay, which indicate that it was written at least in large part when he was well past fifty. The notes are especially revealing, for here Burton was ruminating about himself:

Hájî Abdû has been known to me for more years than I care to record. . . . To a natural facility, a knack of language learning, he added a store of desultory various reading; scraps of Chinese and old Egyptian; of Hebrew and Syriac, of Sanscrit and Prakrit; of Slav, especially Lithuanian; of Latin and Greek, including Romanic; of Berber, the Nubian dialect, and of Zend and Akkadian, besides Persian, his mother-tongue, and Arabic, the classic of the schools. . . . Briefly, his memory was well stored; and he had every talent save that of using his talents. . . . He is weary of wandering over the world, and of finding every petty race wedded to its own opinions; claiming the monopoly of Truth. . . . He evidently aspires to preach a Faith of his own, an Eastern Version of Humanitarianism, blended with the sceptical, or as we now say, the scientific habit of mind. . . . Some will charge the Haji with irreverence, and hold him a "lieutenant of Satan who sits in the chair of pestilence." But he is not intentionally irreverent. . . . he speaks the things that others think and hide.

Burton went on to describe the Haji's philosophy as a "modified fatalism," a rejection of "all popular and mythical explanations by the Fall of 'Adam', the innate depravity of human nature, and the absolute perfection of certain Incarnations, which argues their divinity. He can only wail over the prevalence of evil, assume its foundation to be error, and purpose to abate it by uprooting that Ignorance which bears and feeds it." The Haji believed, said Burton, that the soul was only "a convenient word denoting the sense of personality, of individual identity." Conscience he said was a geographical and chronological accident, and Moslem and Christian notions of heaven merely idealized copies of the present.

The *Kasidah* began with a description of dawn over the desert:

The hour is nigh; the waning Queen walks forth to rule the later night;
Crown'd with the sparkle of a Star, and throned on orb of ashen light:

The Wolf-tail sweeps the paling East to leave a deeper gloom behind,
And dawn uprears her shining head, sighing with semblance of a wind.

The poem goes on to lament the speed with which life quickens as it nears its end. It is punctuated with hints of impotence:

Mine eyes, my brain, my heart are sad—sad is the very core of me:
All wearies, changes, passes, ends; alas! the Birthday's injury! . . .

This House whose frame be flesh and bone, mortar'd with blood and faced
    with skin,
The home of sickness, dolours, age; unclean without, impure within. . . .

This tube, an enigmatic pipe, whose end was laid before begun,
That lengthens, broadens, shrinks and breaks;—puzzle, machine automa-
    ton. . . .

Yes, Life in youth-tide standeth still; in Manhood streameth soft and slow;
See, as it nears th'abysmal goal how fleet the waters flash and flow!

And Deaths are twain; the Deaths we see drop like the leaves in windy Fall;
But ours, our own, are ruined worlds, a globe collapst, last end of all.

Lamentation shifts to philosophy, then to an attack on all sectarian notions of an after-life, with a special attack on Christianity:

Whose sadd'ening creed of herited Sin split o'er the world its cold grey
    spell;
In every vista showed a grave, and 'neath the grave the glare of Hell; . . .

All Faith is false, all Faith is true: Truth is the shattered mirror strown
In myriad bits; while each believes his little bit the whole to own. . . .

There is no Heaven, there is no Hell; these be the dreams of baby minds;
Tools of the wily Fetisher, to 'fright the fools his cunning blinds.

The 268-stanza poem concludes, however, with couplets of affirmation:

"Eat not thy heart," the Sages said; "nor mourn the Past, the buried Past;"
Do what thou dost, be strong, be brave; and, like the Star, nor rest nor haste.

Do what thy manhood bids thee do, from none but self expect applause;
He noblest lives and noblest dies who makes and keeps his self-made laws.

It is singular that this book of poetry which Burton published with such profound lack of faith—with one pseudonym for the poet and another for the "translator" and editor—should in the end prove to be his most enduring "original." The *Kasidah* saw sixteen editions in forty years and is still in print. Inevitably, however, it is called a lesser *Rubaiyat*, as Burton probably feared it would be.

Although Burton looked upon his own poetry with misgivings, he was proud of his ability as a translator of poetry, counting himself specially skilled at drawing the line between "unendurable inaccuracy and intolerable servility." But he always sought out poets for whom he felt a sense of immediate identity—first Camoens, later Catullus and the unknown poets of the *Arabian Nights*. Translation meant wearing the mask of another, if only for a time, and he chose the masks with some care. Luis de Camoens (or Camões) like Burton had led a conspicuously romantic life. Born in Lisbon in 1524, he became a handsome, gallant soldier-poet, a man of many loves, including a Chinese slave girl with whom he was shipwrecked returning from a voyage to Macao. He was blinded in the right eye, imprisoned for wounding a court official in a street brawl, and twice banished from Portugal. He served as a soldier in Africa, the Near East, India and China, and while stationed in Portuguese Goa wrote his epic poem, *The Lusiads* (The Portuguese), based on the adventures of Vasco da Gama. Back in Lisbon at forty, his great poetry behind him, he lapsed into apathy and penury. "Misfortune," he said of himself, "had frozen his genius." He died of the plague at fifty-six.

Burton began his biography of Camoens with a paragraph that could just as easily have been written about himself:

Opening with the fairest and brightest promise; exposed in manhood to the extremes of vicissitude, to intense enjoyment and "terrible abysses"; lapsing about middle age into the weariness of baffled hope; and ending, comparatively early, in the deepest glooms of disappointment, distress, and destitution, the Student, the Soldier, the Traveller, the Patriot, the Poet, the mighty Man of Genius, thus crowded into a single career the efforts, the purposes, the events of half-a-dozen.

As a young soldier convalescing in Goa, Burton had translated several stanzas of Camoens, which had been printed in the *Bombay Times*. Returning to *The Lusiads* in Brazil, he published part of Canto I, but was so dismayed at the look of his translation in print that he tore up the remainder of his manuscript. Later a competition developed between himself and his friend J. J. Aubertin, who had lived for some years in Brazil. Aubertin published his translation of *The Lusiads* in 1878 and received wide critical acclaim. Burton's appeared in 1880, to be followed in 1881 by his two-volume commentary, which included a biography of Camoens, a comparison of six English translations of the first two stanzas of *The Lusiads*, a condensed history of Portugal, and a loving account of the voyages of Vasco da Gama, with interpolations based on his own experiences in the same regions of travel. His two-volume translation of Camoens' *Lyricks* was published in 1884. Burton's erudition was staggering; he made himself master of Camoens' life and times. Nevertheless his poetic ear was inferior to Aubertin's, as the majority of his critics were quick to report.

Camoens for any translator provided great difficulties. Burton wrote that he had the exuberance, vitality, and vehemence of Robert Burns, with love songs flowing "lava-hot from the singer's soul." All translators found his harmonies exceedingly difficult to render into English. Oswald Crawfurd in reviewing Burton's translation of *The Lusiads*, in the *Academy* June 25, 1881, called the epic poem "a farrago of foreign adventure, of geography, of patriotica and inaccurate history, and of doubtful classicism. The attitude of the intelligent foreign critic has mostly been, 'It must be good, for the Portuguese say so, and they ought to know.' The truth is that Camoens wrote an impossible *epos*, but being a great poet and exquisite stylist, he left the mark of genius on his stanzas." Crawfurd called Burton's translation "the closest, the most flexible, and the most poetic version that has yet appeared," concluding generously that it proved Burton himself to be a true poet.

Other critics were less kind. *The Lusiads* had been patterned after the *Aeneid*, and contained many Greek and Latin phrases. In an effort to convey the quality of these interpolations, Burton had resorted to archaisms (asperous, batel, bosky, clepe, digne, eke, fere, hythe, targe, shend, and smaragd, are a fair sampling) and many French words, which served only to infuriate his readers. *The Scotsman* of February 21, 1881 pronounced *The Lusiads* "very prolix, and often exceedingly dull, the epithets tiresome, and the machinery cumbrous."

"Captain Burton is no poet," the reviewer said flatly, "and his translation is nearly the most unendurable we ever saw." The *Manchester
Examiner* of January 17, 1881 said "Captain Burton does not write the
English of today, nor apparently the English which was either written
or spoken at any given period."⁶

Though enraged by the unfriendly critics, Burton himself admitted
that *The Lusiads* was "wood-work, not bronze, and far less that which
outlasts bronze." "Even wood, however," he went on wistfully, "has
claims upon the sympathy and affection of his handler; and I end my
work not without regret."⁷

Isabel once wrote of her husband, "He was born to be rich and he
liked to be thought rich." Though he spoke with contempt of how his
own father had squandered his resources, he became no less profligate
with his own. No one knows how much he lost in his mining ventures
in Brazil, but it is clear that these speculations served only to whet his
appetite. "Gold is better than geography," he wrote, and between 1877
and 1882 he embarked on three ambitious expeditions that were really
glorified treasure hunts.

Returning from India in 1876, the sight of the Arabian coastline
brought back a long buried memory. His old Cairo friend, Haji Wali,
had once told him about stumbling upon a gold deposit in the Midian
desert which he had never exploited. Fired by this recollection, and by
the certainty from his own knowledge of the Bible and of Arabic
literature that the Midian had once seen extensive mining, he stopped
at Cairo to explore the possibility of getting Ismail I, the Khedive of
Egypt, to give him permission to lead a mining expedition into northwestern Arabia. He theorized that modern mining techniques might
uncover considerable treasure below the ancient primitive diggings.

Ismail, by the standards of the past in Egypt, was an enlightened
ruler. He had brought many educational and economic reforms, had
succeeded in gaining virtual independence from the Turks, and had
encouraged construction of the Suez Canal. Aspiring to be as cultured
as any European monarch, he had built an opera house in Cairo and
had commissioned Verdi to write an opera—*Aida*—for its inauguration.
Pretending to be in favour of abolishing the slave trade, he had succeeded in convincing European governments of his sincerity, and few
knew that the traffic was flourishing as never before in Egyptian history. European bankers knew, however, that Ismail defaulted on his
loans, and that his public works and private extravagances, plus his
grandiose schemes for annexing the upper Sudan, had served only to
bleed further an already impoverished people. When Burton asked for
an interview in early 1876, the Khedive's treasury was virtually empty

and his credit worthless. Though he refused to see Burton in person, he did not discourage his ideas, and finally early in 1877 invited him to Cairo for a personal audience.

Burton left Trieste on March 3, and argued so persuasively that the Khedive ordered a ship and soldiers to be put at his immediate disposal.[8] In the meantime Burton had sought out Haji Wali, who was now eighty-two, the husband of several wives and the father of many children, including one shortly to be born. Accompanied by George Maria, a French mining engineer, and three other Europeans, Burton set out with Haji Wali on March 25, 1877. His journal reflected his exultation:

At last! Once more it is my fate to escape the prison-life of civilised Europe, and to refresh body and mind by studying Nature in her noblest and most admirable form—the Nude. Again I am to enjoy a glimpse of the "glorious Desert;" to inhale the sweet pure breath of translucent skies that show the red stars burning upon the very edge and verge of the horizon; and to strengthen myself by a short visit to the Wild Man and his old home.[9]

Though the first expedition, lasting but three weeks, was meant to be only preliminary reconnaissance, there is no doubt that Burton had expectations for an instant bonanza in the long lost wadi of Haji Wali. But the old man turned out to be a California prospector caricature, and led them only to will-o'-the-wisps. They found many ancient diggings, and brought back samples of metalliferous quartz, porphyry, greenstone and basalt, which as subsequent tests showed did contain traces of gold and silver, but only in such minute quantities as to make mining operations uneconomic. Burton discovered evidences of crude oil, too, and had he been prospecting in the twentieth century instead of the nineteenth, he might well have become the Croesus of his fantasies.

The metallurgical tests, made in London and Paris, took several months; meanwhile Burton persuaded the Egyptian ruler to underwrite a second expedition. He was now completely in the confidence of the Khedive, who honoured him publicly and entertained him at palace fetes with Isabel, who had followed her husband to Cairo. In the four months from December 19, 1877 to April 20, 1878 Burton and his engineers, using Muwaila as a base, mapped and explored areas along a 600-mile route, noting the sites of eighteen ruined cities in northern Midian and thirteen in the south, and sending detailed topographical itineraries to the Royal Geographical Society. "We brought back details of an old-new land which the civilized world had clean forgotten."[10]

From the geographer's point of view Burton's second trip to the Midian was more important than his journey to Mecca. But Burton himself, having found no gold in quantity, counted it a failure. Moreover, the Khedive now refused to reimburse him for his expenses as promised, and his losses were considerable. Burton wrote a book about both expeditions. Where the first one, *The Gold Mines of the Midian*, reflected cheerful expectation, the second, *The Land of Midian (Revisited)*, radiated disenchantment. The "glorious desert" of the first book became "a hideous sterile horror"; the enchanting mountains of the Sinaitic shore became "huge rubbish-heaps without even colour to clothe their indecently nude forms; and each strives with its neighbour for the prize of repulsiveness." The valleys, he said, were "mere dust-shunts that shoot out their rubbish, stones, gravel, and sand in a solid flow, like discharges of lava. . . . Such is the near, the real aspect of what, viewed from Makná, appears a scene in fairy-land."

Such revulsion, with its sexual overtones, suggests that Burton's repudiation of the desert was deeply personal. When he left Cairo, he wrote, with its "intrigues, silly reports of the envious . . . the weary waiting . . . a great repose fell upon my spirit; it was like gliding into a smooth port after a storm at sea." In Trieste, he said, "friendly faces smiled a welcome; and, after an absence of some seven months, I found myself once more in the good town which has given us home during the last five years."[11]

The London press occasionally reproached the Foreign Office for keeping Burton in exile in Trieste. One reporter described him as "chained to his post . . . doomed by perverse fate to an isolation that must be almost irksome as the rock of St. Helena to Napoleon."[12] But it is clear that Burton found the pleasant security of his life there increasingly important to him. There was good food, good wine, pleasant company and a variety of travel, with the gaiety of the informal café life Burton had seen and envied as an adolescent. Isabel described the menu of one dinner in Milan: trout with mayonnaise, sausage, gelatine stuffed with truffles and pistachios, boiled fish, fillet of beef with ravioli, game pudding, ice pudding, cheese, dessert, all washed down with Lomabard Gattinara and Piedmontese Barolo wine. There was nothing of this kind in London.

But Burton was eternally restless, and his wife could never be sure that the desert and the male world it symbolized would not again entice him back. A decisive test came in 1877–8. Charles George Gordon, myth-making British general, had accepted a post with the Khedive of Egypt as Governor General of the upper Sudan, with orders to pacify the tribes and annex the million square mile area stretching up to the great Nile lakes. Gordon, who from 1874 to 1876 had added his own chapter of mapping and exploration of the upper Nile, wrote to Burton on June 21, 1877 as follows:

You now, I see have £600 a year, a good climate, quiet life, good food, etc., and are engaged in literary inquiries, etc. etc. I have no doubt that you are comfortable, but I cannot think entirely satisfied with your present small sphere. I have therefore written the Khedive to ask him to give you Darfur as Governor-General, with £1,600 a year, and a couple of secretaries at £300. . . . Now is the time for you to make your indelible mark in the world and in these countries.

Darfur was 140,000 square miles of desert land west of the central Sudan, inhabited by tribes who were being ravaged by slavetraders, and who hated the Egyptians as much as the Turks. Burton, who was at the time lost to his Midian gold fever, sent his polite regrets, implying that the salary was inadequate. Gordon wrote back acidly on October 19, 1877, "£1,600, or indeed £16,000, would never compensate a man for a year spent actively in Darfur. But I considered you, from your independence, one of Nature's nobility, who did not serve for money. Excuse the mistake—if such it is."

Later Gordon met Isabel Burton in Cairo and urged her to persuade her husband to go to Darfur for £3,000 a year. A little giddy herself at the moment with the expectation of great riches, she turned the offer aside, laughing, saying that if the Midian mines turned out as expected, £3,000 would hardly pay for Richard's gloves. But Gordon persisted, writing again on August 8, 1878, "I will give you £5,000 if you will throw up Trieste." By this time Burton was back in Trieste, deflated, bitter, and out of pocket. Still he refused. "You and I are too much alike. I could not serve under you nor you under me. I do not look upon the Soudan as a lasting thing. I have nothing to depend upon but my salary, and I have a wife, and you have not."[13]

It was a fateful decision. Gordon gave the Darfur post to Rudolf Carl von Slatin, a young Austrian officer, and shortly after retired, leaving the Sudan an easy conquest for the fanatical native revolutionary and warrior-priest, Mohammed Ahmed Ibn el-Sayyid Abdullah, known as "the Madhi." Slatin was taken prisoner by the Madhi in 1884, and to save his life pretended to be converted to Islam. He served as the Madhi's slave for fourteen years. Gordon himself, drawn back to Egypt as leader of the British expeditionary force to suppress the Madhi, was lost in the heroic defence of Khartoum, January 1885.

Burton was incredulous at the news of Gordon's death, and refused for a long time to believe it, insisting that he had escaped. Later, when Gordon's journals were published, he wrote a perceptive review, praising the general's truthfulness, integrity and phenomenal unselfishness, but also pointing out what he called the "hallucinations . . . to which all African travellers after a time become subject."[14] Since Gordon knew no Arabic, Burton was inclined to believe that he could have managed better in his place. "Arabic is my native tongue," he said to Frank Harris, "I know it as well as I know English. I know the Arab nature. The Mahdi business could have been settled without striking a blow. If Gordon had known Arabic well, he would have won the Mahdi to friendship." In letters to the *Academy* he deplored the slaughter of the Sudanese Negroes by British troops. For Egypt proper he recommended breaking up the "immense Khedivial domains" and landed estates, with distribution among the peasants, and called for more modern farming methods and industrialization. Damming the Nile would make it possible to support ten million. The British should govern Egypt as a protectorate for ten years, he said, but the country itself should be run by educated Egyptians, competing for office on a merit basis.[15]

Had Burton gone to the Sudan in 1878 he might have changed the course of Egypt's history, or he might have been slain like General Gordon. One can be certain only that he would never, like Rudolf Carl von Slatin, have remained in Darfur for fourteen years as the Mahdi's Moslem slave.

Isabel wrote of their life from 1879 to 1883, "I can never remember to have had a more peaceful and happy time."[16] These were years when Burton was working on eight to ten books, and when for long periods he seemed wholly content with his literary life. Still the time was punctuated by accidents, illness and the still recurring episodes of what seemed to her abandonment. She suffered leg and back injuries in a fall down a freshly waxed staircase in Paris in April 1879, and for months was badly crippled. Massage, mineral and vapour baths in Vienna and Marienbad eased her pain; then a "bone-setter" gave her a course of treatment that left her worse off than before. Later, in 1881, a doctor diagnosed an ovarian tumour, and fearing it to be malignant recommended an operation. This she refused, and made a vow to tell her husband nothing of the diagnosis.

In the autumn of 1879 Burton decided to return to Egypt to try and recover the money he had spent in the fruitless expeditions to the Midian. Ismail had been forced to abdicate in June, 1879, in favour of his son, Tewfik Pasha, and Burton hoped to persuade him either to underwrite a third expedition, or to reimburse him for the expenses Ismail had promised to pay. But Ismail had emptied the state treasury of its remaining £3 million, sailing away with it in his yacht to a palace on the Bosphorus.

Tewfik ignored Burton, leaving him "to eat out his heart in impotent rage and disgust at his bad luck."[17] During this six-month stay in Egypt he spent several weeks exploring the ruins in the El Faiyum oasis and "natron lakes" regions of Cairo with philologist, Bible critic and archaeologist William Robertson Smith,* who was looking for ancient manuscripts. Here they stumbled upon a portion of a slave caravan, consisting of natives captured in the Sudan and marched down the oases of the Nile, obviously with the more or less open connivance of the government. British missionaries had rescued about eighty out of a thousand slaves, mostly children. Burton was appalled at the sight of these destitute youngsters, many of them castrated boys intended for shipment to the harems of Turkey and Arabia.

Romulo Gessi, the Italian Nile explorer who had been on Gordon's staff, had estimated in 1878 that at least 400,000 natives had been taken from Bahr-el-Ghazal, Darfur, and Kordofan from 1860 to 1876—this though the American Civil War had virtually brought an end to the slave traffic in the Atlantic. Burton's research in Cairo and Alexandria now convinced him that three fourths of the inhabitants of Darfur had disappeared into slave caravans intended for Egypt, Arabia and Turkey. He estimated the number of annual "mutilations" at 8,000. "The nature of the subject forbids details in pages intended for the public eye," he wrote in an article, "How to Deal with the Slave Scandal in Egypt," "but in communicating with my Government, I have been as explicit as decency permits, and my description makes the blood run cold." About a quarter of the boys died from the razor, he said, if the operation was performed before the age of five; at the age of ten the loss was seventy per cent. The castration meant a rise in value from £5 or £10 to £25 and £80, depending on the age. Later he wrote more frankly, ". . . the parts are swept off by a single cut of a razor, a tube (tin or wooden) is set in the urethra, the wound is cauterised with boiling oil, and the patient planted in a fresh dunghill. His diet is milk; and if under puberty, he often survives . . ."[18]

Burton now asked Lord Granville for a temporary appointment as roving slave commissioner in the Red Sea, with the necessary gunboats, a salary of £1,600 to £2,000, and the promise that after two years he could return to Trieste. Calling slavery "a blasphemy against humanity," he called for "general and absolute manumission," and "a decree abolishing utterly and for ever the sale of human beings—the 'league with death and covenant with hell.'" Granville may well have been astonished to find Burton quoting William Lloyd Garrison, for he knew that he was contemptuous of the more fanatical abolitionists, in the United States as well as in England. But Gladstone, who at this point was backing away from any kind of commitment in Egypt and ignoring the hue and cry against the slave trade, dismissed Burton's request

* Freud expressed great admiration of Smith's sophisticated analysis of the "totem meal" and the ritual of sacrifice in his *Totem and Taboo*, 1913.

as just one more unnecessary military involvement. Only in 1882 was the Prime Minister forced against his inclination into serious intervention in Egypt.

Shortly before leaving Egypt in May 1880, Burton was attacked one night on an Alexandria street. He bloodied his fists striking back, but was felled by a blow on the head and left for dead. Recovering consciousness, he staggered to his hotel. The gold signet ring on his finger was gone, and the divining rod he carried with him always in Egypt, but his watch and purse were untouched. He kept the incident secret from the police, and sailed home to be nursed by his wife.

Eventually his gold fever flared up again. Despite a stern warning from the Foreign Office in March 1881, forbidding him to "proceed to foreign countries, for the purpose of promoting any specific commercial or industrial undertaking, or of obtaining concessions from a foreign government,"[19] he was off in November 1881 for the Kong Mountains of the Gold Coast. James Irvine of the Guinea Gold Coast Mining Company had promised him all expenses and a share in the profits if he would survey the company concessions and work out treaties with the local chiefs. Verney Lovett Cameron, a young African explorer who had been the first European to cross equatorial Africa from sea to sea, went along to do the surveying work, while Burton negotiated with the natives. After two months both came down with fever. Cameron, who was only thirty-eight, recovered quickly, but Burton, now sixty-one, was forced to go to Madeira to recuperate. From there he wrote to the Foreign Office, proposing that he be made governor of the Gold Coast with half a regiment of West Indian troops to supervise the mining. The reply was a peremptory order to get out of the concession altogether.[20] The whole venture ended in an imbroglio of lawsuits; Burton was forced to pay back even the expenses advanced to him, and found himself, as always, poorer than before.

Actually there was gold in the area; a generation later many Englishmen would become rich by using the hydraulic sluicing methods Burton strongly recommended in 1882. One cannot help wondering why this too, like all of Burton's mining ventures, failed. Isabel believed that he was always tricked by baser men, but it appears that there was something in Burton that courted financial failure. Like the compulsive gambler, he seems to have found relief in losing. Even his books had now become experiments in failure. Once lively, readable, and financially rewarding, they had become lifeless compilations often requiring prodigious labour to produce, but certain to be left unread. After his Gold Coast failure he published a two-volume *To the Gold Coast for Gold*, a shoddy mockery of his earlier African books, much of it a "cannibalization" of his *Wanderings in West Africa* and *Two*

Trips to Gorilla Land. Although Lovett Cameron in writing of Burton
insisted that he was kindness itself towards the unsophisticated natives,[21] Burton's fundamental anti-Negro feeling continued to permeate
even these volumes. The reviewers were hostile; the *Spectator* of
May 19, 1883 slapped at him for his "random thwacks from his self-
opinionative cudgel."

Burton was now forced to suffer agonies of humiliation going from
one publisher to another to market his manuscripts. Still he kept writing. Back in Trieste in 1882 he resumed work on a volume which he
had so far been unable to sell. This was his *Book of the Sword*, the
first of a projected three-volume study.* No other of Burton's books
was so symbolic of "the dual man." Here was the swordsman writing
about the sword, the soldier writing about the history of weaponry,
the explorer patiently sifting the chronicles of scores of explorations of
other men. For Burton the sword was the supreme weapon, what he
called "a prolongation of his own person, a lengthening of the arm."
He recognized it as a phallic symbol, quoting from the Egyptian Ritual
of the Dead, "I came forth as his child from his Sword," and noting
that the sword "at marriages represented the bridegroom in his absence." In commenting on infibulation in Africa he wrote of the bridegroom: ". . . if he can open his bride with the natural weapon, he is a
sworder to whom no woman in the tribe can deny herself." But this
symbolism was secondary.

"The history of the Sword is the history of humanity," he said. It had
been "a creator as well as a destroyer"; it had "carved out history,
formed the nations, and shaped the world." It was "the heroic weapon
. . . the invention and favourite arm of the gods and demi-gods. . . . a
Personage, endowed with human as well as superhuman qualities. . . .
To surrender the Sword was submission; to break the Sword was
degradation."[22] For Burton the sword and the man were one.

His first volume was sub-titled "The Birth, parentage, and early
career of the Sword." There were chapters on the use of the weapon
in ancient Greece, India, Egypt, Persia, Rome and the Near East, as
well as modern Africa. For students of weaponry, anthropology, military history, and the history of science, *The Book of the Sword* was a
source book of dazzling erudition. But almost no one bought it. He
never wrote the second volume, which he had planned to title *The
Sword Fully Grown*, or a third, which was to be *Memoirs of the Sword,
which after long declining revives once more in our day.*

---

* In 1876 Burton had published a 59-page pamphlet, *A New System of Sword
Exercise for Infantry*, which aspired to be the first scientific treatise on the use
of the broadsword or sabre. It had two novelties over other writings on the subject,
the Manchette system, and the reverse or back cut.

Burton himself was in "a long decline" and knew it well. In 1884, shortly after publication of *The Book of the Sword*, he suffered his first heart attack. He had been ill in January and February 1884 with painful attacks of gout. On March 14 a servant came flying to Isabel to tell her that her husband had fainted. "I rushed up," she wrote, "and found him very bad, and sent off for two doctors. They gave him twenty-five drops of digitalis three times at intervals of fifty minutes, and for two days and nights I never left his side. What the doctors had feared was a clot of blood rising to the heart, and I shall never forget the anguish of that time."[23]

No one could have predicted after this attack that Burton—as he suggested in his projected title for his last volume on the sword—would "revive once more." But there remained in his life a long and astonishing chapter.

The Unembarrassed Mind

Know that there are eight things which give strength to and favour the ejaculation. These are: bodily health, the absence of all care and worry, an unembarrassed mind, natural gaiety of spirit, good nourishment, wealth, the variety of faces of women, and the variety of their complexions.

The Perfumed Garden of the Shaykh Nefzawi[1]

RICHARD BURTON, A supremely "unembarrassed mind," was a man of countless secrets. He was also compulsively intent on telling secrets. This was a source of gnawing anxiety for his wife, who during the last years of his life lived in terror lest he be prosecuted under the Obscene Publications Act, passed in 1857. From 1876 to his death in 1890, he was involved in the secret printing of six books of erotica, prosecution for any one of which would have meant a damaging and possibly catastrophic suit, conceivably ending in a jail sentence. The act of 1857 gave British magistrates the power to destroy all books and prints they deemed pornographic, and to give warrants to the police to search out suspected premises. The Society for the Suppression of Vice, in its first 159 prosecutions against printers for publishing obscene literature, had succeeded in getting convictions against all but five. One third of the printers in Holywell street had gone out of business, the others having switched to religious literature.

In 1857 *La Traviata* was being sung at Covent Garden, but the novel upon which it was based was banned in England, and even the English translation of the operatic libretto was "unavailable," as a note on the opera programme informed patrons. By 1877 restrictions were tighter still. In that year Charles Bradlaugh and Annie Besant were prosecuted for publishing a new edition of a pamphlet advocating birth control which had been freely sold in England for forty years. Although the conviction was quashed, the trial was a warning to Burton of the unpleasantness he might face. In 1888 Henry Vizetelly, a 70-year-old publisher, was fined and sentenced to three months in prison for publishing a translation of Zola's *La Terre*. He died a ruined man.[2]

The British public had tolerated Burton's accounts of the sexual habits of the Dahomans and the Sioux, even women reading them without apology, because they were treatises on "savages." But there was a line beyond which Burton dared not step in describing even primitive peoples; this was a discussion of the sexual act itself. Although, as he pointed out, the average educated Briton tolerated the "witty indecencies" of Rabelais, he still counted Balzac prurient and forbade his wife to read his novels, or those of any other contemporary Frenchman. Dr. William Acton, esteemed physician whose text, *The Function and Disorders of the Reproductive Organs*, saw six editions from 1857 to 1875, wrote crisply that the "majority of women (happily for society) are not very much troubled with sexual feeling of any kind." This doctor taught a whole generation of British physicians that masturbation caused insanity, tuberculosis and heart disease, that "marital excess" led to serious disorders, and that women originated gonorrhoea.[3]

Burton, writing and translating at the height of the era of most rigorous suppression, distortion and repression, married to a woman who was in many ways a classic example of the product of all three, once admitted, "I never pretended to understand women." But this was mere masculine cliché. Burton probably knew a good deal more about the psychology of women than the leading physicians in England. He saw that the average educated Englishwoman, far from being without noticeable sexual feeling, lived "in a rustle of (imaginary) copulation." Unable like primitive women to "relieve the brain through the body," she turned instead, he wrote, to French novels and fantasy, "to visions amatory and venereal." Many, he continued, turn to "some counter-agent—religion, pride, or physical frigidity." But "how many a woman 'in Society,'" he wrote, "when stricken by insanity or puerperal fever, breaks out into language that would shame the slums and which makes the hearers marvel where she could have learned such vocabulary. How many an old maid held to be as cold as virgin snow, and how many a matron upon whose fairest fame not a breath of scandal has blown, how many a widow who proudly claims the title *univira*, must relieve their pent-up feelings by what may be called mental prostitution."[4]

Victorian abhorrence of discussion of sex has been amply documented by the generation that revolted against it. Burton's story of "the chloroform'd bride upon whose pillow the bridegroom found a paper pinned and containing the words, 'Mamma says you're to do what you like,'" has become a favourite.[5] What are not so well known are the harassments meted out to writers in both England and France who protested against the pervasive fear. George Eliot was reprimanded in the *Saturday Review* on February 26, 1859, simply for discussing pregnancy at length in *Adam Bede*. Flaubert was legally prosecuted for publishing *Madame Bovary*, and Baudelaire was convicted in 1857 for *Les Fleurs du Mal.* Tennyson was rebuked for his *Maud* in 1855 by a critic who wrote, "If an author pipe of adultery, fornication, murder and suicide, set him down as the practiser of those crimes." To which he replied, "Adulterer I may be, fornicator I may be, suicide I am not yet."[6]

As we have seen, Burton had many of his footnotes deleted as "garbage" by timid or prudish editors. He had helped to found the Anthropological Society of London in 1863, later the Anthropological Institute of Great Britain and Ireland, hoping that it would be a scholarly organ for discreet publication of data which other journals could be counted upon to reject. This society had published his "Notes on an Hermaphrodite," a description of a child in the Cape Verde Islands having deformed genitalia. The natives called it an hermaphrodite; the parents held it to be a boy. Burton, after examination, concluded the child was a girl with "a mere case of deformed clitoris."[7] He used the clinical language of the physician, and had the article appeared in a medical journal it would have raised no eyebrows. As it was, this and subsequent articles frightened the editors.

"Hardly had we begun," he wrote, "when 'Respectability,' that whited sepulchre full of all uncleanness, rose up against us. 'Propriety' cried us down with her brazen, blatant voice and the weak-kneed brethren fell away." He persuaded several members of the society to secede, and they formed the London Anthropological Society, publishing a journal called *Anthropologia.* After three years the societies merged again, and Burton wrote in disgust, "the deadly shade of respectability, the trail of the slow-worm, is over them all."[8]

During his years in India Burton had amassed a collection of erotica, which had been consumed in the Grindlay warehouse fire shortly after his marriage. According to Isabel he shrugged off the loss, saying, "the world will be all the better."[9] Actually he replaced the manuscripts as best he could, and in his later years became increasingly certain that the world would be better off *for* their publication. His own library became a great reservoir of Oriental wisdom on love, a repository of folklore and literature that illuminated the most important cultures of the East.[10] He had been "a stream dammed up with mud" too long, and in the last eight years of his life he flung the floodgates wide.

He defended his private printings with an intensity that suggests it may well have been generated in his own personal agony. The most barbarous tribes of Africa, America and Australia, he pointed out, take boys at puberty and set aside months of priestly tuition for their mastery of "the 'theorick and practick' of social and sexual relations. Amongst the civilised this fruit of the knowledge-tree must be bought

at the price of the bitterest experience, and the consequences of ignorance are peculiarly cruel."[11]

Among western women he found the failure even more damaging.

How often do we hear women in Society lamenting that they have absolutely no knowledge of their own physiology; and what heavy price must
this fruit of the knowledge-tree be bought by the young first entering life.
Shall we ever understand that ignorance is not innocence? . . . She has
feet but no "toes"; ankles but no "calves"; knees but no "thighs"; a stomach
but no "belly" nor "bowels"; hips and no "haunches"; a bust and no
"backside" nor "buttocks"; in fact, she is a monstrum, a figure only to
frighten the crows. . . . Respectability unmakes what nature made. . . .
Moslems and Easterns in general study and intelligently study the art and
mystery of satisfying the physical woman. . . . The mock virtue, the most
immodest modesty of England and of the United States in the xixth century,
pronounces the subject foul and fulsome: "Society" sickens at all details;
and hence it is said abroad that the English have the finest women in Europe
and least know how to use them. Throughout the East such studies are
aided by a long series of volumes, many of them written by learned
physiologists, by men of social standing and by religious dignitaries in high
office. . . .[12]

To the printing of several of these volumes, the nature of which he
had long ago hinted at in his Sindh, and the Races that Inhabit the
Valley of the Indus,[13] Burton now became dedicated. These bride-
books, or pillow-books, usually profusely illustrated, were commonly
presented to the bride and groom in China and Japan as well as in
India. Among the Hindus, who abominated celibacy in any form, instruction in the art of love was considered not only normal but almost
sacramental. Every temple had a phallus at its heart, and the temple
sculpture, as at Khajuraho, was often a choreography on the act of love.

One of the most celebrated of all the Indian manuals of love was
the Ananga Ranga, written in Sanskrit in the 15th or 16th century
by the poet Kalyan Mall (variously spelled Kalyana Malla and
Kalyanamalla). Burton had Hindi, Marathi and Gujarti versions; there
were also Arabic, Persian and Turkish editions. The dangerous project
of printing an English edition was developed jointly by Burton and
Foster Fitzgerald Arbuthnot, a young civil servant in India who was
also a wealthy collector and talented linguist. Arbuthnot was one more
on the list of bright young Englishmen who were attracted by Burton's
flamboyant daring. Six of these men—John Speke, Charles Tyrwhitt-
Drake, Lovett Cameron, Albert Tootal, W. F. Kirby, and Leonard
Smithers—in one way or another collaborated with Burton on at least
one book. Speke was the only one with whom he quarrelled. Arbuthnot
became his best friend; he was also his most important collaborator.

Arbuthnot was born near Bombay in 1833, the son of Sir Robert
Arbuthnot of the Bombay Civil Service. He entered the service himself

in 1862, and except for three furloughs to London, lived continuously in India until 1879, when he retired to England. Burton met him either in India in 1854 in the brief interval between his trips to Mecca and Harar, or on Arbuthnot's furlough to London in 1859–60. In any case the friendship took hold quickly, and they corresponded for many years. Arbuthnot was a quiet, unassertive but nevertheless persistent man, fond of Balzac, painting, and music, but curiously hostile to poetry. Apparently he communicated to Burton his excitement at reading the *Ananga Ranga,* and Burton encouraged him to translate it. This he did with the aid of some Hindu scholars, and he brought the manuscript to London on his furlough, 1872–4, at which time he arranged for the financing and found a printer. Burton was in London during part of 1872, and apparently worked over the manuscript at this time, considerably improving its elegance of style. He also wrote the introduction.

The *Ananga Ranga, Stage of the Bodiless One, or the Hindu Art of Love,* known in Hindustani and Arabic as *The Pleasures of Women,* was a treatise on how to prevent monotony and satiety in marriage. In his preface the poet wrote: "And thus all you who read this book shall know how delicate an instrument is woman, when artfully played upon, how capable she is of producing the most exquisite harmony; of executing the most complicated variations and of giving divinest pleasures. . . . I have shown in this book how the husband, by varying the enjoyment of his wife, may live with her as with thirty-two different women . . . rendering satiety impossible."

The text radiates confidence, exuberant innocence, and a contagious delight in the body. "The lotus woman," supreme of all female types, is described as "pleasing as the full moon." "Her bosom is hard, full and high. Her eyes are bright and beautiful as the orbs of a fawn; well-cut and with reddish corners. . . . Her Yoni resembles the opening lotus-bud, and her Love-seed (Kam-salila, the water of life) is perfumed like the lily which has newly burst." The poet takes for granted, what went largely unrecognized in the western world till the twentieth century, that most marriage difficulties, and many other problems including even those leading to murder, begin with failure to achieve orgasm. He provides much technical advice and several medical recipes on the technique of delaying orgasm for the man—as we have noted earlier, the process called Ismác—and of hastening it for the woman.

Though most of the *Ananga Ranga* is devoted to explicit recommendations for enhancing marriage, in the last chapter the poet assumes realistically that some marriages are beyond saving, and gives genial advice on how to seduce a new partner. He also provides the inevitable recipes for love philters and aphrodisiacs. "Europeans deride these prescriptions," Burton wrote, "but Easterns know better: they affect the fancy, that is, the brain; and often succeed in temporarily relieving impotence. The recipes for this evil, which is incurable only when it comes from heart-affections,* are innumerable in the East; and about half of every medical work is devoted to them."[14]

It is curious that Arbuthnot, who in 1873 was a timid bachelor of forty (he would not marry until forty-six), should have been willing to risk a public lawsuit in order to see the *Ananga Ranga* published. He defended his action with delicacy and conviction:

> The first impression on roughly running through the writings of the old Indian sages is that Europeans and modern society generally would be greatly benefited by some such treatises. . . . Many a life has been wasted and the best feelings of a young woman outraged by the rough exercise of what truly become the husband's "rights", and all the innate delicate sentiments and illusions of the virgin bride are ruthlessly trampled on when the curtains close round the couch on what is vulgarly called the "first night." The master either swoops down on his prey like a vulture or what is just as bad, sins by ignorance, appearing to the trembling creature either as a cruel brute or a stupid bungling fool.[15]

To forestall trouble Burton and Arbuthnot decided on a private printing, and identified themselves as translators only by using their initials in reverse. So the title page read: "Translated from the Sanskrit and Annotated by A.F.F. and B.F.R. For the private use of the Translators only in connection with work on the Hindoo religion and on the manners and customs of the Hindoos." They changed the title to *Kama Shastra*, Kama meaning love, and Shastra scripture or doctrine. Though both men were willing to risk the punishment of the censors, the printers clearly were not. After running off four, possibly six, copies of the proof sheets, they stopped the presses. For a time Burton kept the ill-fated venture secret, but he and Arbuthnot communicated the details to their good friend H. S. Ashbee, who included them in his private printing in 1877 of the *Index Librorum Prohibitorum*, an elaborate descriptive treatise on the banned books of England and France, complete with numerous titillating extracts, written in English rather than Latin as the title suggested. Ashbee, we are told, was "a stoutish, stolid, affable man, with a Maupassantian taste for low life, its humours and its laxities" and an enthusiastic bibliophile. He used the pseudonym Pisanus Fraxi, and was the probable author of the extraordinary eleven-volume anonymous sexual memoir, *My Secret Life*, in which are described one man's affairs with at least 1,250 women.[16]

---

* By "heart affections" Burton meant heart-attacks. Since he wrote this after his own heart attack, the note assumes a peculiarly personal significance.

Burton continued to encourage Arbuthnot, who, back in India, turned to the translation of a still more famous manual of love, Vatsayana's *Kama Sutra*. With the aid of Indian scholars Bhugwuntlal Indraji and Shivaram Parshuram Bhide, he completed the translation in time for Burton's visit to India with Isabel in 1876. Although Arbuthnot later tried to throw the censors off the scent by stating explicitly in Ashbee's second treatise, *Catena Librorum Tacendorum* (1885), that the translation was done entirely by Indian pundits, the vigorous idiomatic English clearly indicates that the two Englishmen were responsible for the final text.* Burton apparently worked through the translation during his holidays in Arbuthnot's country house outside Bombay, giving the manuscript the characteristic boldness and vigour that invariably set Burton's translations apart from others.

It was not until 1882, however, that the two men, probably aided by Monckton Milnes, resolved the printing problem by an ingenious publishing deception, the full nature of which was kept secret for many years. They set up an imaginary publishing house, the Kama Shastra Society of London and Benares, with printers said to be either in Benares (the holy city of Hinduism in northern India), or in Cosmopoli, the ancient name of the capital of the island of Elba. As Burton described it in letters to John Payne on December 23, 1882 and January 15, 1883: "My friend Arbuthnot . . . has founded a society consisting of himself and myself. . . . He and I and the Printer have started a Hindu Kama Shastra (Ars Amoris) Society. It will make the British Public stare. Please encourage him."[17]

Their first publication did not exactly make the British public stare, but it saw two new printings within two years, and quickly became one of the most pirated books in the English language. It would continue to be pirated for eighty years. The *Kama Sutra* was a classic highly respected in India, written by a famous scholar who could also be called "a professional innocent." Written between the first and fourth centuries A.D., it was a compendium based on the writings of still earlier scholars, and it had in turn inspired at least five commentaries.[18]

The book was tender, sage and domestic. Since the author followed the scholarly tradition of making a shastra, or system, he felt compelled, as had his predecessors, to include all the positions of love, however acrobatic or absurd. So also he insisted that the proper education of a young girl should include all of the "sixty-four practices," ranging from the art of playing on musical glasses filled with water to the study of chemistry, mineralogy, architecture, and the art of war.

---

* W. G. Archer, who in 1963 edited with a superb introduction the first publicly printed British edition of the *Kama Sutra*, holds that Arbuthnot "grappled with the original and moulded the translation," with Burton later improving the rhythm and style.

There are passages of extreme gentleness, especially in his chapter "On Creating Confidence in the Girl." Here he recommends no sexual union till at least ten days after the marriage, important advice in a land where many couples never set eyes on each other till the marriage ceremony. "Women being of a tender nature, want tender beginnings," he writes, "and when they are but slightly acquainted, they sometimes suddenly become haters of sexual connection, and sometimes even haters of the male sex." A youth need not be ashamed of humbling himself, he continues, ". . . for it is a universal rule that however bashful or angry a woman may be, she never disregards a man's kneeling at her feet."

Though the author is fundamentally a moralist, he is also realistic, and above all thorough. He includes advice to a courtesan on how to get money out of her lover, or how to get rid of him (for example, by showing small admiration for his learning). He tells a wife living in a harem how to topple her husband's favourite; he lists techniques of "mouth congress" for homosexuals and eunuchs. For men looking for easy conquests he suggests "women who stand at the door of their houses," and women who are "apparently very affectionate with their husbands." Sensibly enough, he advises men to stay away from female lepers, lunatics, women who reveal secrets, bad smelling women, ascetic women, and lastly the wives of relatives, friends, learned Brahmans, and the king.

In translating the most explicit libidinal matters, Burton and Arbuthnot adroitly managed to escape the smell of obscenity. Their words were cool and delicate; they used the Hindu terms for the sexual organs, yoni and lingam, throughout. When in 1962 the book was formally published in England and the United States, reviewers expressed almost unanimous surprise that it should for so many generations have been counted pornographic. The public should be grateful, Francis Watson wrote ironically, "that after whole forests have been felled to publicize a modern rediscovery of the female orgasm we can have the matter settled in a classical dissertation of six pages."[19]

In 1883, emboldened by the success of the secret printing of the *Kama Sutra*, Burton and Arbuthnot dusted off the ill-fated 1873 edition of the *Ananga Ranga* and printed it under this title in 1885, this time daring again to use their reversed initials, A.F.F. and B.F.R. Burton also decided, as we shall see in the following chapter, to use the device of the Kama Shastra Society to print privately but not secretly his unexpurgated translation of the *Arabian Nights*. He had barely finished issuing the first ten volumes of the *Nights* when still another manual of love fell into his hands, which he translated and rushed into print. This, the third secret printing of the Kama Shastra Society, was *The Per-*

fumed Garden of the Cheikh Nefzaoui. Originally written in Arabic, probably in the 15th century, it had been translated into French in 1850, printed secretly in 1876, pirated and again printed in 1886 by Isadore Liseux. It was the Liseux copy that Burton translated. *The Perfumed Garden* was a cheerful book, with a few bawdy stories and much good advice, specific without the deadly clinical aspect of twentieth century marriage manuals. It contained over a score of Arabic words for the male and female genitals, with definitions that were precise, amusing, and graphic. It had the usual remedies for impotence, including great quantities of eggs, a favourite dish, Burton remembered, of Brigham Young—and "a glassful of very thick honey, twenty almonds, and one hundred grains of the pine tree." There were recipes for abortion, some useless, some dangerous, as Burton was careful to point out. By Victorian standards the book was even more pornographic than *Ananga Ranga* or the *Kama Sutra*; today it is counted simply erotic realism. Burton took note of the fact that the last chapter, number twenty-one, was incomplete, cut off because the subject matter dealt with pederasty. Later he would search for the missing portion and translate it.[20]

A question left largely untouched by Burton's biographers is whether or not he took his wife into his confidence concerning his secret printings of the manuals of love. After his death Isabel wrote, "Richard, to save me, used to pretend to his men friends that I knew nothing of these works, and people who want notoriety pretend they can do so *now* with impunity. Richard *did* tell me everything, though he did not allow me to read the works."[21] But Isabel could tell disarming lies with complete unconcern if she thought her own and "Dear Richard's" reputation were at stake. As we shall see, she protested that she never read his unexpurgated *Arabian Nights*, and that he had expressly forbidden her to do so, but both statements were false. The Quentin Keynes collection contains a manuscript in Isabel's hand, "My Deposition Regarding the Scented Garden," in which she stated frankly that the Kama Shastra Society was "a bogie word invented by my husband for the purpose of baffling the world as to the whereabouts of his *Arabian Nights*, whilst it was being printed. I was present at its creation, and many a laugh we had over it."

The question of whether she read the *Kama Sutra*, the *Ananga Ranga* and the first printing of *The Perfumed Garden* may never be resolved. It is possible that Burton took his wife fully into his confidence, and laid these manuscripts at her feet as he had brought shocking tales and adventures home to his mother, anticipating routine scolding, but also intuitively aware that he was generating guilty delight. If Isabel did read them with embarrassed pleasure, like taking the draught of a potent aphrodisiac, she would in all likelihood have died on the rack before admitting it publicly. But the magnitude of her destruction after Richard's death suggests that she would have read any such manuscript more with a sense of sin than liberation. If so, it would only have served to confirm Burton in his sad knowledge that in matters of love mere facts are not enough. In 1877 he wrote in his intimate diary lines that illuminate this without really clarifying it. They were included in one of the rare extracts from his diaries that Isabel permits us to see:

"It is a very curious, and not altogether unpleasant sensation, that of not being believed when you are speaking the truth. I have had great difficulty in training my wife to enjoy it. . . ."[22]

The Nights

Every man at some term or turn of his life has longed for the supernatural powers and a glimpse of Wonderland. Here he is in the midst of it. Here he sees mighty spirits summoned to work the human mite's will, however whimsical, who can transport him in an eye-twinkling whithersoever he wishes; who can ruin cities and build palaces of gold and silver, gems and jacinths; who can serve up delicate viands and delicious drinks in priceless chargers and impossible cups and bring the choicest fruits from the farthest Orient: here he finds magas and magicians who can make kings of his friends, slay armies of his foes and bring any number of beloveds to his arms.

Richard Burton, Preface to *Arabian Nights*

*B*URTON HAD SAT at campfires in Arabia and East Africa listening to the tales of Sheharazade, Sinbad and Aladdin that he had heard as a child, and had learned to tell them himself in Arabic with all the gusto and bravura of the Moslem storyteller. He had found them, he wrote, "an unfailing source of solace and satisfaction . . . a charm, a talisman against ennui and despondency." The *Nights* were the ideal refuge of the romantic, a complicated adult-child fantasy, a labyrinth of wish fulfilment, where the amiable tyrant Harun al Rashid, Charlemagne of the East, ruled as hero. Very early, however, Burton had learned that the complete *Nights* contained tales that would have made his nursemaids redden with embarrassment. In addition to the romance and magic there were stories of homosexuality, bestiality, and simple earthy obscenity. Even the tenderest romances set precedents for explicitness.

"The European novelist," Burton wrote, "marries off his hero and heroine and leaves them to consummate marriage in privacy; even Tom Jones had the decency to bolt the door. But the Eastern storyteller, especially this unknown 'prose Shakespear,' must usher you, with a flourish, into the bridal chamber and narrate to you, with infinite gusto, everything he sees and hears." In the Arab world the *Nights* were considered coffee house entertainment, not polite literature, and though the Turks had made them the basis of a national theatre, most Arab scholars were inclined to dismiss them as fit only for uncultivated men.

The French orientalist Antoine Galland (1646–1715) had introduced the *Nights* to the western world, 1704–17, in a translation of such enchantment that it was shortly pirated all over the continent and even in India.[1] But Galland, as Burton put it, "was compelled to expunge the open repulsive simplicity, the childish indecencies and the wild orgies of the original, contrasting with the gorgeous tints, the elevated morality and the religious tone of the passages which crowd upon them. We miss the odeur du sang which taints the parfums du harem; also the humouristic tale and the Rabelaisian outbreak which relieve and throw out into strong relief the splendour of Empire and the havoc of Time." The English version of Jonathan Scott he called "vapid, frigid, and insipid." Later editions by Henry Torrens and Edward M. Lane he described as "garbled and mutilated, unsexed and unsouled."[2]

The cutting and bowdlerizing of a book was almost as abhorrent to Burton as mutilation of a man, and the idea of restoring what others had cut gave him enormous satisfaction. As early as 1852, he wrote, he had decided to publish "a full, complete, unvarnished, uncastrated copy of the great original." He defended this decision in a witty, brilliant essay on pornography, which he included in his Terminal Essay of volume ten of the *Nights*:

. . . the naive indecencies of the text are rather *gaudisserie* than purience; and, when delivered with mirth and humour, they are rather the "excrements of wit" than designed for debauching the mind. Crude and indelicate with infantile plainness; even gross and at times, "nasty" in their terrible frankness, they cannot be accused of corrupting suggestiveness or subtle insinuation of vicious sentiment. Theirs is a coarseness of language, not of idea; they are indecent, not depraved; and the pure and perfect naturalness of their nudity seems almost to purify it, showing that the matter is rather of manners than of morals. Such throughout the East is the language of every man, woman and child, from prince to peasant, from matron to prostitute. . . .

To those critics who complain of these raw vulgarisms and puerile indecencies in The Nights I can reply only by quoting the words said to have been said by Dr Johnson to the lady who complained of the naughty words in his dictionary—"You must have been looking for them, Madam!"[3]

Burton ridiculed the contention of Edward M. Lane that the *Nights* was the work of a single Arabian author between 1475 and 1525, insisting instead, correctly, that the Alf Laila Wa-Laila, the "Thousand and One Nights" was actually an Arabisation of an ancient Persian masterpiece, *Hazār Afsánah* or *Thousand Tales*.[4] He believed the oldest stories, including Sinbad, dated back to the eighth century, that the thirteen tales common to all the collections dated from the tenth century, and that the latest came from the sixteenth. He gravely warned his readers of the old superstition that no one can read all of *The Nights* without dying. "It is only fair," he said, "that my patrons should know this."[5]

Burton fully expected to be the first scholar to translate the complete *Nights*.[6] But he worked at his translation only "fitfully," and was dismayed to read in the *Athenaeum* of November 5, 1881, that John Payne, thirty-nine-year-old poet, oriental scholar, and translator of François Villon, would bring out the first volumes of the unexpurgated *Nights* in 1882 in a private printing of 500 copies. He wrote at once to Payne wishing him well and offering him "precedence and possession of the field," and his own services if needed. Payne, who had an immense respect for Burton, immediately offered to collaborate with him and give him a share in the royalties. Burton replied, "Your terms about the royalty are more than liberal. I cannot accept them, however, except for value received, and it remains to be seen what time is at my disposal. . . . I must warn you that I am a rolling stone."[7] As it turned out, he refused any compensation whatever.

Burton saw at once, however, in reading Payne's proofs, that he had a formidable rival. Payne was a meticulous scholar with a special gift at translating poetry. But he was timid, and Burton's letters often urged him to translate more literally. "Poor Abu Nuwas is (as it were) castrated," he wrote at one point, "Be bold or *audace*."[8] Payne was a bachelor and recluse, convinced, he once said, "that nearly all the miseries that have befallen empires have resulted from intemperate love of some woman." Even his admiring biographer, Thomas Wright, noted with some wonder that when he travelled on the continent with his two sisters, he insisted on getting a bedroom that could be reached only by going through the bedroom used by the girls. Payne and Burton had numerous friends in common, including Arbuthnot and Ashbee, and met occasionally at dinner parties on Burton's numerous journeys to London. Though Payne professed that he "simply loathed" the erotic publications of the Kama Shastra Society, and urged Burton not to print *The Scented Garden*, which he called "a filthy book without literary value of any kind . . . merely a collection of bawdy tales,"[9] still he translated many in *The Nights* of similar genre and style, and later translated Boccaccio.

Payne's edition of *The Nights* was both praised and condemned, but the author was not prosecuted, and his volumes immediately became collector's items. Burton concluded shrewdly that the field had by no means been pre-empted, and in the autumn of 1882 he began putting together what he called his "old scraps of translation" and collating "a vast heterogeneous collection of notes." "I am going in for notes where they did not suit your scheme," he wrote to Payne, "and shall make the book a perfect répertoire of Eastern knowledge in its most esoteric form."[10] When Burton discovered he could get no more than a meagre £500 from a publisher for his own translation, he decided in disgust to assume all the publishing costs himself and to print the work privately under the imprint of the Kama Shastra Society. It was a serious gamble.

Isabel, at first apprehensive, finally swung behind her husband and with furious energy mailed out 34,000 circulars advertising the proposed ten-volume edition, *A Plain and Literal Translation of the Arabian Nights' Entertainments, Now Entituled The Book of the Thousand Nights and a Night, With Introductory Explanatory Notes on the Manners and Customs of Moslem Men and a Terminal Essay upon the History of the Nights.* It was to be a private printing of 1,000 copies, to be sold by subscription at one guinea per volume, with the promise to the reader that no further copies would be made. Mrs Virginia Maylor was hired to shoulder the burden of copying, and to leave Isabel free for the work of publicity. Fearful at first that they could get no more than 500 names on the subscription list, the Burtons were relieved to see the number swell to one thousand. Then when it continued upwards to two thousand, they regretted bitterly that they had not set the initial figure higher.

Burton's illness in the winter of 1882, culminating in his heart attack in February 1883, kept him bedridden for eight months. But he scribbled furiously at his translation. He used the most reliable of all the *Nights* versions—the Calcutta, or Macnaghten edition—also the Būlāk and Breslau editions, and later in London the Wortley Montagu manuscript,* as well as checking with the new English version

---

* Burton detested working at the Bodleian Library, and asked for the Edward Wortley Montagu manuscript to be sent on loan to the India Office in London. The curators refused, and Burton was forced to have the material photographed. He revenged himself by inscribing Vol. VI of the *Supplemental Nights* as follows:

To the Curators of the Bodleian Library, Oxford, Especially Revd. B. Price and Max Muller:

Gentlemen,

I take the liberty of placing your names at the head of this Volume which owes its rarest and raciest passages to your kindly refusing the temporary transfer of the Wortley Montague MS. from your pleasant library to the care of Dr. Rost, Chief Librarian, India Office. As a sop to 'bigotry and virtue,' as a concession to the 'Scribes and Pharisees,' I had undertaken, in case the loan were granted, not to translate tales and passages which might expose you, the Curators, to unfriendly comment. But possibly anticipating what injury would thereby accrue to the Volume and what sorrow to my subscribers, you were good enough not to sanction the transfer—indeed you refused it to me twice—and for this step my *clientèle* will be (or ought to be) truly thankful to you.

I am, Gentlemen,
Yours obediently
Richard F. Burton

by John Payne. He did much work in London in the summer of 1885, spending long hours in the Athenaeum Club and the India Office, a familiar figure in his white trousers, white linen jacket, and shabby white beaver hat. He worked often the whole day without food, his only diversions being coffee and snuff.

John Payne printed nine volumes between 1882 and 1884, and an additional three volumes, *Tales from the Arabic*, in 1884. Burton printed ten volumes in 1885, with an additional six volumes, the *Supplemental Nights*, from 1886 to 1888—translating altogether seventy-eight more stories than Payne. The degree to which Burton relied on Payne's translation has been a subject of controversy between Payne's admirers and Burton's avid followers. There is general agreement that Burton's was the more exact and literal translation, but the nature of Burton's reliance on Payne needs careful definition, since it has been exaggerated. Because the material is somewhat technical, the discussion is here left to an Appendix.

For the fearlessness and fidelity of his translation Burton has never been excelled and has in fact frightened away all competitors. But the fame of his *Nights* rests also upon his Terminal Essay, and upon his hundreds of footnotes, certainly the most celebrated in English writing. In these notes Burton found finally a vehicle for publishing his enormous secret wealth of anthropological and sexual curiosities. They are hung like precious ornaments at appropriate places, embellishing the body of the tales. He wrote of everything his audience might find even slightly scandalous.

On childbirth among the Moslems of Waday, he described how "a cord is hung from the top of the hut, and the woman in labour holds on to it standing with her legs apart, till the midwife receives the child." He noted the importance of large buttocks as a beauty mark in Somaliland. He discussed inspection of the nuptial sheet among the Persians and Hebrews, and the treatment of madmen in Syrian monastaries. Real hermaphroditism he called an impossibility, though he conceded that medical books had recorded authentic cases of changed sex—at least men changed into women; the reverse he held to be "only apparent." He suggested gingerly that Sapphism and Tribadism were common in harems, and wrote coolly that incest is "physiologically injurious only when the parents have constitutional defects." As always, he discussed eunuchs with special fascination. "There are may ways of making the castrato . . . but in all cases the animal passion remains, for in man, unlike other animals, the *fons veneris* is the brain."

There were three full pages on circumcision, and a detailed account of the invention of the condom. Of defloration he wrote, "Several women have described the pain to me as much resembling the draw-ing of a tooth." He wrote a short history of venereal infection in Europe. He sagely suggested that the idea of demoniac possession arose from erotic dreams. He included an infallible Persian recipe for sobering a drunk: "They hang them up by the heels, as we used to do with the drowned, and stuff their mouths with human ordure which is sure to produce emesis." In a long footnote on the possibility of mating with apes he noted, "During my four years' service on the West African Coast I heard enough to satisfy me that these powerful beasts often kill men and rape women; but I could not convince myself that they ever kept the women as concubines."

There were recipes for hashish, and a classification of aphrodisiacs into medicinal, mechanical, and magical, with appropriate recipes. Rape, infanticide, euthanasia, suicide, adultery, and murder—each got its turn, his discussion of murder including the practice of Egyp-tian wives who murder a husband by tearing out his testicles. There were his usual strictures against Christianity, with its "egoism and degradation of humanity"; there was a long and brilliantly written essay on pornography. In attacking Britain's obscenity laws, which he said, "offer a premium to greedy and unscrupulous publishers," he argued that *Fanny Hill* should be published, since it was worth pence instead of pounds, and he recommended an Arab treatise on birth control, "Kitab Al Bah," as "useful to humanity."

All of this was titillating and Burtonesque, only moderately danger-ous for his reputation, and not much more revealing of the multiple directions of his curiosity than the footnotes of his great travel books. There were, however, two subjects about which he wrote at length in the Terminal Essay of the *Nights* which he had not dared to discuss earlier. One was the sexual education of women, which we have examined briefly in the previous chapter; the other was homosexuality. His 18,000-word essay titled "Pederasty" was one of the first attempts by an Englishman to explore the subject with something like clinical detachment. Havelock Ellis, it will be remembered, published his volume on sexual inversion in 1898, thirteen years later, only to suffer immediate prosecution. The printer was heavily fined.

"I propose to discuss the matter sérieusement, honnêtement, his-toriquement," Burton wrote, "to show it in decent nudity not in sug-gestive fig-leaf." He began with surprising frankness describing the difficulties he had suffered concerning his intelligence report on the male brothels of Karachi back in 1845. Subsequent research, he said, had led him to believe that there was an immense geographical area —the Sotadic zone [named after Sotades, a Greek poet, 276 B.C., notorious for his homosexual verse]—where "le vice contra nature"

was well established. This he described as a belt stretching through
the Mediterranean countries, including southern France, extending
across the Near East to include Mesopotamia and Afghanistan, from
thence to Sind, Punjab and Kashmir in India, and including all of
Indo-China, China, Japan and Turkestan. It included also the South
Sea Islands and the whole of the new world. The belt omitted northern
Europe, Australia, Siberia, southern India and most of Africa. "Within
the Sotadic Zone," he wrote, "the Vice is popular and endemic, held
at the worst to be a mere peccadillo, whilst the races to the North and
South of the limits here defined practice it only sporadically amid the
opprobrium of their fellows who, as a rule, are physically incapable
of performing the operation and look upon it with the liveliest disgust."

Burton's diction occasionally indicated mild distaste. He called
pederasty the vice, the abuse, pathological love, and a great and
growing evil deadly to the birth rate, and noted that in countries
where it was most common, such as Persia, it was a perpetual mortification to the women. He distinguished types of homosexuals, describing the obviously feminine man with womanly gait and gestures, and
quoting Walt Whitman's portrait of the "professed pederast" with
"puffy features and unwholesome complexion . . . and peculiar
cachetic expression." He distinguished them sharply from "the young
priest who honestly refrains from women and their substitutes." In
describing homosexuals who use signals to recognize each other, he
used the term debauchee. But for the most part his account is neither
pejorative nor defensive. One emerges from these pages with the
impression that there was very little on the subject that Burton did
not know.

He reviewed historical attitudes towards homosexuality, his details
showing that in his reading in classical literature he had missed few
references to the subject. The Greeks, he said, professed to regard
youths as "the most cleanly and beautiful objects in this phenomenal
world." He noted that though Mohammed had regarded sodomy
with philosophical indifference, he had nevertheless taken pains to
forbid it in the Koran. The notion that "the Ghilmán or Wuldán, the
beautiful boys of Paradise . . . will be lawful catamites to the True
Believers in a future state of happiness" Burton called vicious, and
emphasized that learned Moslems looked upon the idea as scandalous.
But he went on to point out that "Moslems, even of saintly houses,
are permitted openly to keep catamites, nor do their disciples think
worse of their sanctity for such license." The Turks were "a race of
pederasts," but Hindus held the practice in abhorrence, and the
Negro race, thanks to the indoctrination of their youth in sexual
matters, was "almost untainted by sodomy and tribadism."

Although his writing was for the most part scholarly—in defining twenty-five pederastic terms he frequently used Latin to avoid being offensive—now and then he slipped into the crudest kind of smoking-room story. "A favourite Persian punishment for strangers caught in the harem or gynaeceum," he wrote, "is to strip and throw them and expose them to the embraces of the grooms and negro-slaves. I once asked a Shirazi how penetration was possible if the patient resisted with all the force of the sphincter muscle: he smiled and said, 'Ah, we Persians know a trick to get over that; we apply a sharpened tent-peg to the crupper-bone (os coccygis) and knock till he opens.'"

Burton did not dodge the subject of homosexuality in England. "In our modern capitals, London, Berlin and Paris for instance, the Vice seems subject to periodical outbreaks. For many years, also, England sent her pederasts to Italy, and especially to Naples whence originated the term 'Il vizio Inglese.'" Berlin, he continued, "is not a whit better than her neighbours . . . Paris is by no means more depraved than Berlin and London; but, whilst the latter hushes up the scandal, Frenchmen do not; hence we see a more copious account of it submitted to the public."

"A friend knowledgeable in such matters," he continued, had informed him that many distinguished men of the past had been homosexuals; among them were Alexander, Julius Caesar, Napoleon, and Shakespeare. Among the monarchs he included Henri III, Louis XIII, Louis XVIII, Frederick the Great, Peter the Great, and William II of Holland. The friend was Henry S. Ashbee, whose listing in his *Catena Librorum Tacendorum* (1885) was practically identical, and who—like Burton—failed to cite any historical evidence.

In discussing theories of causation Burton noted that the Persians blamed the high incidence of sodomy in their country upon parental severity. "Youths arrived at puberty find none of the facilities with which Europe supplies fornication," he said, as female brothels were practically unknown. So it was not surprising, with such habits well begun, that later in life "after marrying and begetting heirs, Paterfamilias returns to Ganymede." He went on to examine and to reject the theory that homosexuality resulted from abnormal groupings of the nerves in the rectum and genitalia. He also discounted Plato's mystical grouping of humanity into men, women, and men-women or androgynes. He toyed with the idea that the higher incidence in certain areas was due to climate. Finally, in what was for Burton an unusually tentative manner, he put forward the theory he most trusted, that homosexuality in both men and women resulted from "a blending of the masculine and feminine temperaments."

Burton had a grisly catalogue of the punishments man had inflicted upon inverts since the dawn of history. And he was acutely aware of possible legal penalties in Britain for even discussing the subject in print. Because of the cultural impact of the story of the burning of Sodom in the Old Testament, Jews and Christians had for centuries considered—at least in theory—that sodomy was a crime worthy of punishment by death. The Zoroastrians were equally punitive. In England Henry VIII took the matter out of the jurisdiction of the ecclesiastical courts in 1533 by making sodomy a felony punishable by death, and turning prosecution over to the civil authorities. His law remained in force with minor changes for the next 275 years. But the punishment was for public "indecency" only; private acts between consenting adults were generally ignored by the law. In 1861 the death penalty was changed to imprisonment from ten years to life. Then in 1885 a law was passed which for the first time made private as well as public homosexual acts—such as street solicitation—a criminal offence, with a penalty of up to two years in prison. This gave a free field to blackmailers.[11]

Burton's essay on pederasty appeared in the same year this law was passed, and was in effect though not in intent, a scholarly protest against it. Burton held that homosexuality was not a sin, nor a crime, but simply illness. "This pathological love, this perversion of the erotic sense, one of the marvellous list of amorous vagaries" deserves, he wrote, "not prosecution but the pitiful care of the physician and the study of the psychologist."

Burton realized that he could be brought to court for what he had written about homosexuality as well as for the more robust stories of *The Nights*. "I don't care a button about being prosecuted," he wrote, "and if the matter comes to a fight I will walk into court with my Bible and my Shakespeare and my Rabelais under my arm, and prove to them that, before they condemn me, they must cut half of *them* out."[12] He had carefully marked all the passages in these classics that a British audience would find shocking, including the line in the Old Testament where Jehovah orders the Israelites to mix human dung in their cake flour [Ezekiel IV, 12–15]—and one suspects that he would have loved his day in court.[13]

He was not prosecuted. Even the rumour that the American customs had denied entry of his *Nights* into the United States proved false. Instead he was deluged with acclaim. The *Continental Times* called the *Nights* "singularly robust and healthy." The *Academy* critic wrote warmly, ". . . none I imagine were prepared for the fine force and old-world flavour of the style which he has forged for himself on this occasion, or for the extraordinary richness, variety, and quaintness of his vocabulary." Phrases like "thanks and congratulation," "simply priceless," "masterly," "strong, vital, picturesque" peppered other reviews. The *St James Gazette* called it "one of the most important translations to which a great English scholar has ever devoted himself." The *New York Tribune*, November 2, 1891, described it as "a monument of knowledge and audacity."[14]

But a handful of editors were outraged. The *Echo* called it "a morally filthy book . . . absolutely unfit for the Christian population of the nineteenth century." The *Pall Mall Gazette* attacked it in two articles titled "Pantagruelism or Pornography," and "The Ethics of Dirt." The Boston *Daily Advertiser* of January 26, 1868, described the volumes as "offensive and not only offensive, but grossly and needlessly offensive." Another review called it "the garbage of the brothels."

No editor in Great Britain attacked the *Nights* more venomously than Burton's old enemy, Henry Reeve, of the *Edinburgh Review*. "Probably no European has ever gathered such an appalling collection of degrading customs and statistics of vice," he wrote. "It is a work which no decent gentleman will long permit to stand upon his shelves. . . . Galland is for the nursery, Lane for the library, Payne for the study, and Burton for the sewers."[15]

Burton seized his cudgel and joyously swung back: "I should say that the childish indecencies and the unnatural vice of the original cannot deprave any mind save that which is perfectly prepared to be depraved. . . . The man must be prurient and lecherous as a dog-faced baboon in rut to have aught of passion excited by either."[16]

The Nights were not only a critical but also a financial success. Burton spent 6,000 guineas on printing sixteen volumes, and gained a profit of 10,000 guineas. "I struggled for forty-seven years," he wrote with ironic satisfaction. "I distinguished myself honourably in every way I possibly could. I never had a compliment nor a 'Thank you,' nor a single farthing. I translated a doubtful book in my old age, and immediately made sixteen thousand guineas. Now that I know the tastes of England, we need never be without money."[17]

Burton to the end publicly maintained his elaborate fiction that *The Nights* were intended only for men, and for scholars in particular. But from the beginning he knew who could be counted upon to ferret out his volumes. He wrote to John Payne on September 9, 1884, "My conviction is that all the women in England will read it and half the men will cut me."[18] He was delighted by the popular anonymous verse soon circulating in London:

> What did he say to you, dear aunt?
> That's what I want to know.
> What did he say to you, dear aunt?
> That man at Waterloo!

An Arabian old man, a Nights old man
As Burton, as Burton can be;
Will you ask my papa to tell my mama
The exact words and tell them to me?[19]

Both the Burtons had contributed to the pretence that Isabel had never read the *Nights*. "I have never read, nor do I intend to read, at his own request, and to be true to my promise to him, my husband's 'Arabian Nights,'" she wrote emphatically. When, however, she persuaded Richard to let her issue her own version of the first ten volumes, a nicely cleaned edition every British mother could show to her daughter, there arose the problem of explaining how she could edit out the naughty passages without reading them. Isabel, who was not really adept at bald lying, gave her own explanation as follows: "Richard forbade me to read them till he blotted out with ink the worst words, and desired me to substitute, not English, but Arab Society words, which I did to his complete satisfaction. . . . Mr Justin Huntley McCarthy helped me a little, so that out of the 3,215 original pages, I was able to copyright three thousand pages."[20] Burton put it somewhat differently: "Mr Justin Huntley McCarthy converted the 'grand old barbarian' into a family man to be received by the 'best circles.' His proofs, after due expurgation, were passed on to my wife, who I may say has never read the original, and she struck out all that appeared to her over-free. . . ."[21]

The truth was that Isabel slashed her way through the *Nights* with all the diligence of a member of the Society for the Suppression of Vice. The volumes she covered with sweeping parentheses, exasperated marginal notations, and vigorously written changes, may be seen today in the Royal Anthropological Institute. Burton had inked out nothing. Where her husband had written "satisfying their lusts," Isabel wrote "embracing" in the margin. The sentence "The King arose and did away with his bride's maidenhood" became "The King arose and embraced his bride." A long seduction scene is cut to a single phrase, "disobeying orders." For the word "concubine" she substituted "assistant wife." Out went all the livelier footnotes.

It is clear from the marginal notes that Burton carefully checked her cuts, and at times where he felt her sensibility excessive he wrote an emphatic "Stet" in the margin. In places this became a fascinating dialogue between husband and wife. Isabel wanted to erase the footnote where Richard had written of "the abominable egotism and cruelty of the English mother, who disappoints her daughter's womanly cravings in order to keep her at home for her own comfort"—counting it correctly a slap at her own mother. Burton with a "stet" retained it.

More significant in the dialogue are Isabel's cuts and emendations in passages having to do with homosexuality. The story of the 255th Night contained an attempted seduction of the hero, Ala Al-Din al-Shamat, by an older man. In Burton's version the youth finally repels him, saying, "Of a truth this may never be, take back thy dress and mule . . ." Isabel eliminated most of the attempted seduction scene, and put in the youth's mouth an expression of her own detestation: "Oh man of sin, I cannot abide thy presence."[22]

The unspoken dialogue went on. We learn from a manuscript in the Quentin Keynes collection that Burton put together all the material his wife had cut out and threatened to print it privately as "The Black Book of the Arabian Nights." In this manuscript, intended as a preface to the Black Book, Burton wrote that "a 'bowdlerised' book loses half its influence and bears the same relation to its prototype as a castrato to a male masculant." He believed, he said, that the British public was "slowly but surely emancipating itself from the prurient reticence and the prudish and immoral modesty of the early xixth century." Meanwhile he watched the sales of what he called the "six pretty volumes" edited by his wife. Only 457 copies were sold in two years,[23] a fact Burton noted with obvious satisfaction in his *Supplemental Nights*. "The public would have none of it: even innocent girlhood tossed aside the chaste volumes in utter contempt, and would not condescend to aught save the thing, the whole thing, and nothing but the thing, unexpurgated and uncastrated."

This Final Frailty,
This Sad Eclipse

*E*LATED BY THE initial success of the early volumes of the *Nights*,
which brought immediate international renown, Burton found
his long dampened hopes for a new Foreign Office post rekindled.
Learning that Sir John Drummond-Hay, minister to Morocco, would
shortly retire, he applied for the post. On November 21, 1885 he went
off to Tangier to inspect the area, and also—with his irrepressible
Arcadian optimism—to investigate rumours of a sunken treasure ship
in Vigo Bay on the northeastern Spanish coast. He had now largely
recovered from his first heart attack, writing to William Forrell Kirby
from Gibraltar, December 12, 1885, "I walk 5 miles every day and
soon hope to walk ten."[1] Isabel joined him in time for their silver
wedding anniversary, January 22, 1886.

On February 5 a messenger brought him a telegram addressed,
"Sir Richard Burton." He tossed it over to his wife and said, "Some
fellow is playing me a practical joke, or else it is not for me. I shall
not open it, so you may as well ring the bell and give it back again."
But he did open it, and found a message from Robert Cecil, Lord Salisbury, saying that the Queen, at his recommendation, had made him
Knight Commander of St Michael and St George in reward for his
many services to the crown.

"I shall not accept it," he said uncomfortably.

"You had better accept it, Jemmy," Isabel said, because it is a certain
sign that they are going to give you Tangier."[2]

It is curious that Burton should have greeted with uneasiness a
reward he so justly deserved. "Honour not honours" was a motto he
had chosen to live by, but this only betrayed that he hungered for
recognition far more than most men. He knew that Isabel, pining to
be Lady Burton, had been desperately intent on the K.C.M.G., and
had written scores of letters in the past urging their influential friends
in England to write to the Queen. So his elation was tempered by the
suspicion that the honour came not from his own merit but from her
insistent pleading. And while this may or may not have deepened his
gratitude, it did little for his self-esteem.

Burton described Tangier "a foul Harbour-town," "Home of Dullness," and Isabel was distressed to find the embassy quarters far less attractive than their own pallazone in Trieste. This made it easier later to accept the humiliation when the Foreign Office refused to give him the post. An influential friend and cabinet member wrote to them tactfully, "We don't want to annex Morocco, and we know that you two would be Emperor and Empress in about six months."[3]

Sailing back to Trieste by way of Genoa and Naples aboard the *Saragossa*, the couple encountered a thirty-hour storm that swamped the galley and loosened the cargo of iron in the hold so that the ship developed a nasty cant to starboard. "Richard was knocked down, and had a very heavy fall on the head, forehead and shins," Isabel wrote. "The coal-bunks caught fire, and we shipped seas into the saloon. . . . I shall never forget his kindness and tenderness to me in that gale."

When the sea was calm, Burton went out on the upper deck. Isabel followed, looking for him, not knowing that the storm had washed away part of the ladder leading to the lower deck. "I saw something," Burton wrote "which I took to be a large feather pillow roll lightly into the timbers below. I saw several people rush to pick it up, and, to my horror, found it was my wife. She seemed stunned for a minute, and then she was so frightened that I should be uneasy, that she just shook herself and said she was all right." But it was a bad fall, and as Burton noted in his journal, "she was already not well enough to risk any shaking."[4] So at Naples he put her aboard the train for Trieste, and continued the journey alone by sea, arriving home three days after she did. By then she was well enough to board the boat to receive him.

Byron Farwell cites this act of abandonment as evidence of the inconsiderateness and callousness with which Burton treated his wife. And it is true that though he willingly nursed Speke in East Africa and Lovett Cameron in West Africa when they were fearfully ill, he fled from Isabel's illness and accidents. He was like a small boy who comforts his mother importantly in times of danger, but who cannot face her sickness without overpowering anxiety, which is registered only in annoyance and impatience. Though Isabel would write freely to Mrs Friswell, "I am a poor devil with a tumour in the right ovaria,"[5] she continued to keep it a secret from Richard, sensing correctly that her husband's life was more fragile now than her own.

His gout worsened, keeping him bedridden often for weeks at a time. Fears of his own death deepened, and he recorded painfully in his journal the obituary notices of his friends. Monckton Milnes died of a heart attack on August 11, 1885, aged seventy-six. He had been ailing for some months and knew his sentence. "What is the matter with you?" a concerned friend asked him. "Death," he replied. "That is what is the matter with me. I am going to die. I am going over to the majority, and you know I have always preferred the minority."[6] Burton refused to write an obituary on Milnes for the *Academy*, saying the wound was too sore, but he did write that during the course of a long and fruitful life Milnes had "never said an unkind word, and he never did an unkind deed." Later Burton wrote in the *Academy*, "It is one of the penalties of advancing years to find one's surroundings haunted by the spectres of the passed away, to tread everywhere on the tombstone of some dear friend, and, briefly, to see one's world— the only world known to man—lapsing into ruin."[7]

The fear of Richard's dying at any moment preyed upon Isabel, and she became increasingly desperate at the thought that he would go to his grave without being baptised a Catholic. Ouida wrote derisively of her ever more insistent plaintive cry, "If I could only save Dick's soul!" Isabel remembered and recorded what he had said to the London Anthropological Society in 1865, "My religious opinions are of no importance to anybody but myself; *no one* knows what my religious views are. I object to confessions, and I will *not* confess. My standpoint is, and I hope ever will be, 'The Truth,' as far as it is in me, but known only to myself." She did not find it amusing when, in discussing his own death he told her he wanted no cremation, adding with "his usual joke at a serious thing, 'I do not want to burn before I have got to.' "[8] She had managed to persuade him to buy a lot in the Catholic cemetery at Mortlake, a London suburb, where many of her relatives were buried. After looking at the plot he had agreed, saying whimsically, "It's like a nice little family hotel."

Like almost everyone in the British upper classes, the Burtons toyed with spiritualism, then fashionable, and took part in numerous séances. Burton was fascinated by the table rappings and related phenomena, but suspected fakery and repudiated the mediums as true bridges to the spirit world "if for no other reason than that the spirits were always as illiterate as their invokers." In a letter to *The Times* on November 13, 1876 he accused the mediums of sleight of hand trickery. But he had seen too much evidence of clairvoyance, somnambulism, hypnosis, and occult phenomena associated with what he called the "Jogis" in India, to dismiss the whole movement as based entirely on fraud.[9]

In a speech before the British National Association of Spiritualists on December 2, 1878, he said that he believed perception to be possible without the ordinary channels of the senses, but went on bluntly: "The supernatural is the natural misunderstood or improperly misunderstood . . . no man—positively, absolutely, no man—neither deity nor devil—angel nor spirit—ghost nor goblin—has ever wandered beyond the narrow limits of this world—has ever brought us a single idea or notion which belongs to another and different world. . . . I must be contented to remain, as a facetious friend said, 'a Spiritualist without the Spirits.' . . . Personally I ignore the existence of soul and spirit, feeling no want of self within a self, an I within an I." He held stoutly, he said, to the Gospel of Doubt and Denial. "Lord Beaconsfield is all 'on the side of the Angels.' I cannot but hold to the apes."

Miracles like the stigmata of St Francis he believed could be explained perfectly by "suggestion," just as healings in Arabia that resulted from swallowing a verse of the Koran written upon a scrap of paper.[10] In the Terminal Essay of the *Nights* he wrote, "The more I study religions the more I am convinced that man never worshipped anything but himself."

A visit to the Passion Play at Oberammergau in 1880, which for Isabel had been a profound religious experience, left Burton scornful and unmoved. Each wrote at length about the play, and he suggested that both essays be published together as a small book titled *Ober Ammergau as Seen by Four Eyes.* As it turned out, the publisher accepted only Burton's sardonic piece, which appeared in 1881 as *A Glance at The "Passion-Play."* Isabel's pious pilgrimage account came out posthumously in 1900, edited by W. H. Wilkins with the title, *The Passion Play at Ober-Ammergau.* Burton's scoffing could only have made his wife wring her hands. All notions of heaven, purgatory, hell, devils and angels, he said, were "dishonouring to the Creator" and "debasing" to man. Of Pilate's condemnation of Jesus he wrote irreverently:

I cannot but think that the poor "Pagan" did exactly what would have been done by an Anglo-Indian officer of the last generation in a violent religious quarrel amongst the mild Hindus, with their atrocious accusations against one another. Utterly unable to appreciate the merits and demerits of the case, he would have said, "There'll be an awful row if I don't interfere. Old Charley (the commander-in-chief) doesn't like me, and I don't want to lose my appointment. After all, what matter? Let the nigs do as they please!"[11]

In late February 1887, when the Burtons were on a holiday in Cannes, Richard suffered a second severe heart attack. The doctor, very alarmed, warned Isabel her husband might die at any moment. "I was seized with a panic lest he might not have been properly baptized," she wrote, "and asking Dr Frank if I might do so, he said, 'You may do anything you like.' I got some water, and knelt down and saying some prayers, I baptized him." So she got her wish at last.[12]

Dr F. Grenfell Baker, a young English physician convalescing from his own serious illness in Cannes, who had been called in for consultation, was delegated to tell Burton he was near death. Dr Baker tells us that Sir Richard greeted the news with a shrug, "Ah, well, what must be will be," then launched into a story from the *Arabian Nights*. The ailing young doctor was impressed. Later, when Isabel, informed of the seriousness of her husband's condition, asked Dr Baker to be his full time personal physician, travelling with them everywhere and living with them in Trieste, he accepted. Burton at first fought the idea of a resident physician, resenting the intrusion on his privacy, predicting that Baker "would probably quarrel with us, or hate one or both of us, and make mischief." As it turned out, the thin, mild-mannered doctor proved unobtrusive and able, and became a devoted friend. Except for a brief period when he was replaced by Dr Ralph Leslie, he lived with them until Burton's death.[13]

As Sir Richard's iron constitution was slowly corroded by gout, circulatory ailments, and anginal pain, his fierce independence disappeared, and the long intervals away from his wife, formerly so frequent, diminished now almost to zero. Eventually he came to cling to Isabel as if she were the vital source of life itself. "If it had not been for my wife, I should have died of inanition," he wrote. Though Burton had become fond of his Trieste home, he detested wintering there. After one bad hailstorm he wrote to Leonard Smithers, September 22, 1889, "Last night we had a storm of all the horrors including hail which broke half the window panes in the house. Today Trieste is again smiling—like a whore at a christening."[14] In 1889–90 he travelled almost constantly with his wife and doctor, haunting the spas and resorts of Europe and North Africa as his father had done before him, in search of his old vitality. Geneva, Vévy, Montreux, Berne, Venice, Neuberg, Brindisi, Malta, Tunis, Algiers, Cannes, Innsbruck, Ragatz, Maloja—the list lengthened as he became ever more enfeebled. All his requests for retirement with full pension in advance of his formal retirement after thirty years of Foreign Office service—expected in March 1891—were stonily refused.

Although they spent with reckless exuberance on the best hotels, Burton was never content to stay in one place more than three weeks. "He sucked dry all his surroundings," Isabel wrote, "whether place, scenery, people, or facts, before the rest of us had settled down to realize whether we liked the place or not. When he arrived at this stage everything was flat to him, and he would anxiously say, "Do you think I shall live to get out of this, to see another place?" She tried to make travel easier for him by going alone in advance to get tickets and arrange for baggage, but he would never permit it, and insisted on jumping into the same carriage.

"I am in a very bad way," he once said to her. "I have got to hate everybody except you and myself, and it frightens me, because I know perfectly well that next year I shall get to hate you, and the year after that I shall get to hate myself, and then I don't know what will become of me. We are always wandering, and the places that delight *you* I say to myself 'Dry rot,' and the next place I say, 'Dry rotter,' and the third place I say, 'Dry rottest,' and then *da capo*."[15]

They kept up a pretence of being young and vigorous. Burton for a time dyed his greying hair black, and Isabel took to wearing a blond wig with curls. Burton spent a great deal of money on fashionable clothes, but wore few of them. He fully indulged his curious passion for boots; in his last years he owned as many as a hundred pairs. Everywhere they went he looked for swords, examining, cataloguing, note-taking, for his projected second and third volumes on the subject.

In Maloja they met Henry Stanley, who at forty-nine had finally married, and was honeymooning with his beautiful artist wife, Dorothy Tennant Stanley. "He seems much broken in health," Stanley wrote. "I proposed he should write his reminiscences. He said he could not do so, because he should have to write of so many people. 'Be charitable to them, and write only of their best qualities,' I said. 'I don't care a fig for charity; if I write at all, I must write truthfully, all I know," he replied. Burton told the Stanleys he was writing a book on "Anthropology of Men and Women."[16]

Isabel tells us that she urged Richard to finish the memoir he had begun on his trip to India in 1875. But she was unhappy about portions of it. "I begged to be allowed to erase many little things in the early biography," she wrote, "and his only answer was, 'I will not have it altered. If a biography is written, it must be a true photograph with its good and evil. . . .'"[17] Still, when Francis Hitchman, a stranger to both of them, approached Isabel with plans to write a biography of her husband, she persuaded Richard to loan him the mansucript of his unfinished autobiography. Hitchman, in a scandalous piece of plagiarism, simply changed the pronouns of the manuscript into the third person, publishing only one chapter, "Beatson's Horse," as Burton's own writing. He copied extracts from Burton's books no less shamelessly.

In the face of this literary robbery, Burton lost all heart for the task of writing his own autobiograhy. Isabel wrote contritely to Leonard Smithers that Hitchman had "tricked my heart with tales of poverty, sickness and a large family, and asked me if I could prevail on my husband to let him write his biography, because he would sell it for £150."[18] Even worse, publication of this biography in 1887 brought a personal attack in the *Saturday Review* that left the Burtons paralysed with indignation. It labelled the biography "unfortunate," and called Burton "disrespectful and ungrateful . . . to his official superiors, discontented with his lot, and perpetually whining after more rewards and honours and better paid posts." "We wonder what Consul or other servant of the Foreign Office ever had such long and frequent leaves of absence, and spent so little time at his post (drawing salary all the time, it may be presumed), as Sir Richard Burton." His *Arabian Nights* was dismissed as "a book hitherto by decent folks considered untranslatable."[19]

"My best course is to remain perfectly silent," Isabel wrote to a friend, "and let it blow over with dignity. I do not believe the Saturday Review . . . has harmed my husband."[20] Burton was vulnerable, however, on the matter of leaves. Lord Rosebury reprimanded him early in 1886 for being away from Trieste too often and too long. Lord Salisbury, however, who became Prime Minister in June 1886, judiciously regarded Burton's post as a reward for his services to the crown, and saw to it that he was no longer annoyed with many requests for routine consular work, though he refused to grant him retirement at full pension. The only sufferer was the consular aide, who did most of Burton's work in his last years, with only half Burton's pay in addition to his own.

The Burtons returned briefly to England in 1888, and though they were "asked out immensely into Society," [the phrase, interestingly enough is Burton's] Richard was too ill to accept any invitations after eight in the evening. His niece Georgiana, who had always thought of him as an indestructible deity, was appalled at his appearance. "His eyes wore that strained look which accompanies difficult respiration, his lips were bluish-white, his cheeks livid; the least exertion made him short of breath and sometimes he would pant when quietly seated in his chair.[21]

Still demon-driven, he continued translating at a furious rate, going from one "naughty book" to another. After finishing the six volumes of the *Supplemental Nights* in 1888, he decided to translate an unexpurgated version of Boccaccio's *Decameron*. On learning that John Payne had anticipated him, he turned instead to a collection of lusty Neapolitan folk tales, *Il Pentamerone: or the Tale of Tales*, by Giovanni Batiste Basile, first issued in Naples in 1637. Burton's translation of the more robust passages showed that he had forgotten nothing of the gutter argot he had learned in Naples as a youth. In describing a fight between an old woman and a boy who has broken her pitcher with a stone, he gives us the following dialogue:

Ah, Kindchen, scatterbrains, piss-a-bed, goat-dancer, petticoat-catcher, hangman's rope, mongrel mule, spindle-shanks, whereat if ever the fleas cough, go where a palsy catch thee; and may thy mammy hear the ill news! . . . knave, pimp, son of a whore!

The lad, who had little beard and less discretion, hearing this flow of abuse, repaid her with the same coin, saying 'Wilt thou not hold thy tongue, devil's grandam, bull's vomit, children-smotherer, turd-clout, farting crone?'[22]

Next Burton turned to a group of Latin and Italian poets, who though famous, had all written some poetry which had hitherto been considered too bawdy, prurient, or perverse for the delicate English ear. He considered translating *Orlando Furioso* by the renaissance Italian poet Lodovico Ariosto (1474–1533), the *Epigrammata* of the Roman poet Decimus Magnus Ausonius (310–95), the *Metamorphoses* or *Golden Ass* of Lucius Apuleius, philosopher and rhetorician born in Numidia A.D. 125, the *Carmina* of Catullus, Latin poet, contemporary of Julius Caesar, and the satires of Juvenal, (A.D. 60–140).

First, however, he collaborated with a young Englishman, Leonard Smithers, in printing privately the first English translation of the Latin *Priapeia*, a famous collection of eighty exceedingly explicit poems on the subject of Priapus, the fertility god of the Hellespont, said to have been the son of Dionysus and Aphrodite, who was usually represented in antiquity as a grotesquely ugly man with an enormous erect phallus. Burton never met Smithers: they exchanged many letters, however, which illuminate the nature of their collaboration. Smithers, a young soliciter with a taste for erotic literature, frankly fascinated by sexual pathology, and intent on becoming an "erotic specialist" in his own right, offered to do all the necessary research for the *Priapeia* annotations. He translated it into prose, and suggested that Burton collaborate by translating it into verse. All three versions—Latin, prose, and verse—were printed in the same volume. In the first printing in 1889 they used the pseudonyms Outidanos and Neaniskos; Smithers arranged for the printing under the façade of the so-called Erotika Biblion Society, with headquarters presumably in Athens.[23]

Burton warned Smithers about the possibility of police prosecution, the likelihood of search warrants, and the difficulty of concealing the identity of the printers, noting that "purity people are great at bribery." Smithers, unfrightened, urged Burton to collaborate on a second printing of the Priapeia, with extensive annotations and provocative illustrations, and to identify himself in some fashion on the title page so as to ensure greater sales. At first Burton agreed, and worked out as a sample frontispiece the following:

> The metrical part is by the translator of "the Book of the Thousand Nights and a Night," and the prose portion is by 'Jurand' who has added notes explaining the text and long excursions into pederasty of either sex, bestiality, masturbation, the *cunnilinges* . . . habits of Roman dancing, the tribadism of Roman women, the 'infamous finger' and so forth.[24]

When Isabel learned of this she was consumed with anxiety. She wrote several letters to Smithers without Richard's knowledge, warning him that censors had wind of the first printing and were about to descend on him with search warrants. By May 16, 1890 she was frantic:

My husband is doing *a most quixotic thing*—to him *most dangerous* and his identity *thoroughly put forward*. . . . This is his last year's service. In March he becomes a free man—his official career is ended, and between March and August the question of his pension will be settled and we transfer ourselves from Trieste to London. . . . if there is a row the pension which is to keep him the remainder of his days after an honourable career of 49 years will most likely be withheld or reduced to a minimum. And for what? What madness possesses him I cannot think—to risk a whole future . . . and to do a service by *lending his name* to a man he never saw seems to me equally ridiculous. . . . You must not write my husband of this letter.

Smithers wrote back trying to reassure her. She replied on May 27, 1890:

You are quite mistaken in thinking that Sir Richard will not be prosecuted equally as well as you. We had the greatest . . . difficulty all through the 16 vols. of the Nights, and it was only *Benares* saved us. Sir Richard has warm friends and popular honour, but a few bitter enemies he has quizzed and criticized in early days, and those are near the throne, and always setting the Queen against him. . . . All my life has been spent in trying to control these untoward circumstances, and restraining him to limit his interests. . . . you have no idea of the "fix" I was in. Sir Richard wanted to throw up the Consulate last week, and sell my charming home here, because he could not keep his engagements with you otherwise. . . . I dare not tell my husband I wrote you—he would be very angry with me. . . . Do not write to me again because the letter might fall into his hands.[25]

One cannot but sympathize with poor Lady Burton in this battle. Arbuthnot came to her aid, and the 1890 *Priapeia* was printed under the original pseudonyms. Neither man was prosecuted.

Next Burton turned to Gaius Valerius Catullus, known for his passionate love lyrics to his mistress Clodia (Lesbia of the poems), the brilliant and powerful wife of Metellus. Catullus had also written love poems to boys, and lampoons noted for their anatomical obscenity. Burton's version of the complete *Carmina* contained the original Latin, his own translation into verse, and Smithers' translation into prose.[26]

Burton wrote in the preface, "Discovery is mostly my mania," and admitted somewhat defensively to a "bastard-urging" impulse to publish discoveries of this nature. He finished the translation, but did not live to see it printed. When Isabel took up the manuscript after his death, the first thing she saw was his cruel scrawl across the top, "Never show half-finished work to women or fools." She had a copy made—Smithers said it was swarming with errors—and cut out many passages she thought vulgar, replacing them with asterisks. Then she burned the original.[27]

Before his death Burton had translated four cantos of Ariosto, and done preliminary work on Apuleius and Ausonius. These he temporarily abandoned for a new translation of *The Perfumed Garden*, which had apparently sold well, both private printings of 1886 having been exhausted. Burton now sought out the original Arabic version, intending to retranslate it as *The Scented Garden*, plus the missing chapter on homosexuality. He intended to annotate if fully, including a summary of the ideas of the German scholar Karl Henrich Ulrichs, who under the pseudonym of Numa Numantius had written about, and defended homosexual love. He also intended to include new material on Chinese eunuchs.[28]

So again, to Isabel's dismay, he took up the themes of homosexuality and castration, as if by accumulating details and ever more details he could somehow exorcise the anxieties and frustrations that apparently continued to plague him. He went to Tunis and Algiers with Isabel in December 1889, seeking a warmer climate than Trieste, and hoping also to get aid from Arabic scholars for his notes and translation. "Being amongst Moslems again is a kind of repose to me," he wrote to Smithers on December 10. "The atmosphere of Christiandom demoralizes and distresses me." But his research proved disappointing. "I have done little with the Garden at Tunis where I expected so much," he reported to Smithers on January 5, 1890. Then came the old inevitable reaction against the desert. Before returning he wrote bluntly to John Payne, "The world is growing vile and bête."[29]

At first he held no exaggerated notion of the significance of *The Scented Garden*, and had no real expectation of its financial success, since it had already seen two printings. He wrote to Smithers on January 31, 1890 that he intended to print a thousand copies, adding, "but the public is fickle . . . and a manual of erotology cannot have the interest of the Nights."[30] In his diary entry of March 21, 1890 he wrote, "Began or rather resumed Scented Garden, don't care much about it, but it is a good potboiler." But as he worked upon it, developing what was a rather small book into a manuscript of 1,282 pages,[31] it became increasingly important to him. He told Dr Grenfell Baker, "I have put my whole life and all my life-blood into that *Scented Garden*; it is my great hope that I shall live by it. It is the crown of my life."[32]

When Isabel fretted, he told her all the proceeds were going to be set aside as an annuity for her after his death,[33] but she found this poor solace. Dr Baker, more sensitive than Richard to her hostility, warned Burton that the manuscript might well be burned if he died before it was finished. "Do you really think so?" Burton asked, incredulous. "Then I must write to Arbuthnot at once, and tell him that in the event of my death, the manuscript is to be his." And so he did.[34]

But Burton's mistrust of his wife was momentary, and he named her sole excutrix in his will. Over the years he had moulded her into a special creation; she was no longer Sir Richard Burton's wife— "the mere bellows player to the organist," as she was fond of saying when deprecating her role—but a person in her own right. She had written two successful travel books and numerous articles, and had translated and published a Portuguese manuscript. She could speak French, Arabic, Italian, and Portuguese, with some German and a smattering of Yiddish. "I consider that he *made* me, so to speak," she cheerfully admitted. In turn she had made Richard live, as André Maurois said in describing Disraeli's marriage, "in a paradise of slightly comical adoration." Hers had been a continuous and lasting tenderness.

Once in 1887 an earthquake shook their hotel in Cannes so severely that, as Burton described it, "it split a few walls, shook the soul out of one's body, and terrified strangers out of their wits." Isabel looked out of the window at the panic-stricken guests flocking into the streets in their night clothes and begged him to get out of bed and flee the hotel. "No, my girl," he said, "you and I have been in too many earthquakes to show the white feather at our age."

"All right," she answered.

"So," Burton concluded his account of the event in his own journal, "I turned round and went to sleep again."[35] Nothing he ever wrote was so explicit a statement of his devoted—but also demanding— attachment to his wife.

Back in Trieste in August 1890, Burton, now sixty-nine and increasingly frail, looked apprehensively at the passing of summer. The flight of swallows southwards in September filled him with sadness. "We intend to pass the next summer at home," he wrote to W. F. Kirby on August 16, "but the time is long and Fate is malignant."[36] What he had written earlier about the last years of Camoens—"this final frailty, this sad eclipse"—now aptly described himself. He went to the markets in Trieste with his wife and bought caged birds, took them home, and set them free in his garden. Passing a monkey in a cage outside a neighbour's house, Burton stopped one day and spoke to him morosely while Isabel fed him bits of fruit and cake. "What crime did you commit in some other world, Jocko, that you are caged for now, and tormented, and going through your purgatory?" As they walked away he muttered over and again, "I wonder what he did —I wonder what he did."

Three days before he died he told Isabel that a bird had been tapping at his window all the morning. "That is a bad omen, you know," he said. When she pointed out reassuringly that he fed the birds every morning at seven and they had come to expect the service, he replied, "Ah, it was not that window, but another." Afterwards she found a verse scribbled on the margin of his diary for that day:

> Swallow, pilgrim swallow,
> Beautiful bird with purple plume,
> That, sitting upon my window-sill,
> Repeating each morn at the dawn of day
> That mournful ditty so wild and shrill,—
> Swallow, lovely swallow, what wouldst thou say,
> On my casement-sill at the break of day?[37]

The next day, Sunday October 19, 1890, he rescued a robin drowning in a tank in the garden, warmed it in his hands, put it in his fur coat till he was sure it would live. That night he dined sparingly, but laughed, talked, and joked. At half-past nine he went to bed, assisted by both his wife and the doctor. At midnight Burton complained of "a gouty pain" in his foot. He dozed a little and woke again, saying, "I dreamt I saw our little flat in London, and it had quite a nice large room in it." At four in the morning he was again in pain, but Dr Baker could find nothing wrong of consequence.

At half-past four he complained in alarm of suffocation. His wife flew back once more to summon the doctor, who saw at once that he was dying. Isabel, frantic, woke up the servants and sent them scurrying in all directions for a priest.

"Oh, Puss," Burton cried out at one point, "chloroform—ether— or I am a dead man!"

"My God!" she said, "I would have given the blood out of my veins if it would have saved him." As she held him upright in her arms on the bed, he got ever heavier and more insensible. Finally Dr Baker released her and laid him backwards. He applied an electric battery to Burton's heart as Isabel knelt at his left side feeling desperately for his pulse, and, as she wrote later, "praying my heart out to God to keep his soul there (though he might be dead in appearance) till the priest should arrive."

Burton had stopped breathing at five o'clock. Father Pietro Martelani came at seven. He called Isabel aside and told her he could not give Extreme Unction because her husband had not declared himself a Catholic. Tearfully she begged him not to lose a moment in giving the Sacrament, and assured him that she had evidence to satisfy him that Richard was secretly a convert. The priest looked sharply at the figure on the bed.

"Is he dead?" he asked.

"No," she said stoutly.

At once he administered Extreme Unction and said the prayers for the dying soul. "By the clasp of the hand, and a little trickle of blood running under the finger," Isabel said, "I judged there was a little life until seven, and then I knew that . . . I was alone and desolate forever."[38]

The Burning

A man's wife knows, perhaps, too much about him.

Richard Burton, 1878

"IT WAS A GORGEOUS military funeral," Isabel wrote with satisfaction, and "the Bishop had conceded to him all the greatest ceremonies of the Church." The Diet of Trieste adjourned as a mark of respect, and the crew of a British ship in the harbour joined the cortège. Of the 150,000 citizens of Trieste, she noted, "everyone who could drive or walk, from the highest authorities to the poorest, turned out. . . . every flag in the town and harbour was at half mast." When the local Protestant minister protested to Dr Grenfell Baker that Burton was no Catholic, Baker shunted him aside and warned him to leave Lady Burton alone with her grief.

"Losing the man who had been my earthly God for thirty-five years was like a blow on the head," she wrote, "and for a long time I was completely stunned." A wire from London put an abrupt end, at least momentarily, to her protestations of grief. It was from a publisher offering her six thousand guineas for the manuscript of *The Scented Garden*.

I remained for three days in a state of perfect torture as to what I ought to do about it. . . . "Bury it," said one adviser. . . . I said, "I can take in the world, but I cannot deceive God Almighty, who holds my husband's soul in His hands". . . . I said to myself, "Out of fifteen hundred men, fifteen will probably read it in the spirit of science in which it was written; the other fourteen hundred and eighty-five will read it for filth's sake, and pass it to their friends, and the harm done may be incalculable". . . . what a gentleman, a scholar, a man of the world may write when living, he would see very differently to what the poor soul would see standing naked before its God, with its good or evil deeds alone to answer for. . . . I fetched the manuscript and laid it on the ground before me, two large volumes' worth. . . . It was his *magnum opus*, his last work that he was so proud of, that was to have been finished on the awful morrow—that never came. . . .

And then I said, "Not only for six thousand guineas, but not for six million guineas will I risk it."

So she burned it, "sorrowfully, reverently." Only later did she ask herself, "Will he rise up in his grave and curse me or bless me? The thought will haunt me to death."

All this she wrote in a public letter to the *Morning Post*, published June 19, 1891. Later she told several friends what she had not dared write to the press, that Richard came to her as she sat before the fire, that he pointed to the manuscript saying firmly, "Burn it!" Again he appeared, as she hesitated, with the same command, only to fade into the shadows. The third time his command galvanized her into action. As she fed the flames Richard stood by watching, his face illumined, she said, "by a fresh ray of light and peace." When her friend Daisy Letchford reproached her, she said stoutly, "I wished his name to live forever unsullied and without stain."[1]

Isabel felt it only proper that Richard should be buried in Westminster Abbey. David Livingstone had been buried there on April 18, 1874, his crudely embalmed body having been brought all the way from the banks of the Lulimala River by his devoted native bearers. It had been a wonderful funeral procession, with Henry Stanley and James Grant among those carrying the coffin. Heartened by warm praise for her husband in the obituary notices of the British press —*The Times* described Burton as "one of the most remarkable men of his time"—Lady Burton wrote to the Dean of Westminster "inquiring his intention." But the Dean held the ascetic missionary explorer Livingstone to be a very different kind of hero from the sardonic agnostic Richard Burton, and wrote back politely if not quite exactly that there was no more room.

Vexed but undaunted, she decided to create a monument of her own choosing. Remembering that Richard had once said to her, when they were talking of burial sites, "I should like us both to lie in a tent, side by side," she designed an exotic tomb in the shape of an Arab tent, eighteen feet high and twelve feet square, to be placed among the stone crosses in the Catholic cemetery at Mortlake. It was to be made of Forest of Dean stone, sculptured to create the illusion of canvas, with a door and interior of Cararra marble. She ordered two Moslem stars on top, and a crucifix above the door. Inside she planned to have an altar, and to suspend Arab lanterns and camel bells that would tinkle when the door was open and the wind blowing through. A small stained glass window with Burton's coat of arms would let in subdued sunlight from the rear. It proved expensive; loyal friends contributed £688, but since it could not be finished for some months she remained in Trieste. Burton's embalmed body lay in the *chappelle ardente*; she visited it every day.

On February 7, 1891, four months after her husband's death, Lady

Burton arrived in London. Since the tomb was still unfinished, Burton's body was placed in the crypt of the chapel of St Mary Magdalene at Mortlake. The funeral was finally held on June 15, 1891. Isabel had sent out 850 invitations. Four hundred declined "because of the flu," she wrote lightly.[2] Actually Burton's Protestant friends, outraged at the spectacle of an elaborate Catholic funeral in London eight months after an elaborate Catholic funeral in Trieste, chose to stay at home. Only one Burton relative appeared, a cousin, and only three geographers. Francis Galton stood with Lord Northbrook, a former president of the Royal Geographical Society, quietly indignant. "There were none of Burton's old associates," he wrote. "It was a ceremony quite alien to anything that I could conceive him to care for." Burton's niece wrote icily in her biography, "Rome took formal possession of Richard Burton's corpse, and pretended, moreover, with insufferable insolence, to take under her protection his soul."[3]

Swinburne lashed out at Isabel in his elegy of Burton:

> Priests and the soulless serfs of priests may swarm
> With vulturous acclamation, loud in lies,
> About his dust while yet his dust is warm
> Who mocked as sunlight mocks their base blind eyes.
>
> Their godless ghost of godhead, false and foul
> As fear his dam or hell his throne: but we
> Scarce hearing, heed no carrion church-kites howl:
> The corpse be theirs to mock; the soul is free.

Privately the poet wrote to Eliza Lynn Linton, "It is not my part to strip and whip the popish mendacities of that poor liar Lady Burton. Of course she has befouled Richard Burton's memory like a harpy."[4] Meanwhile Eliza Lynn Linton, whom Isabel had counted a good friend, had written in *Nineteenth Century*, March 1892: "He was no sooner dead than his widow surrounded him with the emblems and rites of her own faith—which was not his. . . . She cared nothing for the integrity of the life she thus stultified—nothing for the grandeur of the intellect she thus belittled."[5] But Isabel had no qualms whatever about her relations with Richard's intellect now that she had satisfied herself about the state of his soul. She visited his tomb every Sunday, and bought a small cottage nearby to make this communication easier. She even held four séances in the stone tent, hoping wistfully that he who had penetrated so many holy places and successfully returned would find some way back to her from death.[6]

The outcry over the Catholic funerals was nothing compared to the abuse heaped upon Lady Burton for burning *The Scented Garden*.

She was called an hysterical, illiterate woman, with "the bigotry of Torquemada, the vandalism of a John Knox." Ouida wrote, "I never spoke or wrote to her after that irreparable act." Many believed she had burned it at the direction of her "peasant priest" in Trieste. Apparently she was sensitive about this accusation, for in a defensive document, never published, called "My Deposition Regarding the Scented Garden," she wrote stoutly, "Although a Catholic, I do not consult priests about my temporal matters, nor yet about my spiritual, unless I doubt whether I am right or wrong, and in this instance I needed no guidance whatever."[7]

Still she had felt the necessity of a public confession, or she would never have written her explanatory letter to the *Morning Post*. Actually this letter was curiously slanted. It said in part:

My husband had been collecting for fourteen years information and materials on a certain subject. His last volume of *The Supplemental Nights* had been finished and out on November 13, 1888. He then gave himself up entirely to the writing of this book, which was called *The Scented Garden*, a translation from the Arabic. It treated of a certain passion. Do not let any one suppose for a moment that Richard Burton ever wrote a thing from the impure point of view. He dissected a passion from every point of view, as a doctor may dissect a body, showing its source, its origin, its evil, and its good, and its proper uses, as designed by Providence and Nature. In private life he was the most pure, the most refined and modest man that ever lived, and he was so guileless himself that he could never be brought to believe that other men said or used things from any other standpoint. I, as a woman, think differently. . . .[8]

There was scarcely a line of this that was factually correct. During the past fourteen years Burton had been collecting, writing, and translating material on human behaviour across a spectrum as broad as life and variegated as history. The *Scented Garden* was not a work treating of a single passion, homosexual love, as she strongly intimated, but a manual of heterosexual love with only the last chapter and certain notes given over to pederasty. All her protestations that her husband was pure, refined, modest, and guileless served only to advertise her extreme anxiety that he was none of these. And her insistence that his interest in homosexual behaviour was merely scientific dissection served only to betray her secret terror that it was not.

The abuse that followed publication of this letter, including many obscene anonymous letters, shocked her into a realization of the possibly irreparable damage she had inflicted on her husband's reputation. Her biographer W. H. Wilkins, who was also her friend, tells us that she was thoroughly aware of the "evil rumour" that had followed Burton from India in his youth. "When I know not, in what way I know not," he wrote, but the fact that sooner or later she did get to know of it is indisputable. How she fought to dispel this none but herself will ever know. Official displeasure she could brave; definite charges she could combat; but this baseless rumour, shadowy, indefinite, intangible, ever eluded her, but eluded her only to reappear. She could not grasp it. . . . at last the calumny died down, as all calumnies must die, for lack of sustenance."[9] Now the revival had been of her own making. Had she described the *Scented Garden* correctly, on the other hand, it would have been a public confession that she had wantonly burned a manuscript devoted primarily to instruction on the art of love as practised by a man and woman, and it is quite likely that she could not face the personal implications of this act even in the solitude of her own bedroom.

At first she flung out explanations in an agony of contrition. She wrote to Lady Guendolen Ramsden, "I see now how mistaken I was to have confessed it, and to imagine it was my duty to confess, which I certainly did. I know that he, being dead, would not have wished it published; if so, why did he leave it to me?"[10] To Burton's collaborator, Leonard Smithers, on the other hand, she wrote an extraordinarily frank letter, quite free from self-deception:

> I wish you would counsel me on one point. Why did he wish the subject of unnatural crime to be so largely aired and expounded? He had such an unbounded contempt for the Vice and its Votaries. I never asked him this question *unfortunately*; and though it may be a safe dissection for a live man to undertake, I think it such a dangerous one for a dead man's memory, who, if his motive be *once misunderstood* cannot defend himself. . . .
>
> The world and I are at daggers drawn, I on a wee island in a surging boiling ocean, take the standpoint only of Richard Burton—how it will affect *him*, and I have no public spirit in the matter. I feel that if a rotten carcass has to be dissected for the public good, let some other living man (with a living to make by the pen) bring in *his* knife and scalpel, not my dead husband.[11]

"Unnatural crime," "rotten carcass,"—the violence of her language suggests the intensity of her outrage at the mere idea of "le vice." Burton had put it succinctly when he described the widespread pederasty in Persia as a "perpetual mortification" for the Persian women. Now for the first time Isabel seems to have realized that her confession had put her own reputation as a wife in serious jeopardy. In a remarkable exhibition of sustained energy, considering that she was slowly dying of cancer, she sat down and in eight months wrote the 1,200-page biography of her husband—dedicated "To My Earthly Master, Who Is Waiting For Me On Heaven's Frontiers"—which she hoped would settle the matter for all time.[12]

Here she tried to fashion her Rabelaisian adventurer into her image not of the man she could wholly have loved but of the man she felt he should have been—a good Catholic, a husband faithful in thought as well as in act, and a refined and modest man. Although she professed to admire Richard as "a spade-truth man," she held rigorously to the rule she had set for herself at marriage, "Hide his faults from everyone." Still the story as it unfolded was rich in intimate detail. The evidences of her devotion pour through it like an engulfing torrent. But we see, too, as never in his books, the evidences of *his* devotion. Isabel wrote confidently, "Loads of books will be written about him, and everyone will be different; and though perhaps it is an unseemly boast, I venture to feel that mine will be the truest one." The publication of ten biographies of Richard Burton has served to demonstrate that his wife's boast was not "unseemly." Hers remains the great source book, overflowing with her own confessions, inadvertently betraying much of the truth about their marriage. Readers and reviewers alike in 1893 were captivated and content with her portrait long before they reached her final, impassioned ending:

> I was wife, and mother, and comrade, and secretary, and aide-de-camp, and agent to him and I was proud, happy, and glad to do it all, and never tired day or night for thirty years. I would rather have had a crust and tent with him, than be a Queen elsewhere. At the moment of his death I had done all I could for the body, and then I tried to follow his soul. I *am* following the soul and I *shall* reach it before long. . . . Be ashamed that History may have to say, that the only honour that England accorded to Richard Burton, having failed to do him justice in this life, was to bespatter his wife with mud after he was dead, and could not defend her. . . .
>
> He said always, "I am gone—pay, pack, and follow." Reader! I have paid, I have packed, I have suffered. I am waiting to join his Caravan. I am waiting for a welcome sound—"The Tinkling of his Camel-Bell."

Still she was not content. The great stack of diaries and journals, largely unmined, apparently filled her with fear, not because they contained open confessions that confirmed her anxiety—for it is inconceivable that Burton would have willed her his journals if they had —but for other reasons. First there was his outspoken honesty. As Norman Penzer, who fell heir to the only journal that escaped burning, wrote later, "Indeed, truth with him was something of an obsession."[13] Isabel herself wrote, "He saw and knew all the recesses of men's minds and actions."[14] As we have seen, the diaries in addition to being franker and more spontaneous than his books, were also studded with perceptive ruminations of the most personal sort. One she elected to put in her biography read as follows:

> When I see a man trying to prove that a woman drinks, or that she is out of her mind, or hysterical, or a liar, if he tells it to me once I may forget it, but if he tells it to me twice I know that that man has got something serious to hide, and that that woman knows his secret. If the

man is effeminate, or deformed, or vain, morbid, or craving for notice and sympathy, be sure it is his own state he describes, and not the woman he wants to run down, who has snubbed him and knows what he wants to hide.[15]

We know from her quotations that his diaries contained many references to her. He wrote in the *Nights* of "the cruelty of a good woman,"[16] and it is likely that in his diaries he was always frank and often merciless about his wife. If so, this would be reason enough for her to burn them, lest they give the lie to the idealized romance she had made their marriage out to be.

Burton believed, mistakenly, that men were far more destructive than women, or at least that he was more destructive than his wife. Master of disguise, he never fully comprehended that he had married a woman with whom dissimulation was a way of life. He knew far better than most men of his time the punishing effects upon a woman of frustration and frigidity, but he had no special insight into the capacity for unconscious revenge of a woman with a blighted sexual life. He failed utterly to anticipate the holocaust that followed his death, or he would never have willed Isabel his manuscripts. One act of his wife's he would have found inconceivable. In her will she ordered her literary executors, in supervising the publication of his posthumous works, to forbid the printing of "a single immodest word." She appointed two trustees to carry out this order; one was a friend, Minnie Grace Plowman; the other was W. A. Coote, a member of the National Vigilance Society. She had, in truth, gone over to the enemy.[17]

Burton

A SUMMARY OF RICHARD BURTON's solid achievements in his many varied fields adds up to an improbable total. He not only stands among the first five of British African explorers—with Livingstone, Stanley, Baker, and Speke—but as scholar-explorer he towers above the rest. None of the others had his curiosity, learning, linguistic gifts or writing talent. None wrote about the native ceremonies of birth, marriage, dying, fetishism, and preparation for war with such fascination and meticulous accuracy. But Burton, though long hailed as explorer, is only recently winning his due recognition as one of the great pioneer anthropologists, mostly because his fame as an explorer has obscured his achievements in this field. The very audacity of his trip to Mecca detracted from the virtues of his *Pilgrimage* as an ethnological classic, and even now he is remembered more for the feat itself than for his descriptions of Bedouin life, or for his still unmatched portrayal of the mass catharsis of the annual Moslem pilgrimage.

Melville Herskovits was the first twentieth century anthropologist to recognize Burton's special gifts, when he spent two years in Dahomey and matched Burton's *Mission to Gelele* against the thin accounts of those who preceded and who followed him to the Amazon kingdom. Herskovits was impressed not only by Burton's translations and phonetic transcriptions of Dahoman words, but also by his general accuracy and sophisticated insight. Moreover, Burton was never merely a theoriser, as were many of his contemporaries who came to call themselves anthropologists, and who mostly spun elaborate speculations about the nature, origin, and differences of the races of mankind. Burton was an empiricist, a true field worker. He theorised at length only about African fetishism, which he believed to be a natural stage in the development of religion among all peoples—a new and no doubt outlandish idea to most Bible-reading Englishmen of his time. When compared with the disciplined but also blander monographs of today's ethnologists, his writings seem less judicious and often bigoted and dogmatic, but they radiate authority. One by one they are being reprinted in our own time.

Burton wrote altogether forty-three volumes about his explorations and travels. Of these his *Pilgrimage to El Medinah and Meccah* and *Lake Regions of Central Africa* are recognized classics. Almost as rewarding are his *First Footsteps in East Africa* and *Zanzibar*. The *City of the Saints* is the best book on the Mormons published in the nineteenth century; his still neglected *Sindh, and the Races that Inhabit the Valley of the Indus* remains one of the great pioneer studies of the peoples of northern India.

In the field of archaeology Burton remained largely a dilettante. Though he is credited with a "first" for his copies of the Hamath stones, which proved to be important Hittite inscriptions, his books on the Syrian ruins and the necropolises of northern Italy were largely the summaries of the discoveries of other men. The British Museum is richer for the skulls, artifacts, shells, and fossils he forwarded to their exhibition rooms, but he usually left the work of evaluation to more carefully trained scientists.

Burton's reputation as a linguist and translator remains formidable. In learning twenty-five languages, with dialects that brought the number to forty, his approach was not that of a scholar of linguistics but of a traveller intent on communication. Wherever he went, he compiled vocabularies for the benefit of the men who would follow him. He wrote a grammar of the Jataki dialect in India, compiled vocabularies in Harar, Dahomey and Brazil, as well as making transliterations of proverbs in ten different West African tongues. In the end translating became his most satisfying occupation. But Burton was no ordinary translator; the inflexible integrity, brilliance, and vigour of his translations are an index to the man himself. One stands in awe of the ease with which he moved from Hindustani for his "Pilpay's Fables" and *Vikram and Vampire*—to Portuguese for his *Camoens* and *Lacerda*—to Arabic for the *Arabian Nights* and the *Perfumed Garden*—to Neapolitan Italian for his *Il Pentamerone*—to Sanscrit for his *Kama Sutra* and *Ananga Ranga*, and to Latin for his *Priapeia* and *Catullus*.

Still, as with every translator, Burton knew he was at best assuming with each work the cloak of a better writer; with every new book he acted out another role, still another of his multiple disguises. His hunger was ever to be a great writer in his own right. More than all else he wished to be a poet. But of his two long original poems the first, *Stone Talk*, is forgotten, and the second, *Kasidah*, though remaining in print for more than ninety years, does not measure up to the *Rubaiyat of Omar Khayyam*, which it resembles. Even these poems Burton published under a pseudonym, as if compelled to mask even what was truly original about himself.

For Burton, who at fifteen assumed the role of *croquemort* to assist in the burial of cholera victims in Naples, disguise was a way of life. Whether in costume—as a Persian merchant in India, Indian doctor in Egypt and Arabia, and Moslem merchant in Somaliland—or out of it, he assumed and shed new roles up to his death. To each role, whether of soldier, swordsman, explorer, anthropologist, archeologist, mining speculator, dignified consul, "man about London," "naughty Frenchman," Arab sheikh, or devoted husband, he brought whatever supported it best—courage and enthusiasm, dramatic flourish, earnestness, or careful scholarship. But the wild diversity of these roles served also to obscure the real man and the nature of the "demon" that drove him from one to another.

In his early years Burton had frankly searched for fame. Later he joined that group of British scientists who in the first flush of excitement of freedom from faith in religion embraced a touching faith in science, believing that to achieve perfection the world had only to conquer ignorance. Burton worked systematically to "raise the platform of his knowledge." So he accumulated languages, sought out the mysteries of the Kaaba and the Nile, explored the nature of Dahoman cruelty, and vainly struggled with the languages of the mysterious dead. Still he suffered from depression, anguish and guilt. In the end he turned to the ancient folklore of love. But even here his faith remained in the amassing of facts—including the most secret and the most shocking. It was as if sheer quantity of facts about coital positions, permutations, aphrodisiacs and an infinitude of stories of love could somehow substitute for the act of loving or make up for the failure of sexuality in his own marriage. Married to a woman who could play skilfully at the role of wife, he came to accept her self-conscious and overpowering adoration as a substitute for sexuality. But he could not have been blind to the fundamental failure or to his own contribution to that failure—else he would not have fled so often from the marriage.

Burton himself once wrote, "The greater the man the warmer are his passions." He also wrote, "I am no hot amorist." Burton was a man of great passions, but they were for the most part translated into curiosity and scholarship. His aggressive impulses, too, were transmuted and made safe by this scholarship, though they burst out now and then in the form of literary quarrels and personal truculence. But beyond this it seems obvious that something had done great damage to his inner life. First and most importantly his mother—and afterward his wife—had subtly encouraged and applauded his wildness and adventurousness, while at the same time disparaging and repudiating his sexuality. His father, a weak and lazy man who dissipated his life in boar-hunting and hypochondria, had provided no admirable image, and Burton had no motivation whatever for imitation or identification with him.

Burton's capacity for loving intimately saw a turning outwards, and a scattering, finding its freest expression among exotic peoples. So we find in his life an Indian mistress, a passionate love affair with a Persian woman, an attempted seduction of a nun, and experimentation with native women in Africa and the Near East, as well as with Fred Hankey's special variety of Paris prostitutes. Hunger for the forbidden was with Burton always, and he indulged his appetite as a man just as he had when a child in gobbling up the forbidden sugar and cream, and the pastries of Madame Fisterre. Finally when he did marry, it was to a woman who was in certain critical respects very like his mother, which may have been one reason—as sometimes happens—that he turned away from her sexually.

Isabel once wrote that she and Richard belonged in different centuries, she in medieval times and he in the twentieth century.[1] In matters of religious conviction and intellectual outlook they truly did go past each other. This was also true of their intimate life, else they would hardly have described themselves as living together like an elder and younger brother. Still the marriage, if hardly "a poem" as W. H. Wilkins called it, was a complicated and viable companionship, peculiarly essential to both. For Isabel Richard Burton served as the bearer of her instinctual life; he did all that she dared not do; he lived out her wildest fantasies. She lived vicariously all his adventures, sharing his exhilaration and exultation, his failure and shame. For Burton himself Isabel, too, served as an important object in his fantasy life. She was the English virgin, pure and chaste; she was the scolding but nevertheless adoring mother, essentially untouchable and therefore endlessly exasperating and provocative, from whom he must flee and to whom he must return. She was the stabilizer and balance without whom he felt his impulses would be uncontrollable. When he wrote cryptically, "I am a spoilt twin and she is the missing fragment," he came as close as he ever would to describe the essential quality of his dependence upon his wife. The Burtons did not live with each other, as an ordinary couple; they lived through each other, both providing a component the loss of which would have been intolerable. The strength and intensity of this fundamental relationship greatly impressed many of the Burtons' friends, who were certain that theirs was a remarkable love marriage. It was also apparent in Isabel's biography, filtering through the exaggeration and sentimentality.

Burtons' passion for the forbidden, no doubt reinforced by more direct tendencies, involved him peripherally in homosexuality. We have seen that the rumour of his homosexual practices began with the

Karachi brothel study and pursued him like an evil phantom. His periodic but close association with sexually marginal characters like Swinburne, or with deviants like Hankey, as well as his explicit and detailed writings on the subject, and his translation of such poetry as that of Catullus, served to keep the suspicion alive. His wife's anxiety on the matter did not help to clear his record. Still, the evidence of overt homosexuality is extremely fragmentary. Foremost in importance is the Karachi episode, for one must doubt that a young man of twenty-four could make an intensive study of a male brothel without some degree of participation. Most men would flee from such an assignment in disgust.

As we have seen, fragments of letters to Monckton Milnes and letters from Swinburne suggest that there may have been an occasional homosexual episode after Burton's marriage. Still, the intensity and almost frantic quality of his searching, especially on matters sexual, would seem to indicate that Burton through most of his life was seeking to resolve an unfulfilled sexuality. Moreover, one should not forget that he was fascinated also with all forms of heterosexuality—which most male homosexuals find utterly repugnant—and that an extraordinary amount of energy went into his "field research" as well as into his translations on the subject. His skill in the symbolically rich sport of fencing, and especially his scholarship on the history of the sword, tend to suggest latent rather than active homosexuality, for active homosexuals do not content themselves with the symbol of the phallus, but seek out the real thing. Though we can be fairly certain that there was a large component of homosexuality in his make-up, it is clear too that much of the compulsive searching that filled his life served in one way or another as a continuing defence against it.

We have good reason to believe that despite his prodigious curiosity about sex there was not much of it in his marriage. That he was attracted by a woman who would be content with this reveals as much about Burton as it does about his wife. Still, Burton's periodic depressions and flights from Isabel suggest a recurring discontent, just as his inevitable returns to her show his deep dependence. But to speculate about what might have happened during these flights, beyond frantic accumulation of data for another book, is to indulge in fantasy.

Burton's preoccupation with castration, whether in the form of multilation, circumcision, or clitoral excision, also defies easy analysis. He may have been exorcising an unconscious anxiety of his own by plunging into meticulous examination of the subject—just as he exorcised his fears of death by courting it—or he may simply have been indulging his sadistic impulses.

The most arresting and significant aspect of Burton's life, however, was his ceaseless search for an identity. We see it in his flight from self, first as a child into lying, then into languages, disguises, translation, and finally into prodigious learning of a very specialized sort. He was always homeless, always rootless. He never settled into a profession or even into a nationality. When Frank Harris asked him late in life if he would have preferred to be Viceroy of India or Consul General of Egypt, he replied passionately, "Egypt, Egypt! In India I should have had the English Civil Servants to deal with, and English prejudices, English formalities, English stupidity, English ignorance. They would have killed me in India, thwarted me, fought me, intrigued against me, murdered me." It was as if he still equated England and Englishmen with punishment, and a lifetime that contained acts of personal heroism in the service of this nation had not served to erase the special anxiety. England, though clearly felt to be his native country rather than the France in which he grew up, was still the land in which he could not feel at home. Though no longer "a waif, a stray," as he described himself as a child in England, he had continued to be "a blaze of light without a focus."

Here Isabel, for all her fulsome praise, had been no true helpmate. Burton had said publicly in a speech in 1878 that a wife should not write her husband's biography. *"A man's wife knows, perhaps, too much about him. I think it scarcely fair to have his character drawn by his wife. I do not think gentlemen would go to their wives, or that wives should go to their husbands, in order to know exactly what they are."*² What Burton failed to comprehend was that Isabel might not know too much about him but far too little. This we see especially in her burning of the *Scented Garden*, by which she was spurning not only his final gift of an annuity, but also his final gesture towards communication, his last attempt to strengthen and mature the structure of his own identity. If he could not be a poet or philosopher, he could at least as translator assume for a time the mantle of authorship and temporarily share an identity. In the last weeks before his death he had become the Arab Shaykh Nefzawi, the wise and compassionate but also virile and earthy scholar of the *Scented Garden* instructing in the art of love. This identity Isabel emphatically rejected.

In going still further to burn his intimate diaries and his journals she was burning the whole Richard Burton, preserving only a mutilated portrait in her biography. "I got my best reward," she wrote, "in a review which said that 'Richard Burton's widow might comfort herself, as England knew the man inside and out, that she had lifted every cloud from his memory, and his fame would shine as a beacon in all future ages.'"[3] But on the contrary it was the complication, the anguish and perplexity, the desperate quest for identity as a man, as well as the heroism, brilliance and erudition, that made Burton's life greater than all his books and adventures and strangely more rewarding for us than the lives of most of his contemporaries who were less haunted, and less demon-driven.

APPENDIX

NOTES

BIBLIOGRAPHY

INDEX

The Burton-Payne Controversy

THOMAS WRIGHT, WHO wrote biographies of both Richard Burton and John Payne, was a friend and ardent admirer of Payne and covertly hostile to Burton. In his biography of Burton, published in 1906, he listed parallel columns from the *Arabian Nights* translations of both men with the intention of trying to prove that Burton's was "largely a paraphrase of Payne." As he admitted in his *Life of John Payne*, "One of my principal objects in writing the book [on Burton] had been to show that Burton had stolen the translation from Payne."[1]

Norman Penzer, Burton's bibliographer, outraged by the accusation, replied that "there is practically no end to Wright's absurdities."[2] He noted that Wright knew no Arabic, and still less the problems of translation. Penzer, who did know Arabic and was a scholar of comparative folklore, pointed out in his own careful comparison of the two translations of the story of "Alaeddin," where Burton's *preceded* that of Payne, that in this instance the similarities were equally numerous. He also exposed Wright in many errors of fact.

Nevertheless, the cry of plagiarism was not stilled. Joseph Campbell in 1952, editing *The Portable Arabian Nights* from Payne's edition, wrote emphatically that "Burton followed it word for word, even semicolon for semicolon, not merely 'often,' but practically throughout." John T. Winterick, on the other hand, editing a two-volume edition from Burton's translation in 1955, wrote as follows: "Burton, the swashbuckling, zestful, frequently indignant, often discursive, invariably omniscient final authority, had the tremendous advantage of appearing last in the lists, and seized that advantage probably for all time." J. Oestrup, in the article on the *Nights*, "Alf Laila Wa-Laila," in the *Encyclopaedia of Islam*, stated emphatically that Burton's translation was "the most complete and exact" of all the translations in European languages. Duncan B. Macdonald, writing for the 1938 Supplement to the *Encyclopaedia of Islam* (I,17–21), states that Burton's edition, which like Payne's was based largely on the Calcutta or Macnaghten manuscript of 1814, "is very largely dependent upon that of Payne, and often reproduces Payne verbatim." Macdonald preferred Torrens's edition to either that of Burton or Payne; yet he writes of Burton's version that it was "his great work—for it is truly great."[3]

Burton was unusually meticulous in granting credits to men who aided him. He acknowledged the help of James F. Blumhardt, Cambridge orientalist, who helped him in translating Vol. III of the *Supplemental Nights* when he fell ill. He spelled out the work done for him by W. A. Clouston, folklorist, who worked on the bibliographical material and wrote one appendix, and by A. G. Ellis of the British Museum, who revised the foreword of volume six. He further thanked M. O. Houdas, Professor of Arabic in Paris, E. J. W. Gibb, orientalist, William H. Chandler of Pembroke College, Oxford, and Alexander J. Cotheal. He wrote that W. F. Kirby had helped with the bibliography, that Yacoub Artin Pasha, minister of Public Instruction in Cairo, had aided with the illustrations, and that Dr F. Steingass, an Arabist, had assisted in putting the whole work through the press and had written the treatise on Arabic prosody, Vol. X, 270–300.

He also admitted his indebtedness to Payne. "He succeeds admirably in the most difficult passages, and he often hits upon choice and special terms and the exact vernacular equivalent of the foreign word so happily and so picturesquely that all future translators must perforce use the same expression under pain of falling far short."[4] Payne and Burton seem to have remained on excellent terms. Payne dedicated Vol. IX of his translation to Burton, and in his preface to Vol. I thanked him profusely for his aid. When the original Arabic version of "Alaeddin and the Enchanted Lamp" was discovered by M. Zotenberg in 1887, Burton published his translation first, as one of the stories of the *Supplemental Nights*. Payne published his own translation in 1889. He inscribed the book to Burton in the warmest terms:

To Captain Sir Richard Francis Burton, K.C.M.G.,
H.B.M. Consul, Trieste

My Dear Burton,
    I give myself the pleasure of placing your name in the forefront of another and final volume of my translation of the Thousand and One Nights, which, if it have brought me no other good has at least been the means of procuring me your friendship.

> Believe me,
> Yours always,
> John Payne[5]

Still the exact nature of Burton's dependence upon Payne, which was real enough, deserves to be spelled out. First, it was limited entirely to the prose. There were 10,000 lines of poetry in the *Nights*, and everyone agrees that Burton's version of it is wholly his own. In the few instances where the lines are identical, he scrupulously acknowledges his indebtedness to Payne in a footnote. Actually Burton failed to match the quality of Payne's mellifluous verses. Striving always for exactness, his verses are usually terser, frequently more harsh, and often needlessly marred by archaic words, as was his translation of Camoens. Arab scholar Ameen Rihani later insisted both men failed to convey "the magic and music, the spirit-stirring lyricism of the original," though admitting that "the Arabic rhythm, do what we may, cannot be produced in English."[6]

As for the prose, since both translators were excellent Arabists and both were intent on translating the Nights "word for word," it is hardly surprising that there should be many identical passages. Payne himself, writing of the sameness of the imagery in *The Nights*, noted that in the tales eyebrows are always a bended bow, lips are always coral, eyes are lakes of jet, and cheeks are blood-red anemones.[7] Mr Quentin Keynes recently came into possession of a good many pages from the same Villon Society Edition (1882–4) of Payne's *Tales from the Arabic* that Burton had consulted in translating some of the tales for his *Supplemental Nights*. These heavily marked pages make clear that Burton did indeed use Payne's version but that he checked it with the Arab texts and made changes in the prose whenever he felt Payne to be inexact, which was often, particularly when he felt Payne to be blurring the essential vulgarity of the original. The existence of these pages indicates that Norman Penzer was probably in error when he wrote that he had examined Burton's copy of Payne's *Nights* and found it scarcely tampered with, concluding by implication that Burton had used Payne's version very little.[8] It now seems likely that Burton had two copies of Payne's *Nights*, one of which was cut up, elaborately marked and edited, as in the case of his *Tales from the Arabic*.

Burton tried to translate, Penzer tells us, "as the Arab would have written in English." His somewhat archaic style actually served to soften the grossness and terrible frankness of the tales, and gave them an esoteric flavour that added greatly to their charm. Still he was always more literal than Payne, as the following extracts, taken from the first story in *The Nights*—the cuckolding of King Shāhzemàn—clearly reveal. Payne described the king coming back unexpectedly to his palace as follows:

"In the middle of the night it chanced that he bethought him of somewhat he had forgotten in his palace: so he returned thither privily and entered his apartments, where he found his wife asleep in his own bed, in the arms of one of his black slaves. When he saw this, the world grew black in his sight, and he said to himself,

'If this is what happens whilst I am yet under the city walls, what will be the condition of this accursed woman during my absence at my brother's court?' Then he drew his sword and smote the twain and slew them and left them in bed and returned presently to his camp, without telling anyone what had happened.

Burton's version is more earthy, also more dramatic:

"But when the night was half spent he bethought him that he had forgotten in his palace somewhat which he should have brought with him, so he returned privily and entered his apartments, where he found the Queen, his wife, asleep on his own carpet-bed, embracing with both arms a black cook of loathsome aspect and foul with kitchen grease and grime. When he saw this the world waxed black before his sight and he said, 'If such case happens while I am yet within sight of the city what will be the doings of this damned whore during my long absence at my brother's court?' So he drew his cymitar and, cutting the two in four pieces with a single blow, left them on the carpet and returned presently to his camp without letting anyone know of what had happened."

Such differences occur throughout the entire edition. Where Payne used the phrase "go into a maid," Burton wrote "abate her maidenhood." When Payne wrote "join thy body to mine," Burton put it more crudely, "glue my body with thy body and strum and belly-bump."[9] In the less vulgar passages, the differences were less striking, but Burton's changes were always in the direction of greater exactness. In the story of Hasan of Bassorah, the 787th Night, for example, Payne described a lovely woman as follows: "She had a polished aquiline nose and cheeks like blood-red anemones." Burton wrote, "She had a polished nose straight as a cane and cheeks like blood-red anemones of Nu'uman." Where Payne wrote somewhat carelessly, "She had a mouth like Solomon's seal," Burton wrote, "She had a mouth magical as Solomon's seal," the seal being the mystical symbol consisting of two interlaced triangles symbolizing the union of soul and body.[10] In the passages describing homosexual episodes, Payne's timidity was most apparent. Here even Thomas Wright admitted that Burton was more faithful to the text.

It is also usually forgotten that Burton translated many more stories than Payne. Though his first ten volumes are a translation of the same 1,001 stories as Payne's nine-volume translation, he went on to translate in his six-volume *Supplemental Nights* (1886–8) seventy-eight stories not included in Payne's three-volume supplement, *Tales from the Arabic* (1884). This counting includes tales within tales.

NOTES

CHAPTER I. The Devil Drives (pp. 15 to 20)

1. Burton to Monckton Milnes (Lord Houghton), May 31, 1863, from the Lord Houghton papers, Trinity College Library, Cambridge.

2. *A Plain and Literal Translation of the Arabian Nights' Entertainments, etc.*, 10 vols (Benares, 1885), printed by the Kama Shastra Society, for Private Subscribers only, IX, 135n. Hereafter this will be referred to as *Arabian Nights*.

3. Arthur Symons, *Dramatis Personae* (Indianapolis, 1923), 251; Earl of Dunraven, *Past Times and Pastimes* (London, 1922), I, 178.

4. Foreword to Burton's translation of the *Carmina of Gaius Valerius Catullus*, privately printed, 1894.

5. *Academy*, obituary, October 25, 1890, 365.

6. Isabel Burton, *Life of Captain Sir Richard F. Burton*, 2 vols (London, 1893), II, 257. Hereafter this will be referred to simply as *Life*.

7. Bram Stoker, *Personal Reminiscences of Henry Irving*, 2 vols (London, 1906), I, 360–1; Lord Redesdale (Algernon Bertram Freeman-Mitford), *Memories*, 2 vols (London, 1915), II, 562–4.

8. These stories were told by Thomas Wright in his *Life of Sir Richard Burton*, 2 vols (London, 1906), II, 166, 48.

9. "Richard Burton," *Fortnightly Review*, LXXIX, 1040, June 1, 1906.

10. *Contemporary Portraits* (New York, 1920), 180–2. See also Harris's *My Life and Loves* (New York, 1963), 616–21.

11. A sampling of Burton's capacity for attack is best seen in Vol. VII of his *Supplemental Nights to the Book of the Thousand Nights and a Night* (London, 1886–8). See VII, 401–2, 444, for the above, also the *Athenaeum*, October 23, 1875.

12. W. H. Wilkins, *The Romance of Isabel Lady Burton*, 2 vols (London, 1897), II, 720; Ouida, "Richard Burton," *Fortnightly Review*, LXXIX, 1042, June 1, 1906.

13. Georgiana Stisted, *The True Life of Captain Sir Richard F. Burton* (London, 1897), 275; Thomas Wright, *Life of John Payne* (London, 1919), 143; Lord Redesdale, *Memories*, I, 574, 563–4; *The Swinburne Letters*, edited by Cecil Y. Lang, 6 vols (Yale University Press, 1959), II, 336.

14. Isabel Burton in a letter to the *Morning Post*, June 19, 1891.

15. *Life*, II, 442. Here Isabel Burton was defending her burning of *The Scented Garden*. She did not confess publicly that she burned his journals and diaries.

CHAPTER II. The Merest Trifles (pp. 21 to 31)

1. *Sind Revisited*, 2 vols (London, 1877), I, 257.

2. Burton erroneously believed he was born at Barham House. The baptismal register at Elstree states he was born at Torquay. His sister Maria's baptism is recorded at Elstree, March 18, 1823, and his brother Edward's, August 31, 1824. See Thomas Wright, *Life of Sir Richard Burton*, I, 37–8, and *Torquay Directory*, March 23, 1921.

3. From Burton's memoir, which describes his life up to 1848, as quoted in Isabel Burton, *Life*, I, 16.

4. Quoted in *Life*, I, 20–1.

5. Quoted in *ibid.*, I, 22.

6. *Scinde; or, The Unhappy Valley*, 2 vols (London, 1851), II, 188.

7. *Ibid.*, I, 248–9; *Vikram and the Vampire, or Tales of Hindu Devilry* (London, 1870), 295n.

8. *Personal Narrative of a Pilgrimage to El-Medinah and Meccah*, 3 vols (London, 1855–6). All quotations in this volume are from the memorial edition, edited by Isabel Burton in 2 vols (London, 1893). For the above quotation see I, 287.

9. Georgiana Stisted, *The True Life of Captain Sir Richard F. Burton*, 22.

10. *Sindh, and the Races that Inhabit the Valley of the Indus* (London, 1851), 197; *Scinde; or, The Unhappy Valley*, I, 269.

11. In a speech honouring Queen Victoria, Trieste, June 23, 1887, *Life*, II, 342.

12. *Pilgrimage to El-Medinah and Meccah*, II, 239.

13. Quoted in *Life*, I, 58.

14. *Arabian Nights*, VIII, 287n.

15. Quoted in *Life*, I, 65–6.

16. *Ibid.*, I, 596.

17. Laura Hain Friswell Myall, *In the Sixties and Seventies* (Boston, 1906), 44; Harold Nicolson, *Portrait of a Diplomatist* (Boston, 1930), 59; Ouida, "Richard Burton," *Fortnightly Review*, LXXIX, 1041, 1906; Arthur Symons, *Dramatis Personae*, 262.

18. See *Trial of Queen Caroline, consort of George IV, for Adulterous Intercourse with Bartolomo Bergami* (London, 1820).

19. Quoted in *Life*, I, 17–18.

20. The Quentin Keynes collection has two accounts of the genealogy, one in Richard's hand and one in that of his wife. It is amusing to see how she altered it in favour of respectability. See also *Life*, I, 24, 397.

21. *Supplemental Nights*, VII, 9n.

CHAPTER III. The Impact of France (pp. 32 to 39)

1. Letter to John Payne, January 19, 1884, quoted in Thomas Wright, *Life of Sir Richard Burton*, II, 71.

2. Except where otherwise noted, all the quotations in this chapter come from Burton's memoir, Isabel Burton, *Life*, 1–75.

3. *The Book of the Sword* (London, 1884), xi.

4. Francis Hitchman, who had the use of Burton's memoir, cut this episode severely in his biography, but Isabel Burton permitted it to remain intact. See her *Life*, I, 52.

CHAPTER IV. Oxford (pp. 40 to 46)

1. Except where otherwise noted, all quotations in this chapter are from Burton's memoir, printed in Isabel Burton, *Life*. See I, 75–90.

2. Article from *Sporting Truth*, without signature, quoted in *Life*, I, 181.

3. Alfred Bates Richards, *A Short Sketch of the Career of Captain Richard F. Burton . . . by an Old Oxonian* (London, 1880). This was reprinted with some additions in 1886; most of it was reproduced in *Life*, II, 4–15.

4. Francis Galton, *Memories of My Life* (London, 1908), 202.

CHAPTER V. Fact and Fiction in India (pp. 47 to 56)

1. Burton published this poem of 121 pages under a pseudonym, Frank Baker, in 1865. The above extract is from the reprint made by the Sutro Branch, California State Library, as *Occasional Papers No. 24* (San Francisco, November 1940), 10.

2. *Falconry in the Valley of the Indus* (London, 1852), 95; *Life*, I, 95.

3. Quoted in *Life*, I, 99.

4. Quoted in *ibid.*, I, 101, 102, 138; *Falconry in the Valley of the Indus*, 95.

5. Quoted in *Life*, I, 101, 107.

6. *Pilgrimage to El-Medinah and Meccah*, II, 100.

7. Norman M. Penzer, *An Annotated Bibliography of Sir Richard Francis Burton* (London, 1923), 7. See also W. N. Evans, "Serendipity," *Psychoanalytic Quarterly*, XXXII, 165–79 (1963), for the story of a linguist whose approach to languages—intense excitement, followed by boredom and then the searching out of a new language—was very like that of Burton. In this case the linguist suffered from impotence.

8. The account of Burton's experiment is detailed by his wife. See *Life*, I, 160. Modern zoologists, making systematic studies with recordings, have identified thirty different "words" among the monkeys of Japan, twenty-two among the gorillas of Africa and fifteen to twenty among the Howler monkeys of tropical America. See *New York Times Magazine*, March 29, 1964, 14*ff.*, for a summary of these studies by Marston Bates, zoologist at the University of Michigan.

9. *Life*, I, 110, 599.

10. Quoted in *ibid.*, I, 132, 103.

11. Quoted in *ibid.*, I, 135.

12. *Ananga-Ranga; (Stage of the Bodiless One) or, the Hindu Art of Love*, translated and annotated by Richard Burton and F. F. Arbuthnot, using the initials A.F.F. and B.F.R., privately printed, 1885, 41n.; *Arabian Nights*, V, 76n.

13. *Falconry in the Valley of the Indus*, 87.

14. *Scinde; or, The Unhappy Valley*, I, 74–8.

15. *The True Life of Captain Sir Richard F. Burton*, 43–4.

16. *Arabian Nights*, X, 127.

17. *Scinde; or, The Unhappy Valley*, II, 203–4; *Sind Revisited*, II, 168.

CHAPTER VI. Sind (pp. 57 to 70)

1. William Napier, *Life and Opinions of General Sir Charles James Napier*, 4 vols (London, 1857), II, 132.

2. *Ibid.*, III, 409–10, 152; IV, 363. The diary extract of August 4, 1845 may be seen in the original diary in the British Museum.

3. Quoted in *Life*, I, 140. Burton's detailed account of his years in India may be seen in this biography, I, 92–151.

4. *Scinde; or, The Unhappy Valley*, I, 34; *Sind Revisited*, II, 281–2.

5. Jean B. Villars, *T. E. Lawrence, or the Search for the Absolute* (London, 1955), 330.

6. *Scinde; or, The Unhappy Valley*, I, 29–30, 147, 152, 217.

7. William Napier, *Life . . . Sir Charles James Napier*, III, 277; Charles Napier, MS. diary in the British Museum, January 1, 1846.

8. Quoted in *Life*, I, 144.

9. *Goa and the Blue Mountains; or, Six Months of Sick Leave* (London, 1851), 316. See also Geoffrey Bibby, *The Testimony of the Spade* (New York, 1956), 201.

10. See *Sind Revisited*, I, 192–3; *Life*, I, 146.

11. See Burton's review of William Napier Bruce, *Life of General Sir Charles Napier, Academy*, February 6, 1886, 85.

12. Charles Napier, MS. diary, August 4, 6, 1845.

13. Burton to Leonard Smithers, August 8, 1888, Huntington Library.

14. *Scinde; or, The Unhappy Valley*, I, 263.

15. *Falconry in the Valley of the Indus*, 99, 101.

16. See Burton's note on this in the *Arabian Nights*, V, 249n., and in *Sind Revisited*, I, 315. In revising portions of *Scinde; or, The Unhappy Valley*, for *Sind Revisited*, Burton wrote this story on the margin of his own copy, now in the Royal Anthropological Institute. See I, 270.

17. William Napier, *Life . . . Sir Charles James Napier*, III, 132, 139.

18. *Goa and the Blue Mountains,* 347; *Sindh, and the Races that inhabit the Valley of the Indus* (London, 1851), 244.

19. *Scinde; or, The Unhappy Valley,* II, 220–1. Parts of this seem to have been copied directly from Burton's journal.

20. William Napier, *Life . . . Sir Charles James Napier,* III, 331.

21. *Scinde; or, The Unhappy Valley,* II, 6.

22. *Ibid.,* II, 70n.

23. See the section on Pederasty, "Terminal Essay," *Arabian Nights,* X.

24. William Napier, *Life . . . Sir Charles James Napier,* IV, 28.

25. Quoted in *Life,* I, 147.

26. *Goa and the Blue Mountains,* 1.

27. William Napier, *Life . . . Sir Charles James Napier,* IV, 73–4.

28. The technical papers, "Notes and Remarks on Dr Dorn's Chrestomathy of the Pushtu or Affghan Language," and "A Grammar of the Játakí or Belohcki Dialect," were published in January 1849 in the Bombay Branch of the *Royal Asiatic Society Journal.* See III, No. 12, 58–69, 84–125. "Brief Notes relative to the Division of Time, and Articles of Cultivation in Sind," and "Notes relative to the Population of Sind; and the Customs, Language, and Literature of the People," were published in the *Bombay Government Records,* No. XVII, New Series, Part II (1855), 613–36, 637–57, 1855.

29. "Terminal Essay," *Arabian Nights,* X, 205. The original of this fateful report seems hopelessly lost. Mr Stanley Sutton, Director of the India Office Library in London ordered a search to be made for me in the India Office archives, and also requested Dr P. M. Joshi, Director of the Bombay Records Office, Delhi, to have a search made in Delhi. When both proved fruitless, Dr Joshi suggested that the report might have been sent to West Pakistan along with many other records in 1936. Mr Mian Mohammad Sadullah, P.C.S., Keeper of the Records, Government of West Pakistan, of the West Pakistan Civil Secretariat in Lahore, also had his records searched, but nothing was found.

A list of Burton's unpublished works, made by Minnie Grace Plowman after his death, included the title "Sind-Karachi," which may have been a copy of the brothel study. If so, it was certainly burned either by Isabel Burton or her sister. See Norman M. Penzer, *An Annotated Bibliography of Sir Richard Francis Burton,* 183, 198.

30. This important letter was preserved in the family, and published by Thomas Wright. See his *Life of Sir Richard Burton,* I, 84–7.

31. Quoted in *Life,* I, 162.

32. Burton had heard this from his father. See Thomas Wright, *Life of Sir Richard Burton,* I, 84, 87.

33. Ouida, "Richard Burton," *Fortnightly Review,* LXXIX, 1044, June 1, 1906.

34. *Arabian Nights,* V, 160n.

CHAPTER VII. Burton Becomes a Writer (pp. 71 to 77)

1. *Pilgrimage to El-Medinah and Meccah,* I, 151. Since this was written before his return to England from Mecca, it clearly refers to his return from India.

2. Georgiana Stisted, "Reminiscences of Sir Richard Burton," *Temple Bar,* July 1891, 335–342; *The True Life of Captain Sir Richard F. Burton,* 58.

3. This is a quote not from the memorandum but from *Pilgrimage to El-Medinah and Meccah,* I, 38. Burton in a footnote indicated that these sentiments were similar to "a much stronger report" which he had sent to the Court of Directors in 1852, "for which I duly suffered." This report was never published.

4. *Goa and the Blue Mountains,* 222.

5. A study of comparable merit was written by a French priest, Abbé J. A. Dubois, a missionary to India from 1792 to 1823. His *Hindu Manners, Customs and Ceremonies* (translated by Henry K. Beauchamp in 1897) was also a forerunner of the ethnological studies of the twentieth century.

6. *Scinde; or, The Unhappy Valley,* II, 7; *Pilgrimage to El-Medinah and Meccah,* I, 40.

7. *Scinde; or, The Unhappy Valley,* I, 182; *Goa and the Blue Mountains,* 158.

8. *Falconry in the Valley of the Indus,* 54.

9. *Goa and the Blue Mountains,* 162, 351. See also *Sindh, and the Races . . . of the Indus,* 333, 406; *Scinde; or, The Unhappy Valley,* I, 120–1.

10. Richard Burton, *The Lake Regions of Central Africa,* 2 vols (New York, 1961), edited with an introduction by Alan Moorehead, xi.

11. *Athenaeum,* April 19, 1851, 423–5; October 25, 1851, 1111–12; July 17, 1852, 765–6.

12. *The Kama Sutra of Vatsyayana,* translated by Sir Richard Burton and F. F. Arbuthnot, edited with a preface by W. G. Archer, and an introduction by K. M. Panikkar (London, 1963), 17.

13. *Sindh, and the Races . . . of the Indus,* 146–7.

CHAPTER VIII. Burton Looks at Marriage (pp. 78 to 88)

1. *Sindh, and the Races . . . of the Indus,* 160.

2. *Ibid.,* 401.

3. Quoted in *Life,* I, 53; see also Georgiana Stisted, *The True Life of Captain Sir Richard F. Burton,* 58–9; "Reminiscences of Sir Richard Burton," *Temple Bar,* July 1891, 335–42.

4. *Life of Sir Richard Burton,* I, 95. For Isabel's account see *Life,* I, 393, 167, 249.

5. *Life,* I, 168.

6. *The True Life of Captain Sir Richard F. Burton,* 63.

7. The most complete account of the courtship is to be found in W. H. Wilkins, *The Romance of Isabel Lady Burton,* based on her manuscript autobiography. Part of it appears also in her own biography of her husband. For the above quotations see Wilkins, I, 22, 53–6, 60; *Life,* I, 166–8.

8. The above quotations are from W. H. Wilkins, *The Romance of Isabel Lady Burton,* I, 16–17, 57.

9. *Life,* I, 332n. The inscribed copy of *Tancred* is in the Royal Anthropological Institute.

10. Isabel Burton, *A.E.I., Arabia, Egypt, India, a Narrative of Travel* (London, 1879), 5.

11. W. H. Wilkins, *The Romance of Isabel Lady Burton,* I, 38–9.

12. *Pilgrimage to El-Medinah and Meccah,* I, 141. For Georgiana Stisted's comments see *The True Life of Captain Sir Richard F. Burton,* 63–4.

13. Georgiana Stisted, *The True Life of Captain Sir Richard F. Burton,* 58, 67.

14. Norman M. Penzer, writing in 1923, said that "until about ten years ago it was impossible to find any work on the subject which was not based on Burton's work." *An Annotated Bibliography of Sir Richard Francis Burton,* 42. Oddly, it has become the rarest of all Burton's writings.

15. *Pilgrimage to El-Medinah and Meccah,* I, 2.

16. *Sindh, and the Races . . . of the Indus,* 358, 413.

CHAPTER IX. The Chartered Vagabond (pp. 89 to 102)

1. *The City of the Saints and Across the Rocky Mountains to California* (London, 1861), 491. See also Dr Ralph Greenson, "The Struggle Against Identification," *Journal of the American Psychoanalytic Association,* II, 200–217, April, 1954.

2. For a detailed summary of these voyages see *Pilgrimage to El-Medinah and Meccah,* Appendices IV, V, VI; R. H. Kiernan, *The Unveiling of Arabia* (London, 1937), 54–161; David G. Hogarth, *The Penetration of Arabia* (Cambridge, 1904); and Penzer, *An Annotated Bibliography of Sir Richard Francis Burton,* 46–8.

Others who visited Mecca include Vincent le Blanc, 1568, Johann Wild, who published a volume about his experiences as captive in Mecca in 1604, Ulrich Seetzen, German botanist and Arabist who went to Mecca disguised as a physician but was killed on his return; Roches, a Frenchman who went in 1841–2, and George A. Wallin, a Swede who visited Mecca in 1845 but whose report was not read before the Royal Geographical Society until 1852. After Burton's voyage there were others: Keane, an Englishman, in 1877–8; a Dutchman Snouck Hurgronje, who lived in Mecca for five months; Gervais-Courtellement, a Frenchman, who was there in 1894; and Archibald Wavell in 1908. There were also others, nameless, Europeans and renegades. The distinguished explorer H. St. John B. Philby actually lived in Mecca for five months, becoming a Moslem for the purpose. See his *The Heart of Arabia* (1922). Anti-infidel regulations are still applied with all the old vigour. See Christina P. Grant, *Syrian Desert Caravans, Travel and Exploration* (New York, 1938), 233.

3. *The Empty Quarter, being a description of the Great South Desert of Arabia* (New York, 1933), xvii.

4. *Pilgrimage to El-Medinah and Meccah*, I, 15, 13, 8.

5. *Arabian Nights*, III, 212n., and *Pilgrimage to El-Medinah and Meccah*, I, 175n.; II, 91.

6. Pierre François Hugues D'Hancarville, *Recherches sur l'origine, l'esprit et les progrès des arts de la Grèce; sur leurs connections avec les arts et la religion des plus anciens peuples connus* . . . (London, 1785). See also *Pilgrimage to El-Medinah and Meccah*, I, 32, 72, 81, 84, 89, 92, 210.

7. *Pilgrimage to El-Medinah and Meccah*, I, 9, 123.

8. *Ibid.*, I, 143, 149.

9. For Burton's quotations see *ibid.*, I, 173, 24, 127; II, 10.

10. Redesdale, *Memories*, II, 572; Bram Stoker, *Personal Reminiscences of Henry Irving*, I, 359. For Burton's denial see Kenneth Walker's compilation of his notes, *Love, War and Fancy* (London, 1964), 260.

11. *Pilgrimage to El-Medinah and Meccah*, II, 128.

12. Ibid., II, 206–9. Isabel Burton's *Life* has a somewhat altered version of this episode. See I, 177.

CHAPTER X. Breaking the Guardian Spell (pp. 103 to 114)

1. *Royal Geographical Society Journal* (1855), XXV, 138.

2. Quoted in *Life*, I, 178–9.

3. *First Footsteps in East Africa; or, An Exploration of Harar* (London, 1856), 118. See also T. E. Lawrence, *Seven Pillars of Wisdom* (New York, 1935), 30–3, 508. When Norman Penzer questioned Colonel Lawrence about the accuracy of Burton's *Pilgrimage*, he described it as "absolutely correct in every detail" and "a most remarkable work of the highest value to a geographer or to a student of the East." *An Annotated Bibliography of Sir Richard Francis Burton*, 7.

4. *Pilgrimage to El-Medinah and Meccah*, II, 93–4.

5. A fact revealed in Stanley Lane-Poole's introduction to the Standard Library edition of *Pilgrimage to El-Medinah and Meccah*, 1914. Later the deleted matter appeared in Burton's footnotes to the *Arabian Nights*.

6. *First Footsteps in East Africa*, 38.

7. *Ibid.*, 130.

8. See Gordon Waterfield's edition of *First Footsteps in East Africa* (London, 1966), 260, quoting from the army physician's official report concerning Burton's injuries at Berbera in 1855. Burton's extensive notes on syphilis in the Terminal Essay of the *Arabian Nights* reflect the absence of correct medical knowledge on the subject even in the 1880s. "Syphilis varies greatly with climate," he wrote. "In Persia it is said to be propagated without contact; in Abyssinia it is often fatal and in Egypt it is readily cured by sand baths and sulphur-unguents." See X, 90n. The

sand bath, where the patient was buried up to his neck in sand in the desert, raised the body temperature like a severe fever. This often cured the syphilis, and sometimes killed the patient. Contracting malaria (which Burton did later in Africa) also had the effect of curing syphilis. See C. C. Dennie, *History of Syphilis* (1962), and William A. Pusey, *History of Syphilis* (1933). There was little precise information on syphilis in Burton's time, as Dr Edward Shapiro pointed out to me, chiefly because "amongst the godly it was considered to be a just retribution for venery."

9. Sigmund Freud, *Leonardo Da Vinci, a Study in Psychosexuality* (Modern Library), 20.

10. "Narrative of a Trip to Harar," *Royal Geographical Society Journal* (1855), XXV, 137.

11. W. H. Wilkins, *The Romance of Isabel Lady Burton*, 72–3.

12. Burton's publication of the *Pilgrimage* was preceded by two rather austere descriptive letters he sent to the Royal Geographical Society. See "Journey to Medina, with route from Yamba," *Royal Geographical Society Journal* (1854), XXIV, 208–25; and "A Journey from El-Medina to Mecca," *Royal Geographical Society Journal* (1855), XXV, 136–50.

13. Burton, incensed that Doughty had not read his own book, pointed out in his ungenerous review of Doughty's book in the *Academy* that had he done so it "would have saved him many an inaccuracy," and hinted that much of Doughty's hardship was brought upon himself by his insistence on parading the fact that he was a Christian. *Academy*, July 28, 1888, 47–8.

14. Speke also had two sisters, Sophia Murdock and Matilda Pine-Coffin, as well as two other brothers. His sisters prepared two "Histories of the Speke family," now in the Royal Geographical Society archives. His eldest brother died without an heir, and the estate went to the youngest brother, Benjamin, as Edward had been killed on September 15, 1858 in the Indian Mutiny.

15. *Zanzibar; City, Island, and Coast*, 2 vols (London, 1872), II, 377.

16. John H. Speke, *What Led to the Discovery of the Source of the Nile* (Edinburgh, 1864), 151.

17. See Burton's *Zanzibar*, II, 378, and Speke's account in *Blackwood's Magazine*, November, 1859, 575.

18. *Zanzibar*, II, 381.

19. The British Resident at Aden, Sir James Outram, old foe of Sir Charles Napier, formally denied Burton's request for permission to explore a wide area in Somaliland, and greatly curtailed his plans. Burton eventually revenged himself by writing in his *First Footsteps in East Africa* that in Aden "the business of life is comprised in ignoble squabbles . . . where, briefly, the march of mind is at a dead halt." See 38–9.

20. *First Footsteps in East Africa*, 15n., 42, 74, 119.

21. *Arabian Nights*, V, 279n.

22. The appendix was meant to include pp. 593–8; my copy contains pp. 593–5. When I learned that Mr Gordon Waterfield was editing a new edition of *First Footsteps in East Africa*, I sent him photostats of these pages. He had them translated and included in full in his Appendix 2, "Excision and Infibulation." Back in 1893 when Leonard Smithers was helping to edit the memorial edition of Burton's chief works, he wrote to Isabel Burton as follows: ". . . have you discovered aught of the missing appendix?" Apparently she did not—or would not—find it for him. The Smithers letter is in the collection of Edwards Metcalf.

23. *Arabian Nights*, V, 279n.

24. "Narrative of a Trip to Harar," *Royal Geographical Society Journal* (1855), XXV, 137; *First Footsteps in East Africa*, 240.

25. *First Footsteps in East Africa*, 303, 360. J. Spencer Trimingham, visiting Harar almost a century later, found Burton's description of the wadads still valid. See his *Islam in Ethiopia* (Oxford University Press, 1952), 216. Dr. Ioan Myrddin Lewis, in his *A Pastoral Democracy*, (Oxford, 1961), wrote that Burton's *First*

Footsteps in East Africa "remains the best general description of northern Somali society." See p. 32.

26. *First Footsteps in East Africa*, 364–5.

CHAPTER XI. First Footsteps Towards the Nile (pp. 115 to 125)

1. This account, published by Isabel Burton in *Life*, I, 214–15, was taken from the original journal. Burton's shorter more austere account in *First Footsteps in East Africa* omits the story of the *katta*. In describing his trip before the Royal Geographical Society he dismissed the dramatic crossing of the desert as "a mere adventure of uncommon hardship." See *Royal Geographical Society Journal* (1855), XXV, 148.

2. *What Led to the Discovery of the Source of the Nile*, 88. See also Burton's *First Footsteps in East Africa*, 500.

3. *First Footsteps in East Africa*, 502.

4. Georgiana Stisted, *The True Life of Captain Sir Richard F. Burton*, 164, 412; *Supplemental Nights*, VI, 326n.

5. *First Footsteps in East Africa*, 234–6. See also Georgiana Stisted, *The True Life of Captain Sir Richard F. Burton*, 159.

6. The original letter is in the archives of the Royal Geographical Society. It was quoted in part by Dorothy Middleton, "Burton and Speke Centenary," *The Geographical Journal*, September, 1957, CXXIII, 414.

7. Burton to Norton Shaw, February 25, 1855, Royal Geographical Society; *First Footsteps in East Africa*, 312n.

8. See Henry M. Stanley, *In Darkest Africa*, 2 vols (New York, 1890), II, 302–5; and James Bruce, *Travels to Discover the Source of the Nile in the Years 1768, 1769, 1770, 1771, 1772, and 1773*, 5 vols (Edinburgh, 1890), III, 609.

9. See Father Jerome Lobo, *A Short Relation of the River Nile* (London, 1673), and *A Voyage to Abyssinia*, as translated from the French by Samuel Johnson (London, 1789), 110–11, 209–10. James Bruce in his *Travels to Discover the Source of the Nile* dates Father Paez's visit as 1618 rather than 1613. See III, 618. The Paez account was told through Father Kercher, another Jesuit missionary.

10. *Travels to Discover the Source of the Nile*, III, 596–7, 640–1.

11. For Burton's account see *First Footsteps in East Africa*, and for Speke's version see *What Led to the Discovery of the Source of the Nile*, especially 132–40. Speke in his book blamed Burton's failure to hire an Abban for "all the mishaps which befell the expedition," see 112n. When Burton read this, he wrote in the margin of his copy of Speke's book, "Not a word true." This copy may be seen in the Royal Anthropological Institute.

12. See the 1966 edition of *First Footsteps in East Africa*, edited by Gordon Waterfield, 260.

13. *Life*, I, 219. Gordon Waterfield, whose research uncovered much new material, has examined the whole question of Burton's laxity with extreme care in his introduction to *First Footsteps in East Africa*. He holds that while the posting of only two guards would seem to indicate irresponsibility, actually Burton often won success by sheer bravado, and made a point of not showing obvious fear to natives. Waterfield holds, however, that Burton's superiors were convinced he had been imprudent, and never forgave him for this.

CHAPTER XII. Crimea (pp. 126 to 132)

1. Isabel Burton, *Life*, I, 226, a quotation from Burton's own account of his Crimean experience, called "With Beatson's Horse." Most of the material in this chapter comes from this brief memoir.

2. See Cecil Woodham-Smith, *The Reason Why* (London, 1963), 21–2, 140,

225*ff.*, and Christopher Hibbert, *The Destruction of Lord Raglan* (Boston, 1961), 137.

3. Letter to *The Times*, December 6, 1855, and *Life*, I, 238.
4. As quoted in Cecil Woodham-Smith, *The Reason Why*, 275.
5. Quoted in *Life*, I, 228.
6. *First Footsteps in East Africa*, 457n.
7. Royal Geographical Society archives.
8. Quoted in *Life*, I, 241.
9. Ibid., I, 242, 234–5. See also Humphry Sandwith, *A Narrative of the Siege of Kars* (London, 1856), 300. Stanley Lane-Poole, in a letter to the *Athenaeum*, August 25, 1888, objected to Burton's statement implying that Stratford had frustrated the relief of Kars, as published in Burton's biography by Francis Hitchman. Burton replied angrily in a letter to the *Academy*, September 1, 1888, 137. The letter, dated August 26, 1888, refers to Lane-Poole's "silly, saltless, sneering way." Nevertheless Burton did accept the fact that it was the Foreign Office and not Lord Stratford who had been responsible. See also Burton's review of Stanley Lane-Poole's biography of Lord Stratford, as published in the *Academy*, November 24, 1888, 329–30.
10. William Howard Russell, *The War from the Death of Lord Raglan to the Evacuation of the Crimea* (London, 1856), 181. Dispatch of September 12, 1855.
11. Quoted in *Life*, I, 244.
12. *Zanzibar*, I, 5; and *Life*, I, 247.

CHAPTER XIII. The Courtship (pp. 133 to 140)

1. For all the extracts from Isabel Burton's diary quoted in this chapter, see W. H. Wilkins, *The Romance of Isabel Lady Burton*, I, 65–9, 81–8, 95, 97, 112.
2. Compare the diary extracts quoted by Wilkins, I, 83–8, with Isabel Burton's *Life*, I, 250.
3. *Gypsy Lore Society Journal*, and obituary of Burton, reprinted in *Life*, I, 251–2.
4. According to Thomas Wright. See his *Life of Sir Richard Burton*, I, 147.
5. W. H. Wilkins, *The Romance of Isabel Lady Burton*, I, 86.
6. *Ibid.*, I, 84, 97, and *Life*, I, 333.
7. Isabel later repeated this with minor variations in a letter to her mother, October 1859. See *Life*, I, 335, and compare with the diary extracts in W. H. Wilkins, *The Romance of Isabel Lady Burton*, I, 91, 112.

CHAPTER XIV. The Impact of Africa (pp. 141 to 153)

1. Burton tells us that he quoted this direct from his journal. See *Zanzibar*, I, 16–17. Isabel Burton, also writing that the quotation came from his journal, nevertheless reproduced it differently. The "slavery of Home" becomes "slavery of Civilization." See *Life*, I, 258.
2. A quotation from his Sir Henry Morton Stanley's African notebook of 1876, reproduced in his *Autobiography*, (London, 1912), 533.
3. George Seaver, *David Livingstone: His Life and Letters* (London, 1957), 583, 594.
4. Quoted in Alan Moorehead, *The White Nile*, 91–2.
5. *Zanzibar*, II, 382.
6. Speke's letter to Norton Shaw, October 28, 1859, is in the Royal Geographical Society archives. Speke's Taunton speech is quoted in part in Richard Burton's *The Nile Basin*, 2 Parts (London, 1864), Pt I, 28.
7. See *Zanzibar*, II, 382, 385, and *The Lake Regions of Central Africa, A Picture of Exploration*, 2 vols (London, 1860), I, 25.
8. Quoted in *Life*, I, 315.

9. Speke to Norton Shaw, October 28, 1859 and December 12, 1860. Royal Geographical Society archives.

10. Farwell bases his judgment largely on Speke's letters to C. P. Rigby, published in Mrs C. E. B. Russell's *General Rigby, Zanzibar and the Slave Trade* (London, 1935), but these letters were all written after the estrangement. See Byron Farwell, *Burton* (London, 1963), 138, and Richard Burton, *The Nile Basin*, Pt I, 6.

11. These letters, May 20, 1857 and July 2, 1858, are in the Royal Geographical Society archives.

12. *Zanzibar*, I, 37.

13. *Ibid.*, I, 457–458, 353, 464, 95–6.

14. *Ibid.*, I, 184–5.

15. *The Lake Regions of Central Africa*, I, 269.

16. *Ibid.*, I, 24.

17. *Ibid.*, I, 84, 192–3, 325, 323.

18. See Alan Moorehead, *The White Nile*, 34, and Burton, *The Lake Regions of Central Africa*, I, 97, 161, 194.

19. *The Lake Regions of Central Africa*, II, 161–2, I, 35, 234; *Zanzibar*, II, 95.

20. See Burton's own copy of Speke's *Journal of the Discovery of the Source of the Nile* (Edinburgh, 1863), xiii, and 546. Burton wrote "Humbug," and then "Beastly Humbug," in the margins of both these pages. This copy is in the Royal Anthropological Institute library.

21. *The Lake Regions of Central Africa*, II, 340, 372, 324; I, 106.

22. *Zanzibar*, II, 84–5, and *The Lake Regions of Central Africa*, II, 340–60.

23. *Zanzibar*, II, 92.

24. There are several manuscript pages filed in Volume II of Burton's own copy of his *Abeokuta and the Cameroons Mountains. An Exploration*, 2 vols (London, 1863), in the Royal Anthropological Institute library. By matching the pages with the published *Zanzibar*, one can see that this extract was meant to be included in Vol. I, 379–80.

25. *Arabian Nights*, I, 6n. This note was prompted by the fact that the first tale in *The Nights*, the framework upon which all the others hang, is a story of fury over the infidelity of wives, a fury compounded by the fact that the lovers of the wives of both King Shahryar and his brother were black men. Burton implies that only this kind of adultery would have turned the king into a mass murderer, who killed more than a thousand girls before he found the celebrated Shehrazade, or, as Burton also spells the name, Shahrázád.

26. Speke, *What Led to the Discovery of the Source of the Nile*, 68, and *Blackwood's Magazine*, Vol. 86, 353, September 1859; *Journal of the Discovery of the Source of the Nile*, 181.

27. See Burton's copy of Speke's *What Led to the Discovery of the Source of the Nile*, 296, in the Royal Anthropological Institute library.

28. See Speke's letter describing a dancing party in Madeira, on his way to Africa in 1860, quoted by Dorothy Middleton, "Burton and Speke Centenary," *Geographical Journal*, CXXIII, 414, September 1957.

29. *Journal of the Discovery of the Source of the Nile*, 518, 361, 369.

30. *The Lake Regions of Central Africa*, I, 389.

CHAPTER XV. Tanganyika (pp. 154 to 166)

1. Quoted in *Life*, I, 304.

2. Burton wrote back to the Royal Geographical Society, June 24, 1858, correctly, that there were at least four lakes, the Nyanza, Chama, Ujiji and Ukerewe—actually Nyassa, Bangweulu, Tanganyika and Victoria.

3. *The Lake Regions of Central Africa*, I, 404.

4. *Ibid.*, II, 42, 44, 85–90.

5. Speke's account first appeared in *Blackwood's Magazine*, September 1859, and was reprinted in Burton's *The Lake Regions of Central Africa*, II, 91–2n.

6. *Blackwood's Magazine*, October 1859, Vol. 86, 351; *Royal Geographical Society Proceedings*, 1859, Vol. 29, 17.

7. *Blackwood's Magazine*, October 1859, Vol. 86, 391.

8. *The Lake Regions of Central Africa*, II, 114, 118.

9. *Ibid.*, II, 117–18.

10. As quoted by Burton in *Two Trips to Gorilla Land and the Cataracts of the Congo* (London, 1876), II, 188, after he had himself canoed a hundred miles up the Congo from its mouth. Livingstone had written in his journal, May 21, 1872, "I am oppressed with the apprehension that after all it may turn out that I have been following the Congo; and who shall risk being put into a cannibal pot and converted to a black man for it?" Quoted in George Seaver, *David Livingstone: His Life and Letters*, 606.

11. From Burton's journal, quoted in *Life*, I, 305.

12. *The Lake Regions of Central Africa*, II, 156.

13. *The Highlands of Brazil*, 2 vols (London, 1869), I, 297. See also *Life*, I, 308, and *The Lake Regions of Central Africa*, II, 167.

14. Quoted in *Life*, I, 290, 309.

15. See *Blackwood's Magazine*, October 1859, Vol. 86, 392, for the first quotation, and *What Led to the Discovery of the Source of the Nile*, 251, for the second. James A. Grant later wrote that Speke told him that "Burton, using strong language, declared 'he was not going to see any more lakes.'" Letter to *The Times*, October 28, 1890.

16. Speke to Dr Norton Shaw, July 2, 1858, Royal Geographical Society archives.

17. *Blackwood's Magazine*, September and October 1859, Vol. 86, 395–7, 412n.; *What Led to the Discovery of the Source of the Nile*, 309.

18. See *Life*, I, 312, where the account is taken from the original journal. Burton's shortened description may be seen in *The Lake Regions of Central Africa*, II, 209.

19. Burton, "The Lake Regions of Central Equatorial Africa," *Royal Geographical Society Journal*, XXIX, 20 (1859).

20. *Blackwood's Magazine*, September 1859, Vol. 86, 341.

21. *Life*, II, 424.

22. The most revealing parts of this story were not included in Burton's *The Lake Regions of Central Africa*, II, 235, but published from the original journal by Isabel Burton. See *Life*, I, 322–3.

23. Quoted in *Life*, I, 326.

24. Quoted in *Ibid.*, I, 327.

25. W. E. Frere, searching the strong box in February 1865, found the manuscript and returned it to Burton by way of the Royal Geographical Society, to whom it had been addressed. He stated that he did not know how it found its way there, but suspected that it was the manuscript Burton had sent to Colonel Rigby at Zanzibar, and which had disappeared. Burton said, "The white population of Zanzibar had in those days a great horror of publiction." This was the closest he came to accusing Rigby publicly. A second manuscript, describing Burton's visit to Sa'adani and Kilwa, was stolen from him in Fernando Po, considerably later. It too reappeared. After being missing six years it was purchased by a British colonel in a London bookshop and then left by mistake in Lord Derby's hall. Lord Derby recognized Burton's handwriting and persuaded the colonel to restore it to Burton. "Who shall say there is no destiny in this?" Burton wrote. And he proceeded to publish both lost manuscripts as his two-volume *Zanzibar* in 1872, fifteen years later. See *Zanzibar*, preface, and *Life*, I, 280n., for details.

26. Mrs C. E. B. Russell, *General Rigby, Zanzibar and the Slave Trade*, 243n.

27. Speke, already planning to return with his own expedition, was worried lest these men refuse to accompany him. As he put it later in a letter to Dr Norton Shaw, "I shall have to pay them if the Govt: do not." (Royal Geographical Society

archives.) And on the trip to London he wrote to Rigby urging a formal investigation, one which would minimize his role as "informer" aganst Burton, but which would nevertheless let "justice run its course." (As reported later by Speke in a letter to the Under-Secretary of State for India, December 1, 1859. Quoted in Russell, *General Rigby, Zanzibar and the Slave Trade*, 252.)

28. *Zanzibar*, II, 389–90.

29. *The Lake Regions of Central Africa*, II, 384.

30. The italics are Burton's. See *Life*, I, 327.

CHAPTER XVI. Betrayal and Attack (pp. 167 to 178)

1. Philip Henderson, *The Life of Laurence Oliphant* (London, 1956), 13, 188, 254.

2. *Zanzibar*, II, 390; *Life*, I, 328.

3. *Journal of the Discovery of the Source of the Nile* (New York, 1864), 31.

4. *Zanzibar*, II, 391.

5. *Royal Geographical Society Proceedings* (1858–9), III, 219; *Royal Geographical Society Journal*, (1859), XXIX, xcvii.

6. Speke to Rigby, October 6, 1860 and May 12, 1861, in Mrs C. E. B. Russell, *General Rigby, Zanzibar and the Slave Trade*, 235, 237; Speke obituary, *Blackwood's Magazine*, October 1864, Vol. 96, 514ff.

7. *The Romance of Isabel Lady Burton*, I, 144.

8. Burton published the correspondence in full in Appendix II of *The Lake Regions of Central Africa*. For additional material, see Mrs C. E. B. Russell, *General Rigby, Zanzibar and the Slave Trade*. Unfortunately, Mrs Russell, Rigby's daughter, did not publish the letters in full, as she frankly admits.

9. Philip Henderson, *The Life of Laurence Oliphant*, 125.

10. *Zanzibar*, II, 392, 321.

11. Royal Geographical Society archives.

12. Mrs C. E. B. Russell, *General Rigby, Zanzibar and the Slave Trade*, 255.

13. Speke to Burton, January 17, 1860. Quentin Keynes collection.

14. Quentin Keynes collection. The reply Burton wrote at the end of the letter was dated February 3, 1860.

15. Speke to Shaw, February 6, 1860. Quentin Keynes collection.

16. *Life*, I, 331.

17. Benjamin Speke to Dr Norton Shaw, August 21, 1860. Quentin Keynes collection.

18. April 16, 1860. Quentin Keynes collection.

19. Quoted in *Life*, I, 316.

20. *The True Life of Captain Sir Richard F. Burton*, 163–4.

21. Thomas Wright, *Life of Sir Richard Burton*, I, 241.

22. *Life*, I, 332.

23. *Ibid.*, I, 329n.; W. H. Wilkins, *The Romance of Isabel Lady Burton*, I, 149.

24. W. H. Wilkins, *The Romance of Isabel Lady Burton*, I, 149–51.

25. *Life*, I, 333–6.

26. This letter is in the Houghton collection, Trinity College Library, Cambridge. See also James Pope-Hennessy, *Monckton Milnes: The Flight of Youth, 1851–1885* (London, 1951), 118–19, and Edmond and Jules de Goncourt, *Journal, Mémoires de la vie littéraire* (Monaco, 1956), V, 89–93, (1861–3).

27. January 22, 1860. Trinity College Library.

28. Burton, *The Lake Regions of Central Africa*, II, 206.

29. *Ibid.*, II, 207. Speke's first map, sent to the Royal Geographical Society from Africa, had shown the Kivira to be an influent.

30. This lake, later named Bangeulu, would be "discovered" and mapped by Livingstone in 1868.

31. Royal Geographical Society archives.

32. *The Lake Regions of Central Africa*, I, xiv–xv.

33. Speke to Dr Norton Shaw, October 28, 1859. Royal Geographical Society archives.

34. Royal Geographical Society archives. See also James Augustus Grant, *A Walk Across Africa* (London, 1864), ix. Grant dedicated the book to Speke's memory.

35. Speke to Blackwood, February 1, 1861. By courtesy of Alexander Maitland.

36. *Life*, I, 337–8.

CHAPTER XVII. Salt Lake City (pp. 179 to 189)

1. They were saved from burning by Daisy Letchford Nicastro, who was living with the Burtons in Trieste at the time of Richard Burton's death. A note accompanying the pages indicates that they were sent direct to the British Museum by Mrs. Evelyn Lindenmann Letchford. Isabel Burton describes Burton's two sets of journals in "Sir Richard Burton: an Explanation and Defence," *New Review*, November 1892, 569n.

2. See *Deseret News*, August 29, 1860.

3. See *A Mission to Gelele, King of Dahome, etc.*, 2 vols (London, 1864), II, 186, 189n., and *Zanzibar*, I, 14.

4. *Zanzibar*, I, 14–15.

5. Marcy's book had been published in New York in 1859. Burton's edition appeared in London in 1863.

6. *The City of the Saints*, 68–9, 83, 186, 143.

7. *Ibid.*, 240–1.

8. Mr Dale L. Morgan informs me that the Manuscript History of Brigham Young, in the Historian's Office of the Church of Jesus Christ of Latter-Day Saints, Salt Lake City, states that Burton was in the Historian's Office taking copious notes September 3, 11 and 13, 1860.

9. Richard Walden Hale wrote in his 11-page pamphlet, *Richard F. Burton, a footnote to history* (Boston, 1930), "Burton when soused was a great brawler. His friends were kept busy hunting up influence with Bishop John Lee, Orson Pratt, Tom Kane and others of the Avenging Angels. It took Bishop Lee . . . to keep Burton out of the calaboose." Kane was not even a Mormon; Pratt was a respected "Apostle"; John D. Lee was living at the time in a remote village in southern Utah. For an account of Lee's activities, see Juanita Brooks, *John D. Lee* (Glendale, California, 1962).

10. *The City of the Saints*, 254, 494, 524–534.

11. *Arabian Nights*, X, 199–200; *City of the Saints*, 523.

12. *Royal Geographical Society Proceedings*, (1860), V, 1–2.

13. *The City of the Saints*, 300, 293.

14. This anecdote is told by Thomas Wright in *Life of Sir Richard Burton*, I, 163–4. Monckton Milnes stated that he had heard many Mormon anecdotes from Burton too ribald for publication. See Wemyss Reid, *Life, Letters, and Friendships of Richard Monckton Milnes*, 2 vols (London, 1891), II, 77. Milnes wrote a glowing review of *The City of the Saints* for the *Edinburgh Review*, January 1862, 185–210.

15. See also Fawn M. Brodie, *No Man Knows My History: the life of Joseph Smith, the Mormon Prophet* (New York, 1945) [English edition, *No Man Knows My History (Joseph Smith)* (London, 1963).]

16. *The City of the Saints*, 491, 497.

17. *Ibid.*, 438, 443.

CHAPTER XVIII. The First Seven Months (pp. 190 to 203)

1. W. H. Wilkins, *The Romance of Isabel Lady Burton*, I, 154–5, 158–9.

2. *Arabian Nights*, I, 212n.

3. W. H. Wilkins, *The Romance of Isabel Lady Burton*, I, 162–5.

4. *Life*, I, 342.

5. Georgiana Stisted tells us that her mother was informed only a few days before the ceremony. *The True Life of Captain Sir Richard F. Burton*, 275.

6. *Life*, I, 343. Here Isabel reproduces a photostat of the letter from Richard to her father.

7. *The True Life of Captain Sir Richard F. Burton*, 275.

8. *Ibid.*, 274–5, 309–11. The letters to Mrs Lynn Linton, April 5 and 8, 1896, are in the Quentin Keynes collection.

9. *Life*, I, 344.

10. W. H. Wilkins, *The Romance of Isabel Lady Burton*, I, 161.

11. Written from Dovercourt, Essex. Trinity College collection.

12. *Life*, I, 347–8.

13. James Pope-Hennessy, *Monckton Milnes; The Flight of Youth, 1851–1885*, 6, 133.

14. Edmond and Jules de Goncourt, *Journal, Mémoires de la vie littéraire*, V, 93. James Pope-Hennessy, quoting from a different edition of the journal, writes, "un peau comme sa . . . sur une négresse vivante," *Monckton Milnes: The Flight of Youth, 1851–1885*, 118. Burton's letters asking about Hankey are in Trinity College Library.

15. Trinity College collection. Dr Heinrich Barth, a German explorer, had been in Central Africa, 1850–5, publishing his *Travels and Discoveries in North and Central Africa*, 1857–8. But it is clear from Burton's own letters that it was he and not Barth to whom Hankey was referring.

16. Burton to Leonard Smithers, February 17, 1889. Huntington Library.

17. *Life of Sir Richard Burton*, I, 141–2.

18. Swinburne to Milnes, February 10, 1863, *The Swinburne Letters*, edited by Cecil Y. Lang, 6 vols (Yale University Press, 1959), I, 78.

19. Gosse's essay was first published in *The Swinburne Letters*, 1959, see VI, 244. See also Robert J. Clements, reviewing a 1965 edition of Sade's works, *Saturday Review*, September 11, 1865, 46.

20. *Transatlantic Review*, March 1924, 24.

21. *The Swinburne Letters*, No. 78, I, 124.

22. *Ibid.*, I, xlix.

23. *Ibid.*, No. 79, I, 125.

24. *Abeokuta and the Cameroons Mountains*, I, 110–11.

25. *The Romance of Isabel Lady Burton*, I, 176.

26. *Ibid.*, I, 178.

27. *Life*, I, 348.

28. See Burton's edition of Randolph B. Marcy's *The Prairie Traveller, a Handbook for Overland Expeditions* (London, 1863), 140n.

29. Trinity College collection. These extracts are from two letters.

30. *My Diaries*, 2 vols (New York, 1921), II, 128.

31. *The Amberley Papers*, edited by Bertrand Russell (3rd Earl Russell, grandson of 1st Viscount Amberley), 2 vols (New York, 1937), I, 349–50, January 8–9, 1865.

32. Cf. *Zanzibar*, I, 183, and Burton's letter, January 25, 1861, published in *The Times*, January 30, 1861.

33. August 23, 1861. Trinity College collection.

34. *Wanderings in West Africa, From Liverpool to Fernando Po* (Anon., by F.R.G.S.), 2 vols (London, 1863), I, 1, 3; II, 295.

35. Isabel Burton writes that this poem was written in 1852, but it was not published until 1880, and internal evidence relating to the death of his parents indicates that it could not have been written before 1859. The success of Edward Fitzgerald's *Rubaiyat of Omar Khayyam*, published 1859, unquestionably stimulated Burton in writing the *Kasidah*. There is no way of knowing how much he revised it before publication in 1880.

CHAPTER XIX. The Desperate Quest (pp. 204 to 216)

1. *Wanderings in West Africa*, I, 65–6.
2. *Abeokuta and the Cameroons Mountains*, I, 88.
3. *Wanderings in West Africa*, I, 296.
4. December 22, 1862. Quentin Keynes collection.
5. "Notes on Certain Matters Connected with the Dahoman," *Anthropological Society of London Memoirs*, (1863–4), I, 308. The paper was read on November 18, 1864.
6. W. H. Wilkins, *The Romance of Isabel Lady Burton*, I, 188.
7. Royal Geographical Society archives.
8. Burton to Monckton Milnes, February 17 and March 29, 1863. Trinity College collection. When Burton returned to Madeira in 1881 with Lovett Cameron, en route to the Gold Coast, he wrote nostalgically of his first visit with Isabel, "I need hardly say that we thoroughly enjoyed ourselves; the impressions of that good old time were deep and durable." *To the Gold Coast for Gold*, 2 vols (London, 1883), I, 54.
9. This copy may be seen in the Royal Anthropological Institute library. Isabel Burton's copy of *A Mission to Gelele, King of Dahome* may also be examined there; it is inscribed by Burton, "To my darling wife."
10. *Anthropological Society of London Memoirs* (1863–4), I, 320.
11. *Wanderings in West Africa*, II, 136n., 211.
12. *Ibid.*, I, 274, 222, 239, 267.
13. A damaged brig, the *Harriet*, was sold by auction at Freetown at the request of three Aku natives who had inherited it upon the death of one William Johnson. The brig was sold for £ 280. Burton signed the receipt but left it to the acting-consul, an English trading agent, to remit the money. The agent paid over only £ 29, alleging that the rest of the purchase money had gone into expenses. Rainy complained to the Foreign Office, which sent a naval officer to make an official inquiry. By this time Burton was in Brazil, but was officially blamed for carelessness and forced to pay out of his own salary. Isabel, even more hostile to the Negro than her husband, published a crude caricature of Rainy in her biography of Burton. See I, 355. Christopher Fyfe, *A History of Sierra Leone* (Oxford University Press, 1962), 342, tells the story, as does William Rainy in *The Censor Censured, or the Calumnies of Captain Burton on the Africans of Sierra Leone Refuted and his Conduct Relative to the Purchase Money of the Brig "Harriet" Tested and Examined* (London, 1865).
14. See *Two Trips to Gorilla Land*, II, 318, 320, and *Abeokuta and the Cameroons Mountains*, II, 172.
15. *Abeokuta and the Cameroons Mountains*, I, 43–4.
16. See Christopher Fyfe, *A History of Sierra Leone*, 337; C. W. Newbury, *The Western Slave Coast and its Rulers* (Oxford University Press, 1961), 74; and *Parliamentary Papers* (1865), Q, 294, 512.
17. Trinity College collection.
18. At a meeting of the London Ethnological Society, Chaillu, angered when T. A. Malone intimated that he was a liar, knocked him down. Burton in a letter to *The Times*, July 8, 1861, defended the Frenchman and said Malone had grossly insulted him. Chaillu's mounted gorilla specimens, when exhibited in London in 1861–2, caused a sensation. The first man to give a scientific account of the gorilla anatomy had been Dr Jeffries Wyman, Harvard anatomist, who described it in 1847.
19. *Two Trips to Gorilla Land and the Cataracts of the Congo*, 2 vols (London, 1876), II, 251–2.
20. Trinity College collection.
21. *Two Trips to Gorilla Land*, I, 217–18.
22. Trinity College collection.

23. They were William Snelgrave, 1734, William Smith, 1744, Robert Norris, 1789, Archibald Dalzel, 1793, John M'Leod, 1820, John Duncan, 1847, and Frederick E. Forbes, 1851.

24. May 31, 1863. Trinity College collection.

25. *Ibid.*

26. *A Mission to Gelele, King of Dahome,* II, 72–3. See also Melville J. Herskovits, *Dahomey,* 2 vols (New York, 1938), I, 86n.

27. *Abeokuta and the Cameroons Mountains,* I, 121n.

28. *Anthropological Society of London Memoirs,* (1863–4), I, 319.

29. This item appeared not in *A Mission to Gelele, King of Dahome,* but later in a footnote to Burton's translation of *The Lands of Cazembe, Lacerda's Journey to Cazembe in 1798* (London, 1873), 40n.

30. *A Mission to Gelele, King of Dahome,* II, 20–1, 279, 285, 250.

CHAPTER XX. September Tragedy, 1864 (pp. 217 to 231)

1. *Journal of the Discovery of the Source of the Nile,* 231.

2. A copy of the letter, which never reached Petherick, was printed in the *Royal Geographical Society Proceedings,* VII, 235.

3. *Journal of the Discovery of the Source of the Nile,* 373, 458, 461, 466–7.

4. Speke to William Blackwood, February 1, 1861. A copy of this letter was furnished me through the courtesy of Mr Alexander Maitland. The italics are Speke's.

5. *A Walk Across Africa,* 248.

6. Speke's map turned out to be extremely accurate, far more so than the one drawn by Samuel Baker who, after pressing north to the Lúta Nzigé, greatly exaggerated its size, so anxious was he to claim the glory of the discovery of the Nile source for himself.

7. Speke to Norton Shaw, February 19, 1864, Royal Geographical Society archives; Speke in a public address at Taunton, late December 1863. For a detailed account of Speke's first meeting with Petherick, see also John Petherick, *Travels in Central Africa,* 2 vols (London, 1869), James Macqueen's article in the *Morning Advertiser,* as reproduced in Richard Burton, *The Nile Basin,* 169, as well as Speke's own *Journal of the Discovery of the Source of the Nile.* Harry Johnston, *The Nile Quest* (New York, 1903), 100, exonerates Petherick of any complicity in the slave trade, noting that it was his anti-slave trade activities that had caused the Arab traders to start a campaign of intrigue against him. This, plus Speke's charges, had resulted in his consulship being revoked.

8. *Royal Geographical Society Proceedings,* June 22, 1863, VII, 218.

9. Charles Beke, quoting the *Taunton Courier,* which reported Speke's speech of December 23, 1863, cited Speke's phrase about being ungenerous in a letter to the *Athenaeum,* written December 28, 1863 and published January 2, 1864, 22–3. Speke's letter to the *Athenaeum* was published on January 23, 1864, 121. It was dated January 14, 1864.

10. *Zanzibar,* II, 395.

11. Moreover, Speke had revised his original estimate of the altitude of Lake Victoria from 3,550 to 3,745 feet (a remarkably close measurement to the actual height of 3,720), but had estimated the height of the Nile below Ripon Falls as 3,308 feet, which would have necessitated a waterfall measuring several hundred feet. Ripon Falls was only twelve feet high, as Macqueen was quick to note. Speke had pointed out however that any thermometer such as the one he used could be inaccurate by as much as 300 feet; and he placed a question mark by his Ripon Falls, and had warned that his Nile readings were doubtful. Still, since he stated his altitude readings with extreme precision, he laid himself open to attack on this matter. For Macqueen's attack, see Burton, *The Nile Basin,* 67–195.

12. Philip Henderson, *The Life of Laurence Oliphant,* 125.

13. Speke argued this in a dispatch to Sir Roderick Murchison even before arriving home. See *Royal Geographical Society Proceedings*, May 25, 1863, VI, 185–7, where Murchison read the dispatch.

14. *Life*, II, 426.

15. Burton later defensively admitted in a speech to the Royal Geographical Society, November 29, 1875, that from Arab accounts in 1858 he had "laid down the lake as 240 miles in length by 80 miles in breadth," but in his publications would allow only that part to be put in which had actually been surveyed. *Royal Geographical Society Proceedings* (1875–6), XX, 49–50.

16. When asked about the height of Tanganyika, at the Royal Geographical Society, December 11, 1871, Burton stated that Speke had supposed the height to be 1,800 feet, but he had found a pencilled note by Speke, never before published, that his thermometer was 1,000 feet below actuality, and the height was therefore 2,800 feet, considerably above that of the Lüta Nzigé (Albert Nyanza). The actual height of Tanganyika, as it turned out, was 2,536 feet. See *Royal Geographical Society Proceedings*, XVI, 131.

17. *Life*, II, 426.

18. *Zanzibar*, II, 398, and *Life*, II, 426.

19. See Dr Karl Menninger, *Man Against Himself* (New York, 1938), a classic study of suicide.

20. *Life of Sir Richard Burton*, I, 192.

21. The first letter, September 21, 1864, written from Bath, is in the Quentin Keynes collection; the second was quoted by Byron Farwell in *Burton*, 241.

22. *Zanzibar*, II, 398.

23. James A. Grant, *A Walk Across Africa*, 347.

24. *The Times* obituary appeared September 19, 1864, Burton's reply September 23, 1864.

25. See *Blackwood's Magazine*, January 1865, Vol 97, 100, 104, 116, and Burton's own copy of *The Nile Basin*, Royal Anthropological Institute library, which contains many of the critical reviews.

26. *Life*, II, 426.

27. The elegy differs markedly in style and shows far more poetic talent than the single example of Isabel's poetry, a poem in praise of her husband which she published somewhat timorously in the appendix of her first book, *The Inner Life of Syria, Palestine, and the Holy Land*, 2 vols (London, 1876), II, 307–8. The elegy appeared in *Fraser's Magazine*, February 1869, 165–8, with the title, "Who Last Wins." Isabel ostensibly described the circumstances of the visit to the studio as an introduction. Burton reproduced both the introduction and the poem in his *Zanzibar*, II, 399–404.

28. Henry Stanley, *How I Found Livingstone* (New York, 1887), 455. See also George Seaver, *David Livingstone: His Life and Letters*, 606, 625.

29. *Royal Geographical Society Proceedings* (1875–6), XX, 50.

30. See his *Supplementary Papers to the Mwáta Cazembe*. A few copies of this controversial material on the Nile, rejected by his editor in publishing his *Lands of the Cazembe*, were struck off in 1873. There is a copy in the Royal Anthropological Institute library. See especially xiii. This 43-page pamphlet is now extremely rare.

31. See the *Athenaeum*, November 3, 1877, 568–9, and Richard Burton, *Camoens: His Life and His Lusiads*, 2 vols (London, 1881), II, 514–17n.

CHAPTER XXI. The Taming (pp. 232 to 246)

1. W. H. Wilkins, *The Romance of Isabel Lady Burton*, I, 264.

2. *Portraits of the Sixties* (London, 1903), 174.

3. W. H. Wilkins, *The Romance of Isabel Lady Burton*, I, 227.

4. Quentin Keynes collection.

5. *Life*, I, 395–7.

6. Redesdale, *Memories*, II, 562–4; V. Lovett Cameron, "Burton as I knew Him," *Fortnightly Review*, LIV, 878–84, December 1890.

7. *Life*, I, 392–5. Only a few copies were preserved. The poem was reprinted, November 1940, by the Sutro Branch, California State Library, as *Occasional Papers*, Reprint Series No. 24. Burton's own copy is in the Royal Anthropological Institute library.

8. W. H. Wilkins, *The Romance of Isabel Lady Burton*, I, 242–3.

9. For Isabel Burton's letters to her mother, December 15, 1865, January 17, May 14, 1866 and April 13, 1867, see *ibid.*, I, 251–2, 257, 270.

10. This is Burton's spelling. A more common one, Vetālapañchaviṁśati.

11. See *Vikram and the Vampire, or Tales of Hindu Devilry* (London, 1870), 71. This paragraph, from the story, "In Which a Man Deceives a Woman," cannot be found in Arthur W. Ryder, *Twenty-Two Goblins*, translated from the Sanskrit, London, 1917, or in M. B. Emeneau, *Jambhaladatta's Version of the Vetālapañcaviṁśati* (American Oriental Society series, IV, New Haven, 1934).

12. *Life*, I, 425.

13. *The Highlands of Brazil*, I, 189.

14. *Life*, I, 445.

15. W. H. Wilkins, *The Romance of Isabel Lady Burton*, I, 340, 348. Wilkins had the benefit of a long manuscript which Isabel had written about this journey, which was never published.

16. *The Highlands of Brazil*, II, 444–6, 457.

17. *My Diaries*, II, 128.

18. W. H. Wilkins, *The Romance of Isabel Lady Burton*, I, 343, and *Life*, I, 449.

19. Isabel Burton to her mother, May 3, 1868. Quoted in *The Romance of Isabel Lady Burton*, I, 345.

20. *Letters from the Battle-fields of Paraguay* (London, 1870), 32.

21. *The Highlands of Brazil*, I, 332, 397.

22. *Letters from the Battle-fields of Paraguay*, 168.

23. *Ibid.*, 31, 27.

24. *My Diaries*, II, 129–31.

25. The Tichborne Claimant was probably originally a London butcher named Arthur Orton. Roger Tichborne had been drowned off the coast of South America in 1854. His mother, who refused to believe him dead, fell easy victim to Orton's impersonation. Orton pursued his claim for seven years with amazing success, but was finally, 1874, sentenced to fourteen years in prison. Byron Farwell obtained a copy of Burton's testimony in this trial, Tichborne v. Lushington. See *Burton*, 293–4. Burton indicated at the trial that he had spent only a single evening with the Claimant, but Isabel Burton stated that he had travelled wih him for a week. Blunt wrote that he saw them together often in Buenos Aires. He added, quite incorrectly, that they had travelled together westwards across the Pampas and on to the Pacific. See *Life*, I, 453, 593, 596, and Douglas Woodruff, *The Tichborne Claimant, a Victorian Mystery* (London, 1957).

26. "Memories of Richard Burton," *Transatlantic Review*, March 1924.

27. *Letters from the Battle-fields of Paraguay*, 414. Burton in testifying at the Tichborne trial was questioned about his trip across the Andes, and spoke of his brush with the natives as "a very near thing." See Byron Farwell, *Burton*, 294.

28. *Unexplored Syria*, 2 vols (London, 1872), I, 3.

29. *Life*, I, 455. Burton had crossed the Andes on mules to Santiago, pushed on to Valparaiso, and then sailed to Lima.

30. Isabel to Richard Burton, January 7, 1869, in W. H. Wilkins, *The Romance of Isabel Lady Burton*, I, 352. Lord Stanley (Edward Henry Stanley, 15th Earl of Derby) was Secretary of State for Foreign Affairs, 1866–8 and again, 1874–8, under Disraeli.

CHAPTER XXII. Damascus (pp. 247 to 262)

1. *Life*, I, 485.
2. The elegy was first published in *Fortnightly Review*, July 1, 1892, LVIII, 1–5. For the letters to Alice Swinburne and James McNeill Whistler, see *The Swinburne Letters*, II, 23, 21.
3. *Ibid.*, II, 24.
4. *Ibid.*, I, 223–4.
5. "Verses on the Death of Richard Burton," *New Review*, IV, 97–9, February 1891.
6. *The Swinburne Letters*, VI, 235.
7. *Life*, I, 459.
8. *Arabian Nights*, VI, 206n.
9. Quoted in *Life*, I, 507.
10. Elliot's role was not apparent to Burton until the publication in March 1872 by the Foreign Office of *The Case of Captain Burton, late H.B.M.'s Consul at Damascus*, which included much of the official correspondence relating to Burton's troubled time as consul.
11. *The Inner Life of Syria*, II, 305. It was written when Richard was away on a long trip to Iceland. Burton wrote a short account of his Damascus stay, which appeared posthumously in *Wanderings in Three Continents*, edited 1901 by W. H. Wilkins. It appears under the heading, "Through Syria to Palmyra."
12. *Life*, I, 572, and *The Inner Life of Syria*, II, 248.
13. *The Inner Life of Syria*, I, 223, 165, 154.
14. *Ibid.*, I, 365, and *Life*, I, 506.
15. *A Mission to Gelele, King of Dahome*, II, 73.
16. Richard Burton, *The Jew, The Gypsy, and El Islam*, published posthumously, edited W. H. Wilkins (London, 1898), 327.
17. *Unexplored Syria*, I, 3; II, 258. In the latter quotation Burton was paraphrasing and "reversing" a line by Francis Palgrave.
18. Edward Henry Palmer, in August 1882, was ambushed and murdered in the Sinai desert when on a mission for the British government. For a time it was thought he had escaped, and Burton was officially commissioned to search for him. But his death was confirmed by Sir Charles Warren before Burton could get beyond Ghazzeh. For Burton's own story of this search and his obituary of Palmer, see *Life*, II, 242 and 591–616.
19. *Ibid.*, I, 478, 505, 511; *The Inner Life of Syria*, I, 133.
20. *Life*, I, 503–4.
21. *Ibid.*, I, 577. Isabel here quotes from an article written anonymously by a Damascus missionary, who counted Burton "a fearless and honest friend." One missionary, Mentor Mott, superintendent of the British school at Beirut, remained a bitter enemy. Burton had forbidden him to distribute Christian tracts in Damascus, believing them incendiary and dangerous.
22. Isabel Burton, *The Inner Life of Syria*, I, 143; II, 8.
23. *Life*, I, 534, 600–1.
24. *Ibid.*, I, 537; *The Case of Captain Burton, late H.B.M.'s Consul at Damascus*, 23. Eldridge's letter was dated November 30, 1870.
25. *The Inner Life of Syria*, II, 29–30, 76.
26. *Ibid.*, II, 112–63.
27. *Burton*, 279; Isabel Burton, *The Inner Life of Syria*, II, 219–27.
28. *Life*, I, 517–20. Here Isabel reproduced Burton's original letter, and a copy of the Wali's forgery, which Burton had obtained from the Foreign Office in London. See also Burton, *Unexplored Syria*, I, 252.
29. For this correspondence, see *The Case of Captain Burton, late H.B.M.'s Consul at Damascus*, 99ff.
30. For details of this story, see *Life*, I, 546–65, 597–8.

31. For details of the dismissal, see *ibid.*, 548, 568–9, 597; and Isabel Burton, *The Inner Life of Syria*, II, 277–8.

32. *The Inner Life of Syria*, II, 282–3.

CHAPTER XXIII. "This Desperately Learned Man" (pp. 263 to 275)

1. As quoted by Thomas Wright, *Life of Sir Richard Burton*, I, 249.

2. *The True Life of Captain Sir Richard F. Burton*, 363.

3. *Life*, I, 589.

4. Laura Friswell Myall. *In the Sixties and Seventies, Impressions of Literary People and Others* (Boston, 1906), 44. Isabel Burton's letter to Mrs Friswell is now in the Edwards Metcalf collection.

5. Thomas Wright, *Life of Sir Richard Burton*, I, 249.

6. *The Highlands of Brazil*, I, 403n.

7. Edwards Metcalf has a letter from Burton to a publisher, Grattan Geary, May 12, 1877, saying that his manuscript on the Jews was ready, but adding, "you must tell me that you want it, or rather that you are not afraid of it." The essay, as finally published in *The Jew, The Gypsy, and El Islam*, 1898, has always been an embarrassment to Burton biographers, who usually skirt the issue of his anti-semitism, overlooking its importance as evidence of his own guilt and self-hatred. Even Wilkins could not bring himself to publish the most offensive portion of "The Jew"—a section on the alleged ritual murder among the Sephardic Jews of Damascus, and the murder of one Padro Tomaso in 1840. The manuscript of this portion was "sold" in 1908 to Manners Sutton, who tried to publish it. But a suit brought by Isabel Burton's literary trustee, D. L. Alexander, who held that the manuscript had been only loaned to Wilkins, prevented publication. See *The Times*, March 28, 1911.

Isabel Burton, embittered no less than her husband towards the Jews of Damascus, lashed out at them in *The Inner Life of Syria*, published 1876.

8. Quoted in *Life*, I, 591.

9. Thomas Wright, *Life of Sir Richard Burton*, II, 47.

10. "Brimstone's" letters were published August 29 and September 19, 1874, in reply to Burton's account of the sulphur mines as published in the *Mining Standard*, November 1, 1872. Burton republished part of the correspondence in *Ultima Thule; or A Summer in Iceland*, II, 300.

11. *Ibid.*, II, 160; I, 353.

12. *Life*, II, 3.

13. Thomas Wright, *Life of Sir Richard Burton*, I, 251.

14. Isabel reproduced the *World* article, "Captain Richard F. Burton at Trieste," in *Life*, II, 4ff. See also *ibid.*, II, 17.

15. *Life*, 269, reprinted from an article on Burton by Edwin de Leon, in the *Argonaut*.

16. Seaton Dearden, *Burton of Arabia* (New York, 1937), 313.

17. See A. H. Sayce, *The Hittites, the story of a forgotten empire* (London, 1890), 57; Curt W. Marek, *The Secret of the Hittites* (New York, 1956), 17; William Wright, *The Empire of the Hittites* (New York, 1884). H. V. Hilprecht, in *Explorations in Bible Lands During the Nineteenth Century* (Philadelphia, 1903), credits Burton with a "first" in the publication of his Hamath inscriptions. See 756.

18. *Unexplored Syria*, II, 329–30; *Athenaeum*, April 13, 1872, 464–7; James B. Pritchard, ed., *Ancient Near Eastern Texts Relating to the Old Testament* (Princeton, 1955), 320ff., and *Archaeology of the Old Testament* (Princeton, 1958), 103–6.

19. The Italics are my own. A collection of these reviews are in Burton's copy in the Royal Anthropological Institute library. A note from his publisher indicates that by February 6, 1877, out of 1,500 copies only 230 had been sold. The contract

provided that Burton would get three shillings each after the sale of 750 copies. *Etruscan Bologna* suffered by comparison with the elegantly written *Cities and Cemeteries of Western Etruria*, by George Dennis, British consul in Italy, describing discoveries made between 1842 and 1847.

20. *Life*, II, 255.

21. Burton had theorized about the origin of the gypsies in *Sindh, and the Races that Inhabit the Valley of the Indus*. His essay on the gypsies was published after his death as a part of *The Jew, The Gypsy, and El Islam*, 1898.

22. Isabel Burton, *A.E.I., Arabia, Egypt, India*, 95.

23. *Sind Revisited*, I, 47, 257.

24. *A.E.I., Arabia, Egypt, India*, 235. In 1879 she published a 31-page pamphlet, "Prevention of Cruelty and Anti-Vivisection," in London. Much of it appeared in *A.E.I.*

25. *Life*, II, 258–9.

26. *A.E.I.*, 248–9.

CHAPTER XXIV. The Dual Man (pp. 276 to 289)

1. *Life*, II, 268.

2. *Lord Beaconsfield, A Sketch by Captain Richard F. Burton*, 12 pp. (1881), 7. Isabel Burton dates the writing of this indirectly in *Life*, II, 212. Norman Penzer was uncertain of the date.

3. Thomas Wright, *Life of Sir Richard Burton*, II, 23.

4. Quentin Keynes possesses the copy of this review, which was at one time among Burton's papers.

5. Edwards Metcalf collection.

6. Subsequent translators of Camoens have acknowledged indebtedness to Burton. Aubrey F. G. Bell wrote, "Burton made a fine poem out of his translation, but it has perhaps as much of himself as of Camoens." See his *Luis de Camões* (Oxford University Press, 1923), ix. Jeremiah D. M. Ford wrote that Burton "has himself a leading place among those who have brought the *Lusiadas* into English verse." See his introduction to *The Lusiad by Luis de Camoens*, translated by Sir Richard Fanshawe (Harvard, 1946), xxvii.

Leonard Bacon, who translated *The Lusiads* for the Hispanic Society of America, 1950, and Geoffrey Bullough, who edited Sir Richard Fanshawe's translation, with an introduction, 1963, both acknowledged that Burton's translation had been of much value to them.

7. *Camoens: His Life and His Lusiads*, II, 677.

8. Edwards Metcalf has a letter from Khedive to Burton, signed simply Ismail, promising him concessions in the Midian area.

9. *The Gold-Mines of Midian and the Ruined Midianite Cities* (London, 1878), 1.

10. *Land of the Midian (Revisited)*, 2 vols (London, 1879), I, ix. For the itineraries, see *Royal Geographical Society Journal* (1878–9), XLIX, 1–150.

11. *Land of the Midian (Revisited)*, II, 260.

12. Article from *West African Mines*, quoted in *Life*, II, 229.

13. For Gordon's letters to Burton, see W. H. Wilkins, *The Romance of Isabel Lady Burton*, II, 645–75. See also *Life*, II, 43.

14. *Academy*, July 11, 1885, 19.

15. See Frank Harris, *Contemporary Portraits*, 194, and two of Burton's book reviews in the *Academy*, January 19, 1884, 46, and October 20, 1888, 249–50.

16. *Life*, II, 181.

17. *Ibid.*, II, 177.

18. *Supplemental Nights*, I, 70–2n. For Burton's article, "How to Deal with the Slave Scandal in Egypt," and several of his letters to Lord Granville, see *Life*, II, 195–210.

19. Quoted in Francis Hitchman, *Richard F. Burton*, II, 402.
20. *Ibid.*, II, 427.
21. "Burton as I knew Him," *Fortnightly Review*, December 1890, LIV, 878–84.
22. *The Book of the Sword*, xiii, xv, xviii, 184; *Arabian Nights*, X, 108.
23. *Life*, II, 273.

CHAPTER XXV. The Unembarrassed Mind (pp. 290 to 299)

1. From Burton's 1886 edition, as reprinted (London, 1963) with introduction and notes by Alan Hull Walton, 230.
2. See Norman St John-Stevas, *Obscenity and the Law* (London, 1956), and Alec Craig, *The Banned Books of England* (London, 1937), 46.
3. See Wayland Young, *Eros Denied* (London, 1965), 197.
4. *Supplemental Nights*, VII, 404, 439.
5. *Ibid.*, V, 42n.
6. For details, see Norman St John-Stevas, *Obscenity and the Law*, 59.
7. *Anthropological Society of London Memoirs* (1865–6), II, 262–3.
8. Quoted by E. W. Braybrook, *Royal Anthropological Institute Journal* (1891), XX, 295–8. See also Burton's Preface to *Arabian Nights*.
9. *Life*, II, 439–40.
10. Burton listed in *Arabian Nights*, X, 201, nine or ten works commonly held to be pornography, but which he insisted were sober medical treatises of the East.
11. Foreword, *Arabian Nights*.
12. *Supplemental Nights*, VII, 438; *Arabian Nights*, X, 200.
13. Pp. 158–9.
14. *Arabian Nights*, IV, 32n.
15. See his account in Henry S. Ashbee (who used the pseudonym Pisanus Fraxi), *Catena Librorum Tacendorum* (London, 1885), 462–3. (Privately printed.)
16. Thomas Wright, *Life of John Payne*, 96. See also Gerhson Legman's introduction to *My Secret Life*, 1966, published by Grove Press.
17. Thomas Wright, *Life of Sir Richard Burton*, II, 62, 66.
18. See John W. Spellman's introduction to the *Kama Sutra*, published (New York, 1962) with a foreword by Santha Rama Rau. The phrase "professional innocent" is Robert J. Clements'. See his "More Wisdom from the Orient," *Saturday Review*, August 25, 1962, 23.
19. "Must We Burn Vatsayana," *Encounter*, March 1964, 70.
20. Burton was already familiar with the Arabic original; he had referred to it in *Pilgrimage to El-Medinah and Meccah* (II, 19–20) as the work of Shaykh al-Nafzawi. For details of the printing history, see Alan Hull Walton's introduction to *The Perfumed Garden of Shaykh Nefzawi* (1963), based on Burton's 1886 translation. Walton amended the spelling of Burton's original title and expurgated his version slightly.

Burton would supervise the printing of two other secret books by the Kama Shastra Society, *The Beharistan*, 1887, and *The Gulistan*, 1888. Both were translated by Edward Rehatsek, scholar of Indian lore who spent most of his life in India. See F. F. Arbuthnot, "Life and Labours of Mr Rehatsek," *Journal of the Royal Asiatic Society*, July 1892; also, Norman M. Penzer, *An Annotated Bibliography of Sir Richard Francis Burton*, 162.
21. *Life*, II, 443n.
22. *Ibid.*, II, 348.

CHAPTER XXVI. The Nights (pp. 300 to 311)

1. Burton, in *Academy*, October 23, 1886, wrote that he had found three separate translations of Galland in Hindustani.
2. *Arabian Nights*, X, 110–11; *Supplemental Nights*, VII, 422.

3. *Arabian Nights*, X, 203–4.

4. Also spelled Hezār efsāneh. See Alf Laila Wa-Laila, an account by J. Oestrup, in *Encyclopaedia of Islam*.

5. *Arabian Nights*, X, 166.

6. Burton had originally planned to collaborate on the translation with Dr John Steinhaeuser, with himself translating the poetry and Steinhaeuser the prose. These plans were laid as early as 1852. After Steinhaeuser's untimely death Burton fell heir to only a few of his papers. In a letter to the *Athenaeum*, November 26, 1881, he stated that he began to work "fitfully," "amid a host of obstructions," and that "in the spring of 1879 the tedious process of copying began and the book commenced to take finished form." But it could not, he added, be finished without "a year's hard labour." Biographer Thomas Wright, however, insists that Burton told Payne in May 1882 when they met in London that he had no manuscript of any kind beyond "a sheet or two of notes" (see Wright, *Life of Sir Richard Burton*, II, 37). There must have been more than this, for Burton showed Lord Redesdale "the first two or three chapters" in Damascus in 1871 (see Redesdale, *Memories*, II, 573).

7. Thomas Wright, *Life of Sir Richard Burton*, II, 35.

8. *Ibid.*, II, 42.

9. Thomas Wright, *Life of John Payne*, 102.

10. Thomas Wright, *Life of Sir Richard Burton*, II, 53. See also *Supplemental Nights*, VII, 390.

11. See Derrick S. Bailey, *Homosexuality and the Western Christian Tradition* (London, 1955), 152.

12. *Life*, II, 284. The printer of Havelock Ellis's volume on sexual inversion was prosecuted and heavily fined, in 1898. Ellis had hoped to defend his book in court but the printer capitulated without a struggle. The book was denounced as "lewd, wicked, bawdy, scandalous, and obscene." See Alec Craig, *The Banned Books of England*, 61.

13. See his long footnote on "the immorality of the Old Testament," complete with chapter and verse. *Arabian Nights*, X, 180–1n.

14. Burton included extracts from seventy-eight reviews in his *Supplemental Nights*. They range from good to ecstatic. See VII, 457–500.

15. *Edinburgh Review*, Vol. 164, 166ff., July 1886.

16. *Supplemental Nights*, VII, 431.

17. *Life*, II, 442.

18. Thomas Wright, *Life of Sir Richard Burton*, II, 54.

19. *Life*, II, 262.

20. *Ibid.*, II, 285, 290.

21. *Supplemental Nights*, VII, 452.

22. See the changes in her own hand in the copy in the Royal Anthropological Institute. Actually Isabel emended the story still more to make it appear that the old man had attempted to murder the youth. Compare Isabel's edition, II, 456, with Burton's, IV, 45. After her husband's death she issued a "library edition" of the *Nights* with all the material on homosexuality expunged, but very little else. See *The Book of the Thousand Nights and a Night, Lady Burton's Edition of her Husband's Arabian Nights* . . . 6 vols (London, 1886–8[?]).

23. As noted in *Supplemental Nights*, VII, 452. "The Black Book of the Arabian Nights" was not printed in Burton's lifetime. In 1964 a book comprising very much the same material was published as *Love, War and Fancy, the social and sexual customs of the East*, edited by D. Kenneth Walker.

CHAPTER XXVII. This Final Frailty, This Sad Eclipse (pp. 312 to 324)

1. Edwards Metcalf collection.

2. *Life*, II, 311.

3. *Ibid.*, II, 324.

4. *Ibid.*, II, 313.

5. The letter to Mrs Friswell, July 28, 1885, is in the Edwards Metcalf papers. See also W. H. Wilkins, *The Romance of Isabel Lady Burton*, II, 634.

6. James Pope-Hennessy, *Monckton Milnes: The Flight of Youth, 1851–1885*, 253.

7. *Academy*, August 22, 1885, 118; and March 27, 1886, 212.

8. *Life*, II, 448, 267.

9. For his discussion of Yoga, see his speech, "Spiritualism in Eastern Lands," reprinted in *Life*, II, 137–59. Norman Penzer also published the speech, *Selected Papers on Anthropology, Travel and Exploration, by Sir Richard Burton* (London, 1924), 184–210. For the ironic comment on spiritualism, see *Life*, II, 137.

10. Burton to Dr Charles Tuckey, April 24, 1889, quoted in Thomas Wright, *Life of Sir Richard Burton*, II, 208; *Life*, 139–42.

11. *A Glance at the "Passion-Play"* (London, 1881), 166, 139.

12. *Life*, II, 337.

13. See F. Grenfell Baker, "Sir Richard Burton as I Knew Him," *Cornhill Magazine*, No. 304; October 1921, 411–23; and *Life*, II, 338.

14. Edwards Metcalf collection. See also *Life*, II, 339.

15. *Life*, II, 364, 401.

16. If so, it was burned with his diaries. See Henry M. Stanley, *Autobiography*, edited by his wife Dorothy Stanley (London, 1912), 423–4.

17. Isabel Burton to Leonard Smithers, February 18, 1888. Huntington Library.

18. *Ibid.*

19. *Saturday Review*, LXV, 110–11, January 28, 1888.

20. Isabel Burton to Leonard Smithers, February 18, 1888. Huntington Library.

21. Georgiana Stisted, *The True Life of Captain Sir Richard F. Burton*, 409; and *Life*, II, 364.

22. Burton's edition was published after his death, in 1893. Apparently Isabel did not tamper with the manuscript. Leonard Smithers wrote to her, December 12, 1893, "I'm glad you saw no reason to alter Pentamerone." This letter is in the Edwards Metcalf collection. A new edition, with a foreword by William A. Drake, appeared in 1943.

23. A brochure from the Erotica Biblion Society advertising the *Priapeia* at £2 12s, reducible on payment before December 1, 1888 to £2 2s net, may be seen among the Burton manuscripts in the British Museum.

24. See his letters, May 12 and 19, 1890, in the Huntington Library. The last quotation is from an undated letter, also in the Huntington Library.

25. These letters are in the Huntington Library. Edwards Metcalf owns the copy of the *Priapeia* which he and Burton at one time planned to publish, complete with numerous pasted in illustrations, which Isabel Burton would have considered extremely pornographic. The 1890 edition reproduced none of them.

26. E. A. Havelock, *The Lyric Genius of Catullus* (Oxford, 1939), 117, in referring to the poems to boys says that "to place the label homosexual on these expressions of feeling is totally misleading." Burton seems to have felt otherwise. Smithers stated in his preface that "Sir Richard laid great stress on the necessity of thoroughly annotating each translation from an erotic (and especially a paederastic) point of view, but subsequent circumstances caused me to abandon that intention." *Catullus* was privately printed in 1894, with prefaces by Isabel Burton and Smithers, as well as by Burton.

27. The Edwards Metcalf collection contains numerous letters between Isabel Burton and Leonard Smithers concerning the *Catullus* publication. Despite great tact, he was unable to prevent her mutilation. By this time Smithers was acting as Lady Burton's lawyer and literary agent. The Huntington Library also has a collection of letters which Isabel Burton exchanged with Smithers.

28. From the *Journal* of the North-China Branch of the Royal Asiatic Society, New Series, XI, 143–84 (1877).

29. The letters to Smithers are in the Huntington Library; the letter to Payne, January 28, 1890, is in Thomas Wright, *Life of John Payne*, 103.

30. Huntington Library. A pirated edition, almost but not quite identical, had also appeared in 1886.

31. Quentin Keynes has an important four-page typewritten document, Isabel Burton, "My Deposition Regarding the Scented Garden," in which she threatens prosecution to anyone who should print *The Scented Garden* and claim it to be a translation by her husband. This manuscript includes a printer's statement which bears out her contention that the manuscript she burned was indeed almost finished. It called for 882 pages in the main text, with a preface of 100 pages, 50 pages of a "parody of sermons," an excursus of 200 pages, with an extra 50 pages identified as "Law & Prophets." Burton's diary entry, March 21, 1890, was quoted in *Life*, II, 441.

32. Thomas Wright, *Life of Sir Richard Burton*, II, 217.

33. W. H. Wilkins, *The Romance of Isabel Lady Burton*, II, 723, quoting Isabel Burton's letter to the *Morning Post*, January 19, 1891.

34. Thomas Wright, *Life of Sir Richard Burton*, II, 217. Wright says that Arbuthnot received the letter and that Isabel knew about it.

35. *Life*, II, 335.

36. Edwards Metcalf collection.

37. *Life*, II, 378n., 408.

38. *Ibid.*, II, 413–14.

CHAPTER XXVIII. The Burning (pp. 325 to 331)

1. These stories are told by Thomas Wright, *Life of Sir Richard Burton*, II, 252–5.

2. See *Life*, II, 416–21, 426–33, for details of the two funerals and Burton's tomb. The marble door was broken by vandals in 1952, thanks to rumours that the coffins were covered with gold and jewels. Monsignor H. Gibney bricked up the door and covered it with cement to prevent further desecration.

3. Francis Galton, *Memories of My Life*, 202; Georgiana Stisted, *The True Life of Captain Sir Richard F. Burton*, 414.

4. November 24, 1892, *The Swinburne Letters*, VI, 45. The elegy appeared in *Fortnightly Review*, LVIII, 1–5, July 1, 1892.

5. Isabel replied indignantly in "Sir Richard Burton: an Explanation and a Defence," *New Review*, VII, 562–78, November 1892.

6. *Journal of the Society for Psychical Research*, 1897–8, VIII, 3–7. Isabel also had a canvas tent erected in her garden at Mortlake, where in the summer she entertained friends. Here séances were also held.

7. Quentin Keynes collection. At some time during her last years Isabel Burton wrote a document called "Divine Hands of Our Saviour," which she did send to Cardinal Vaughan and Father Cafferata in London for revision. This we learn from the correspondence between Isabel Burton and Leonard Smithers now in the Edwards Metcalf collection. The letters indicate that 1,000 copies of "Divine Hands" were printed in 1893. Curiously, there is no mention of this publication anywhere else, and its nature remains as mysterious as the disposition of the entire printing.

8. Reproduced in full in W. H. Wilkins, *The Romance of Isabel Lady Burton*, II, 722–6.

9. *Ibid.*, II, 731–2.

10. *Ibid.*, II, 759.

11. Isabel Burton to Leonard Smithers, July 17, 1892. Huntington Library.

12. Edwards Metcalf possesses the contract Isabel signed with Chapman and Hall. She was given £ 1,500 outright for an edition of 2,500 copies. Later she was granted a royalty of five shillings per copy on the American edition.

13. *An Annotated Bibliography of Sir Richard Francis Burton*, ix. Burton's jour-

nal, which burned when Penzer's home was destroyed in the London blitz during World War II, was apparently written in 1876. Photostats of four pages from this journal, entitled "Pages from the only remaining Burton Note-Book," appeared in a 95-page pamphlet, "Anthropological Notes on The Sotadic Zone of Sexual Inversion Throughout the World, including some observations on Social and Sexual Relations of the Mohammedan Empire, by Sir Richard Burton," issued privately by the Falstaff Press. This pamphlet, undated, comes from Burton's Terminal Essay in *Arabian Nights*. What makes it rare are the illustrations, photographs taken from "Dr Magnus Hirschfeld's Institute of Sexual Science and Rare Burton Collectanea." A note following the photographs of Burton's 1876 journal states, "From the author's collection. Presented by Madame Nicastro, sister of Albert Letchford." This would indicate that the pamphlet was edited by Norman Penzer himself.

14. *Life*, II, 409.
15. *Ibid.*, II, 261.
16. *Arabian Nights*, X, 156.
17. A clipping from the *Westminster Gazette* prints the will dated December 28, 1895 (Quentin Keynes collection). Lady Burton also directed that most of her husband's remaining private papers were to be burned, according to instructions.

CHAPTER XXIX. Burton (pp. 332 to 338)

1. Isabel Burton, "The Reviewer Reviewed," *Camoens: His Life and His Lusiads*, II, 719–20.
2. "Spiritualism in Eastern Lands," reprinted in *Life*, II, 154. The Italics are Isabel Burton's.
3. Letter to Lady Guendolen Ramsden, October 31, 1893, quoted in W. H. Wilkins, *The Romance of Isabel Lady Burton*, II, 759–60.

APPENDIX. The Burton-Payne Controversy (pp. 341 to 343)

1. Thomas Wright, *Life of John Payne*, 186.
2. *An Annotated Bibliography of Sir Richard Francis Burton*, 319.
3. See Duncan B. Macdonald, "On Translating the Arabian Nights," *Nation*, Vol. 71, 167–8, 185–6, August 30 and September 6, 1900.
4. *Arabian Nights*, I, xii.
5. *Alaeddin and the Enchanted Lamp; Zein ul Asnan and the King of the Jinn: Two Stories Done Into English from the Recently Discovered Arabic Text* (London, Villon Society, 1889). A copy may be seen in the Royal Anthropological Society library among Burton's books.
6. Ameen Rihani, "The Coming of the Arabian Nights," *Bookman*, XXXV, 503–8, June 1912.
7. John Payne, *The Book of the Thousand Nights and One Night*, 1901 edition, IX, 375.
8. *An Annotated Bibliography of Sir Richard Francis Burton*, 317.
9. "The Ensorcelled Prince," *Arabian Nights*, I, 72. Cf. John Payne, 1901 edition, I, 160.
10. See Norman M. Penzer, *An Annotated Bibliography of Sir Richard Francis Burton*, 318–20, for his own listing of examples of the superiority of Burton's choices and the extreme precision of his translation.

BIBLIOGRAPHY

NORMAN M. PENZER, in an act of devotion, compiled and published in 1923 a remarkable annotated bibliography of Richard Burton's works which for many years made any other bibliography superfluous. It contained all the editions of Burton's books and translations up to 1923, as well as listings of Burton's pamphlets, articles, book reviews, and letters to the press. Penzer also included a critical analysis of the first six biographies of Burton, and cited references to many reviews of Burton's books. The bibliography did contain some errors and omissions; in some respects it is now out of date. Burton admirers will welcome the forthcoming publication of a new comprehensive bibliography by Miss B. J. Kirkpatrick, Librarian of the Royal Anthropological Institute.

The Burton library was once housed in Kensington Library, where much of it suffered damage when the basement of the library was accidentally flooded. Miss Kirkpatrick, who has cared for the collection ever since it was transferred to the Royal Anthropological Institute, has supervised the meticulous restoration of these volumes to their original condition. She has, moreover, mastered Burton's baffling handwriting, and is in other respects uniquely equipped to compile the definitive bibliography. My own bibliography is not designed either to duplicate that of Norman Penzer, or in any way to anticipate that of Miss Kirkpatrick. It is intended to supplement information given in my own footnotes, which are intended to be comprehensive.

It is curious that until now no biography of Burton—whose own scholarship was memorable and whose footnotes were famous—contains more than a handful of footnotes. Even *Burton* by Mr Byron Farwell, the best of the biographies, contains none at all. Burton himself was meticulous in acknowledging his sources; he deserves careful annotation.

Recent reprintings of many of his books suggest that a Burton revival is well under way, and attest a solid respect for his genius. See, for example, Alan Moorehead's 1961 edition of Burton's *The Lake Regions of Central Africa*, my own 1963 edition of *The City of the Saints*, Gordon Waterfield's 1966 edition of *First Footsteps in East Africa*, the 1965 edition of *Pilgrimage to El-Medinah and Meccah*, Alan Hull Walton's *The Perfumed Garden of the Shaykh Nefzawi* (1963), and the two new editions of Burton's translation of the *Kama Sutra*, one edited by W. G. Archer, the other by John W. Spellman, as well as a new edition, in three volumes, of his *Arabian Nights*.

Burton as Author, Translator, and Editor

1851—*Goa and the Blue Mountains; or, Six Months of Sick Leave*, London.

1851—*Scinde; or, The Unhappy Valley*, 2 vols, London.

1851—*Sindh, and the Races that Inhabit the Valley of the Indus; With Notices of the Topography and History of the Province*, London.

1852—*Falconry in the Valley of the Indus*, London.

1853—*A Complete System of Bayonet Exercise*, London.

1855-6—*Personal Narrative of a Pilgrimage to El-Medinah and Meccah*, 3 vols, London. Except where noted, all citations in this biography are from the Memorial edition, published in London in 1893, in two volumes, with eight appendices.

1856—*First Footsteps in East Africa; or, An Exploration of Harar*, London.

1860—*The Lake Regions of Central Africa, A Picture of Exploration*, 2 vols, London.

1861—*The City of the Saints and Across the Rocky Mountains to California*, London.

1863—*The Prairie Traveller, a Hand-book for Overland Expeditions . . .* by Randolph B. Marcy . . . Edited (with notes) by Richard F. Burton, London.

1863—*Abeokuta and the Cameroons Mountains. An Exploration*, 2 vols, London.

1863—*Wanderings in West Africa, From Liverpool to Fernando Po* (Anon., by F.R.G.S.), 2 vols, London.

1864—*A Mission to Gelele, King of Dahome, With Notices of the So-called "Amazons," the Grand Customs, the Yearly Customs, the Human Sacrifices, the Present State of the Slave Trade, and the Negro's Place in Nature*, 2 vols, London.

1864—*The Nile Basin. Part I. Showing Tanganyika to be Ptolemy's Western Lake Reservoir. A Memoir read before the Royal Geographical Society, November 14, 1864. With Prefatory Remarks, by Richard F. Burton. Part II. Captain Speke's Discovery of the Source of the Nile. A Review. By James M'Queen . . .*, London [more commonly spelled Macqueen].

1865—*Wit and Wisdom from West Africa; or, A Book of Proverbial Philosophy, Idioms, Enigmas, and Laconisms. Compiled by Richard F. Burton . . .*, London.

1865—*The Guide-book. A Pictorial Pilgrimage to Mecca and Medina. Including Some of the More Remarkable Incidents in the Life of Mohammed, the Arab Lawgiver . . .*, London.

1865—*Stone Talk . . . Being Some of the Marvellous Sayings of a Petral Portion Fleet Street, London, to One Doctor Polyglott, Ph.D., By Frank Baker, D.O.N.*, London. (Baker is a pseudonym for Burton.)

1869—*The Highlands of Brazil*, 2 vols, London.

1870—*Vikram and the Vampire, or Tales of Hindu Devilry. Adapted by Richard F. Burton . . .*, London.

1870—*Letters from the Battle-fields of Paraguay*, London.

1871—*Unexplored Syria, Visits to The Libanus, The Tulúl el Safá, The Anti-

Libanus, The Northern Libanus, and The 'Aláh. By Richard F. Burton and Charles F. Tyrwhitt-Drake, 2 vols, London.

1872—*Zanzibar; City, Island, and Coast,* 2 vols, London.

1873—*The Lands of Cazembe. Lacerda's Journey to Cazembe in 1798. Translated and Annotated by Captain R. F. Burton . . . ,* London.

1874—*The Captivity of Hans Stade of Hesse, in A.D. 1547–1555, Among the Wild Tribes of Eastern Brazil. Translated by Albert Tootal . . . and Annotated by Richard F. Burton,* London.

1875—*Ultima Thule; or A Summer in Iceland,* 2 vols, London.

1876—*Etruscan Bologna: A Study,* London.

1876—*A New System of Sword Exercise for Infantry,* London.

1876—*Two Trips to Gorilla Land and the Cataracts of the Congo,* 2 vols, London.

1877—*Sind Revisited; With Notices of the Anglo-Indian Army; Railroads; Past, Present, and Future, etc.,* 2 vols, London.

1878—*The Gold-Mines of Midian and The Ruined Midianite Cities. A Fortnight's Tour in Northwestern Arabia,* London.

1879—*The Land of Midian (revisited),* 2 vols, London.

1880—*The Kasidah of Hâjî Abdû El-Yezdî a Lay of the Higher Law Translated and Annotated by His Friend and Pupil F.B.,* London. Privately printed. (Burton is author of both the poem and the annotations.)

1880—*Os Lusiadas (The Lusiads): Englished by Richard Francis Burton: (Edited by His Wife, Isabel Burton).* 2 vols, London.

1881—*Camoens: His Life and His Lusiads. A Commentary By Richard F. Burton,* 2 vols, London.

1881—*A Glance at the "Passion-Play,"* London.

1883—*To the Gold Coast for Gold. A Personal Narrative by Richard F. Burton and Verney Lovett Cameron,* 2 vols, London.

1883—*The Kama Sutra of Vatsyayana . . . With a Preface and Introduction.* Printed for the Hindoo Kama Shastra Society, London and Benares. (This was translated by Richard F. Burton and F. F. Arbuthnot.)

1884—*Camoens. The Lyricks. Part I, Part II (Sonnets, Canzons, Odes, and Sextines). Englished by Richard F. Burton.* London.

1884—*The Book of the Sword,* London.

1885—*Ananga Ranga; (Stage of the Bodiless One) or, The Hindu Art of Love. (Ars Amoris Indica). Translated from the Sanskrit, and Annotated by A.F.F. & B.F.R. . . .* Cosmopoli, for the Kama Shastra Society of London and Benares, and for private circulation only.

(This volume, translated by Richard F. Burton and F. F. Arbuthnot, was first issued in 1873 under the title *Kâma-Shâstra or The Hindoo Art of Love (Ars Amoris Indica) . . . ,* and privately printed. But after printing four or six copies the printers became alarmed and refused to print more for fear of prosecution.)

1885—*A Plain and Literal Translation of the Arabian Nights' Entertainments, Now Entituled The Book of The Thousand Nights and a Night. With Introduction Explanatory Notes on the Manners and Customs of Moslem Men and a Terminal Essay upon the History of the Nights.* By Richard F. Burton. Printed by the Kama-shastra Society For Private Subscribers Only. 10 vols.

1886–8—*Supplemental Nights to the Book of The Thousand Nights and a Night. With Notes Anthropological and Explanatory By Richard F. Burton.* Printed by the Kama Shastra Society for Private Subscribers Only. 6 vols.

1886—*Iracéma, The Honey-lips,* By J. De Alencar, Translated by Isabel Burton and *Maluel De Moraes, A Chronicle of the Seventeenth Century,* by J. M. Pereira Da Silva, Translated by Richard F. and Isabel Burton, London.

1886—*The Perfumed Garden of the Cheikh Nefzaoui, A Manual of Arabian Erotology* (xvi. Century) Revised and Corrected Translation. Cosmopoli, 1886, for the Kama Shastra Society of London and Benares, and for Private circulation only. (This was translated from the French by Richard F. Burton. Two printings were exhausted in 1886; Burton was working on an enlarged and annotated version and translating from the original Arabic, when he died. This version his wife burned.

1887—*The Behâristân (Abode of Spring) By Jâmi, A Literal Translation from the Persian.* Printed by the Kama Shastra Society for Private Subscribers only. Benares. (This was translated by Edward Rehatsek, but Burton seems to have supervised the editing.)

1888—*The Gulistân or Rose Garden of Sa'di. Faithfully Translated Into English.* Printed by the Kama Shastra Society for Private Subscribers only. Benares. (This too was translated by Edward Rehatsek, with Burton supervising the editing.)

1890—*Priapeia or the Sportive Epigrams of divers Poets on Priapus: the Latin Text now for the first time Englished in Verse and Prose (the Metrical Verson by "Outidanos") with Introduction, Notes Explanatory and Illustrative, and Excursus, by "Neaniskos."* Cosmopoli. For private subscribers only. (Burton is responsible for the translation into poetry; the remainder of the volume seems to be largely the work of his collaborator, Leonard Smithers.)

POSTHUMOUS WORKS OF RICHARD BURTON

1891—*Marocco and the Moors: Being an Account of Travels, with a General Description of the Country and Its People,* by Arthur Leared. Second edition, revised and edited by Sir Richard Burton, London.

1893—*Il Pentamerone; or, the Tale of Tales. Being a Translation by the Late Sir Richard Burton . . . ,* London.

1894—*The Carmina of Gaius Valerius Catullus, Now first completely Englished into Verse and Prose, the Metrical Part by Capt. Sir Richard F. Burton . . . and the Prose Portion, Introduction, and Notes Explanatory and Illustrative by Leonard C. Smithers,* London.

1898—*The Jew, The Gypsy, and El Islam, By the Late Captain Sir Richard Burton . . . ,* edited with a preface and brief notes by W. H. Wilkins, London.

1901—*Wanderings in Three Continents, By the Late Captain Sir Richard F. Burton,* edited with a preface by W. H. Wilkins, London.

Books and Articles

Amberley Papers, edited by Bertrand Russell, 2 vols, New York, 1937.

Arberry, A. J., *Oriental Essays, portraits of seven scholars*, London, 1960.

————, *Sufism, an account of the mystics of Islam*, London, 1950.

Archer, W. G., "Reflections on the 'Kama Sutra,'" *The Listener*, April 18, 1963, 665–7.

————, Ed., *The Kama Sutra of Vatsyayana*, translated by Sir Richard Burton and F. F. Arbuthnot, London, 1963.

Ashbee, Henry S. (Pisanus Fraxi), *Catena Librorum Tacendorum*, privately printed, London, 1885.

————, *Index Librorum Prohibitorum*, privately printed, London, 1877.

Bacon, Leonard, trans., The Lusiads of Luiz de Camões, translated with introduction and notes by Leonard Bacon, New York, 1950.

Baker, F. Grenfell, "Sir Richard Burton as I Knew Him," *Cornhill Magazine*, No. 304, October 1921, 411–23.

Baker, J. N. L., "Sir Richard Burton and the Nile Sources," *English Historical Review*, Vol 59, 1944.

Baker, Sir Samuel W., *The Albert N'Yanza, Great Basin of the Nile*, London, 1866. Citations here are from the 1885 edition.

Bailey, Derrick Sherwin, *Homosexuality and the Western Christian Tradition*, London, 1955.

Bell, Aubrey F. G., *Luis de Camões*, Oxford Press, 1923.

Bercovici, Alfred, *That Blackguard Burton!*, New York, 1962.

Blanch, Lesley, *The Wilder Shores of Love*, London, 1954.

Blunt, Wilfrid Scawen, *My Diaries*, 2 vols, New York, 1921.

Brockelman, Carl, *History of the Islamic Peoples*, New York, 1947.

Brodie, Fawn M., ed., *The City of the Saints by Richard F. Burton*, New York, 1963; London, 1964.

————, *No Man Knows My History, the Life of Joseph Smith the Mormon Prophet*, New York, 1945. [English edition, *No Man Knows My History (Joseph Smith)*, London, 1963.]

Browne, W. G., *Travels in Africa, Egypt, and Syria from the Year 1792 to 1798*, London, 1799.

Bruce, James, *Travels to Discover the Source of the Nile, 1768–1773*, 5 vols, Edinburgh, 1790.

Burnes, James, *Narrative of a Visit to the Court of Sinde at Hyderabad on the Indus*, Edinburgh, 1839.

Burton, Isabel, *A.E.I., Arabia, Egypt, India*, London, 1879.

————, *Inner Life of Syria, Palestine and the Holy Land*, 2 vols, London, 1876.

————, *Life of Captain Sir Richard F. Burton*, 2 vols, London, 1893.

————, "Sir Richard Burton: an Explanation and a Defence," *New Review*, VII, 572–8, November 1892.

————, *The Passion-Play at Ober-Ammergau*, London, 1900.

Burton, Jean, *Sir Richard Burton's Wife*, New York, 1941.

Cameron, Vernon Lovett, "Burton as I Knew Him," *Fortnightly Review*, LIV, 878–84, December 1890.

Campbell, R. J., *Livingstone*, London, 1929.

Case of Captain Burton, late H.B.M.'s Consul at Damascus, published by the British Foreign Office, March 1872.

Coupland, R., *Exploitation of East Africa, 1856–90*, London, 1939.

Craig, Alec, *The Banned Books of England*, London, 1937.

Crowder, Michael, *The Story of Nigeria*, London, 1962.

Davidson, Basil, *Black Mother, Africa: The Years of Trial*, London, 1961.

Dearden, Seton, *Burton of Arabia*, New York, 1937.

Dodge, Walter Phelps, *The Real Sir Richard Burton*, London, 1907.

Downey, Fairfax, *Burton, Arabian Nights Adventurer*, New York, 1931.

Du Chaillu, Paul B., *Explorations and Adventures in Equatorial Africa*, London, 1861.

Dunraven, Earl of (Windham Thomas Wyndham-Quin), *Past Times and Pastimes*, 2 vols, London, 1922.

Dupee, F. W., "Sir Richard and Ruffian Dick," *New York Review of Books*, April 16, 1964, 3ff.

Edwardes, Allen, *Death Rides a Camel*, New York, 1963.

Emeneau, M. B., trans., *Jambhaladatta's Version of the Vetālapañchaviṁśati*, American Oriental Society, New Haven 1934.

Evans, W. N., "Serendipity," *Psychoanalytic Quarterly*, XXXII, 165–79, 1963.

Farwell, Byron, *Burton*, London, 1963.

————, *The Man Who Presumed, a Biography of Henry M. Stanley*, New York, 1957.

Fenichel, Otto, "The Counter-Phobic Attitude," and "Neurotic Acting Out," in *Collected Papers of Otto Fenichel*, 2nd series, New York, 1954.

Forbes, Frederick E., *Dahomey and the Dahomans*, 2 vols, London, 1851.

Ford, Jeremiah D. M., eds., *Os Lusiades*, edited with introduction and notes by J. D. M. Ford, Harvard Press, 1946.

Fyfe, Christopher, *A History of Sierra Leone*, Oxford University Press, 1962.

Galton, Francis, *Memories of My Life*, London, 1908.

Goncourt, Edmond et Jules de, *Journal, Mémoires de la vie littéraire*, Vol 5, 1861–3, Monaco, 1956.

Grant, Christina P., *Syrian Desert Caravans, Travel and Exploration*, New York, 1938.

Grant, James A., *A Walk Across Africa*, London, 1864.

Greenson, Ralph R. "The Struggle Against Identification," *American Journal of the Psychoanalytic Association*, II, 200–16, April 1954.

Hale, Richard Walden, *Sir Richard F. Burton, a footnote to history*, Boston, 1930, 11 pp.

Hancarville, Pierre François d', *Recherches sur l'origin, l'esprit, et les progrès des arts de la Grèce. . . .* London, 1785.

Haring, C. H., *Empire in Brazil*, Harvard University Press, 1958.

Harris, Frank, *Contemporary Portraits*, New York, 1920.

————, *My Life and Loves*, New York, 1963.

Henderson, Philip, *The Life of Laurence Oliphant*, London, 1956.

Herskovits, Melville J., *Dahomey*, 2 vols, New York, 1938.

Hilprecht, H. V., *Exploration in Bible Lands During the Nineteenth Century*, Philadelphia, 1903.

Hitchman, Francis, *Richard F. Burton*, 2 vols, London, 1887.

Howard, C., and J. H. Plumb, *West African Explorers*, Oxford University Press, 1951.

Huttenback, Robert A., *British Relations with Sind, 1799–1843*, University of California Press, 1962.

Ionides, Luke, "Memories of Richard Burton," *Transatlantic Review*, March 1924.

Johnston, Sir Harry, *The Nile Quest*, New York, 1903.

Kiernan, R. H., *The Unveiling of Arabia*, London, 1937.

Lambrick, H. T., *Sir Charles Napier and Sind*, Oxford, 1952.

Lawrence, T. E., *Seven Pillars of Wisdom*, New York, 1935.

Lewis, Ioan M., *A Pastoral Democracy*, Oxford, 1961.

Linton, Eliza Lynn, "The Partisans of Wild Women," *Nineteenth Century*, March 1892.

Livingstone, David, *Missionary Travels and Researches in South Africa*, London, 1857.

Lobo, Father Jerome, *A Short Relation of the River Nile*, London, 1673.

————, *A Voyage to Abyssinia*, edited by Samuel Johnson, London, 1789.

McCarthy, Justin, *Portraits of the Sixties*, London, 1903.

Macdonald, Duncan B., "Alf Laila Wa-Laila," *Encyclopaedia of Islam*, Supplement, I, 17–21.

————, "On Translating the Arabian Nights," *Nation*, Vol 71, 167–8, 185–6, August 30 and September 6, 1900.

Marek, Curt W., *The Secret of the Hittites*, New York, 1956.

Maurois, André, *Disraeli*, New York, 1939.

Moorehead, Alan, *The Blue Nile*, New York, 1962.

————, *The White Nile*, New York, 1960.

————, *The Lake Regions of Central Africa*, by Sir Richard F. Burton, edited with an introduction by Alan Moorehead, New York, 1961.

Moscati, Sabatino, *Ancient Semitic Civilizations*, London, 1957.

Murray, Douglas, *Sir Samuel Baker, a Memoir*, London, 1895.

Myall, Laura Hain Friswell, *In the Sixties and Seventies*, Boston, 1906.

Napier, William, *Life and Opinions of General Sir Charles James Napier*, 4 vols, London, 1857.

Newbury, C. W., *The Western Slave Coast and its Rulers*, Oxford, 1961.

Nicolson, Harold, *Portrait of a Diplomatist*, Boston, 1930.

Oestrup, J., "Alf Laila Wa-Laila, Thousand and One Nights," *Encyclopaedia of Islam*, 1913.

Ouida, "Richard Burton," *Fortnightly Review*, Vol 85, 1039–45, June 1906.

Payne, John, *The Book of the Thousand Nights and One Night*, London, 1882.

————, *Tales from the Arabic*, London, 1884.

————, *Alaeddin and the Enchanted Lamp; Zein ul Asnan and the King of the Jinn . . .*, London, 1889.

Penniman, T. K., *A Hundred Years of Anthropology*, London, 1935.

Penzer, Norman M., *An Annotated Bibliography of Sir Richard Francis Burton*, London, 1923.

————, *Anthropological Notes on the Sotadic Zone, etc., by Sir Richard F. Burton, with Photographs of anthropological rarities . . . and Rare Burton Collectanea*, 95 pp., edited anonymously by Norman Penzer, and privately printed.

————, *Selected Papers on Anthropology, Travel and Exploration, by Sir Richard Burton*, edited by Norman Penzer, London, 1924.

Philby, H. St John, *The Empty Quarter, being a description of the Great South Desert of Arabia*, New York, 1933.

————, *The Heart of Arabia*, London, 1922.

Pope-Hennessy, James, *Monckton Milnes: The Years of Promise, 1809–1851*, London, 1940.

————, *Monckton Milnes: The Flight of Youth, 1851–1885*, London, 1951.

Pritchard, James B., ed., *Ancient Near Eastern Texts Relating to the Old Testament*, Princeton University Press, 1955.

————, *Archaeology and the Old Testament*, Princeton University Press, 1958.

Pusey, William Allen, *History of Syphilis*, London, 1933.

Rainy, William, *The Censor Censured, or the Calumnies of Captain Burton on the Africans of Sierra Leone Refuted . . .*, London, 1865.

Redesdale, Lord (Algernon Bertram Freeman-Mitford), *Memories*, 2 vols, London, 1915.

Reid, T. Wemyss, *Life, Letters, and Friendships of Richard Monckton Milnes, First Lord Houghton*, 2 vols, London, 1891.

Richards, Alfred Bates, *A Short Sketch of the Career of Captain Richard F. Burton*, London, 1886, first published in 1880.

Richards, Vyvyan, *Portrait of T. E. Lawrence*, London, 1936.

Robinson, Ronald, with John Gallagher and Alice Denny, *Africa and the Victorians*, New York, 1961.

Russell, Mrs Charles E. B., *General Rigby, Zanzibar and the Slave Trade*, London, 1935.

Russell, William Howard, *The War from the Death of Lord Raglan to the Evacuation of the Crimea*, London, 1856.

Ryder, Arthur W., *Twenty-Two Goblins*, London, 1917.

St John-Stevas, Norman, *Obscenity and the Law*, London, 1956.

Sayce, A. H., *The Hittites, the story of a forgotten empire*, London, 1890.

Schneider, Herbert W., and George Lawton, *A Prophet and a Pilgrim, being the incredible history of Thomas Lake Harris and Laurence Oliphant*, Columbia University Press, 1942.

Schonfield, Hugh J., *Richard Burton, Explorer*, London, 1936.

Seaver, George, *David Livingstone: His Life and Letters*, London, 1957.

Speke, John Hanning, *Journal of the Discovery of the Source of the Nile*, New York, 1864.

————, *What Led to the Discovery of the Source of the Nile*, Edinburgh, 1864.

Spellman, John W., ed., *The Kama Sutra of Vatsyayana . . . translated by Sir Richard F. Burton*, foreword by Santha Rama Rau, introduction by John W. Spellman, New York, 1962.

Stanley, Sir Henry Morton, *Autobiography*, London, 1912.

————, *In Darkest Africa*, 2 vols, New York, 1890.

————, *How I Found Livingstone*, New York, 1887.

Stisted, Georgiana, "Reminiscences of Sir Richard Burton," *Temple Bar*, July 1891, reproduced in *Living Age*, August 15, 1891.

————, *The True Life of Captain Sir Richard F. Burton*, New York, 1897.

Stoker, Bram, *Personal Reminiscences of Henry Irving*, 2 vols, London, 1906.

Suson, E. W. A., *The British Consul's Manual of 1856*, London, 1856.

Swinburne, Algernon Charles, "Elegy," *Fortnightly Review*, Vol 58, 1–5, July 1, 1892.

————, *The Swinburne Letters*, ed. Cecil Y. Lang, 6 vols, Yale University Press, 1959.

Symons, Arthur, "A Neglected Genius: Sir Richard Burton," *Dramatis Personae*, Indianapolis, 1923.

Trimingham, J. Spencer, *Islam in Ethiopia*, Oxford Press, 1952.

Villars, Jean B., *T. E. Lawrence, or the Search for the Absolute*, London, 1955.

Walker, Kenneth, ed., *Love, War and Fancy, the social and sexual customs of the East*, by Sir Richard Burton, London, 1964.

Walton, Alan Hull, ed., *The Perfumed Garden of the Shaykh Nefzawi, translated by Sir Richard F. Burton*, London, 1963.

Waterfield, Gordon, ed., *First Footsteps in East Africa*, by Sir Richard F. Burton, London, 1966.

Watson, Francis, "Must We Burn Vatsayana," *Encounter*, March 1964, 67–74.

Wilkins, W. H., *The Romance of Isabel Lady Burton*, 2 vols, London, 1897.

Wilson, Sir Arnold, *Richard Burton*, fifth Burton Memorial lecture, London, 1937.

Woodham-Smith, Cecil, *The Reason Why*, London, 1953.

Woodruff, Douglas, *The Tichborne Claimant, a Victorian Mystery*, London, 1957.

Wright, Thomas, *The Life of John Payne*, London, 1919.

————, *The Life of Sir Richard Burton*, 2 vols, London, 1906.

Wright, William, *The Empire of the Hittites*, New York, 1884.

Young, Wayland, *Eros Denied*, London, 1965.

INDEX